WHATCHA GONNA DO WITH THAT DUCK?

ALSO BY SETH GODIN

The Icarus Deception
V Is for Vulnerable
Linchpin
Tribes
Meatball Sundae
All Marketers Are Liars
The Dip
Free Prize Inside
Purple Cow
Survival Is Not Enough
Unleashing the Ideavirus
Permission Marketing
Big Red Fez
The Big Moo (editor)
Small Is the New Big
Poke the Box
We Are All Weird

Find them all at sethgodin.com

WHATCHA GONNA DO WITH THAT DUCK?

AND OTHER
PROVOCATIONS,
2006–2012

Seth Godin

COMPILED BY BERNADETTE JIWA

PORTFOLIO / PENGUIN

PORTFOLIO / PENGUIN
Published by the Penguin Group
Penguin Group (USA) Inc., 375 Hudson Street, New York, New York 10014, U.S.A. • Penguin Group (Canada), 90 Eglinton Avenue East, Suite 700, Toronto, Ontario, Canada M4P 2Y3 (a division of Pearson Penguin Canada Inc.) • Penguin Books Ltd, 80 Strand, London WC2R 0RL, England • Penguin Ireland, 25 St. Stephen's Green, Dublin 2, Ireland (a division of Penguin Books Ltd) • Penguin Group (Australia), 707 Collins Street, Melbourne, Victoria 3008 Australia (a division of Pearson Australia Group Pty Ltd) • Penguin Books India Pvt Ltd, 11 Community Centre, Panchsheel Park, New Delhi – 110 017, India • Penguin Group (NZ), 67 Apollo Drive, Rosedale, Auckland 0632, New Zealand (a division of Pearson New Zealand Ltd) • Penguin Books, Rosebank Office Park, 181 Jan Smuts Avenue, Parktown North 2193, South Africa • Penguin China, B7 Jaiming Center, 27 East Th ird Ring Road North, Chaoyang District, Beijing 100020, China

Penguin Books Ltd, Registered Offi ces:
80 Strand, London WC2R 0RL, England

First published in 2012 by Portfolio / Penguin,
a member of Penguin Group (USA) Inc.

"Stop Stealing Dreams" was published as an ebook by the author. "Th e Future Is Arriving" appeared on Th e Domino Project website. Th e other selections appeared on the author's website.

Photograph: Don Emmert / AFP / Getty Images

LIBRARY OF CONGRESS CATALOGING IN PUBLICATION DATA

Godin, Seth.
Whatcha gonna do with that duck? : and other provocations, 2006-2012 / Seth Godin.
p. cm.
ISBN 978-1-59184-609-3
1. Marketing.   2. Management.   I. Title.
HF5415.G5784 2013
658—dc23   2012036873

Pro with Helvetica Neue LT Std
Designed by Daniel Lagin

Paperback ISBN: 9780593853917

147141878

For Helene, always

Thanks to Bernadette Jiwa and Niki Papadopoulos for the herculean task of culling six years' worth of writing into this book. I couldn't (and wouldn't) have done it without you.

I don't remember writing most of these posts.

I read them and I shake my head in agreement (most of the time). Sometimes I wonder what I was thinking at the time. But yes, I wrote them, every word, over the course of the last five or six years.

I've collected them in this handy set not because you can read them more easily during takeoff or landing, or in the tub or at the beach. No, I've collected them because there's (still) something magical about the linear, permanent nature of a book. Even an ebook feels less evanescent than the disconnected, temporary nature of a blog post.

One of my creative heroes, Gary Larson, was generous enough to let us read the collected *Far Side*, thousands of brilliant little cartoons connected into permanent volumes. And the experience of reading them is different than the way he intended when he drew them. A cartoon or a blog post emailed to you now and then might break your stride or make you do a double take, but the relentless force of an entire book of them can have a genuine impact on you and those that you care to share with.

I guess that this is the real reason I collected these posts. So those that have been keeping up with the daily blog have a handy tool they can use to proselytize. Hand this to the heathen, see if you can get them to join the tribe.

Thanks for reading. Thanks for sharing. And most of all, thanks for doing difficult work.

Whatcha Gonna Do with That Duck?

We're surrounded by people who are busy getting their ducks in a row, waiting for just the right moment.

Getting your ducks in a row is a fine thing to do. But deciding what you are going to do with that duck is a far more important issue.

CONTENTS

INTRODUCTION: MAY 2004

Five Years from Now . . .

Assume that:

Hard drive space is free.
Wifi-like connections are everywhere.
Connections speeds are 10 to 100 times faster.
Everyone has a digital camera.
Everyone carries a device that is sort of like a laptop, but cheap and tiny.
The number of new products introduced every day is five times greater
    than now.
Walmart's sales are three times as big as they are now.
Any manufactured product that's more than five years old in design sells
    at commodity pricing.
The retirement age will be five years higher than it is now.
Your current profession will either be gone or be totally different.

What then?

WHATCHA GONNA DO WITH THAT DUCK?

NOW WAS ALWAYS A GOOD TIME TO START

Opportunity. Choosing and Doing. Picking Yourself.

Make Something Happen

If I had to pick one piece of marketing advice to give you, that would be it.

Now.

Make something happen today, before you go home, before the end of the week. Launch that idea, post that post, run that ad, call that customer. Go to the edge, that edge you've been holding back from . . . and do it today. Without waiting for the committee or your boss or the market. Just go.

When to Start

- **The best time to start** is when you've got enough money in the bank to support all contingencies.
- **The best time to start** is when the competition is far behind in technology, sophistication, and market acceptance.
- **The best time to start** is when the competition isn't *too far* behind, because then you'll spend too long educating the market.
- **The best time to start** is when everything at home is stable and you can really focus.
- **The best time to start** is when you're out of debt.

- **The best time to start** is when no one is already working on your idea.
- **The best time to start** is when your patent comes through.
- **The best time to start** is after you've got all your VC funding.
- **The best time to start** is when the political environment is more friendly than it is now.
- **The best time to start** is after you've got your degree.
- **The best time to start** is after you've worked all the kinks out of your plan.
- **The best time to start** is when you're sure it's going to work.
- **The best time to start** is after you've hired the key marketing person for the new division.
- **The best time to start** was last year. The best opportunities are already gone.
- **The best time to start** is before some pundit declares your segment passé. Too late.
- **The best time to start** is when the new generation of processors is shipping.
- **The best time to start** is when the geopolitical environment settles down.

Actually, as you've probably guessed, **the best time to start** was last year. The second best time to start is *right now*.

The Reason

The reason they teach biology before they teach chemistry in high school is that biology was invented first. Even though you need chemistry to do biology, but not vice versa.

The reason that you have a water bubbler in your office is that it used to be difficult to filter water effectively.

The reason that Blockbuster exists is that VCR tapes used to cost more than $100.

The reason that SUVs have a truck chassis is that the government regulates vehicles with a truck chassis differently.

The reason you have a front lawn is to demonstrate to your friends and neighbors how much time and energy you're prepared to waste.

The reason the typewriter keyboard is in a weird order is that original typewriters jammed, and they needed to rearrange the letters to keep common letters far apart.

The reason we don't have school in the summer is so our kids can help with farm work. Or because it's too hot and there's no air conditioning . . .

The reason there's a toll on that bridge but not on that road is that there used to be a ferry on that river, and the ferryman needed to make a living.

The reason you go to a building to go to work every day is that steam or water power used to turn a giant winch-like structure that went right through the factory building. Every workman used that power to do his work. As factories got more sophisticated, it remained efficient to move the workers, not the stuff.

What's your reason?

Is There a First-Mover Advantage?

Some conventional wisdom says that you need to be first to win. People will point to eBay and Microsoft and Starbucks and the William Morris Agency and say, "if it's a natural monopoly or a market where switching costs are high, the first person in, wins."

This argument has been amplified lately by the high cost of building a name for yourself (it would just cost too much to build a brand bigger than Starbucks in a post-TV world) as well as the network effects of things like eBay and Hotmail.

Skeptics scream foul. They point out that not one of the examples I gave above was actually the first mover. There were plenty of others that came first, and, they argue, the fast follower won by learning from the mistakes of the innovator. They argue that innovation is overrated, and low costs and good service are the key.

I think both sides are wrong (and right) and the mistake is caused by the erroneous belief that there's a market.

There isn't a market.

There are a million markets. Markets of one, or markets of small groups, or markets of cohorts that communicate.

If you're an eBay user, my guess is that eBay was the first auction site you used. If you use Windows, my guess is that you never used CPM. And if you are a Starbucks junkie, my guess is that you don't live near a Peet's.

What happens: the market often belongs to the first person who brings you the right story on the right day.

Yes, you must be first (and right) in that market or this market.

But that doesn't mean you have to be first (and right) in the universe.

The market is splintering more than even some pundits predicted in 1998 (that would be me). Which means that the idea of monolithic marketing messages to monolithic markets makes no sense. The race is now to be the first mover in the micro-markets where attention matters.

Of course, those micro-markets are leaky. People don't cooperate. They talk to each other. So pretty quickly, that splintered market coalesces into something bigger.

Trial and Error

Most learning, especially most organizational learning, occurs through trial and error.

Error occurs whether you want it to or not. Error is difficult to avoid. It's not clear that research or preparation have an enormous impact on error, especially marketing error. Error is clearly not in short supply.

Trial, on the other hand, is quite scarce, especially in some organizations. People mistakenly believe that one way to successfully avoid error is to avoid trial.

We need more trial.

"No" to Average

One of my favorite conversations goes like this.

"Oh, by the way, I read your book, *Purple Cow*. I liked it a lot. I even underlined some paragraphs."

"Thanks!" I say. Underlining is the goal of people in my line of work.

"I can imagine that it's really helpful to a lot of people. Unfortunately, in my [business/organization/line of work], most of what you write about doesn't really work."

The reason it's such a good conversation is that people in every possible line of work have managed to tell me that the ideas don't apply to them, and that gives me a chance to ask them more details about what they do—and within a minute or two, we're both jumping up and down, excited with the possibilities of how it *does* work in their line of work. Ministers, freelance photographers, real estate agents, middle managers, website marketers—doesn't matter, it always seems to come down to one thing:

Say "no" to being average.

This morning, Bradley was explaining to me that it couldn't work in his profession as a freelance writer. It seems that almost all the clients want average stuff. Which is no surprise, since average is, by definition, the stuff most people want. I asked, "Are there any writers in your field who you hate because they get paid way too much compared to your perception of the effort they put in and the talent they have?"

"Sure," he said, feeling a little sheepish about being annoyed by their success.

"And how do they get those gigs?"

It's because they stand for something. Because they are at the edges. Because if an editor wants a "Bob-Jones-type" article, she has to call Bob Jones for it . . . and pay Bob's fees. Bob would fail if he did average work for average editors just to make a living. But by turning down the average stuff and insisting on standing for something on the edge, he profits. By challenging his clients to run stuff that makes them nervous (and then having them discover that it's great), he profits.

This is scary. It's really scary to turn down most (the average) of what comes your way and hold out for the remarkable opportunities. Scary to quit your job at an average company doing average work just because you know that if you stay, you'll end up just like them. Scary to go way out on an edge and intentionally make what you do unattractive to some.

Which is why it's such a great opportunity.

Done

What happens when your inbox is empty?

What happens when all the agenda items and all the incoming emails are cleared?

Time to go home.

A job well done. Congratulations, you earned your paycheck.

This is the factory mindset that has been drilled into us since kindergarten. You get assignments, you do your best, and you finish them.

It is at this point that we draw the line between workers and entrepreneurs, between people who work in marketing and marketers.

The challenge is NOT to empty your inbox. The challenge is not to get your boss to tell you what to do.

The challenge is to ask a two-part question:

What next? What now?

Asking is the hard part.

The Intuition Vs. Analysis Conundrum

Let's say you've got a really good idea. And you've had good ideas before.

You show it to your colleagues. They analyze it. They tell you why it's *not* a good idea.

Hmmm.

Do you go with your instinct? Is your gut reaction to be trusted? After all, you've been right before. After all, you've been wrong before.

The analysis, based on past events, certainly seems sound. But following your instincts is the only way you're going to do something *unsound*.

And unsound things become hits. Sound ones never do.

Who Moved My Cheese? was unsound. So was publishing a book two years after you started blogging every chapter. So was an expensive, unfitted, almost untailored suit from Milan. So was running against Joe Lieberman.

The challenge is not to somehow persuade those in search of soundness to change their minds. The challenge is to do enough of a gut check to decide whether you should defend your instinct. And then do it.

Advice for Authors

It happened again. There I was, meeting with someone who I thought had nothing to do with books or publishing, and it turns out his new book just came out.

With more than 75,000 books published every year (not counting ebooks or blogs), the odds are actually pretty good that you've either written a book, are writing a book, or want to write one.

Hence this short list:

1. Lower your expectations. The happiest authors are the ones that don't expect much.

2. The best time to start promoting your book is three years before it comes out. Three years to build a reputation, build a permission asset, build a blog, build a following, build credibility, and build the connections you'll need later.

3. Pay for an editor. Not just to fix the typos, but to actually make your ramblings into something that people will choose to read. I found someone I like working with at the EFA (Editorial Freelancers Association). One of the things traditional publishers used to do is provide really insightful, even brilliant editors (people like Fred Hills and Megan Casey), but alas, that doesn't happen very often. And hiring your own editor means you'll value the process more.

4. Understand that a nonfiction book is a souvenir, just a vessel for the ideas themselves. You don't want the ideas to get stuck in the book; you want them to spread. Which means that you shouldn't hoard the idea! The more you give away, the better you will do.

5. Don't try to sell your book to everyone. First, consider this statistic from Dan Poynter: "58% of the U.S. adult population never reads another book after high school." Then, consider the fact that among people even willing to buy a book, yours is just a tiny little needle in a very big haystack. Far better to obsess about a little subset of the market—that subset that you have permission to talk with, that subset where you have credibility, and most important, that subset where people just can't live without your book.

6. Resist with all your might the temptation to hire a publicist to get you on *Oprah*. First, you won't get on *Oprah* (if you do, drop me a note and I'll mention you as the exception). Second, it's expensive. You're way better off spending the time and money to do #5 instead, going after the little micro-markets. There are some very talented publicists out there (thanks, Allison), but in general, see #1.

7. Think really hard before you spend a year trying to please one person in New York to get your book published by a "real" publisher. You give up a lot of time. You give up a lot of the upside. You give up control over what your book reads like and feels like and how it's promoted. Of course, a contract from Knopf and a seat on Jon Stewart's couch are great things, but so is being the Queen of England. That doesn't mean it's going to happen to you. Far more likely is that you discover how to efficiently publish (either electronically or using POD or a small-run press) a brilliant book that spreads like wildfire among a select group of people.

8. Your cover matters. Way more than you think. If it didn't, you wouldn't need a book; you could just email people the text.

9. If you have a "real" publisher (#7), it's worth investing in a few things to help them do a better job for you. Like editing the book before you submit it. Like putting the right to work on the cover with them in the contract. And most of all, getting the ability to buy hundreds of books at cost that you can use as samples and promotional pieces.

10. In case you skipped it, please check #2 again. That's the most important one, by far.

11. Blurbs are overrated, IMHO.

12. Blog mentions, on the other hand, matter a lot.

13. If you've got the patience, bookstore signings and talking to book clubs by phone are the two lowest-paid but most-guaranteed-to-work methods you have for promoting a really, really good book. If you do it 200 times a year, it will pay.

14. Consider the free PDF alternative. Some PDFs have gotten millions of downloads. No hassles, no time wasted, no trying to make a living on it. All the joy, in other words, without debating whether you should quit your day job (you shouldn't!).

15. If you want to reach people who don't normally buy books, show up in places where people who don't usually buy books are. Media places, virtual places, and real places, too.

16. Most books that sell by the truckload sell by the caseload. In other words, sell to organizations that buy on behalf of their members/ employees.

17. Publishing a book is not the same as printing a book. Publishing is about marketing and sales and distribution and risk. If you don't want to be in that business, don't be! Printing a book is trivially easy. Don't let anyone tell you it's not. You'll find plenty of printers who can match the look and feel of the bestselling book of your choice for just a few dollars a copy. That's not the hard part.

18. Bookstores, in general, are run by absolutely terrific people. Bookstores, in general, are really lousy businesses. They are often where books go to die. While some readers will discover your book in a store, it's way more likely they will discover the book before they get to the store, and the store is just there hoping to have the right book for the right person at the time she wants it. If the match isn't made, no sale.

19. Writing a book is a tremendous experience. It pays off intellectually. It clarifies your thinking. It builds credibility. It is a living engine of marketing and idea spreading, working every day to deliver your message with authority. You should write one.

Good Enough

So, just about everything that can be improved, *is* being improved. If you define "improved" to mean more features, more buttons, more choices, more power, more cost.

The washing machine I used this morning had more than 125 different combinations of ways to do the wash . . . don't get me started about the dryer. Clearly, an arms race is a good way to encourage people to upgrade.

I wonder, though, if "good enough" might be the next big idea. Audio players, cars, dryers, accounting . . . not the best ever made, not the most complicated, and certainly not the most energy consuming. Just good enough.

For some people, a clean towel is a clean towel.

Listen to This . . .

What's the point of talking to a group?

I'm serious. We spend a lot of time in presentations, or at the United Nations, or sending our kids to school. We have orientation sessions and keynote speeches and long-winded oratory on the floor of the Senate. Why?

One reason: to incite. To share emotion. To sell. And that's never going to go out of fashion, as far as I can tell.

But most of the speeches I'm talking about don't incite. I heard an excerpt on the radio the other day . . . someone at the EU going on at length about admitting Romania and Bulgaria to the EU. There was even a mention of food safety issues. Thousands of people listening to one person drone on about food safety. This wasn't an emotional speech designed to sell us on an idea. Instead, it was designed to teach us.

To teach us the way a schoolteacher I heard recently teaches: by reading a text. She stands up at the front of the room and, along with showing a few Web images, reads a text to the class.

Here's my point: In our scan-and-skip world, in a world where technology makes it obvious that we can treat different people differently, how can we possibly justify teaching via a speech?

Speech is both linear and unpaceable. You can't skip around and you can't speed it up. When the speaker covers something you know, you are bored. When he quickly covers something you don't understand, you are lost.

If marketing is the art of spreading ideas, then teaching is a kind of marketing. And live teaching to groups is broken, perhaps beyond repair. Consumers of information won't stand for it. We're learning less every time we are confronted with this technique, because we've been spoiled by the remote control and the Web.

If you teach—teach anything—I think you need to start by acknowledging that there's a need to sell your ideas emotionally. So you need to use whatever tools are available to you—an evocative PowerPoint image, say, or a truly impassioned speech.

Then, and this is the hard part, if you're teaching to a group of more than three people, you need to find a way to engage that is nonlinear. Q&A doesn't work for a large group, because only the questioner is engaged at any given moment (if you're lucky, the questioner represents more than a few, but she rarely represents all).

If it's worth teaching, it's worth teaching well. If it's worth investing the time of 30 or 230 or 3,330 people, then it's worth investing the effort to actually figure out how to get the message across. School is broken. Legislative politics are broken. Linear is broken. YouTube and Bloglines, on the other hand, are new platforms, platforms that enable the education of millions of people every day, quickly and for free.

Mañana

If you could do tomorrow over again, would you?

Most of us live programmed lives. Tomorrow is set, finished, done, and you haven't even started it yet.

And we accept that as part of the deal in setting goals and reaching them.

But what about the tomorrow thirty days from now? Or a year?

If you could do those over, would you? How?

Creativity

Ninety-nine percent of the time, in my experience, the hard part about creativity isn't coming up with something no one has ever thought of before. The hard part is actually executing the thing you've thought of.

The devil doesn't need an advocate. The brave need supporters, not critics.

Sheepwalking

I define "sheepwalking" as the outcome of hiring people who have been raised to be obedient and giving them a brain-dead job and enough fear to keep them in line.

You've probably encountered someone who is sheepwalking.

The TSA "screener" who forces a mom to drink from a bottle of breast milk because any other action is not in the manual. A "customer service" rep who will happily reread a company policy six or seven times but never stop to actually consider what the policy means. A marketing executive who buys millions of dollars' worth of TV time even though she knows it's not working—she does it because her boss told her to.

It's ironic but not surprising that in our age of increased reliance on new ideas, rapid change, and innovation, sheepwalking is actually on the rise. That's because we can no longer rely on machines to do the brain-dead stuff.

We've mechanized what we could mechanize. What's left is to cost-reduce the manual labor that must be done by a human. So we write manuals and race to the bottom in our search for the cheapest possible labor. And it's not surprising that when we go to hire that labor, we search for people who have already been trained to be sheepish.

Training a student to be sheepish is a lot easier than the alternative. Teaching to the test, ensuring compliant behavior, and using fear as a motivator are the easiest and fastest ways to get a kid through school. So why does it surprise us that we graduate so many sheep?

And graduate school? Since the stakes are higher (opportunity cost, tuition, and the job market), students fall back on what they've been taught. To be sheep. Well-educated, of course, but compliant nonetheless.

And many organizations go out of their way to hire people that color inside the lines, that demonstrate consistency and compliance. And then they give these people jobs where they are managed via fear. Which leads to sheepwalking. ("I might get fired!")

The fault doesn't lie with the employee, at least not at first. And of course, the pain is often shouldered by both the employee and the customer.

Is it less efficient to pursue the alternative? What happens when you build an organization like W. L. Gore and Associates (makers of Gore-Tex) or the Acumen Fund? At first, it seems crazy. There's too much overhead, there are too many cats to herd, there is too little predictability, and there is way too much noise. Then, over and over, we see something happen. When you hire amazing people and give them freedom, they do amazing stuff.

And the sheepwalkers and their bosses just watch and shake their heads, certain that this is just an exception, and that it is way too risky for their industry or their customer base.

I was at a Google conference last month, and I spent some time in a room filled with (pretty newly minted) Google sales reps. I talked to a few of them for a while about the state of the industry. And it broke my heart to discover that they were sheepwalking.

Just like the receptionist at a company I visited a week later. She acknowledged that the front office is very slow, and that she just sits there, reading romance novels and waiting. And she's been doing it for two years.

Just like the MBA student I met yesterday who is taking a job at a major packaged-goods company . . . because they offered her a great salary and promised her a well-known brand. She's going to stay "for just ten years, then have a baby and leave and start my own gig. . . ." She'll get really good at running coupons in the Sunday paper, but not particularly good at solving new problems.

What a waste.

Step one is to give the problem a name. Done. Step two is for anyone who sees themselves in this mirror to realize that you can always stop. You can always claim the career you deserve merely by refusing to walk down the same path as everyone else just because everyone else is already doing it.

Advice for Nathan (and Anyone Who Wants to Be a Marketer)

I just got a note from Nathan, who asks,

> I recently realized that I want to be a marketer. So now with a résumé that includes "Research Analyst" for an economics professor, "Finance Director" for a Nevada governor candidate, and a degree in physics from Harvard, I find myself applying for jobs in marketing. Ultimately, I would like to be VP of Product Development or perhaps CEO at a new company (I love

bringing remarkable ideas to fruition), and I have suddenly realized marketing, not finance, is the way to go for me. And, as I search for jobs and try to find an entry point for my newfound path, I have a few questions:

1. Where do I start? Most of what I read online seems to say I should have had a marketing internship in college. Can I get an Assistant Brand Manager position with no experience?

2. Do you have company suggestions? Which companies get that some of the millions they are spending on TV ads could be better spent improving their products/services?

3. Which books should form the backbone of my marketing education?

My answer is easy to write, harder to implement. In my experience, the single best way to become a marketer is to market. And since marketing isn't expensive any longer (it takes more guts than money), there's no need to work for Procter & Gamble. None. In the old days, you could argue that you needed to apprentice with an expert and that you needed access to millions (or billions) to spend. No longer.

So, start your own gig. Even if you're 12 years old, start a store on eBay. You'll learn just about everything you need to learn about digital marketing by building an electronic storefront, doing permission-based email campaigns, writing a blog, etc. Who knows more about marketing—Scoble or some mid-level marketing guy in Redmond?

You don't need a lot of time or a lot of money. You can start with six hours every weekend. Over time, if (and when) you get good at it, take on clients. Paying clients. Folks that need brilliant marketers will beat down the door to get at you. After a while, you may decide you like that life. Or, more likely, you'll decide you'd rather be your own client.

People who want to become great fishermen don't go to work on a salmon trawler. And people who want to become marketers ought to just start marketing.

That Moment

When you are sitting right on the edge of something daring and scary and creative and powerful and perhaps wonderful . . . and you blink and take a step back.

That's the moment. The moment between you and remarkable. Most people blink. Most people get stuck.

All the hard work and preparation and daring and luck are nothing compared with the ability to not blink.

Everyone Is Lonely

People spend money (and make money) and join organizations and invest time and enormous energy to solve this problem. Every day.

Labor Day

I'm working today. In fact, if I'm conscious, I'm working. That's largely because it doesn't seem like "work" today. I'd write this blog even if no one read it.

More and more people are lucky enough to have a gig like mine—work you'd do even if you didn't have to, even if you didn't get paid to do it. This is a bigger idea than it seems, because it changes the posture of what you do. Different motivations ought to lead to different results.

My version goes like this: If I'm doing this for fun (and I am), then I might as well be doing something remarkable/great/worth doing. Otherwise, why bother?

Here's something I wrote in 2003, shortly before *Purple Cow* came out. I reference it a lot; I guess I think it's good:

Your great-grandfather knew what it meant to work hard. He hauled hay all day long, making sure that the cows got fed. In *Fast Food Nation*, Eric Schlosser writes about a worker who ruptured his vertebrae, wrecked his hands, burned his lungs, and was eventually hit by a train as part of his 15-year-career at a slaughterhouse. Now that's hard work.

The meaning of hard work in a manual economy is clear. Without the leverage of machines and organizations, working hard meant producing more. Producing more, of course, was the best way to feed your family.

Those days are long gone. Most of us don't use our bodies as a replacement for a machine—unless we're paying for the privilege and getting a workout at the gym. These days, 35% of the American workforce sits at a desk. Yes, we sit there a lot of hours, but the only heavy lifting that we're likely to do is restricted to putting a new water bottle on the cooler. So do you still think that you work hard?

You could argue, "Hey, I work weekends and pull all-nighters. I start early and stay late. I'm always on, always connected with a BlackBerry. The FedEx guy knows which hotel to visit when I'm on vacation." Sorry. Even if you're a workaholic, you're not working very hard at all.

Sure, you're working long, but "long" and "hard" are now two different things. In the old days, we could measure how much grain someone harvested or how many pieces of steel he made. Hard work meant more work. But the past doesn't lead to the future. The future is not about time at all. The future is about work that's really and truly hard, not time-consuming. It's about the kind of work that requires us to push ourselves, not just punch the clock. Hard work is where our job security, our financial profit, and our future joy lie.

It's hard work to make difficult emotional decisions, such as quitting a job and setting out on your own. It's hard work to invent a new system, service, or process that's remarkable. It's hard work to tell your boss that he's being intellectually and emotionally lazy. It's easier to stand by and watch the company fade into oblivion. It's hard work to tell senior management to abandon something that it has been doing for a long time in favor of a new and apparently risky alternative. It's hard work to make good decisions with less than all of the data.

Today, working hard is about taking apparent risk. Not a crazy risk like betting the entire company on an untested product. No, an apparent risk: something that the competition (and your coworkers) believe is unsafe but that you realize is far more conservative than sticking with the status quo.

Richard Branson doesn't work more hours than you do. Neither does Steve Ballmer or Carly Fiorina. Robyn Waters, the woman who revolutionized what Target sells—and helped the company trounce Kmart—probably worked fewer hours than you do in an average week.

None of the people who are racking up amazing success stories and creating cool stuff are doing it just by working more hours than you are. And I hate to say it, but they're not smarter than you, either. They're succeeding by doing hard work.

As the economy plods along, many of us are choosing to take the easy way out. We're going to work for the Man, letting him do the hard work while we work the long hours. We're going back to the future, to a definition of work that embraces the grindstone.

Some people (a precious few, so far) are realizing that this temporary recession is the best opportunity that they've ever had. They're working harder than ever—mentally—and taking all sorts of emotional and personal risks that are bound to pay off.

Hard work is about risk. It begins when you deal with the things that you'd rather not deal with: fear of failure, fear of standing out, fear of rejection. Hard work is about training yourself to leap over this barrier, tunnel under that barrier, drive through the other barrier. And after you've done that, to do it again the next day.

The big insight: the riskier your (smart) coworker's hard work appears to be, the safer it really is. It's the people having difficult conversations, inventing remarkable products, and pushing the envelope (and, perhaps, still going home at 5 P.M.) who are building a recession-proof future for themselves.

So tomorrow, when you go to work, really sweat. Your time is worth the effort.

Random Acts of Initiative

As a young, first-year student at the Stanford MBA program (most of the other 300 students had wasted a few years working at a bank, but he came straight from undergrad), Chip Conley picked out four other students—strangers to him and to each other—and invited them to a weekly brainstorming session. He explained to us that once a week we'd meet for four hours and brainstorm business plans and entrepreneurial ventures.

A year later, we had compiled more than 500 great ideas and countless lousy ones, and we had figured out how to think about the structure of a business. I think the five of us would all agree we learned more in that room in the anthropology department than we did in the classes we were paying for.

The extraordinary thing about Chip's little bit of initiative in setting up the group is how rare it is. Successful people have this in common. It's not the giant breakthroughs, it's the willingness to take little chances.

Chip has gone on to be the most successful of our team, running one of the largest independent hotel chains in California. We had a deal: I agreed not to open hotels; he agreed not to write books. He's written a book [update: now it's a few], and they're worth checking out.

Even if you don't have an anthropology department nearby, there's no doubt that there's some small piece of initiative you can grab ahold of tomorrow.

Big Ideas

Padmanabhan wrote me a nice note today, asking why I so freely give away ideas. (It was nice because he thought some of the ideas were actually good ones.)

I responded that ideas are easy; doing stuff is hard.

My feeling is that the more often you create and share ideas, the better you get at it. The process of manipulating and ultimately spreading ideas improves both the quality and the quantity of what you create; at least it does for me.

History is littered with inventors who had "great" ideas but kept them quiet and then poorly executed them. And history is lit up with doers who took ideas that were floating around in the ether and actually made something happen. In fact, just about every successful venture is based on an unoriginal idea, beautifully executed.

So, if you've got ideas, let them go. They're probably holding you back from the hard work of actually executing.

Sweet-Spot Marketing

Golf (or maybe tennis) has the true myth of the sweet spot. That special part of the club (racket) that magically makes the ball go farther and straighter.

There's a sweet spot in promotion and PR as well. Let me give you a few examples from the book world to get us started:

Peter Drucker was in the sweet spot for the *Harvard Business Review*. His background, reputation, and style of writing contributed to his writing more pieces for them than anyone else. (My stuff, on the other hand, is blacklisted by the *HBR*. They won't even consider my work.)

If you want to get reviewed by the *New York Times Book Review*, don't even consider self-publishing. Don't write a how-to book. Don't write something particularly funny, either. But it sure helps to be published by Knopf. Literary fiction by respected writers published by Knopf is the sweet spot (history comes in a close second).

There's a sweet spot for getting on *Oprah* and for being on NPR as well. You rarely hear about romance novels on *All Things Considered*.

My point isn't that you shouldn't try to get these middlemen to broaden their horizons or that you should give up on something you're passionate about. It's just that it might be easier to build a new sweet spot than it is to persuade an established middleman to change his rules for you.

I never had a chance with existing magazines, so I invented a writing style for myself that worked well with *Fast Company*, which until then had never had a columnist. Bloggers around the world are discovering that it's cheaper and faster and more effective to build their own media channels than it is to waste time arguing with the old ones.

So I guess my advice would be to either build your product and network along the way to align with exactly what the middlemen want, or reject them and live/thrive without them. It's the middle ground that's really frustrating.

The First Thing to Do This Year

Google yourself.

If you're a salesperson, your prospects already do.

If you're looking for a job, your prospective employers already do.

If you've got a job, your coworkers already do.

What do they see? Do you know?

If you don't like it, you can fix it. Start a blog, even if it's just a few pages' worth. Have some colleagues suggest you for Wikipedia (if the powers that be think you're notable enough), or make sure you're represented on HubPages or Squidwho, or write an article for ChangeThis.

You can be finished by tonight. It's worth it.

Have to Vs. Get To

Someone asked me the other day if posting a blog post every day is intimidating or a grind.

I view it as something I *get* to do. I spend most of my blogging time deciding what not to post.

The best work, at least for me, is the stuff you get to do. If you are really good at that, you're lucky enough to have very little of the *have-to* stuff left.

The Forces of Mediocrity

Maybe it should be "the forces for mediocrity . . ."

There's a myth that all you need to do is outline your vision and prove it's right—then, quite suddenly, people will line up and support you.

In fact, the opposite is true. Remarkable visions and genuine insight are always met with resistance. And when you start to make progress, your efforts are met with even more resistance. Products, services, career paths . . . whatever it is, the forces for mediocrity will align to stop you, forgiving no errors and never backing down until it's over.

If it were any other way, it would be easy. And if it were any other way, everyone would do it and your work would ultimately be devalued. The yin and yang are clear: without people pushing against your quest to do something worth talking about, it's unlikely that it would be worth the journey. Persist.

Persistence

Persistence isn't using the same tactics over and over. That's just annoying.

Persistence is having the same goal over and over.

Getting Vs. Taking

Most people spend a lot of time to get an education.

They wait for the teacher (hopefully a great one) to give them something of value.

Many employees do the same thing at work. They wait for a boss (hopefully a great one) to give them responsibility or authority or experiences that add up to a career.

A few people—not many, but a few—take. They take the best education they can get, pushing teachers for more, finding things to do, exploring non-defined niches. They take more courses than the minimum, they invent new projects, and they show up with questions.

A few people, not many, take opportunities at work. Marketers have the easiest time of this (it's sort of hard to commandeer the chain saw) but don't do it nearly as often as they should.

What have you taken today?

Drip, Drip, Drip Goes the Twit

I trust Sara Fishko.

I don't know her, I've never bought anything from her, and I wouldn't recognize her if we met, but I trust her.

Every once in a while, over the last few years, Sara's voice has come out of my radio, telling me about one interesting cultural event or another. She's consistent. She shows up. She has built a body of work over time, taking her time, that has led to trust.

Twitter can do that for you.

Not for a million New Yorkers, but perhaps for a hundred or a thousand people you want to reach. Blogs do the same thing.

The best time to look for a job next year is right now. The best time to plan for a sale in three years is right now. The mistake so many marketers make is that they conflate the urgency of making another sale with the timing of earning the right to make that sale. In other words, you must build trust before you need it. Building trust right when you want to make a sale is just too late.

Publishing your ideas—in books, or on a blog, or in little twits on Twitter—and doing it with patience, over time, is the best way I can think of to lay a foundation for whatever it is you hope to do next.

How to Read a Business Book

I like reading magic books.

I don't do magic. Not often (and not well). But reading the books is fun. It's a vicarious thing, imagining how a trick might work, visualizing the effect, and then smiling at how the technique is done. One trick after another, it's a pleasant adventure.

A lot of people read business books in just the same way. They cruise through the case studies or the insights or examples and imagine what it would be like to be that brilliant entrepreneur or that successful CEO or that great sales rep. A pleasant adventure.

There's a huge gap between most how-to books (cookbooks, gardening, magic, etc.) and business books, though. The gap is motivation. Gardening books don't push you to actually do something. Cookbooks don't spend a lot of time trying to sell you on why making a roast chicken isn't as risky as you might think.

The stakes are a lot higher when it comes to business.

Wreck a roast chicken and it's $12 down the drain. Wreck a product launch and there goes your career.

I'm passionate about writing business books precisely for this reason. There are more business books sold than most other nonfiction categories for the same reason. High stakes, high rewards.

The fascinating thing is this: I spend 95% of my time persuading people to take action and just 5% of the time on the recipes.

The recipe that makes up just about any business book can be condensed to just two or three pages. The rest is the sell. The proof. The persuasion.

Which leads to your role as the reader. How to read a business book—it's not as obvious as it seems.

- Bullet points are not the point.

If you're reading for the recipe, and just the recipe, you can get through a business book in just a few minutes. But most people who do that get very little out of the experience. Take a look at the widely divergent reviews for *The Dip*. The people who "got it" understood that it was a book about getting you to change your perspective and thus your behavior. Those who didn't get it were looking for bullet points. They wasted their money.

Computer books, of course, are nothing but bullet points. Programmers get amazing value because for $30 they are presented with everything they need to program with a certain tool. Yet most programmers are not world class, precisely because the bullet points aren't enough to get them to see things the way the author does, and aren't enough to get them motivated enough to actually program great code.

So, how to read a business book:

1. Decide, before you start, that you're going to change three things about what you do all day at work. Then, as you're reading, find the three things and do them. The goal of the reading, then, isn't to persuade you to change; it's to help you choose *what* to change.

2. If you're going to invest a valuable asset (like time), go ahead and make it productive. Use a Post-it or two, or some index cards or a highlighter. Not to write down stuff so you can forget it later, but to create marching orders. It's simple: if three weeks go by and you haven't taken action on what you've written down, you've wasted your time.

3. It's not about you, it's about the next person. The single best use of a business book is to help someone else. Sharing what you read, handing the book to a person who needs it—pushing those around you to get in sync and to take action—that's the main reason it's a book, not a video or a seminar. A book is a souvenir and a container and a motivator and an easily leveraged tool. Hoarding books makes them worth less, not more.

Effective managers hand books to their teams. Not so they can be reminded of high school, but so that next week she can say to them, "Are we there yet?"

Like Your Hair Is on Fire

In the U.S., the next two weeks are traditionally the slowest of the year. Plenty of vacations, half-day Fridays, casual Mondays, martini Tuesdays . . . you get the idea.

What if you and your team go against type? What if you spend the two weeks while your competitors (and the forces for the status quo) are snoozing—and turn whatever you're working on into a completed project?

So, here's the challenge: assemble your team (it might be just you) on Monday and focus like your hair is on fire (I have no direct experience in this area, but I'm told that hair flammability is quite urgent).

Do nothing except finish the project. Hey, you could have been on vacation, so it's okay to neglect everything else, to put your email on vacation auto respond, and your phone on voice mail and to beg off on the sleepy weekly all-hands meeting and to avoid the interactions with those who might say no.

And then finish it. Finish the website or the manuscript or the business plan or the suite of tools. No, this isn't a great week to do outreach or make a pitch. That's not the goal. It's to finish that project that's been stuck too long. Finish it or cancel it.

Looking for a Reason to Hide

I've seen it before and I'm sure I'll see it again.

Whenever a business cycle starts to falter, the media start wringing their hands. Then big businesses do, then freelancers, then entrepreneurs, and soon everyone is keening.

People and organizations that have no real financial stress start to pull back "because it's prudent." Now is not the time, they say. They cut budgets and put off investments. It's almost as if everyone is just waiting for an excuse to do less.

In fact, they are.

Growth is frightening for a lot of people. It brings change and the opportunity for public failure. So if the astrological signs aren't right or the water is too cold or we've got a twinge in our elbow, we find an excuse. We decide to do it later, or not at all.

What a shame. What a waste.

Inc. magazine reports that a huge percentage of companies in this year's *Inc.* 500 were founded within months of 9/11. Talk about uncertain times.

But uncertain times, frozen liquidity, political change, and poor astrological forecasts (not to mention chicken entrails) all lead to less competition, more available talent, and a do-or-die attitude that causes real change to happen.

If I weren't already running my own business, today is the day I'd start one.

Is Effort a Myth?

People really want to believe that effort is a myth, at least if we consider what we consume in the media:

- politicians and beauty queens who get by on a smile and a wink
- lottery winners who turn a lifetime of lousy jobs into one big payday
- sports stars who are born with skills we could never hope to acquire
- Hollywood celebrities with the talent of being in the right place at the right time
- failed CEOs with $40 million buyouts

It really seems (at least if you read popular media) that who you know and whether you get "picked" are the two keys to success. Luck.

The thing about luck is this: we're already lucky. We're insanely lucky that we weren't born during the Black Plague or in a country with no freedom. We're lucky that we've got access to highly leveraged tools and terrific opportunities. If we set that luck aside, though, something interesting shows up.

Delete the outliers—the people who are hit by a bus or win the lottery, the people who luck out in a big way—and we're left with everyone else. And for everyone else, effort is directly related to success. Not all the time, but as much as you would expect. Smarter, harder-working, better-informed, and better-liked people do better than other people, most of the time.

Effort takes many forms. Showing up, certainly. Knowing stuff (being smart might be the luck of the draw, but knowing stuff is the result of effort). Being kind when it's more fun not to be. Paying forward when there's no hope of tangible reward. Doing the right thing. You've heard these things a hundred times before, of course, but I guess it's easier to bet on luck.

If people aren't betting on luck, then why do we make so many dumb choices? Why aren't useful books selling at fifty times the rate they sell now? Why does anyone, ever, watch reality TV shows? Why do people do such dumb stuff with their money?

I think we've been tricked by the veneer of lucky people on the top of the heap. We see the folks who manage to skate by, or who get so much more than we think they deserve, and it's easy to forget that:

A. these guys are the exceptions,

and

B. there's nothing you can do about it anyway.

And that's the key to the paradox of effort: while luck may be more appealing than effort, you don't get to choose luck. Effort, on the other hand, is totally available, all the time.

This is a hard sell. Diet books that say "eat less, exercise more" may work, but they don't sell many copies.

With that forewarning, here's a bootstrapper's/marketer's/entrepreneur's/fast-rising executive's effort diet. Go through the list and decide whether each item is worth it. Or make up your own diet. Effort is a choice, so at least make it on purpose:

1. Delete 120 minutes a day of "spare time" from your life. This can include watching TV, reading the newspaper, commuting, wasting time in social networks, and going to meetings. Up to you.
2. Spend the 120 minutes doing this instead:
   - Exercise for 30 minutes.
   - Read relevant nonfiction (trade magazines, journals, business books, blogs, etc.).

- Send three thank-you notes.
- Learn new digital techniques (spreadsheet macros, Firefox short-cuts, productivity tools, graphic design, HTML coding).
- Volunteer.
- Blog for five minutes about something you learned.
- Give a speech once a month about something you don't currently know a lot about.

3. Spend at least one weekend day doing absolutely nothing but being with people you love.

4. For one year, spend money on only the things you absolutely need to get by. Save the rest of your money, relentlessly.

If you somehow pulled this off, then six months from now, you would be the fittest, best-rested, most intelligent, best-funded, and most motivated person in your office or your field. You would know how to do things that other people don't, you'd have a wider network, and you'd be more focused.

It's entirely possible that this effort won't be sufficient and you will continue to need better luck. But it's a lot more likely that you'll get lucky, I bet.

Maybe You Can't Make Money Doing What You Love

The thing is, it's far easier than ever before to surface your ideas. Far easier to have someone notice your art or your writing or your photography. Which means that people who might have hidden their talents are now finding them noticed.

That blog you've built, the one with a lot of traffic . . . perhaps it can't be monetized.

That nonprofit you work with, the one where you are able to change lives . . . perhaps turning it into a career will ruin it.

That passion you have for art . . . perhaps making your painting commercial enough to sell will squeeze the joy out of it.

When what you do is what you love, you're able to invest more effort and care and time. That means you're more likely to win, to gain share, to profit. On the other hand, poets don't get paid. Even worse, poets that try to get paid end up writing jingles and failing and hating it at the same time.

Today, there are more ways than ever to share your talents and hobbies in public. And if you're driven, talented, and focused, you may discover that the market loves what you do. That people read your blog or click on your cartoons or listen to your MP3s. But, alas, that doesn't mean you can monetize it, quit your day job, and spend all day writing songs.

The pitfalls:

1. In order to monetize your work, you'll probably corrupt it, taking out the magic in search of dollars;

and

2. Attention doesn't always equal significant cash flow.

I think it makes sense to make your art, your art, to give yourself over to it without regard for commerce.

Doing what you love is as important as ever, but if you're going to make a living at it, it helps to find a niche where money flows as a regular consequence of the success of your idea. Loving what you do is almost as important as doing what you love, especially if you need to make a living at it. Go find a job you can commit to, a career or a business you can fall in love with.

A friend who loved music, who wanted to spend his life doing it, got a job doing PR for a record label. He hated doing PR, realized that just because he was in the record business didn't mean he had anything at all to do with music. Instead of finding a job he could love, he ended up being in proximity to, but nowhere involved with, something he cared about. I wish he had become a committed schoolteacher instead, spending every minute of his spare time making music and sharing it online for free. Instead, he's a frazzled publicity hound working twice as many hours for less money and doing no music at all.

Maybe you can't make money doing what you love (at least what you love right now). But I bet you can figure out how to love what you do to make money (if you choose wisely).

Do your art. But don't wreck your art if it doesn't lend itself to paying the bills. That would be a tragedy.

(And the twist, because there is always a twist, is that as soon as you focus on your art and leave the money behind, you may just discover that this focus turns out to be the secret of actually breaking through and making money.)

Be Careful of Who You Work For

The single most important marketing decision most people make is also the one we spend precious little time on: where we work.

Think about this for a second. Your boss and your job determine not only what you do all day, but what you learn and whom you interact with. Where you work is what you market. Work in a high-stress place and you're likely to become a highly stressed person, and your interactions will display that. Work for a narcissist and you'll develop into someone who's good at shining a light on someone else, not into someone who can lead. Work for someone who plays the fads and you'll discover that instead of building a steadily improving brand, you're jumping from one thing to another, enduring layoffs in between gold rushes. Work for a bully and be prepared to be bullied.

And yet, there are plenty of books about getting a job, but no books I know of about *choosing* a job. There are hundreds of sites where job seekers can go to find a new job, and virtually none where you can find reviews of bosses or companies or jobs.

Ted Zoromski really needed a job, so he took one doing human spam (outbound telemarketing). That was his first mistake. That kind of work isn't a stepping stone to something better, it doesn't teach you much, it grinds you down, and it doesn't make you more marketable. When he found that he was also making calls he found offensive, he quit.

Years ago, when I had ten people working for me at my book packaging company, one client accounted for about half our revenue. They were difficult, constantly threatening litigation, sending lawyers to otherwise productive meetings, questioning our ethics, and more. It was clearly the culture of their organization to be at war. So I fired them. I gave them the rights and walked away, even though it meant a huge hit to our organization. Why do it? Because if we had stuck with them, it would have changed who we were, who we hired, and how we marketed ourselves going forward. We would have had a lifetime of this.

How many job offers with good pay have you turned down in your lifetime? How many clients? Compare that to how many times you've been rejected. That's totally out of whack. Great marketing involves having a great product, and not every job (or every client) is worth your time or attention or love.

If you want to become the kind of person that any company would kill to have as an employee, you need to be the kind of employee that's really picky about whom you align with.

Reacting, Responding, and Initiating

Most knowledge workers spend their day doing one of three things:

- Reacting (badly) to external situations
- Responding (well) to external inputs
- Initiating new events or ideas

Zig taught me the difference between the first two. When you react to a medication, that's a bad thing. When you respond to treatment, that's a plus.

So, think about your team or your front-line staff or your CEO. Something happens in the outside world: an angry comment on Twitter or a disappointed passenger on your airline or a change in the stock price.

Do you react to it? How much of your time is spent reacting to what people say in meetings or emails?

The rest of your day may be spent responding. Responding to a request for proposals. Responding to a form in your inbox. Responding to emails or responding to status updates on Facebook. Responding is gratifying, because you go from having something to do to having something done. There's a pile in a different spot on your desk at the end of the day. You responded to the needs of the tribe you lead, or you responded to password-change requests or you responded to the boss's punch list.

And that's it. You go home having done virtually nothing in the third bucket.

We tend to reserve the third bucket, initiate, for quiet times, good times, down times, or desperate times. We wait until the inbox is empty or the new product lines are due (at which point the initiative is more of a response). It's possible to spend an entire day blogging and Twittering and Facebooking and never initiate a thing; just respond to what's coming in. It's possible to spend an entire day at P&G (actually it's possible to spend an entire career) doing nothing but responding.

Take a look at your Sent folder. Is it filled with subject lines that start with "RE:"? Consider your job at the university—do you actively recruit people who don't even apply for professorships? What about your blog—does it start conversations or just continue them?

What did your brand or organization initiate today?

What did *you* initiate?

Think about the changes you'd have to make (uh-oh, initiate) in your work day in order to dramatically change the quantity and scale of the initiatives you create.

Some marketing jobs are about responding. None are about reacting. The best ones are about initiating.

How to Make Money Using the Internet

Make money: not by building an Internet company, but by using the 'Net as a tool to create value and get paid. Use the Internet as a tool, not as an end. Do it when you are part of a big organization or do it as a soloist. The dramatic leverage of the 'Net more than overcomes the downs of the current economy.

The essence is this: **connect**.

Connect the disconnected to each other, and you create value.

- Connect advertisers to people who want to be advertised to.
- Connect job hunters with jobs.
- Connect information seekers with information.
- Connect teams to each other.
- Connect those seeking similar.

- Connect to partners and those that can leverage your work.
- Connect people who are proximate geographically.
- Connect organizations spending money with ways to save money.
- Connect like-minded people into a movement.
- Connect people buying with people who are selling.

Some examples? I think it's worth delineating these so you can see that the opportunity can be big, if that's your taste, or small, if you don't want to invest heavily just yet.

Connect advertisers to people who want to be advertised to.

Dany Levy did this with Daily Candy, a company she recently sold for more than a hundred million dollars. Daily Candy uses simple email software; there are no technology tricks involved. Instead, it's a simple permission marketing business: hundreds of thousands of the right people, getting an anticipated, personal, and relevant email every day. (Note! This works only if you earn true permission, not that sort of fake half-and-half version that's so common.)

Connect job hunters with jobs.

My friend Tara has made hundreds of thousands of dollars (in good years) working as an executive recruiter. But what did she actually do all day? She stayed connected with a cadre of people. She kept track of the all-stars. She connected with the right people, investing time in them that her clients never thought was worth it. So, when it was time to hire, it was easier for them to call Tara than it was for them to start from scratch. The best time to start a gig like this is right now, when no one in particular wants to connect with and help out the superstars. Later, when the economy bounces back, your position will be extremely valuable. (Note! This works only if you have insane focus and if the people you interact with are the true superstars, not just numbers.)

Connect information seekers with information.

At a large scale, this is what Bloomberg did to make his fortune. Spending \$\$\$ on a Bloomberg terminal guarantees a user at least a 15-minute head start on people who don't have one. But consider the number of micro-markets where this connection doesn't occur. Michael Cader offers it to book publishers and does quite well. Which industry needs you to channel and collect and connect?

On a micro level, there are now people making thousands of dollars a month running their pages on Squidoo. That's almost enough to be a full-time job for a curious person with the generosity to share useful information.

Connect teams to each other.

How much is on the line when a company puts ten people in three offices on a quest to launch a major new product in record time? The question, then, is why wouldn't they be willing to spend a little more to hire a team concierge? Someone to manage Basecamp and conference calls and scheduling and document source control to be sure the right people have the right information at the right time? I don't think most organizations can hire someone to do this full-time, but I bet this is a great specialty for someone who is good at it.

Connect those seeking similar.

Who's running the ad hoc association of green residential architects? Or connecting the hundred CFOs at the hundred largest banks in the U.S.? It's amazing how isolated most people are, even in a world crowded with people. I know of a guy who built an insanely profitable business around connecting C-level executives at the *Fortune* 500. After all, there are only 500 of them. They want to know what the others are doing.

Connect to partners and those that can leverage your work.

Freelancers had no power because they depended on the client to hook them up with the rest of the team that could leverage their work. But what if you do that before you approach the client? What if you, the graphic designer, have a virtual partner who is an award-winning copywriter, and another partner who is a well-known illustrator? You could walk in the door and offer detailed PDFs or other high-impact viral electronic media in a turnkey package.

Connect people who are proximate geographically.

We all know that newspapers are tanking. Yet news, it appears, is on the rise. This paradox is an opportunity. Who is connecting the 10,000 people in your little community/suburb/town/ZIP code to each other? One person who spends all day at school board meetings, breaking stories about a dumping scandal, profiling a local businessperson or teacher? If you did that, and built an audience of thousands by RSS and email, do you think you'd have any trouble selling out the monthly cocktail party/mixers? Any trouble finding sponsors among local businesses for a media property that actually and truly reaches everyone?

Connect organizations spending money with ways to save money.

During the last recession, plenty of entrepreneurs scored by selling businesses on doing a phone bill audit. They took 30% of the first year's savings and did the work for free. Today, there are countless ways that businesses can save money by using technology and outsourcing, but few take full advantage. You can train them to do this and keep a share of the savings.

Connect like-minded people into a movement.

We've seen plenty of headstrong bootstrapped entrepreneurs turn a blog into the cornerstone of a multimillion-dollar empire. The secret: they don't write their blog for everyone. Instead, they use the blog as the center connecting point for a niche, and then go from there. It's easy to list the tech successes, but there are literally 10,000 other niches just waiting for someone to connect them.

Connect people buying with people who are selling.

Sure, you know how to use Craigslist and eBay to buy and sell, but most people don't. How about finding people in your town with junk that needs removing, items that need selling, odd jobs that need filling, and then, for a fee, solve their problems, using your laptop and these existing networks? Imagine the power, to pick just one example, of building an email alert list of 500 garage-sale bargain hunters. Every time you email them, they show up. Now, you can walk into any home in any town and guarantee the biggest garage sale success they've ever seen, and you have the photos to prove it. As long as you protect the list and do for your subscribers, not to them, this asset increases in value.

The best time to do any of these projects was five years ago, so that today you'd be earning thousands of dollars a week. Too late. The second best time to start: now.

Time to Start a Newspaper

What should not-so-busy real estate brokers do?

Why not start a local newspaper?

Here's how I would do it. Assume you've got six people in your office. Each person needs to do two things each day:

- Interview a local business, a local student, or a local political activist. You can do it by phone, it can be very short, and it might take you ten minutes.
- Get 20 households to "subscribe" by giving you their email addresses and asking for a free subscription. You can use direct contact or fly-ers or speeches to get your list.

Twice a week, send out the "newspaper" by email. After one week, it will have more than 500 subscribers and contain more than 20 interesting short articles or quotes about people in the neighborhood. Within a month (if it's any good), every single person in town who matters will be reading it and forwarding it along to others.

It will cost you nothing. It will become your gift to the community. And it will be a long-lasting asset that belongs to you, not to the competition. (And yes, you can do this if you're a plumber or a chiropractor. And yes, you can do this if "local" isn't geographic for you, but vertical.)

Own your ZIP code. The next frontier is local, and this is a great way to start.

The Goals You Never Hear About

Doing goal-setting with friends and colleagues is always motivating and invigorating for me. You hear things ranging from "I want to help this village get out of poverty" to "I want to double our market share" or "I want to be financially independent."

What you rarely hear is, "I don't want to fail," "I don't want to look stupid," or "I don't want to make any mistakes."

The problem is that those goals are really common, and when they're left unsaid, they dominate. If your goal is not to be called on in class, that's a largely achievable goal, right?

Think about how often your goal at a conference or a meeting or in a project is "don't screw up!" or "don't make a fool of yourself and say the wrong thing." These are very easy goals to achieve, of course. Just do as little as possible. The problem is that they sabotage your real goals, the achievement ones.

It's not stupid to have a stated goal of starting several ventures that will fail, or asking three stupid questions a week, or posting a blog post that the world disagrees with. If you don't have goals like this, how exactly are you going to luck into being remarkable?

What Are You Good At?

As you consider marketing yourself for your next gig, consider the difference between process and content.

Content is domain knowledge. People you know or skills you've developed. Playing the piano or writing copy about furniture sales. A Rolodex of movers in a given industry, or your ability to compute stress ratios in your head.

Domain knowledge is important, but it's (often) easily learnable.

Process, on the other hand, refers to the emotional-intelligence skills you have about managing projects, visualizing success, persuading other people of your point of view, dealing with multiple priorities, etc. This stuff is insanely valuable and hard to learn. Unfortunately, it's usually overlooked by headhunters and HR folks, partly because it's hard to accredit or check off in a database.

Venture capitalists like hiring second- or third-time entrepreneurs because they understand process, not because they can do a spreadsheet.

As the world changes ever faster, as industries shrink and others grow, this process ability becomes priceless. Figure out which sort of process you're world-class at and get even better at it. Then, learn the domain—that's what the Internet is for.

One of the reasons that super-talented people become entrepreneurs is that they can put their process expertise to work in a world that often undervalues it.

Solving a Different Problem

The telephone destroyed the telegraph.

Here's why people liked the telegraph: it was universal, inexpensive, and asynchronous and it left a paper trail.

The telephone offered not one of these four attributes. It was far from universal, and if someone didn't have a phone, you couldn't call them. It was expensive, even before someone called you. It was synchronous—if you weren't home, no call got made or received. And of course, there was no paper trail.

If the telephone guys had set out to make something that did what the telegraph does, but better, they probably would have failed. Instead, they solved a different problem, in such an overwhelmingly useful way that they eliminated the feature set of the competition.

The list of examples is long (YouTube vs. television, Web vs. newspapers, Nike vs. sneakers). Your turn.

Do You Deserve It?

Do you deserve the luck you've been handed? The place you were born, the education you were given, the job you've got? Do you deserve your tribe, your customer base, your brand?

Not at all. "Deserve" is such a loaded word. Most of us don't deserve the great opportunities we have, or the lucky breaks that got us here.

The question shouldn't be "Do you deserve it?" I think it should be "What are you going to do with it now that you've got it?"

Slack

A lot of corporations have seen dramatic decreases in revenue and have cut back projects as well. In many cases, these cutbacks were accompanied by layoffs, and so everyone who's left is working far harder.

But in other organizations, and for a lot of freelancers, there's more time than work. In other words, slack time.

Assume for a moment that you don't have money to develop and launch something new. So, what are you going to do with the slack?

What can you build over the next year that will take time now and pay off later? How can you invest the slack to build a marketing asset that you'll own forever?

May I offer two suggestions:

1. Learn something. Become an expert. For free, using nothing but time, you can become a master of CSS or HTML or learn Python. You can hit the library and read the entire works of important authors, or you can borrow some books from a friend and master analytics or discover case studies and corporate histories that will be invaluable in a year. You could learn to become fluent in Spanish.

If you're a glass blower without a job, you can't do much glass blowing. But if you're a digital marketer between gigs, you can do a lot of digital marketing. Build a tribe for your favorite nonprofit and make it a case study for an entire industry.

2. Earn a following and a reputation. Use social networking tools to connect to people for no good reason. Post tons of useful answers on discussion boards where your expertise is valued. Build a permission asset in the form of an email newsletter or a fascinating blog that people want to read. Do résumé makeovers for 100 friends. Start a neighborhood or industry book group. Don't go to conventions; earn the right to speak at them.

If you were as serious about these two endeavors as you are about doing your job (eight hours a day on a slow day), imagine how much more powerful and in demand you'll be a year from now.

Beats the alternative, by far.

First, Ten

This, in two words, is the secret of the new marketing.

Find ten people. Ten people who trust you/respect you/need you/ listen to you.

Those ten people need what you have to sell, or want it. And if they love it, you win. If they love it, they'll each find you ten more people (or a hundred or a thousand or, perhaps, just three). Repeat.

If they don't love it, you need a new product. Start over.

Your idea spreads. Your business grows. Not as fast as you want, but faster than you could ever imagine.

This approach changes the posture and timing of everything you do.

You can no longer market to the anonymous masses. They're not anonymous and they're not masses. You can market only to people who are willing participants. Like this group of ten.

The timing means that the idea of a "launch" and press releases and the big unveiling is nuts. Instead, plan on the gradual build that turns into a tidal wave. Organize for it and spend money appropriately. The fact is, the curve of money spent (big hump, then it tails off) is precisely backward from what you actually need.

Three years from now, this advice will be so common as to be boring. Today, it's almost certainly the opposite of what you're doing.

Can You Change Everything?

You might not be as permanently stuck in a rut as you think. The rut you're in isn't permanent, nor is it perfect. There are certainly less-perfect ruts, but there may be better ones as well. The certain thing is that you can change everything.

1. Buy a competitor.
2. Sell to a competitor.
3. Publish your best work for free online.
4. Close your worst-performing locations.
5. Open a new branch in a high-traffic location.
6. Hire the best salesperson away from the competition.
7. Join the competition.
8. Host a conference for your competitors.
9. Connect your best customers and organize a tribe.
10. Fire the 80% of your customers that account for 20% of your sales.
11. Start a blog.
12. Start a digital bootstrap business on the weekends.

13. While looking for a job, spend 40 hours a week volunteering and freelancing for good causes.
14. Go on tour and visit your best customers in person.
15. Answer the customer service line for a day.
16. Learn to be a killer presenter.
17. Let the most junior person in the organization run things for a day.
18. Delete your website and start over with the simplest possible site.
19. Call former employees and ask for advice.
20. Move to Thailand.
21. Listen to audiobooks, instead of the radio, in your car.
22. Sell your cash-cow division to the competition and invest everything in the new thing.
23. Find more products for your existing customers to buy.
24. Become a gadfly and tell the truth about your industry.
25. Quit your job.
26. Move your operations to another city.
27. Become a vegan.
28. Have all meetings in a room with no chairs, and have everyone wear a bathrobe over their clothes.
29. Open your offices only four hours a day.
30. Open your offices 24 hours a day for a week.
31. Find every project that is near the danger zone (in terms of P&L or deadlines) and cancel it; no appeals.
32. Go for a walk during lunch.
33. Get an RSS reader and read a lot more blogs.
34. Go offline for longer than you thought possible.
35. Write five thank-you notes every day.
36. Stop sending spam.
37. Do your work somewhere else. Set up your chiropractic table at the mall.
38. Have everyone at work switch offices.
39. Give your most valuable possessions to a stranger.
40. Go see live music.
41. Start a company scrapbook and take daily notes.
42. Hire a firm to make a documentary about your organization.
43. Buy some art.

44. Make some art.

45. Do the work.

Graduate School for Unemployed College Students

Fewer college grads have jobs than at any other time in recent memory—a report by the National Association of Colleges and Employers annual student survey said that 20% of 2009 college graduates who applied for a job actually have one. So, what should the unfortunate 80% do?

How about a postgraduate year doing some combination of the following (not just one, how about all):

- Spend twenty hours a week running a project for a nonprofit.
- Teach yourself Java, HTML, Flash, PHP, *and* SQL. Not a little, but to the point of mastery. [Clarification: I know you can't become a master programmer of all these in a year. I used the word "mastery" to distinguish it from "familiarity," which is what you get from one of those *Dummies*-type books. I would hope you could write code that solves problems, works, and is reasonably clear, not that you could program well enough to work for Joel Spolsky. Sorry if I ruffled feathers.]
- Volunteer to coach or assistant coach a kids' sports team.
- Start, run, and grow an online community.
- Give a speech a week to local organizations.
- Write a regular newsletter or blog about an industry you care about.
- Learn a foreign language fluently.
- Write three detailed business plans for projects in the industry you care about.
- Self-publish a book.
- Run a marathon.

Beats law school.

If you wake up every morning at six, give up TV, and treat this list like a job, you'll have no trouble accomplishing everything on it. Everything! When you do, what happens to your job prospects?

Crowded at the Top

In the 260 weeks from 1966 to 1970, there were only *thirteen* musical acts responsible for every #1 album on the Billboard charts.

In the 260 weeks that accounted for the first half of the 1970s, it was 26. (Hat tip to John Marks for the stat.)

Sometimes, we define a golden age in a market as a time of stability, when one or a few giants capture all of our attention. AT&T telephones, Superman comics, Beatles records, IBM computers, *The New York Times* . . . and now Google. Choices are easy, the market grows without a lot of effort, and we marvel over the ease of success. Ironically, the success of these winners attracts quixotic entrepreneurs, people who set out to challenge the few who are winning. While we might root for these underdogs, it turns out that they're not the ones who usually change everything. The powerful are still too powerful.

The real growth and development and the foundations for the next era are laid during the chaotic times, the times that come *after* the leaders have stumbled. Harry Chapin didn't trip up the Beatles, but the breakup of the Beatles allowed Harry Chapin his chance. The next golden ages of journalism, of communications, of fashion, of car design— those are being established now, in a moment when it's not so crowded at the top.

The very best time to launch a new product or service is when the market appears exhausted or depleted. There's more room at the top and there are fewer people in a hurry to get there.

Without Them

One of the most common things I hear is, "I'd like to do something re-markable like that, but my xyz won't let me," where "my xyz" = my boss, my publisher, my partner, my licensor, my franchisor, etc.

Well, you can fail by going along with that and not doing it, or you can do it, cause a ruckus, and work things out later.

In my experience, once it's clear that you're willing to do something remarkable (not just willing, but itching, moving, and yes, implementing) without them, things start to happen. People are rarely willing to step up and stop you, and are often just waiting to follow someone crazy enough to actually do something.

I'm going. Come along if you like.

No, Everything Is Not Going to Be Okay

It's natural to seek reassurance. Most of us want to believe that the choices we make will work out, that everything will be okay.

Artists and those that launch the untested, the new and the emotional (and I'd put marketers into all of these categories) wrestle with this need all the time. How can we proceed, knowing that there's a good chance that our actions will fail, that things might get worse, that everything won't end up okay? In search of solace, we seek reassurance.

So people lie to us. So we lie to ourselves.

No, everything is not going to be okay. It never is. It isn't okay now. Change, by definition, changes things. It makes some things better and some things worse. But everything is never okay.

Finding the bravery to shun faux reassurance is a critical step in producing important change. Once you free yourself from the need for perfect acceptance, it's a lot easier to launch work that matters.

Modern Procrastination

The lizard brain adores a deadline that slips, an item that doesn't ship and, most of all, busywork.

These represent safety, because if you don't challenge the status quo, you can't be made fun of, can't fail, can't be laughed at. And so the Resistance looks for ways to appear busy while not actually doing anything.

I'd like to posit that for idea workers, misusing Twitter, Facebook, and various forms of digital networking is the ultimate expression of procrastination. You can be busy, very busy, forever. The more you do, the longer the queue gets. The bigger your circle, the more connections are available.

Laziness in a white-collar job has nothing to do with avoiding hard physical labor. "Who wants to help me move this box?" Instead, it has to do with avoiding difficult (and apparently risky) intellectual labor.

"Honey, how was your day?"

"Oh, I was busy, incredibly busy."

"I get that you were busy. But did you do anything important?"

Busy does not equal important. Measured doesn't mean mattered.

When the Resistance pushes you to do the quick reaction, the instant message, the "ping-are-you-still-there," perhaps it pays to push in precisely the opposite direction. Perhaps it's time for the blank sheet of paper, the cancellation of a long-time money loser, the difficult conversation, the creative breakthrough . . .

Or you could check your email.

Genius Is Misunderstood as a Bolt of Lightning

Genius is the act of solving a problem in a way no one has solved it before. It has nothing to do with winning a Nobel Prize in physics or completing certain levels of schooling. It's about using human insight and initiative to find original solutions that matter.

Genius is actually the eventual public recognition of dozens (or hundreds) of failed attempts at solving a problem. Sometimes we fail in public, often we fail in private, but people who are doing creative work are constantly failing.

When the lizard brain kicks in and the Resistance slows you down, the only correct response is to push back again and again and again with one failure after another. Sooner or later, the lizard will get bored and give up.

Do You Make Slush?

A few months ago, *The Wall Street Journal* wrote a piece about the demise of the slush pile, that undifferentiated mass of unsolicited manuscripts from authors and screenwriters in search of a publisher or studio.

In the words of Michael Brooke, "I'm not interested in creating slush."

If you have something good, really good, what's it doing in the slush pile?

Bring it to the world directly, make your own video, write your own ebook, post your own blog, record your own music.

Or find an agent, a great agent, a selective agent, one that's almost impossible to get through to, one that commands respect and acts as a filter because after all, that's what you're seeking: a filtered, amplified way to spread your idea.

But slush?

Good riddance.

One in a Million

The chances of a high school student's eventually becoming first-chair violinist for the Boston Philharmonic: one in a million.

The chances of a high school student's eventually playing basketball in the NBA? About the same.

In fact, the chances of someone's growing up and getting a job precisely like yours, whatever it is, are similarly slim. (Head of development at an ad agency, director of admissions for a great college . . . you get the idea.) Every good gig is a long shot, but in the end, a lot of talented people get good gigs. The odds of being happy and productive and well compensated aren't one in a million at all, because there are many good gigs down the road. The odds are slim only if you pick precisely one job.

Here's the lesson: the ardent or insane pursuit of a particular goal is a good idea if the steps you take along the way also prep you for other outcomes, with each one almost as good as (or better than) the original. If pushing through the Dip and bending the market to your will and shipping on time and doing important and scary work are all skills you need to develop along the way, then it doesn't really matter so much if you don't make the goal you set out to reach.

On the other hand, if you live a life of privation and spend serious time and money on a dead-end path with only one desired outcome, you've described a path likely to leave you broken and bitter. Does spending your teenage years (and your twenties) in a room practicing the violin teach you anything about being a violin teacher or a concert promoter or some other job associated with music? If your happiness depends on your draft pick or a single audition, that's giving way too much power to someone else.

Incoming!

Perhaps the biggest change in your work life is one that snuck up on you.

Every morning, before you even take off your slippers, there's a pile of incoming work. You might not think of it as work, because it doesn't involve stuffing envelopes or making sales calls, but it's part of your career and your job.

That email, Facebook, and text message queue is a lot longer than it used to be. For some people, it's now a hundred or even a thousand distinct social electronic interactions a day. It's as if a genie is whispering in your ear, "I have an envelope, and it might contain really good or really bad news. Want to open it?"

The relevant discussion here: Are the incoming messages helping? After all, most of them aren't initiated by you, but they have the power to change your mood or your energy or even how you spend your non-electronic time. And they're addictive. When, for some random reason, they ebb and you have a really light few hours—admit it, you check more often.

What's up? Is anyone out there?

It's like living near Niagara Falls and then one night it freezes. You miss the noise. Is it possible that the noise is helping you hide from the stuff that scares you?

If you're actually going to do the work, the real work, the work of producing and shipping the things that matter, I'm afraid you're going to have to be brutally honest about whether keeping up with this stream of electronic interactions is merely a fun habit or actually a useful lever. Once the fun habit reaches a significant portion of your day (try tracking it today), it might be time to take charge instead of being a willing victim.

Two years ago, I started taking a lot of flak for being choosy about which incoming media I was willing to embrace. What I've recently seen is that this is a choice that's gaining momentum.

It's your day, and *you* get to decide, not the cloud. I could go on and on about this, but I know you've got email to check . . .

The Paralysis of Unlimited Opportunity

There aren't just a few options open to you; there are thousands (or more).

You can spend your marketing money in more ways than ever, live in more places while still working electronically, contact different people, launch different initiatives, hire different freelancers. You can post your ideas in dozens of ways, interact with millions of people, launch any sort of product or service without a permit or a factory.

Too many choices.

If it's thrilling to imagine the wide open spaces, go for it.

If it's slowing you down and keeping you up at night, consider artificially limiting your choices. Don't get on planes. Don't do spec work. Don't work for jerks. Work on paper, not on film. Work on film, not on video. Don't work weekends.

Whatever rule you want . . .

But no matter what, don't do nothing.

Do You Have a Media Channel Strategy? (You Should)

Twenty years ago, only big companies and TV stars worried about media channels.

Oprah was on TV; then she added radio. Two channels. Then a magazine.

Pepsi set out to dominate TV with their message, and then added billboards and vending machines. Newspapers, not so much. The media you chose for spreading your message mattered. In fact, it could change what you made and how you made it. [Stop for a second and consider that—the media channel often drove the product and pricing and distribution.]

Today, of course, everyone has access to a media channel. You can create a series of YouTube videos or have a blog. You can be a big-time tweeter, or lead a significant tribe on Facebook.

Harder to grapple with is the idea that the media channel you choose changes who you are and what you do. Tom Peters gives a hundred or more speeches a year, around the world, for good money (and well earned). But this channel, this place where he can spread his message, determines what he does all day, affects the pace of the work he does, informs all of his decisions.

Oprah lives a life that revolves around a daily TV show. Of course it would be difficult for her to write a book; that's a life dictated by a different channel. And she's a lapsed Twitter user because it demands different staffing and a different mindset than she has now.

This principle applies to non-celebs, to people with jobs, to entrepreneurs, to job seekers. We all spread our ideas, at least a little, and the medium you choose will *change* your ideas. If you pay attention to the world only when you need a new job (your channel is stamps, and your message is your résumé), you'll spend your day differently than you will if you are leading a tribe, participating in organizations, or giving local speeches all the time.

We've come a long way from a worker having just two channels (a résumé and a few references) to a worker having the choice of a dozen or more significant ways to spread her ideas. Choose or lose.

Simple Five-Step Plan for Just About Everyone and Everything

The number of people you need to ask for permission keeps going down:

1. Go, make something happen.
2. Do work you're proud of.
3. Treat people with respect.
4. Make big promises and keep them.
5. Ship it out the door.

When in doubt, see #1.

16 Questions for Free Agents

If you're starting out as an entrepreneur or a freelancer or a project manager, the most important choice you'll make is: what to do? As in the answer to the question, "what do you do?"

Some questions to help you get started:

1. Who are you trying to please?
2. Are you trying to make a living, make a difference, or leave a legacy?
3. How will the world be different when you've succeeded?
4. Is it more important to add new customers or to increase your interactions with existing ones?
5. Do you want a team? How big? (I know, that's two questions.)
6. Would you rather have an open-ended project that's never done, or one where you hit natural end points? (How high is high enough?)
7. Are you prepared to actively sell your stuff, or are you expecting that buyers will walk in the door and ask for it?
8. Which: to invent a category, or to be just like Bob/Sue, but better?
9. If you take someone else's investment, are you prepared to sell out to pay it back?
10. Are you done personally growing, or is this project going to force you to change and develop yourself?
11. Choose: teach and lead and challenge your customers, or do what they ask.
12. How long can you wait before it feels as though you're succeeding?
13. Is perfect important? (Do you feel the need to fail privately, not in public?)
14. Do you want your customers to know each other (a tribe), or is it better that they be anonymous and separate?
15. How close to failure, wipe-out, and humiliation are you willing to fly? (And while we're on the topic, how open to criticism are you willing to be?)
16. What does busy look like?

In my experience, people skip all of these questions and ask instead: "What can I do that will be sure to work?" The problem, of course, is that there is no *sure*, and even worse, you and I have no agreement at all on what it means for something to work.

You're Already Self-Employed

When are you going to start acting like it?

The idea that you are a faceless cog in a benevolent system that cares about you and that can't tell particularly whether you are worth a day's pay or not, is, like it or not, over.

In the long run, we're all dead. In the medium-long run, though, we're all self-employed. In the medium-long run, the decisions and actions we take each day determine what we'll be doing next.

And yet it's so easy to revert to "I just work here."

Self-Marketing Might Be the Most Important Kind

What story do you tell yourself about yourself?

I know that marketers tell stories. We tell them to clients, prospects, bosses, suppliers, partners, and voters. If the stories resonate and spread and seduce, then we succeed.

But what about the story you tell yourself?

Do you have an elevator pitch that reminds you that you're a struggling fraud, certain to be caught and destined to fail? Are you marketing a perspective and an attitude of generosity? When you talk to yourself, what do you say? Is anyone listening?

You've learned through experience that frequency works. That minds can be changed. That powerful stories have impact.

I guess, then, the challenge is to use those very same tools on yourself.

Finding Inspiration Instead of It Finding You

One approach to innovation and brainstorming is to wait for the muse to appear, to hope that it alights on your shoulder, to be ready to write down whatever comes to you.

The other is to seek it out, will it to appear, train it to arrive on time and on command.

The first method plays into our fears. After all, if you're not inspired, it's not your fault if you don't ship, it's not your fault if you don't do anything remarkable—hey, I don't have any good ideas, you can't expect me to speak up if I don't have any good ideas.

The second method challenges the fear and announces that you've abandoned the Resistance and instead prepared to ship. Your first idea might not be good, or even your second or your tenth, but once you dedicate yourself to this cycle, yes, in fact, you will ship and make a difference.

Simple example: start a blog and post once a day on how your favorite company can improve its products or its service. Do it every day for a month; post one new, actionable idea each and every day. Within a few weeks, you'll notice the change in the way you find, process, and ship ideas.

The Myth of Preparation

There are three stages of preparation. (For a speech, a product, an interview, a sporting event . . .)

The first I'll call the beginner stage. This is where you make huge progress as a result of incremental effort.

The second is the novice stage. This is the stage in which incremental effort leads to a not-so-visible increase in quality.

And the third is the expert stage. Here's where races are won, conversations are started, and sales are made. A huge amount of effort, off-limits to most people, earns you just a tiny bit of quality. But it's enough to get through the Dip and be seen as the obvious winner.

Here's the myth: The novice stage is useful.

If all you're going to do is go through the novice stage before you ship, don't bother. If you're not prepared to put in the grinding work of the expert stage, just do the beginner stuff and stop screwing around. Make it good enough and ship it and move on.

We diddle around in the novice stage because we're afraid. We polish (but not too much) and go to meetings (plenty of them) and look for deniability, spending hours and hours instead of shipping. And the product, in the end, is not so much better.

I'm all for expertise. Experts, people who push through and make something stunning—we need more of them. But let's be honest: if you're not in the habit of being an expert, it's unlikely that your current mode of operation is going to change that any time soon.

Go, give a speech. Go, start a blog. Go, ship that thing that you've been hiding. Begin, begin, begin, and then improve. Being a novice is way overrated.

Do You Need a Permit?

Where, precisely, do you go in order to get permission to make a dent in the universe?

The accepted state is to be a cog. The preferred career is to follow the well-worn path, to read the instructions, to do what we're told. It's safer that way. Less responsibility. More people to blame.

When someone comes along and says, "not me, I'm going down a different path," we flinch. We're not organized to encourage and celebrate the unproven strivers. It's safer to tear them down (with their best interests at heart, of course). Better, we think, to let them down easy, to encourage them to take a safer path, to be realistic, to hear it from us rather than from the marketplace.

Perhaps, years ago, this was good advice. Today, it's clearly not. In fact, it's disrespectful, ill-advised, and shortsighted. How dare we cheer when a bold change-maker stumbles? Our obligation today isn't to spare the feelings of our peers and shield them from future disappointment. It's to establish an expectation that of course they're going to do something that matters.

If you think there's a chance you can make a dent, GO.

Now.

Hurry.

You have my permission. Not that you needed it.

Laziness

I think laziness has changed.

It used to be about avoiding physical labor. The lazy person could nap or have a cup of tea while others got hot and sweaty and exhausted.

Part of the reason society frowns on the lazy is that this behavior means more work for the rest of us.

When it came time to carry the canoe over the portage, I was always hard to find. The effort and the pain gave me two good reasons to be lazy.

But the new laziness has nothing to do with physical labor and everything to do with fear. If you're not going to make those sales calls or invent that innovation or push that insight, you're not avoiding it because you need physical rest. You're hiding out because you're afraid of expending emotional labor.

This is great news, because it's much easier to become brave about extending yourself than it is to become strong enough to haul an 80-pound canoe.

Reasons to Work

1. For the money
2. To be challenged
3. For the pleasure/calling of doing the work
4. For the impact it makes on the world
5. For the reputation you build in the community
6. To solve interesting problems
7. To be part of a group and to experience the mission
8. To be appreciated

Why do we always focus on the first? Why do we advertise jobs or promotions as being generic on items #2 through #8 and differentiated only by #1?

In fact, unless you're a drug kingpin or a Wall Street trader, my guess is that the other factors are at work every time you think about your work.

Where's Your Platform?

That needs to be the goal when you seek a job.

Bob Dylan earned the right to make records, and instead of using it to create ever more commercial versions of his old stuff, he used it as a platform to do art.

A brilliant programmer finds a job in a small company, and instead of seeing it as a grind, churning out what's asked, he uses it as a platform to hone his skills and to ship code that changes everything.

A waiter uses his job serving patrons as a platform for engagement, for building a reputation, and for learning how to delight.

A blogger starts measuring page views and ends up racing to the bottom with nothing but scintillating gossip and pandering. Or perhaps she decides to use the blog as a platform to take herself and her readers somewhere they will be glad to go.

There's no rigid line between a job and art. Instead, there's an opportunity. Both you and your boss get to decide if your job is a platform or just a set of tasks.

The First Rule of Doing Work That Matters

Go to work on a regular basis.

Art is hard. Selling is hard. Writing is hard. Making a difference is hard.

When you're doing hard work, getting rejected, failing, working it out—this is a dumb time to make a situational decision about whether it's time for a nap or a day off or a coffee break.

Zig taught me this twenty years ago. Make your schedule *before* you start. Don't allow setbacks or blocks or anxiety to push you to say, "hey, maybe I should check my email for a while, or you know, I could use a nap." If you do that, the lizard brain is quickly trained to use that escape hatch again and again.

Isaac Asimov wrote and published 400 (!) books by using this scheduling technique.

The first five years of my solo business, when the struggle seemed never ending, I never missed a day, never took a nap. (I also committed to ending the day at a certain time and not working on the weekends. It cuts both ways.)

In short: show up.

Maybe Next Year . . .

The economy will be going gangbusters.

Your knowledge will reach critical mass.

Your boss will give you the go-ahead (and agree to take the heat if things don't work out).

Your family situation will be stable.

The competition will stop innovating.

Someone else will drive the carpool, freeing up a few hours a week.

There won't be any computer viruses to deal with, and

Your neighbor will return the lawnmower.

Then . . .

You can ship, you can launch your project, you can make the impact you've been planning on.

Of course, all of these things *won't* happen. Why not ship anyway?

[While others were hiding last year, new products were launched, new subscriptions were sold, and new companies came into being. While others were lying low, websites got new traffic, organizations grew, and contracts were signed. While others were stuck, money was being lent, star employees were hired, and trust was built.

Most of all, art got created.

That's okay, though, because it's all going to happen again in 2011. It's not too late, just later than it was.]

Texting While Working

No, you shouldn't text while driving, or talk on the cell phone, or argue with your dog, or drive blindfolded. It's an idiot move, one that often leads to death (yours or someone else's).

I don't think you should text while working, either. Or use social networking software of any kind, for that matter. And you probably shouldn't eat crunchy chips, either.

I don't think there's anything wrong with doing all that at work (in moderation). But not while you're *working*. Not if working is the act that leads to the scarce output, the hard stuff, the creative uniqueness they actually pay you for.

You're competing against people in a state of flow, people who are truly committed, people who care deeply about the outcome. You can't merely wing it and expect to keep up with them. Setting aside all the safety valves and pleasant distractions is the first way to send yourself the message that you're playing for keeps. After all, if you sit for an hour and do exactly nothing, not one thing, you'll be ashamed of yourself. But if you waste that hour updating, pinging, being pinged, and crunching, well, hey, at least you stayed in touch.

Raise the stakes.

In and Out

That's one of the most important decisions you'll make today.

How much time and effort should be spent on intake, on inbound messages, on absorbing data . . .

. . . and how much time and effort should be invested in output, in creating something new.

There used to be a significant limit on available intake. Once you read all the books in the college library on your topic, it was time to start writing.

Now that the availability of opinions, expertise, and email is infinite, I think the last part of that sentence is the most important:

Time to start writing.

Or whatever it is you're not doing, but merely planning on doing.

Reject the Tyranny of Being Picked: Pick Yourself

Amanda Hocking is making a million dollars a year publishing her own work to the Kindle. No publisher.

Rebecca Black has reached more than 15 million listeners, like it or not, without a record label.

Are we better off without gatekeepers? Well, it was gatekeepers that brought us the unforgettable lyrics of Terry Jacks in 1974, and it's gate-keepers that are spending a fortune bringing out pop songs and books that don't sell.

I'm not sure that this is even the right question. Whether or not we're better off, the fact is that the gatekeepers—the pickers—are reel-ing, losing power, and fading away. What are you going to do about it?

It's a cultural instinct to wait to get picked. To seek out the permis-sion and authority that come from a publisher or a talk-show host or even a blogger saying, "I pick you." Once you reject that impulse and realize that no one is going to select you—that Prince Charming has chosen another house—then you can get to work.

If you're hoping that the HR people you sent your résumé to are about to pick you, it's going to be a long wait. Once you understand that there are problems just waiting to be solved, once you realize that you have all the tools and all the permission you need, then opportunities to contribute abound.

No one is going to pick you. Pick yourself.

Are You Making Something?

Making something is work. Let's define work, for a moment, as some-thing you create that has a lasting value in the market.

Twenty years ago, my friend Jill discovered Tetris. Unfortunately, she was working on her PhD thesis at the time. On any given day, the attention she spent on the game felt right to her. It was a choice, and she made it. It was more fun to move blocks than it was to write her thesis. Day by day this time adds up . . . she wasted so much time that she had to stay in school and pay for another six months to finish her doctorate.

Two weeks ago, I took a five-hour plane ride. That's enough time for me to get a huge amount of productive writing done. Instead, I turned on the Wi-Fi connection and accomplished precisely no new measurable work between New York and Los Angeles.

More and more, we're finding it easy to get engaged with activities that feel like work, but aren't. I can appear just as engaged (and probably enjoy some of the same endorphins) when I beat someone in Words With Friends as I do when I'm writing the chapter for a new book. The challenge is that the pleasure from winning a game fades fast, but writing a book contributes to readers (and to me) for years to come.

One reason for this confusion is that we're often *using precisely the same device to do our work as we are to* distract *ourselves from our work*. The distractions come along with the productivity. The boss (and even our honest selves) would probably freak out if we took hours of ping pong breaks while at the office, but spending the same amount of time engaged with others online is easier to rationalize. Hence this proposal:

THE TWO-DEVICE SOLUTION

Simple but bold: Use your computer only for work. Real work. The work of making something.

Have a second device, perhaps an iPad, and use it for games, Web commenting, online shopping, networking . . . anything that doesn't directly create valued output. (No need to have an argument here about what is work and what is not-work—draw a line, any line, and separate the two of them. If you don't like the results from that line, draw a new line.)

Now, when you pick up the iPad, you can say to yourself, "break time." And if you find yourself taking a lot of that break time, you've just learned something important.

Go, make something. We need it!

Which of the Four Are Getting in the Way?

You don't know what to do.

You don't know how to do it.

You don't have the authority or the resources to do it.

You're afraid.

Once you figure out what's getting in the way, it's far easier to find the answer (or decide to work on a different problem).

Stuck is a state of mind, and it's curable.

Waiting for the Fear to Subside

There are two problems with this strategy:

A. By the time the fear subsides, it will be too late. By the time you're not afraid of what you were planning to start/say/do, someone else will have already done it, it will already be said, or it will be irrelevant. The reason you're afraid is that there's leverage here—something might happen. Which is exactly the signal you're looking for.

B. The fear certainly helps you do it better. The fear-less one might sleep better, but sleeping well doesn't always lead to your best work. The fear can be your compass: it can set you on the right path and actually improve the quality of what you do.

Listen to your fear but don't obey it.

Building a Job Vs. Building a Business

Either can work, both do, but don't confuse them.

The shoemaker/copywriter/plumber who seeks a regular itinerary of gigs is building a job—a job with multiple bosses at the same time there is no boss, but still a job. You wake up in the morning and you do your craft, with occasional interruptions to do the dreaded looking-for-work dance.

The entrepreneur is in a different game. For her, the gig is building the gig.

Easy Vs. Do-Able Vs. Impossible

Often we consider an opportunity based on how easy it is. The problem with this analysis is that if it's easy, it's often not worth doing. It's easy to start a blog, but of course, starting a blog doesn't really deliver a lot of value. Posting 4,100 blog posts in a row, though, isn't easy. It's do-able, clearly do-able, and might just be worth it.

Successful organizations seek out the do-able. When Amazon went after the big bookstore chains, analysts ridiculed them for doing something insanely difficult. But it was clearly do-able. Requiring persistence and talent and a bit of luck, sure, but do-able.

Sometimes we seek out things that are impossible. Building a search engine that's just like Google but better is impossible (if your goal is to dominate the market with it). It's fun to do impossible projects because then you don't have to worry about what happens if you succeed—you have a safety net because you're dreaming the impossible dream.

Do-able, though, is within our reach. Ignore easy.

The Warning Signs of Defending the Status Quo

When confronted with a new idea, do you:

- Consider the cost of switching before you consider the benefits?
- Highlight the pain for a few instead of the benefits for the many?
- Exaggerate how good things are now in order to reduce your fear of change?
- Undercut the credibility, authority, or experience of the people behind the change?
- Grab onto the rare thing that could go wrong, instead of amplifying the likely thing that will go right?
- Focus on short-term costs instead of long-term benefits, because the short term is more vivid for you?
- Fight to retain benefits and status earned only through tenure and longevity?
- Embrace an instinct to accept consistent ongoing costs instead of swallowing a one-time expense?
- Slow implementation and decision making down instead of speeding them up?
- Embrace sunk costs?
- Imagine that your competition is going to be as afraid of change as you are? Even the competition that hasn't entered the market yet and has nothing to lose?

- Emphasize emergency preparation at the expense of handling a chronic and degenerative condition?
- Compare the best of what you have now with the possible worst of what a change might bring?

Calling it out when you see it might give your team the strength to make a leap.

Talker's Block

No one ever gets talker's block. No one wakes up in the morning, discovers he has nothing to say, and sits quietly, for days or weeks, until the muse hits, until the moment is right, until all the craziness in his life has died down.

Why, then, is writer's block endemic?

The reason we don't get talker's block is that we're in the habit of talking without a lot of concern about whether our inane blather will come back to haunt us. Talk is cheap. Talk is ephemeral. Talk can be easily denied.

We talk poorly, and then eventually (or sometimes), we talk smart. We get better at talking precisely because we talk. We see what works and what doesn't, and if we're insightful, do more of what works. How can we get talker's block after all this practice?

Writer's block isn't hard to cure.

Just write poorly. Continue to write poorly, in public, until you can write better.

I believe that everyone should write in public. Get a blog. Or use Squidoo or Tumblr or a microblogging site. Use an alias if you like. Turn off comments, certainly—you don't need more criticism, you need more writing.

Do it every day. Every single day. Not a diary, not fiction, but analysis. Clear, crisp, honest writing about what you see in the world. Or want to see. Or teach (in writing). Tell us how to do something.

If you know you have to write *something* every single day, even a paragraph, you will improve your writing. If you're concerned with quality, of course, then not writing is not a problem, because zero is perfect and without defects. Shipping nothing is safe.

The second best thing to zero is something better than bad. So if you know you have to write tomorrow, your brain will start working on something better than bad. And then you'll inevitably redefine bad, and tomorrow will be better than that. And on and on.

Write like you talk. Often.

Your Competitive Advantage

Are you going to succeed because you return emails a few minutes faster, tweet a bit more often, and stay at work an hour longer than anyone else?

I think that's unlikely. When you push to turn intellectual work into factory work (which means more showing up and more following instructions), you're racing to the bottom.

It seems to me that you will succeed because you confronted and overcame anxiety and the lizard brain better than anyone else. Perhaps because you overcame inertia and got significantly better at your craft, even when it was uncomfortable because you were risking failure. When you increase your discernment, maximize your awareness of the available options, and then go ahead and ship work that scares others—that's when you succeed.

More time on the problem isn't the way. More guts is. When you expose yourself to the opportunities that scare you, you create something scarce, something others won't do.

The More or Less Choice

I think it comes down to one or the other:

How little can I get away with?

vs.

How much can I do?

Surprisingly, they both take a lot of work. The closer you get to either edge, the more it takes. That's why most people settle for the simplest path, which is to do just enough to remain unnoticed.

No one can maximize on every engagement, every project, every customer, and every opportunity. The art of it, I think, is to be rigorous about where you're prepared to overdeliver, and not get hooked on doing it for all, because otherwise you just become another mediocrity, easily overlooked.

That means more "no." More "No, I can't take that on, because to do so would mean not dramatically overdelivering on what I'm doing now."

And it means more "yes." More "Yes, I'm able to confront my fear and my competing priorities and dramatically step up my promises and my willingness to keep them."

Trading in Your Pain

The pain of a lousy boss, of careless mistakes, of insufficient credit. The pain of instability, of bullying, of inadequate tools. The pain of poor cash flow, corrosive feedback, and work that isn't worthy of you.

Pain is part of work. And it leads to two mistakes.

The notion that you can trade your way out of pain.

"If I just get a little bigger, a little more famous, a little richer—then the pain will go away."

This notion creates a cycle of dissatisfaction, an unwillingness to stick it out. There's always a pain-free gig right around the corner, so screw this, let's go try that.

The truth is that pain is everywhere, in every project and in every relationship and in every job. Wandering from one to another merely wastes your energy.

The other choice, though, is:

Embracing your current pain and avoiding newer, unknown pains.

This is precisely the opposite mistake. This leads to paralysis. Falling in love with the pain you've got as a way of avoiding unknown future pains gets you stuck, wasting your potential.

As usual, when you're confronted with two obvious choices, it's the third choice that pays.

Extending the Narrative

Did you wake up fresh today, a new start, a blank slate with resources and opportunities . . . or is today yet another day of living out the narrative you've been engaged in for years?

For all of us, it's the latter. We maintain our worldview, our biases, our grudges, and our affections. We nurse our grudges and see the very same person (and situation) in the mirror today that we did yesterday. We may have a tiny break, a bit of freshness, but no, there's no complete fresh start available to us.

Marketers have been using this persistence to their advantage forever. They sell us a car or a trip or a service that fits the story we tell ourselves. I don't buy the thing because it's the right thing for everyone; I buy it because it's right for me, for the us I invented, the I that's part of the story I've been telling myself for a long time.

The socialite walks into the ski shop and buys a $3,000 ski jacket she'll wear once. Why? Not because she'll stay warmer in it than in a different jacket, but because that's what someone like her does. It's part of her story. In fact, *it's easier for her to buy the jacket than it is to change her story.*

If you went to bed as a loyal company man or an impatient entrepreneur or as the put-upon retiree or the lady who lunches, chances are you woke up that way as well. Which is certainly safe and easy and consistent and non-confusing. But is it helping?

We dismiss the midlife crisis as an aberration to be avoided or ridiculed, as a dangerous blip in a consistent narrative. But what if we had them all the time? What if we took the trust and momentum and resources that help us and decided to let the other stuff go?

It's painful to even consider giving up the narrative we use to navigate our life. We vividly remember the last time we made an investment that didn't match our self-story, or the last time we went to the "wrong" restaurant or acted the "wrong" way in a sales call. No, that's too risky, especially now, in this economy.

So we play it safe and go back to our story.

The truth, though, is that doing what you've been doing is going to get you what you've been getting. If the narrative is getting in the way, if the archetypes you've been modeling and the worldview you've been nursing no longer match the culture, the economy, or your goals, something's got to give.

When decisions roll around—from what to have for breakfast, to whether to make that investment, to what TV show (or none) to watch tonight—the question to ask is: Is this decision a reflex that's part of my long-told story, or is this actually a good decision? When patterns in engagements with the people around you become well worn and ineffective, are they persistent because they have to be or because the story demands it?

Making Big Decisions About Money

We're bad at it. And marketers know this.

Consider: you're buying a $30,000 car and you have the option of upgrading the stereo to the 18-speaker, 100-watt version for just $500 more. Should you?

Or perhaps you're considering two jobs, one that you love and one that pays $2,000 more. Which to choose?

Or . . .

You are lucky enough to be able to choose between two colleges. One, the one with the nice campus and slightly more famous name, will cost your parents (and your long-term debt) about $200,000 for four years, and the other ("lesser") school has offered you a full scholarship.

Which should you take?

In a surprisingly large number of cases, we take the stereo, even though we'd never buy a nice stereo at home, or we choose to "go with our heart because college is so important" and pick the expensive college. (This is, of course, a good choice to have to make, as most people can't possibly find the money.)

Here's one reason we mess up: money is just a number.

Comparing dreams of a great stereo (four years of driving long distances, listening to great music!) compared with the daily reminder of our cheapness makes picking the better stereo feel easier. After all, we're not giving up anything but a number.

The college case is even more clear: $200,000 is a number that's big, sure, but it doesn't have much substance. It's not a number we play with or encounter very often. The feeling about the story of a compromise involving something tied up in our self-esteem, though, that feeling is something we deal with daily.

Here's how to undo the self-marketing. *Stop using numbers.*

You can have the stereo if you give up going to Starbucks every work-day for the next year and a half. Worth it?

If you go to the free school, you can drive there in a brand-new Mini convertible, and every summer you can spend $25,000 on a top-of-the-line internship/experience, and you can create a jazz series and pay your favorite musicians to come to campus to play for you and your fifty coolest friends, and you can have Herbie Hancock give you piano lessons and you can still have enough money left over to live without debt for a year after you graduate while you look for the perfect gig.

Suddenly, you're not comparing "this is my dream" with a number that means very little. You're comparing one version of your dream with another version.

If Your Happiness Is Based on Always Getting a Little More Than You've Got . . .

. . . then you've handed control of your happiness to the gatekeepers, built a system that doesn't scale, and prevented yourself from doing the brave work that leads to a quantum leap.

The industrial system and the marketing regime adore the mindset of "a little bit more, please," because it furthers their power. A slightly higher paycheck, a slightly more famous college, an incrementally better car—it's easy to be seduced by this safe, stepwise progress, and if marketers and bosses can make you feel dissatisfied at every step along the way, even better for them.

Their rules, their increments, and you are always on a treadmill, unhappy today, imagining that the answer lies just over the next hill.

All the data shows us that the people on that hill are just as frustrated as the people on your hill. It demonstrates that the people at that college are just as envious as the people at this college. The never-ending cycle (no surprise) never ends.

An alternative is to be happy wherever you are, with whatever you've got, but always hungry for the thrill of creating art, of being missed if you're gone, and, most of all, of doing important work.

Don't Expect Applause

Accept applause, sure, please do.

But when you *expect* applause, when you do your work in order to get (and because of) applause, you have sold yourself short. That's because your work is depending on something out of your control. You have given away part of your art. If your work is filled with the hope and longing for applause, it's no longer your work—the dependence on approval has corrupted it, turned it into a process in which you are striving for ever more approval.

Who decides if your work is good? When you are at your best, you do. If the work doesn't deliver on its purpose, if the pot you made leaks or the hammer you forged breaks, then you should learn to make a better one. But we don't blame the nail for breaking the hammer, or the water for leaking from the pot. They are part of the system, just as the market embracing your product is part of marketing.

"Here, here it is, it's finished."

If it's finished, the applause, the thanks, the gratitude are something else. Something extra and not part of what you created. If you play a beautiful song for two people or a thousand, it's the same song, and the amount of thanks you receive isn't part of that song.

Hard Work on the Right Things

I don't think winners beat the competition because they work harder. And it's not even clear that they win because they have more creativity. The secret, I think, is in understanding what matters.

It's not obvious, and it changes. It changes by culture, by buyer, by product, and even by the day of the week. But those who manage to capture the imagination, make sales, and grow are doing it by perfecting the things that matter and *ignoring the rest*.

Both parts are difficult, particularly when you are surrounded by people who insist on fretting about and working on the stuff that makes no difference at all.

CARE MORE THAN THE COMPETITION

Respect and Authenticity.

How to Deal with an Angry Customer

Every business encounters angry people. Not disappointed or confused, but actually angry. Here are a few steps you might want to try:

- Acknowledge the anger. You don't have to agree with it, but in order to have a chance at making it go away, you need to empathize with the person's anger. *You cannot sell something (even a solution) to, nor can you negotiate with, an angry person.*
- Talk more quietly and more slowly than the person you're talking with. Not an exaggerated mantra, but just enough that you will be de-escalating, not escalating.
- Ask the person what it will take to help them not be angry. Repeat what they're asking for, in your own words.
- Ask them if that will not only solve their problem, but give your organization a chance to delight them.
- If no, then ask again what it will take. (But only once. You'll settle for a benign grudge if you can get one.)

[It's important to note that so far I haven't asked you to give them anything or to actually agree with their point of view. Just to understand it and recognize it. You cannot negotiate with an angry person. Doesn't work.]

- Now, summarize. Human to human, not as a manipulator or someone following a list of steps read on a blog. "Sue, I'm really sorry you're upset. I can imagine that having one of our room service people walk into your room at 11 P.M., uninvited, and wake you up before a big conference could cost you a lot of sleep and really ruin your visit with us. It sounds like you're hoping for an apology from our manager and a waiver of our Internet fee as a way of showing you we really blew it. Would that help?"

Bingo. You've changed the dynamic. You've made it clear which side of the discussion you're on. You haven't set any expectations, but you've built a connection.

At this point, you have two options. You can describe what you CAN do, right now, in an attempt to make it up to the person. Or you can ask for time and promise to get back to the person after you've checked in with the higher-ups.

It's entirely possible that the steps above won't work. It's entirely possible that Sue is so angry she'll never, ever return to your hotel again. That's okay. You did what you could . . . but more important, you didn't waste a lot of time and emotion and energy trying to solve a problem that's not solvable.

Where Do You Park?

The manager of the Chase Bank in Pleasantville parks right out front. Her branch is on a quiet street with parking meters available for customers to use. Figure there are perhaps a dozen spaces convenient enough to make it worth going to the bank; if they're full, keep on driving, because there's always another bank coming up soon.

And yet, the manager parks right out front (in fact, I saw her move her car from two spaces away to an even closer spot today). She has four or five people working in the branch, so if they follow her lead, that's half the spaces.

Of course, it's a far bigger issue than parking spaces. It's about eating lunch with your employees, handing out free samples to customers instead of to your friends, or answering the phone yourself when Customer Service gets backed up.

I'm increasingly coming to the conclusion that there are really only two attitudes that people bring to work with them. Either they park right out front, or they park down the street in order to send a signal to their staff, their customers, and themselves.

What Do I Get?

Most marketing (and most business) is usually like this:

Do *this* and get *that.*

Figure out what you want, figure out what you need to do to get it, and go do it.

I was thinking about the way my Dad does business the other day. He's been a successful executive (and then entrepreneur) for more than 50 years. I realized that I can't remember one time when he did *this* to get *that.*

When he volunteered to run the United Way or the local theater, or when he helped a local church raise money for a new building, he didn't have an ulterior motive. When he negotiated with the UAW to create a different sort of workforce structure for his plant, it wasn't so he could get more. It was so they could get more. Same thing when he helped dozens of people emigrate from the Soviet Union a few decades ago.

It's been a consistent approach, and it sure seems to work. Consistent as in all the time, not just when it's convenient. It works for a factory in Buffalo (HARD Manufacturing Co.), but it also seems to work for others—for successful marketers all over the world. Now, more than ever, it's easier to give even when it seems like you're not going to get. The happy irony is that this turns out to be a very effective marketing approach, even though that's not the point.

Expectations

Word of mouth comes directly from expectations.

Low expectations are a terrific shortcut, because when you exceed them, people are so amazed that they can't help but talk about it.

But low expectations are dangerous, because if you fly too low, you're invisible. Worse, when people expect little of you, they often don't bother listening at all.

So most of the time, you're challenged with this: high expectations that must be beat.

Broadway shows. Apple products. Expensive consulting services. Promise big and deliver bigger seems to be the only reliable strategy.

Small Before Big

One of the luxuries of being in a low-cost business or in having access to capital is that you can scale quickly. You can go from one salesperson to a hundred, one store to twenty, no franchises to a thousand.

In our rush to scale, sometimes we forget something essential: if it doesn't work when you've got one, it's extremely unlikely to work when you have dozens.

If a political candidate can't sway the audience with one speech, how will doing the speech across the district do anything but waste time?

If a direct-mail letter doesn't work when you mail it to a hundred people, it won't work any better when you mail it to a thousand.

All a roundabout way of saying that you get big dividends when you obsess about that tiny moment when someone decides to buy. Rejiggering or even overhauling a single example of what you do is almost always a better way to spend your time than is trying to double the number of places you do what you do.

The One Thing

If you didn't want anything in return, nothing at all, what's the most generous thing you could do for your best customer, your best friend, your most important prospect?

Give it a try.

How to Spend $20 Million

Treating different customers differently is important.

Customers actually like it if you do it right. People in coach don't mind the folks in first class getting more service, because they'd like to be there one day. (Or because they like the fact that the people paying too much for a fancy seat are subsidizing their flight.) People at nightclubs like watching celebrities being whisked to the front of the line, because it reinforces their belief that they're at a special place.

The trouble kicks in not when you treat different people differently but if it's random or unfair or unpredictable.

When Steve Jobs gave a $200 discount to the late adopters of the iPhone, the early adopters were incensed. They were being treated differently, but in the wrong way. My guess is that his $100 store credit and personal note helped a great deal, but it also cost about $20 million in profit. If Apple had thought it through, Jobs could have offered any of the following (and done it during the presentation he did of the new products):

- Free exclusive ringtones, commissioned from Bob Dylan and U2, available only to the people who already had a phone. (This is my favorite because it announces to your friends—every time the phone rings—that you got in early.)
- A free pass to get to the head of the line the next time a new hot product comes out.
- The ability to buy a specially colored iPod, or an iPod with limited-edition music, that no one else can buy.

The key is not to give price protection to early buyers (that's unsustainable as a business model) but to make them feel more exclusive, not less.

As for being capricious, consider the U.S. Open. The Open doesn't allow spectators to bring in backpacks of any size—IF the straps are padded. They don't announce this rule, and they enforce it somewhat randomly.

If it were really a security issue, they'd have to enforce it completely. If it's just a silly policy that someone dreamed up one day, it's sure to annoy people. Because it's irrational. Because it's not enforced in a way that makes sense.

So yes, treat different customers differently. The more the better, actually. But do it consistently and in a way that your customers respect and understand.

Two Kinds of "Don't Know"

I don't know French. I can't play the piano. I have no clue how to catch a bony spinefish. This is the first kind of "don't know." Stuff you don't know because you haven't been taught it yet. Books are awfully good at solving this problem; so are good teachers.

The second kind of "don't know" is often confused with the first type, but it's really quite different. This is the person who says that they don't know how to cook or that they can't balance a checkbook. This isn't about technique or a lack of knowledge. It's usually either fear or lack of interest. People with this type of deficit won't find the answer in a book or (usually) in a seminar, either. You don't learn how to cook from a cookbook.

The answer lies in trial and error and in motivation and in overcoming the fear that makes us avoid the topic in the first place.

And why should a marketer care?

You need to care because if you try to solve the second kind of ignorance with a manual or a PDF or a blog post or even a long infomercial, you're going to fail. If you discover that users are afraid or resistant to what you're trying to get them to do, presenting more information is almost always the incorrect response. The effective technique involves peer pressure and support and requires changing the design and inputs of what you're doing so that this group is more receptive to what's on offer. For example, Internet penetration isn't up by a factor of

20 because people read a lot of copies of *Internet for Dummies*. It happened because of what peers said to each other over time, and because the act of getting online is a lot easier than it used to be. And you can help that happen.

People Don't Truly Care About Privacy

There's been a lot of noise about privacy over the last decade, but what most pundits miss is that most people don't care about privacy, not at all.

If they did, they wouldn't have credit cards. Your credit card company knows an insane amount about you.

What people care about is being surprised.

If your credit card company called you up and said, "we've been looking over your records and we see that you've been having an extramarital affair. We'd like to offer you a free coupon for VD testing," you'd freak out, and for good reason.

If the local authorities started using what's on the corner surveillance cameras to sell you a new kind of commuter token, you'd be a little annoyed at that as well.

So far, government and big companies have gotten away with taking virtually all our privacy away by not surprising most of us, at least not in a vivid way. Libertarians are worried (probably with cause) that once the surprises start happening, it'll be too late.

This leads us to Ask.com's new Eraser service, which promises to not remember stuff about your searching. The problem they face: most people want Google and Yahoo! and Amazon to remember their searches, because it leads to better results and (so far) rarely leads to surprises.

The irony is that the people who most want privacy are almost certainly the worst possible customers for a search engine. These are the folks who are unlikely to click on ads and most likely to visit the dark corners of the 'Net. If I were running a Web property, I'd work hard to attract the people who least want privacy and who want to share their ideas with everyone else.

Make promises, keep them, avoid surprises. That's what most people (and the profitable people) want.

What's the Point of This Interaction?

Every time you interact with a customer, you're engaging in marketing. Doesn't matter if you're instituting a policy, gaining some data, delivering an invoice—it's a marketing interaction.

So . . .

When you bother 100 customers to get useful data from two, you just paid a marketing cost.

When you yell at a classroom full of kids because one kid misbehaved, that's a marketing decision.

When you make 5,000 non-smugglers wait in a steaming customs hall at a resort destination, you may think you're doing your job and collecting those little white forms, but what you're really doing is marketing (negatively).

And . . .

When you bring a little candy (which wasn't required) with the check (which was), you're using the transaction as an opportunity to do positive marketing.

Here's a little thought experiment that will show how your managers are misjudging these interactions: Go ask your front-line people what they're doing when they're doing what they think is their jobs. Like when they're ripping tickets or answering the phone or filling out a form with a customer. How many people say, "I'm using this as an excuse to market to our best customers"?

The Posture of a Communicator

If you buy my product but don't read the instructions, that's not your fault; it's mine.

If you read a blog post and misinterpret what I said, that's my choice, not your error.

If you attend my presentation and you're bored, that's my failure.

If you are a student in my class and you don't learn what I'm teaching, I've let you down.

It's really easy to insist that people read the friggin' manual. It's really easy to blame the user/student/prospect/customer for not trying hard, for being too stupid to get it, or for not caring enough to pay attention. Sometimes (often) that might even be a valid complaint. But it's not helpful.

What's helpful is to realize that you have a choice when you communicate. You can design your products to be easy to use.

You can write so your audience hears you. You can present in a place and in a way that guarantees that the people who you want to listen will hear you. Most of all, you get to choose who will understand (and who won't).

The Bad Table

I saw a marketing dilemma at the hot new restaurant I went to the other night.

We got there on time at 6:30 and the restaurant was about a third full. We were promptly seated at the worst table in the place, in the back, in the corner, cramped by the kitchen.

We were first-time patrons, having secured a reservation via Open Table. That made us doubly second-class citizens, I guess.

We asked for a better table, pointing to one a few feet away. "Oh, I'm sorry, that one is reserved."

The chances, of course, that a particular table is reserved are close to zero. What he meant was, "Oh, we have a regular customer who deserves that table more than you."

Hence the marketing dilemma: *Who should get your best effort?* Should it be the new customer, whom you just might be able to convert into a long-term customer? Or should it be the loyal customer, who is already valuable?

Sorry, but the answer is this: *you can't have a bad table.*

No one wants to settle for the bad table, your worst salesperson, your second-rate items. Not the new customers and not the loyal ones.

Which means you need to figure out how to improve your lesser offerings. Maybe the table in the worst location comes with a special menu or a special wine list or even a visit from the chef. Maybe the worst table, for some people, becomes the best table because of the way you treat people when they sit there.

Treat different people differently. But don't treat anyone worse.

You're Right!

You probably get feedback from customers. Sometimes you even get letters.

Occasionally (unfortunately), it's negative.

Two weeks ago, I left my car at an expensive parking garage in midtown New York. When I got back four hours later, I discovered that they had left the engine running the entire time. That, combined with the $30 fee and the nasty attitude of the attendant, led me to write a letter to the management company.

The response: it was my fault. When I dropped off the car, I should have taught the attendant how to turn off my Prius.

What's the point of a letter like that? Why bother taking the time? It's not even worth the stamp. Does the writer expect me to say, "Oh, great point! Sorry to have bothered you. I'm an idiot! In fact, I'm so stupid, I'll go out of my way to park there again next time."

It's pretty simple. The only productive response to a critical letter or piece of feedback from a customer is, "You're right. . . ."

You're right, I can see that you are annoyed.

You're right, that is frustrating.

You're right, with the expectations you had, it's totally understandable to feel the way you do.

You're right, and we're really sorry that you feel that way.

Every one of these statements is true; each one is something you are willing to put into writing. It validates the writer, thanks him for sharing the frustration, and gives you a foundation for an actual dialogue.

But isn't this pandering? I don't think so. The writer *is* right. He *is* frustrated. His opinion is his opinion, and if you don't value it, you're shutting down something useful.

How about, "You're right, it's reasonable to expect that we would have turned off your Prius. We'll post a note for all our attendants so they pay better attention in the future." A note like this makes the customer happy and it makes your garage work better.

Someone wrote to me last week, complaining that the handwritten inscription in a book I had signed for his colleague wasn't warm enough.

I responded that he was right to be frustrated, and that if his expectations had been so high, I should have either lowered them or exceeded them. Of course he was right: with expectations like that, it's not surprising that he was disappointed.

Arguing with a customer who takes the time to write to you does two things: it keeps them from ever writing again, and it costs you (at least) one customer. Perhaps that's your goal. Just take a moment before you launch an unhappy former customer into the world.

Time

Here's the #1 most overlooked secret of marketing, of growing your organization, of building trust and creating for the long haul. Actually, it has two parts:

Show up on time. It doesn't cost anything to keep your promises when it comes to time. Show up for the meeting when the meeting starts. Have the dry cleaning ready when you promise. Ship on time. Return that phone call. Finish the renovation ahead of schedule.

Boy, that's simple. Apparently, it's also incredibly difficult.

If you want to build trust, you need to be trustworthy. The simplest test of trustworthiness for most people is whether or not you keep your promises, and the first promises you make are about time.

Cherish my time. The second part is closely related. It has to do with respect. You respect my time when you don't waste it. When you don't spam me. When you worry about the 100 cars backed up on the road and figure out how to get us moving more quickly. You respect me when you value my time more highly than your own.

If you want someone to think you're selfish, just ask for a minute of their time and then waste it or use it for your own ends. Or automate the process so three minutes of your time wastes three minutes of time for the 1,000 or 1 million people on your list.

In a society where so many people have enough, few people have time to spare. When you waste it (by breaking a promise and being late) or abuse it (by viewing your time as worth more than mine), we respond by distrusting you, ignoring you, and eventually moving on.

When You Stand for Something

People and brands and organizations that stand for something benefit as a result. Standing for something helps you build trust, makes it easier to manage expectations, and aids in daily decision making. Standing for something also makes it more fun to do your gig, because you're on a mission, doing something that matters. Of course, there's a cost. You can't get something for nothing.

It's frustrating to watch marketers, politicians, and individuals fall into the obvious trap of trying to stand for something at the same time they try to please everyone or do everything.

You can't be the low-price, high-value, wide-selection, convenient, green, all-in-one corner market. Sorry.

You also can't be the high-ethics CEO who just this one time lets an accounting fraud slide. "Because it's urgent."

You can't be the big-government-fighting, low-taxes-for-everyone, high-services-for-everyone, safety-net, pro-science, faith-based, anti-deficit candidate, either.

You can't be the work-smart, life-in-balance, available-at-all-hours, high-output, do-what-you're-told employee.

To really stand for something, you must make difficult decisions, mostly about what you don't do. We don't ship products like that, we don't stand for employees like that ("you're fired"), we don't fix problems like that.

It's so hard to stand up, to not compromise, to give up an account or lose a vote or not tell a journalist what she wants to hear.

But those are the only moments where standing for something actually counts, the only times that people will actually come to believe that you do in fact actually stand for something.

If you have to change your story because your audience is different (oh, I'm on national TV today!) (oh, this big customer wants me to cut some key corners), you're going to get caught. That's because the audience is now unknown to you, everything is public sooner or later, and if you want to build a brand for the ages, you need to stand for something today and tomorrow and every day.

Authenticity

If it acts like a duck (all the time), it's a duck. Doesn't matter if the duck thinks it's a dog; it's still a duck as far as the rest of us are concerned.

Authenticity, for me, is doing what you promise, not "being who you are."

That's because "being" is too amorphous and we are notoriously bad at judging that. Internal vision is always blurry. Doing, on the other hand, is an act that can be seen by all.

As the Internet and a connected culture place a higher premium on authenticity (because if you're inconsistent, you're going to get caught), it's easy to confuse authentic behavior with an existential crisis. Are you really good enough, kind enough, generous enough, and brave enough to be authentically a hero or leader?

Mother Teresa was filled with self-doubt. But she was an authentic saint, because she always acted like one.

You could spend your time wondering if what you say you are is really you. Or you could just act like that all the time. That's good enough, thanks. Save the angst for later.

What You Say, What You Do, and Who You Are

We no longer care what you say.

We care a great deal about what you do.

If you charge for hand raking but use a leaf blower when the client isn't home;

If you sneak into an exercise class because you were on the wait list and it isn't fair 'cause you never get a bike;

If you snicker behind the boss's back;

If you don't pay attention in meetings;

If you argue with customers instead of delighting them;

If you copy work and pass it off as your own;

If you shade the truth a little;

If you lobby to preserve the unsustainable status quo;

If you network to get, not to give;

If you do as little as you can get away with;

. . . then we already know who you are.

You Matter

- When you love the work you do and the people you do it with, you matter.
- When you are so gracious and generous and aware that you think of other people before yourself, you matter.
- When you leave the world a better place than you found it, you matter.
- When you continue to raise the bar on what you do and how you do it, you matter.
- When you teach and forgive and teach more before you rush to judge and demean, you matter.
- When you touch the people in your life through your actions (and your words), you matter.
- When kids grow up wanting to be you, you matter.
- When you see the world as it is, but insist on making it more like it could be, you matter.
- When you inspire a Nobel Prize winner or a slum dweller, you matter.
- When the room brightens when you walk in, you matter.
- And when the legacy you leave behind lasts for hours, days, or a lifetime, you matter.

Lessons from Very Tiny Businesses

1. Go where your customers are.

Jacquelyn runs a tiny juice company called ChakWave. I met her in Los Angeles, standing next to an organic lunch truck. Like the little birds that clean the teeth of the hippo, there's synergy here. The kind of person that visits the truck for lunch is the sort of person that would happily pay for something as wonderfully weird as her juice. And the truck owners benefit from the rolling festival farmer's-market feel that comes from having a synergistic partner set up on a bridge table right next door.

2. Be micro-focused and the search engines will find you.

My friend Patti Jo is an extraordinary teacher and tutor. Her new business, The Scarsdale Tutor, doesn't need many clients in order to be successful. This fact permits her to focus obsessively, and that gets rewarded with front-page results on Google. Not because she's tried to manipulate the SEO (she hasn't), but because this is exactly the page you'd hope to find if you typed "scarsdale tutor" into a search engine. Could she do this nationwide? Of course not. But she doesn't want to or need to. Living on the long tail can be profitable.

3. Outlast the competition.

I was amazed at all the empty storefronts I saw in LA on my last visit. On one particular block, three or four of the ten lunch places were shut down. And the others? Doing great. That's because the remaining office workers who used to eat lunch at the shuttered places had to eat somewhere, and so the survivors watched their businesses *grow*. A war of attrition is never pretty, but if you're smart about overhead and scale, you'll win it.

4. Leverage.

Rick Toone runs a tiny guitar-making operation. His lack of scale makes it easy for him to share. When others start using his designs, he doesn't suffer (he can't make any more guitars than he's already making); he benefits. Because he's the originator of the design, his originals become more coveted, not less valuable. He leverages his insight and shares it as a free marketing device.

5. Respond.

This is the single biggest advantage you have over the big guys. Not only are you in charge, but you also answer the phone and read your email and man the desk and set the prices.

So don't pretend you have a policy. Just be human.

The Big Drop-off

We try so hard to build the first circle.

This is the circle of followers, friends, subscribers, customers, media outlets, and others willing to hear our pitch. This is the group we tell about our new product, our new record, our upcoming big sale. We want more of their attention and more people on the list.

Which takes our attention away from the circle that matters, which is the second circle.

The second circle is the set of people who hear about us from the first circle.

If the first circle is excited about what we do and it's remarkable enough to talk about, they'll tell two or six or ten friends each. And if we're really good, the second circle, the people we don't even know— they'll tell the third circle. And it's the third circle that makes you a hit, gets you elected, and tips your idea.

The big drop-off is the natural state of affairs. The big drop-off is the huge decline that occurs between our enthusiasm (HEY! BUY THIS!) and the tepid actions of the first circle (yawn). Great marketers don't spend their time making the first circle bigger. They spend all their time crafting services, products, and stories that don't drop off.

"Notice Me"

If the new Web has a mantra, that's it.

So much time and effort are now put into finding followers, accumulating comments, and generating controversy—all so that people will notice you. People say and do things that don't benefit them, just because they're hooked on attention.

Attention is fine, as long as you have a goal that is reached in exchange for all this effort.

Far better than being noticed:

- Trusted
- Engaged with
- Purchased from

- Discussed
- Echoed
- Teaching us
- Leading

Empathy

I have no idea what it's like to be pregnant.

And for most of us, we have no idea what it's like to have $3 to spend on a day's food, or $4 million to spend on a jet. We have no idea what it feels like to be lost in a big city, no idea how confusing it is to go online for the first time, no idea what it's like to own four houses.

Marketers and pundits and writers and bloggers and bosses pretend they are empathetic, but we never can be. Sure, we can try, we can be open to cues and sensitive to clues, but no, we don't really know.

Being certain about how someone else feels or what motivates them is foolish. Don't declare that you know exactly why someone made a choice, or predict what someone is going to do next, and why. It's a great parlor trick, but you're probably going to be wrong. (I think the one universal exception is fear. We all know what it means to be afraid, and fear doesn't change based on income or gender. The causes change, but the fear remains the same.)

Empathy is a hugely powerful marketing tool if we use it gently, being sure to leave lots of room for error. When we say, "oh, you did that to make a quick buck" or "you did that because you hate that guy" or "you did that because you're a man," we've closed the door to allowing people to write their own stories, and we make it difficult to learn what actually makes them tick.

The First Transaction

Do you really expect that the first time we transact, it will involve me giving you money in exchange for a product or service?

Perhaps this is a good strategy for a pretzel vendor on the street, but is that the best *you* can hope for?

Digital transactions are essentially free for you to provide. I can give you permission to teach me something. I can watch a video. I can engage in a conversation. We can connect, transfer knowledge, engage in a way that builds trust—all of these things make it more likely that I'll trust you enough to send you some money one day. I can contribute to a project you're building, ask you a difficult question, discover what others have already learned.

But send you money on the first date? No way.

The question then, is how much time and effort does your nonprofit/consulting firm/widget factory spend on pre-purchase transactions, and how much do you spend on trying to simply close the sale?

Eight Questions and a Why

Whom are you trying to please?
What are you promising?
How much money are you trying to make?
How much freedom are you willing to trade for opportunity?
What are you trying to change?
What do you want people to say about you?
Which people?
Do we care about you?

(And after each answer, ask "why?")

What the Industry Wants

It's easy to get trapped in wondering what consumers want, and then being frustrated when you can't get what you cook up in front of the people who want to buy it.

It's easy to forget what *industry* wants.

Supermarkets don't want unbranded fruits and vegetables because handling is expensive and it's hard to differentiate and charge extra. On the other hand, supermarkets love nationally advertised packaged goods because they bring in shoppers, they have promotional support, they come with shelf allowances (money for shelf space), and new SKUs can create excitement.

Fashion stores don't want sensible clothes that don't change from year to year. Hard to make a living selling that. They like zingy designer names and ever-changing fashion and fads. That's how fashion stores make a living.

Governments don't like buying at retail prices. They prefer custom stuff from high-touch organizations that can bring them the mountain, instead of the other way around. They'd rather pay 10x for an office supply that's customized just for them, instead of modifying what they want to match what the market sells. It gives them something to do. And all those salespeople! The trips, the bribes, the attention . . .

Doctors don't like prescribing lifestyle changes or natural cures, because many patients demand a scrip and it's easily defended and it comes with a sales rep.

If the industry can't make money selling what you're selling, why will they help you?

You can view these things as ridiculous peccadilloes. Or you can see them as parts of the system as permanent and as important as the gatekeepers who rely on them.

On the other hand, fall in love with the system and you might forget the end user. And we know how poorly that approach works.

The Hidden Power of a Gift

If I sell you something, we exchange items of value. You give me money, I give you stuff, or a service. The deal is done. We're even. Even-Steven, in fact.

That's fine, but it doesn't explain potlatch or the mystery of art or the power of a gift.

If I give you something, or way more than you paid for, an imbalance is created. That imbalance must be resolved.

Perhaps we resolve it, as the ancient Native Americans did, by acknowledging the power of the giver. In the Pacific Northwest, a powerful chief would engage in potlatch, giving away everything he owned as a sign of his wealth and power. Since he had more to give away, and the power to get more, the gifts carried real power, and others had to accept his power in order to engage.

Or we resolve it by acknowledging the creativity and insight of the giver. Artists do this every time they put a painting in a museum or a song on the radio. We don't pay for the idea, but we acknowledge it. And then, if it's particularly powerful, it changes us enough that we become givers, contributing to someone else, passing it along.

Sometimes we resolve the imbalance by becoming closer to the brand or the provider. We like getting gifts; we like being close to people who have given us a gift and might do it again.

And sometimes, in the case of international aid, we resent the rich giver, the one with so much more power, and thus create a cycle of dependence that does neither side any good. This sort of gift isn't much of a gift at all.

When done properly, gifts work like nothing else. A gift gladly accepted changes everything. The imbalance creates motion, motion that pushes us to a new equilibrium, motion that creates connection.

The key is that the gift must be freely and gladly accepted. Sending someone a gift over the transom isn't a gift, it's marketing. Gifts have to be truly given, not given in anticipation of a repayment. True gifts are part of being in a community (willingly paying taxes for a school you will never again send your grown kids to) and part of being an artist (because the giving motivates you to do ever better work).

Plus, giving a gift feels good.

Quid Pro Quo (Santa Math)

Walk up to the falafel stand and hand the guy $3. He hands you a falafel, no onions.

This for *that*.

Something for something.

The time between surrendering the money and getting the sandwich is tiny. You gave him something, you got something. It's simple.

Now, stretch it out a bit. You order dinner in a restaurant. They treat you nicely, the room is beautiful, you enjoy the evening, *then* you pay the bill. This, pause, pause, pause, that.

Go to law school. Pay a lot of money. Spend a lot of time. Be taught a bunch of things you don't particularly want to know, things you probably don't need. Get a degree with a modicum of scarcity. Pay for a bar-review course. Pass the bar. Then you get a job that pays a lot of money.

This, then a multi-year pause, then, in return, *that* for the next forty years. We call it "return on investment."

Online, though, I'm not sure the math is so obvious. You don't write a blog to get gigs. You don't help people out in a forum to build a free-lance business. Sure, that might happen, but that's not why you do it. If you are busy calculating quid pro quo, that means your heart isn't in it, and the math won't work out anyway.

Online, the something, the quid, the *this*, doesn't cost cash. It takes heart and energy and caring, which are scarce but renewable resources. As a result, many people are able to spend them without seeking any-thing external in return. Even better, the act of generosity, of giving without expectation, makes it easier to do art, to create work that mat-ters on its own.

I think it's more like Santa math. Santa flies around the world, giving stuff away, and for what? He earns gratitude, trust, and friendship, that's what. Sure, one day he might decide to license his image or try to sell you something. But right here, right now, gratitude, trust, and friendship are plenty. Especially if you enjoy doing what you're doing. Quid, no quo.

Surely Not Everyone

A newspaper asked me the following, which practically set my hair on fire:

What inherent traits would make it easier for someone to become a linchpin? Surely not everyone can be a linchpin?

Why not? How dare anyone say that some people aren't somehow *qualified* to bring emotional labor to their work, somehow aren't ge-netically or culturally endowed with the seeds or instincts or desires to invent new techniques or ideas, or aren't chosen to connect with other human beings in a way that changes them for the better?

Perhaps some people will insist that there are jobs where no human-ity is possible. But you don't have to take those jobs.

Some people want to tell you that your DNA isn't right, or you're not from the right family or neighborhood. I think that's wrongheaded.

Bob Marley grew up in one of the poorest villages in the world. Sir Richard Branson has dyslexia, which makes it difficult for him to read. Hugh Masekela grew up in Witbank, a coal mining town in South Africa. It's not just musicians and entrepreneurs, of course. The Internet makes it possible for a programmer in Russia or a commentator in South Africa to have an impact on a large group of people as well.

We've been culturally brainwashed to believe that the factory approach (average products for average people, compliance, focus on speed and cost) is the one and only way. It's not.

We make a difference to other people when we give gifts to them, when we bring emotional labor to the table and do work that matters. It's hard for me to imagine that this way of living and working is available to only a few. Yes, the cards are unfairly stacked against too many people. Yes, there are too many barriers and not enough support. But no, your ability to create and contribute isn't determined at birth. It's a choice.

Your Smile Didn't Matter

If you worked on the line, we cared about your productivity, not your smile or your approach to the work. You could walk in downcast, walk out defeated, and get a raise if your productivity was good.

No longer.

Your attitude is now what's on offer; it's what you sell. When you pass by those big office buildings and watch the young junior executives sneaking into work with a grimace on their face, it's tempting to tell them to save everyone time and just go home.

The emotional labor of engaging with the work and increasing the energy in the room is precisely what you sell. So sell it.

Organizing for Joy

Traditional corporations, particularly large-scale service and manufacturing businesses, are organized for efficiency. Or consistency. But not joy.

McDonald's, Hertz, Dell, and others crank it out. They show up. They lower costs. They use a stopwatch to measure output.

The problem with this mindset is that as you approach the asymptote of maximum efficiency, there's not a lot of room left for improvement. Making a Chicken McNugget for .00001 cent less isn't going to boost your profit a whole lot.

Worse, the nature of the work is inherently unremarkable. If you fear special requests, if you staff with cogs, if you have to put it all in a manual, then the chances of amazing someone are really quite low.

These organizations have people who will try to patch problems over after the fact, instead of motivated people eager to delight on the spot.

The alternative, it seems, is to organize for joy. These are the companies that give their people the freedom (and yes, the expectation) that they will create, connect, and surprise. These are the organizations that embrace someone who makes a difference, as opposed to searching for a clause in the employee handbook that was violated.

"I've Got Your Back"

These are the words that entrepreneurs, painters, artists, statesmen, customer service pioneers, and writers need to hear.

Not true. They don't need to hear them, they need to *feel* them.

No artist needs a fair-weather friend, an employee or customer or partner who waits to do the calculus before deciding if they're going to be there for the artist.

No, if you want her to go all in, if you want her to take the risk and brave the fear, then it sure helps if you're there, too, no matter what. There's a cost to that, a kind of pain and risk that comes from that sort of trust. After all, this particular bit of art might not work. Failure (or worse! embarrassment) might ensue. That's precisely why art is worth so much. Because it's difficult and scarce.

Later, when it's all good and it's all working, your offer of support means very little. The artist never forgets the few who came through when it really mattered.

Who's got your back? More important, whose back do you have?

How Should You Treat Your Best Customers?

Here's what most businesses do with their best customers: They take the money.

The biggest fan of that Broadway show, the one who comes a lot and sits up front? She's paying three times what the person just three rows back paid.

That loyal Verizon customer, the one who hasn't traded in his phone and has had a contract for six years running? He's generating far more profit than the guy who switches every time a contract expires and a better offer comes along.

Or consider the loyal customer of a local business. The business chooses to offer new customers a coupon for half off—but makes repeat customers pay full price.

If you define "best customer" as the customer who pays you the most, then I guess it's not surprising that your first instinct is to charge him more. After all, he's happy to pay.

But what if you define "best customer" as the person who brings you new customers through frequent referrals, and who sticks with you through thick and thin? That customer, I think, is worth far more than what she might pay you in any one transaction. In fact, if you think of that customer as your *best marketer* instead, it might change everything.

Date Certain

A powerful marketing tactic: tell me *exactly* when I'm going to get it.

"This project will be done noon on Tuesday."

"You'll get the shipment at 4 P.M."

FedEx has made billions shipping packages that didn't even have to be there fast. They merely needed to arrive at a time that we knew about in advance.

We don't want to hear "up to 11 business days." We hope you care more about our project than that.

Assuming Goodwill

Productivity comes from interactivity and the exchange of ideas and talents.

People are happiest when they're encouraged and trusted.

An airport functions far better when we don't strip-search passengers. Tiffany's may post guards at the door, but the salespeople are happy to let you hold priceless jewels. Art museums let you stand close enough to paintings to see them. Restaurants don't charge you until after you eat.

Compare this environment of trust with the world that PayPal has to live in. Every day, thousands of mobsters in various parts of the world sit down intent on scamming the company out of millions of dollars. If the site makes one mistake, permits just one security hole to linger, they're going to be taken for a fortune. As a result, the company isn't just paranoid—they know that people really *are* out to get them.

This is the fork in the road that just about all of us face, whether as individuals or as organizations. We have to make an assumption about whether people are going to steal our ideas, break their promises, void their contracts, and steal from us, or assume, perhaps, that people are basically honest, trustworthy, and generous. It's very hard to have both postures simultaneously. I have no idea how those pistol-packing guys in the movies ever get a good night's sleep.

In just about every industry (except electronic money transfer, apparently), assuming goodwill is not only more productive but is also likely to be an accurate forecast.

Trust pays.

Why You Might Choose to Be in Favor of Transparency

Thousands of doctors have signed up for a service that, among other things, they can use to try to prohibit patients from posting reviews.

In Iowa, in a surprisingly similar move, the state government is moving ahead with a law that will make it a crime to take or possess videotapes of factory farming that might harm the commercial interests of the farmer.

In both cases, an organization is trying to maintain power by hiding information from the public. Can you imagine being arrested for possession of a photo of a pig?

It's easy to argue that from the public's point of view, laws like this are a bad idea. The public certainly benefits from the outing of bad doctors and from the improved hygiene of factory farms. In that sense, it's unethical for doctors and legislators to subvert their responsibilities by ordering the unempowered to shut up.

I think this issue is interesting to think about from the doc's point of view (and the chicken farmer's), as well. The temptation is for those in charge to defend the status quo by fighting transparency. But doing this ignores a simple truth:

When book reviews are posted, book sales go up.

Yes, the argument of fairness matters. The patients have no choice, the chickens certainly have no choice, and the consumers don't have much choice either. There's an argument that goes beyond choice, though: it turns out that transparency increases profitability.

If every chicken coop has a video camera in it, quality will obviously go up. Confidence in the product will go up. Employee behavior will improve as well, because it's hard to torture a chicken if you know you're going to get caught.

But wait, you might argue . . . if we have to take better care of the chickens, our costs will go up as well.

Here's the thing: when consumers get used to transparency, they're also more interested in the quality of what you sell, and are more likely to willingly pay extra. They'll certainly cross the street to buy from an ethical provider. And once people start moving in that direction, the cost of being an unethical provider gets so high that you either change your ways or fade away.

Chicken farms don't need a law prohibiting possession of images. They need a producer who will make a ton of great (true) chicken movies. Inundate us with images of cleanliness and quality instead of blacking us out. Don't race to the bottom (you might win). Instead, force your competition to race you to the top.

[Aside: the same objection arose when we started regulating hygiene in restaurant kitchens. Yes, it got more expensive to clean the pots and kill the rodents, but it was okay, because post–Duncan Hines, demand for quality went up enough to more than pay for it.]

The same argument holds true for doctors. Once information about good doctors becomes widespread, patients will be more willing to seek out those doctors, rewarding the ones who consistently take better care of their patients. The entire profession won't suffer (we'll still go to a doctor)—merely the careless doctors will.

One more: A leading politician in India is arguing that bribery (in certain transactions) ought to be legalized. Why? Because if the briber feels free to rat out the bureaucrat, bribery goes down.

In all three cases, sunlight is an antiseptic and the marketplace rewards those that behave well—and the entire market grows when the standards increase.

Consumers and those that want their admiration ought to reward those in favor of transparency (what a great opportunity for McDonald's). And the antidote for speech that a provider doesn't like isn't a contract or a law. The antidote to speech you don't like is more speech.

What (People) Want

What do customers, friends, the socially networked, users, neighbors, classmates, servers, administrators, employees, and maybe even brands, want?

notice me
like me
touch me
do what I say
miss me if I'm gone

Synchronicity, Intimacy, and Productivity

A shortcut to customer and coworker intimacy is to respond in real time.

A phone call is more human than an email, a personal meeting has more impact than a letter.

On the other hand, when you do your work on someone else's schedule, your productivity plummets because you are responding to the urgent, not the important, and your rhythm is shot.

The shortcut analysis, it seems to me, is to sort your work by how important it is that your interactions be intimate. If it's not vitally important that you increase the energy and realism of the relationship, then insert a buffer. Build blocks of time to do serious work, work that's not interrupted by people who need to hear from you in real time, right now.

On the other hand, for interactions when only a hug or a smile will do, allocate the time and the scheduling to be present.

Confusing urgency with intimacy is getting easier than ever, and it's killing your ability to do great work.

The Professional's Platform

If you show up only when you want something, we'll catch on.

If you learn only the minimum amount necessary to get over the next hurdle, you'll fall behind.

If these short-term choices leave you focused on the urgent, you'll almost never get around to doing the important.

A professional salesperson refuses to engage in the short-cycle process of cold calling, selling, and moving on. An urgent plea from the boss before the end of the quarter isn't enough reason to abandon your consistent approach. That's because cold calls are painful and rarely lead to sales. The professional salesperson realizes that closing a sale and then moving on wastes an opportunity for both you and the person you're working with.

A flustered programmer who grabs the relevant library without understanding its context or the role of the libraries around it will be in the same urgent state in just another few days.

The politician who shows up only when it's time to raise money, probably won't.

We remember what you did when you didn't need us so urgently.

If you're going to make a career of whatever it is you do (and of course, if you want to excel, you will), that means taking the time to understand the texture of your field. It means investing, perhaps over-investing, in relationships long before it's in your interest to do so.

When it comes down to decisions that matter, your town, every town, is far more likely to support the one who has moved in, put down roots, and contributed than it is to rush to whatever bright, shiny object shows up for a few days before moving on.

No Such Thing as Business Ethics

The happy theory of business ethics is this: do the right thing and you will also maximize your long-term profit.

After all, the thinking goes, doing the right thing builds your brand, burnishes your reputation, helps you attract better staff, and gives back to the community, the very community that will in turn buy from you. Do all of that and of course you'll make more money. Problem solved.

The unhappy theory of business ethics is this: you have a fiduciary responsibility to maximize profit. Period. To do anything other than that is to cheat your investors. And in a competitive world, you don't have much wiggle room here.

If you would like to believe in business ethics, the unhappy theory is a huge problem.

As the world gets more complex, as it gets harder to see the long term given the huge short-term bets that are made, as business gets less transparent ("which company made that, exactly?"), and as the web of interactions makes it harder for any one person to stand up and take responsibility, the happy theory begins to fall apart. After all, if the long-term effects of a decision today can't possibly have any impact on the profit of this project (which will end in six weeks), then it's difficult to argue that maximizing profit and doing the right thing are aligned. The local store gets very little long-term profit for its good behavior if it goes out of business before the long term arrives.

It comes down to this: *only people can have ethics*. Ethics, as in doing the right thing for the community even though it might not benefit you or your company financially. Pointing to the numbers (or to the boss) is an easy refuge for someone who would like to duck the issue, but the fork in the road is really clear. Either you do work you are proud of, or you work to make the maximum amount of money. (It would be nice if those goals overlapped every time, but they rarely do.)

"I just work here" is the worst sort of ethical excuse. I'd rather work with a company filled with ethical people than try to find a company that's ethical. In fact, companies we think of as ethical got that way because ethical people made them so.

I worry that we absolve ourselves of responsibility when we talk about business ethics and corporate social responsibility. Corporations are collections of people, and we ought to insist that those people (that would be us) do the right thing. Business is too powerful for us to leave our humanity at the door of the office. *It's not business, it's personal.*

[I learned this lesson from my Dad. Every single day he leads by example, building a career and a company based on taking personal responsibility, not on blaming the heartless, profit-focused system.]

Trustiness

We're all looking for someone to trust. People and institutions that will do what they say and say what they mean.

Banks used to use marble pillars and armed guards to make it clear that our money was safe. Doctors put diplomas on the wall and wear white smocks. Institutions and relationships don't work without trust. It's not an accident that a gold standard in business is being able to do business on a handshake.

Today, though, it's easier than ever to build a facade of trust but not actually deliver. "Read the fine print," the financial institutions, cruise ship operators, and business partners tell us after they've failed to honor what we thought they promised.

It's incredibly difficult to build a civil society on the back of "read the fine print." *Emptor fidem* works so much better than caveat emptor. When we have to spend all our time watching our backs and working with lawyers, it's far more challenging to get anything done—and it makes building a business and a brand infinitely more difficult.

The question that needs to be asked by the marketer is, "are we doing this to create the appearance of trust, or is this actually something trustworthy, something we're proud to do?"

Building trust is expensive. You can call it an expense or an investment, or merely cut corners and work on trustiness instead.

Trust is built when no one is looking, when you think you have the option of cutting corners and when you find a loophole. Trustiness is what happens when you use trust as a PR tool.

The difference should be obvious. Trust experienced is remarkable; trustiness, once discovered, leaves a bad taste for even your most valued customers.

The perverse irony is this: the more you work on your trustiness, the harder you fall once people discover that they were tricked.

(With a hat tip to Stephen Colbert.)

One Option Is to Struggle to Be Heard Whenever You're in the Room . . .

Another is to be the sort of person who is missed when you're not.

The first involves making noise. The second involves making a difference.

The Honest Broker

It really is a choice: one or the other.

Either you happily recommend the best option for your customer, or you give preference to your own items first.

Either you believe in what you sell, or you don't.

Either you treat your best partners better, or you treat everyone the same.

Either you shade the truth when it's painful to do otherwise, or you consistently share what's important.

Either you always keep your promises, or you don't.

Either you give me the best price the first time, or you make me jump through hoops to get there.

Earning the position of the honest broker is time consuming and expensive. Losing it takes just a moment.

An Endless Series of Difficult but Achievable Hills

Lightning rarely strikes. Instead, achievement is often the result of step-wise progress, of doing something increasingly difficult until you get the result you seek.

For a comedian to get on *The Tonight Show* in 1980 was a triumph. How to get there? A series of steps: open-mike nights, sleeping in vans, gigging, polishing, working up the ladder until the booker both sees you and likes you.

Same thing goes for the CEO job, the TED talk on the main stage, the line outside the restaurant after a great review in the local paper.

Repeating easy tasks again and again gets you not very far. Attacking only steep cliffs where no progress is made isn't particularly effective, either. No, the best path is an endless series of difficult (but achievable) hills.

Just about all of the stuck projects and failed endeavors I see are the result of poor hill choices. I still remember meeting a guy 30 years ago who had a new kind of controller for the Atari game system. He told me that he had raised $500,000 and was going to spend it all (every penny) on a single ad during the Cosby show. His exact words: "My product will be on fire, like a thresher through a wheat field, like a hot knife through butter!" He was praying for lightning, and of course, it didn't strike.

There are plenty of obvious reasons why we avoid picking the right interim steps, why we either settle for too little or foolishly shoot for too much. Mostly it comes down to fear and impatience.

The craft of your career comes in picking the right hills. Hills just challenging enough that you can barely make it over. A series of hills becomes a mountain, and a series of mountains is a career.

The End of the Diva Paradox

Great surgeons don't need to be respectful or to have a talented, kind, or alert front-desk staff. They're great at the surgery part, and you're not here for the service, you're here to get well (if you believe that the surgery part is what matters). In fact, gruffness might be a clue to their skill for some people.

Great opera singers don't have to be reasonable or kind. They sing like no one else—that's why you hired them, and why they get to (are expected to) act like divas. Get over it.

So the thinking goes.

The traditional scarcity model implied some sort of inverse relationship between service and quality. Not for service businesses like hotels, of course, but for the other stuff. If someone was truly gifted, of course they didn't have the time or focus to also be kind or reasonable or good at understanding your needs. A diva was great partly because, we decided, she was a jerk.

I think that's changing, possibly forever, for a bunch of reasons:

- The state of the art is now easier to find. Word spreads about behavior and service faster than ever. As a result, customers quickly become aware of what a raw deal they're getting from this supposedly gifted individual.
- It's so much easier to deliver better service (Dr. Diva, please send me an email if you're running late!) that we're far less forgiving.
- Since just about any intelligent and caring person can use technology and a bit of humility to deliver better service (see above), we start to wonder whether that diva provider actually is intelligent and caring. And if he isn't, it doesn't really matter if he has some sort of skill, because uncaring hands are worth avoiding.
- With fewer great gigs available (even in opera), it's not so easy to act like a jerk (or be insulated and uncaring) and still get work.

A Simple Antidote to a Corporatized, Unfeeling, Profit-Maximizing World

Care.

Care more than you need to, more often than expected, more completely than the other guy.

No one reports liking Steve Jobs very much, yet he was as embraced as any businessperson since Walt Disney. Because he cared. He cared deeply about what he was making and how it would be used. Of course, he didn't just care in a general, amorphous, whiny way; he cared and then actually delivered.

Politicians are held in astonishingly low esteem. Congress in particular is setting record lows in approval ratings, but it's an endemic problem. The reason? Members of Congress consistently act as if they don't care. They don't care about their peers, certainly, and as we see by their actions, apparently they don't care about us. Money first.

Many salespeople face a similar problem—perhaps because for years they've used a shallow version of caring as a marketing technique to boost their commissions. One report by the National Association of Realtors found that more than 90% of all home owners are never again contacted by their real estate agent after the contracts for the home are signed. Why bother . . . there's no money in it, just the possibility of complaints. Well, the reason is obvious—you'd come by with cookies and intros to the neighbors if you cared.

Economists tell us that the reason to care is that it increases customer retention, profitability, and brand value. For me, though, that's beside the point (and even counter to the real goal). Caring gives you a compass, a direction to head in, and most of all, a reason to do the work you do in the first place.

Care More.

It's only two words, but it's hard to think of a better mantra for the organization that is smart enough to understand the core underpinning of their business, as well as one in search of a reason for being. No need to get all tied up in subcycles of "this leads to this which leads to that so therefore I care . . ." Instead, there's the opportunity to follow the direct and difficult road of someone who truly cares about what's being made and who it is for.

"If I Were You . . ."

But of course, you're not.

And this is the most important component of strategic marketing: we're not our customers.

Empathy isn't dictated to us by a focus group or a statistical analysis. Empathy is the powerful (and rare) ability to imagine what motivates someone else to act.

When a politician or a pundit vilifies someone for her actions, he's missed the point, because all he can do is imagine what he would do in that situation, completely avoiding an opportunity to see the world through someone else's eyes, to try on a new worldview, to attempt to imagine the circumstances that would lead to any action other than the one he would take.

When a teacher can't see why a student is stuck, or when an interface designer dismisses the 12% of the users who can't find the "off" switch, we're seeing a failure of empathy, not a flaw in the user base.

When we call a prospect stupid for not choosing us, when we resort to blunt promotional tactics to get attention we could have earned with a more graceful approach—these are the symptoms that we've forgotten how to be empathetic.

You don't have to wear panty hose to be a great brand manager at L'eggs, nor do you need to be unemployed to work on a task force on getting people back to work. What is required, though, is a persistent effort to understand how other people see the world, and to care about it.

TELLING STORIES AND SPREADING IDEAS

Marketing.

Farming and Hunting

Five thousand years ago, every human was a hunter. If you were hungry, you got a rock or a stick and you went hunting.

The problem was that all of the animals were either dead or really good at hiding.

Fortunately, we discovered/invented the idea of farming. Plant seeds, fertilize 'em, water 'em, watch 'em grow, and then you harvest them.

The idea spread and it led to the birth of civilization.

Everyone got the idea . . . except for marketers.

Marketers still like to hunt.

What we're discovering, though, is that the good prospects are getting really good at hiding.

Wait!

Stop!

Please?!

Fact: about half the visitors to your website leave after less than five seconds.

Fact: the percentage that spend less than that on your ad or your packaging is even greater.

Two choices:

grab the quickie browsers FAST and turn them into interested prospects (somehow);

or

ignore them and realize that you get a chance to talk to only those people who are going to stay for more than five seconds anyway. The rest of the population is ignoring you; don't let them distract you from your real mission, which is to amplify interest, not create it.

If you can do the first, more power to you. Please let the rest of us know what you come up with.

How Can I Get More Traffic?

That's the number-one request (other than "pass the salad dressing") of most of the people I meet.

The problem, of course, is in the "get." The request has at its foundation the assumption that what you've built has somehow earned attention. "Our business model is working great—we just need more traffic. . . ."

People never say "How can I earn more traffic?" or "How can I rethink the core of what I'm offering so that it organically attracts people who want to see it?"

Getting traffic is a little like getting a date. You can probably manipulate the system for a little while (I had a roommate in college who was great at it), but self-reinvention is a markedly better long-term strategy.

The Problem with "Global Warming"

We are facing what might be the greatest threat ever to the future of mankind.

And yet no one is marching in the streets, the outrage is largely intellectual, and action is slow. (If you want to argue about the science, please visit the Wikipedia page for "global warming"; this is a post about the marketing!)

Is the lack of outrage because of the population's decision that this is bad science or perhaps a thoughtful reading of the existing data?

Actually, the vast majority of the population hasn't even thought about the issue. The muted reaction to our impending disaster comes down to two things:

1. The name.
Global is good.
Warm is good.
Even *greenhouses* are good places.

How can "global warming" be bad?

I'm not being facetious. If the problem were called "Atmosphere cancer" or "Pollution death," the entire conversation would be framed in a different way.

2. The pace and the images.

One degree every few years doesn't make good TV. Because activists have been unable to tell their story with vivid images about immediate actions, it's just human nature to avoid the issue. Why give up something we enjoy now to make an infinitesimal change in something that is going to happen far in the future?

Lady Bird Johnson understood this when she invested her efforts into a campaign against litter and pollution. The problem was easy to see. The messaging was emotional and immediate. You could see how your contribution (or efforts) mattered.

Because you don't see your coal being burned (it accounts for more than 50% of U.S. electricity) and because the stuff coming out of your car is invisible, and because you don't live near a glacier, it's all invisible.

Doesn't matter what you market. Human beings want:

totems and icons

meters (put a real-time mpg or CO2 meter in every car and watch what happens)

fashion

stories

and

pictures

Ninety-five percent of the new ideas that don't spread—even though their founders and fans believe they should—fail because of the list above.

Vocabulary: "Landing Page"

I first started talking about landing pages in <gasp> 1991, but there's probably someone out there who can pre-date me. Sometimes when you've been riffing on an idea for so long, it's easy to believe that everyone gets it, but my mail says otherwise.

A landing page is the first page a visitor to your site sees.

Landing pages were important back in the day of email marketing, because if you included a link in your email, that was the page the permission marketee would land on if he clicked through.

Landing pages are even more important today because they are the pages that people see after clicking on Google AdWords ads.

A landing page (in fact, every page) can cause one of five actions:

- Get a visitor to click (to go to another page, on your site or someone else's).
- Get a visitor to buy.
- Get a visitor to give permission for you to follow up (by email, phone, etc.). This includes registration, of course.
- Get a visitor to tell a friend.
- (and the more subtle) Get a visitor to learn something, an action which could even include posting a comment or giving you some sort of feedback.

I think that's the entire list of options.

So, if you build a landing page, and you're going to invest time and money to get people to visit it, it makes sense to optimize that page to accomplish just one of the things above. Perhaps two, but no more.

When you review a landing page, the thing to ask yourself is, "What does the person who built this page want me to do?" If you can optimize for that, you should. If there are two versions of a landing page and one performs better than the other, use that one! This sounds obvious, but how often are you doing the test? How long does a landing page last in your shop before it gets toppled by a better one? And do you have a different landing page for every single ad, every single offer? Why not?

Landing pages are not wandering generalities. They are specific, measurable offers. You can tell if they're working or not. You can improve the metrics and make them work better. Landing pages are the new direct marketing, and everyone with a website is a direct marketer.

Ode: How to Tell a Great Story

Chris Fralic reminded me of this piece I wrote for *Ode*.

Great stories succeed because they are able to capture the imagination of large or important audiences.

A great story is true. Not necessarily because it's factual, but because it's consistent and authentic. Consumers are too good at sniffing out inconsistencies for a marketer to get away with a story that's just slapped on.

Great stories make a promise. They promise fun, safety, or a shortcut. The promise needs to be bold and audacious. Either it's exceptional or it's not worth listening to.

Great stories are trusted. Trust is the scarcest resource we've got left. No one trusts anyone. People don't trust the beautiful women ordering vodka at the corner bar (they're getting paid by the liquor company). People don't trust the spokespeople on commercials (who exactly is Rula Lenska?). And they certainly don't trust the companies that make pharmaceuticals (Vioxx, apparently, can kill you). As a result, no marketer succeeds in telling a story unless he has earned the credibility to tell that story.

Great stories are subtle. Surprisingly, the fewer details a marketer spells out, the more powerful the story becomes. Talented marketers understand that allowing people to draw their own conclusions is far more effective than announcing the punch line.

Great stories happen fast. First impressions are far more powerful than we give them credit for.

Great stories don't always need eight-page color brochures or a face-to-face meeting. Either you are ready to listen or you aren't.

Great stories don't appeal to logic, but they often appeal to our senses. Pheromones aren't a myth. People decide if they like someone after just a sniff.

Great stories are rarely aimed at everyone. Average people are good at ignoring you. Average people have too many different points of view about life, and average people are, by and large, satisfied. If you need to water down your story to appeal to everyone, it will appeal to no one. The most effective stories match the worldview of a tiny audience—and then that tiny audience spreads the story.

Great stories don't contradict themselves. If your restaurant is in the right location but has the wrong menu, you lose. If your art gallery carries the right artists but your staff is made up of rejects from a used-car lot, you lose. Consumers are clever and they'll see through your deceit at once.

Most of all, great stories agree with our worldview. The best stories don't teach people anything new. Instead, the best stories agree with what the audience already believes and makes the members of the audience feel smart and secure when reminded how right they were in the first place.

The Customer Is Always Right

Greg writes in and wants to know if that's really true. What if the customer is an amnesiac, a jerk, a difficult blowhard bad-mouther? What if the customer is the sort that wears his L.L. Bean khakis for a year and then sends them back?

In our ultracompetitive markets, how can you possibly have a chance in the face of enormous consumer power?

The answer might surprise you. It's the unwritten Rule 3 on Stew Leonard's famous granite rock:

If the customer is wrong, they're not your customer anymore.

In other words, if it's not worth making the customer right, fire her.

Successful organizations (and I include churches and political parties on the list) fire the 1% of their constituents that cause 95% of the pain.

Fire them?

Fire them. Politely decline to do business with them. Refer them to your arch-competitors. Take them off the mailing list. Don't make promises you can't keep, don't be rude, just move on.

If you've got something worth paying for, you gain power when you refuse to offer it to every single person who is willing to pay you.

In 1988, my book packaging company had about six weeks' worth of payroll in the bank. Yet we fired our biggest customer, someone who accounted for more than half our revenue. I still believe it was the right thing to do. We ended up happier and more successful, making up the business in a few months' time.

If you treat a customer like he's wrong, he's going to leave and probably tell a bunch of other people. Before you take that route, be direct, straightforward, polite, and firm, and decline to sell to them.

So yes, the customer is always right. And if they're not, then one way or the other, they're not your customer anymore.

Three Big Barriers

It's not always the stories that we tell to prospects and consumers that matter. It's often the stories we tell ourselves.

In talking with companies that are unhappy with the way they are growing, I find two common themes (and one a little less often):

1. A belief that they *deserve* more attention. That their product or their service is so good and so beneficial and so fairly priced that the story they tell and the way they tell it shouldn't matter. I don't think this is arrogance. I think it is a natural by-product of hard work and high pressure.

2. A lack of authenticity. This is almost the flip side of the first, but, surprisingly, it often shows up at the same time. This is the feeling

that you don't have to tell the truth, that it's "just marketing." But talk to someone at a company on a mission—Southwest or JetBlue or Acumen Fund—and you'll hear the same story, told with desire and belief and honesty. These are people on a mission to really do something. Contrast that with someone who wants to know the ROI on a monthly basis from a blog—they're busy doing the math, not living the story.

3. The third theme, which shows up a bit less often, is the marketer who doesn't believe that she deserves success. This is the self-critical marketer who is being brutally honest—and is frustrated at the state of her market and of her product. The obvious but often difficult solution is to either change the product, change the story, or get a new gig. The wrong but most common response is to just be frustrated.

You've certainly met people who have all three things taken care of. They approach a marketplace or a consumer with an appropriate amount of humility. They tell a story that is true, that they believe, that they live. And they do it with confidence, knowing that the story they are telling is bound to benefit most of the people who hear it.

The fascinating thing is that all three of these items happen *before* the consumer is even involved. They are internal and they're under your control, direction, or influence.

Habits, Making and Breaking

Habits are essential to marketing and to profits.

Starbucks in the morning is a habit. So is having your law firm do a trademark search every time you invent a new name. Buying bottled water is a habit, but it didn't used to be.

Making a habit is a lot easier than breaking one (ask a smoker), and habits often come in surprising ways (ask Jerry, who now has a manicure habit).

If you want to grow, you're going to have to either get more people to adopt your habit (which might require breaking a different habit) or somehow increase habitual behavior among your happy customers.

Marketing Pothole (#1 of 3): I'll Know It When I See It

Here is the first of three common pitfalls that wreck your marketing efforts:

Lots of marketers (and most of their bosses) like to say, "I'll know it when I see it."

That's why they want to see three or five or twenty executions of an ad. Or ten or fifteen mock-ups of a car or a facade. That's why marketers put their staff and their freelancers and their agencies through an infinite loop of versioning.

"I'll know it when I see it."

Actually, you won't.

You didn't know it when you saw the first iPod or the first iteration of Google. You didn't know it when you were first exposed to email or JetBlue or the Macarena or Britney Spears. No, in fact, you hardly ever "know it." If you did, you'd be a lot smarter than the rest of us, and we'd all be eagerly watching for your next product.

What *is* true is that we often know success when it smashes us in the face. We didn't "know it" when Google went public at $85 a share (did you buy shares with your house as collateral?), but we sure knew it when it hit $300.

Perhaps Clive Davis knows a hit song when he hears one, and certainly Giorgio Armani has the magic eye. But, just speaking for myself, I don't have Clive's ears or Giorgio's eyes.

Marketing campaigns are frequently crippled by managers who are sure that they know "it" when they see it—and this isn't it. Some of my favorite stories are the ones about all the naysayers who tried to kill the stuff that ends up being great. They just didn't know what it was.

Marketing Pothole (#2 of 3): I'm Too Busy

I can count on one hand the number of marketers I know who get to do "Marketing" (with a capital M) every day.

Accountants do accounting all the time. Salespeople spend a lot of time selling. But marketers, it seems, have a long list of things they do (budgets, coupons, projections, photo shoots, bizdev meetings, meet-and-greets, etc.) that is technically marketing—'cause I think everything an organization does is marketing—but is hardly in the sweet spot.

Think about the giant marketing successes of our time. From Disney to CAA to Boston Consulting Group . . . from Ronald Reagan to the Mormon Church to Habitat for Humanity . . . in every case, these organizations won big-time because of a kernel of an idea, a marketing insight that they built upon.

There are more than 50,000 restaurants in New York City. Perhaps 200 of them are marketing success stories. Yet at the other 49,800 restaurants, the owners spend very little time working on their breakout idea, and tons of time doing stuff that feels a lot more important.

Once an organization is up and running, it's almost impossible to carve out the time to find the marketing vision that will make all the difference. Are you too busy working to make any money?

Marketing Pothole (#3 of 3): What Will the Boss Think?

This is the biggest one, and the reason for the whole series.

I now believe that almost all marketing decisions are first and foremost made without the marketplace in mind.

That's a pretty bold statement, but here goes.

I think that most marketers, most of the time, make their marketing decisions based on what *they think* the committee, or their boss, or their family, or their friends, or the blog readers with email, will say.

When I speak to groups, the folks who are stuck or who are not finding the growth they are hoping for, rarely say, "We don't know how to get the market to respond." Instead, they say, "My boss or the factory or the committee or the design folks or the CFO won't . . ."

Now, of course most of this is whining. Most of this is nonsense. It's not everyone else's fault. But that's not my point. My point is that if you market intending to please those people, you have only yourself to blame.

Great marketing pleases everyone on the team, sooner or later. But at the beginning, great marketing pleases almost no one. At the beginning, great marketing is counterintuitive, non-obvious, challenging, and apparently risky. Of course your friends, shareholders, stakeholders, and bosses won't like it. But they're not doing the marketing, you are.

What People Want

The same thing everyone else is having, but different.

A menu where the prices aren't all the same.

More attention than the person sitting next to them.

A slightly lower price than anyone else.

A new model, just moments before anyone else, but only if everyone else is really going to like it.

A seat at a sold-out movie.

Access to the best customer-service person in the shop, preferably the owner.

Being treated better, but not too much better.

Being noticed, but not too noticed.

Being right.

Marketing Morality

Is that an oxymoron? Is it possible to hold a marketer morally responsible?

Let's start at the beginning:

Marketing works.

Marketing (the use of time and money to create a story and spread it) works. Human beings don't make rational decisions, they make emotional ones, and we've seen time and again that those decisions are influenced by the time and money spent by marketers.

So, assuming you've got no argument with that (and if you're a marketer who doesn't believe marketing works, we need to have a longer discussion), then we get to the next part of the argument:

Your marketing changes the way people act.

Not completely. Of course not. You can't get babies to start smoking cigars and you can't turn Oklahoma into a blue state. But on the margins, especially if your product or service has some sort of archetypal connection to your customers, you can change what people do.

Now it gets tricky. It gets tricky because you can no longer use the argument, "We're just giving intelligent adults the ability to make a free choice." No, actually you're not. You're marketing something so that your product will have an edge over the alternative.

Everyone knows about milk. The milk people don't need to spend $60 million a year advertising milk in order to be sure we all get a free choice about whether to buy milk or not. No, they do it because it makes milk sales go up.

What a huge responsibility.

If you're a good marketer (or even worse, a great marketer), it means that you're responsible for what you sell. When you choose to sell it, more of it gets sold.

I have no standing to sit here and tell you that it's wrong for you to market cigarettes or SUVs, vodka or other habit-forming drugs. What we do need to realize, though, is that it's our choice and our responsibility. As marketers, we have the power to change things, and the way we use that power is our responsibility—not the market's, not our boss's. Ours.

The morality of marketing is this: you need to be able to stand up and acknowledge that you're doing what you're doing. "By marketing this product in this beautiful packaging, I'm causing a landfill to get filled a lot faster, but that's okay with me." Marketers can't say, "Hey, the market spoke. It's not my decision."

The phone rang yesterday. The recording said, "We're sorry to disturb you. This call was meant for an answering machine." Then it hung up. Actually, the marketer wasn't sorry. The marketer was using his market power to violate the Do Not Call Registry and to interrupt my day (on my machine or otherwise) so he could selfishly try to sell me something. While it may or may not be legal to do this, it's irrelevant. What's relevant is that the marketer decided that the ends justified the means, and he needs to acknowledge that on his way to work today.

The same way the marketer at Marlboro needs to acknowledge that by being a good marketer, she's putting her kids through college at the same time she's killing thousands of people. It's a choice—her choice.

We're responsible for what we sell and how we sell it. We're responsible for the effects (and the side effects) of our actions.

It is our decision. Whatever the decision is, you need to own it. If you can't look that decision in the mirror, market something else.

Top 10 Secrets of the Marketing Process

1. **Don't run out of money.** It always takes longer and costs more than you expect to spread your idea. You can budget for it or you can fail.
2. **You won't get it right the first time.** Your campaign will need to be reinvented, adjusted, or scrapped. Count on it.
3. **Convenient choices are not often the best choices.** Just because an agency, an asset, or a bizdev deal is easy to do doesn't mean that it is your best choice.
4. **Irrational, strongly held beliefs of close advisors should be ignored.** It doesn't matter if they don't like your logo.
5. **If it makes you nervous, it's probably a good idea.** If you're sure you're right, you probably aren't.
6. **Focusing obsessively** on one niche, one feature, and one market is almost always a better idea than trying to satisfy everyone.
7. **At some point, you're going to have to either stick to your convictions or do what the market tells you.** It's hard to do both.
8. **Compromise in marketing is almost always a bad idea.** Extreme A could work. Extreme B could work. The average of A and B will almost never work.
9. **Test, measure, and optimize.** Figure out what's working and do it more.
10. **Read and learn.** There are a million clues, case studies, books, and proven tactics out there. You can't profitably ignore them until you know them, and you don't have the time or the money to make the same mistake someone else made last week. It's cheaper and faster to read about it than it is to do it.

Godin on Trademark*

*What every entrepreneur, geek, brand manager, and marketer needs to know about trademarks . . .

If you Google "generic trademarks," you'll find a list on Wikipedia that includes "aspirin, bikini, brassiere, cola, crock pot, dry ice, escalator, granola, heroin, hula hoop, jungle gym, kiwi fruit, pilates exercise system, trampoline, videotape, Webster's dictionary, yo-yo, and zipper." Each of these trademarks was worth many millions of dollars, and then, poof, it belonged to everyone.

Some people are worried about this. Jeroen sent me a note and asked me to riff about it. It even has a name: genericide.

In 1999, I invented a trademark and wrote a book, *Permission Marketing*, about it. Yahoo still owns the trademark for Permission Marketing®, but a quick search will show you more than a million matches for the expression. What's going on?

I had to make a decision. I could have pushed the world to call the ideas I wrote about "Permission-based Marketing." Or I could have been really flexible and encouraged people to call the approach the same thing I did. I figured it was better to be the coiner of a phrase used by millions than to have a little corner of the world all to myself.

And that's part of the paradox of a trademark.

The purpose of a trademark is to help consumers by allowing them to be certain of the source of a good or service. When you go to the store and buy some Mentos, you know you're getting real Mentos, the kind that fizz really well with Coke, not some sort of inferior mento with a small "m." The trademark doesn't just help the Perfetti Van Melle company in Kentucky; it helps you, too.

If everyone knows your trademark, it means that your idea has spread. It means that people are interested in what you sell and may very well decide to buy it from you.

In order to make a word or phrase a trademark, most lawyers agree you need to follow a few superstitions (superstitions because there's no official manual with definitive answers). The first is that you ought to make it clear to the world that you know it's a trademark, that it indicates that your product comes from a specific source. So, putting ™ after your mark helps . . . and once per page/interaction is generally considered to be enough. So you don't have to repeat the ™ over and over and over again in your copy or brochure. It's tacky.

Adding © after your name is just dumb. It doesn't mean a thing.

You can trademark just about any word or phrase, but that doesn't mean it will hold up. The best trademarks are fanciful, words like Yahoo! or Verizon. Next down the list are words that are a bit descriptive, like Whoopie Cushion, Wikipedia, or JetBlue. The worst kind of words are descriptive. Yes, you can trademark the brand American Motors, but don't expect it to be particularly valuable or long lasting.

Some lawyers will get all excited and encourage (demand!) that you register your trademark. This involves paying a bunch of money, filing a bunch of forms, and earning an ® after your name instead of the ™. While the ® does give you some benefits by the time you get to court, it doesn't actually increase the value of your trademark. And you can wait. So, when you come up with a great name, just ™ it.

One thing that has changed dramatically about trademarks is the world of domains. If you own heroin.com, the brand's becoming generic doesn't hurt you so much, because you're the only one who gets the traffic from the domain.

But now we get to the juicy part. Let's say you've invented a trademark and you fear it will become generic. What now?

My first advice is not to worry. By the time aspirin became generic, the guys who developed it were super rich. If actively protecting your trademark is going to get in the way of making your idea spread, the choice is obvious—spread the idea.

Every trademark that turns generic does so for the same reason: because it's the easiest way to describe something. People didn't say, "That's a sexy Bikini®-brand bathing suit." Because the idea itself was bigger (or smaller) than a bathing suit, the new thing needed a name. And the name we picked was bikini.

An iPod is an iPod, not an iPod-brand MP3 player. This is a long-term problem for Apple, and suing people who use the word "pod" to describe other devices isn't really going to help them. The challenge they have is that they invented a brand name for an item that needed a word. Of course, it's not just a problem; it's also a huge advantage.

If you had the chance to work at Apple five years ago, knowing what you know now, what would you do? Pick a name like "the Deluxe Apple-Brand MP3 player"? Would you hassle the folks who coined the term "podcast"? Not me. Yes, it's a great idea to think big, to ensure that you don't make mistakes early on that haunt you later. But no, I don't think you should spend a lot of time imagining the bad things that will happen if you succeed and your idea and your name become intertwined.

You can *Digg* this article. Notice that Digg is a verb, because there's really no easy way to say, "You can recommend this article in a branded social news service like Digg™ by clicking here." So Digg gets the power of spreading their idea. Nobody says, "reddit this article."

Back to the paradox. Would you rather be Digg or reddit? Is it better to have Google's problem (notice that I used "Google" as a verb in the second paragraph?) or to be Ask.com and never get talked about?

The best thing you can invent, as far as I can tell, is an idea that needs a name. When they invented the Jeep®, there was no such thing as the SUV. The Jeep became the name for that idea. The lawyers at Chrysler worked super hard to keep the brand from becoming generic. When the engineers cooked up the Xerox®, they had the same problem. Now, people are happy to call it a copier.

You can recover from impending genericide. What you can't recover from is a clumsy name, or hindering your idea so it doesn't spread, or coming up with a slightly better idea for something that already has a quite good enough name and idea.

Disclaimers: I'm not a lawyer. I don't even play one on TV. If you rely on my legal advice, you're getting exactly what you paid for. I called this post "Godin on Trademark" as a riff on *Nimmer on Copyright*. The irony, of course, is that "Nimmer" became the almost generic phrase for expertise on the topic; you can look it up in Nimmer.

Two Kinds of People in the World . . .

The folks that want (need!) an iPhone, and those that couldn't care less. And of course it's not just Apple and it's not just phones. It's every single industry in the world.

You're not likely to convert one group into the other. What you can do is decide which group you'd like to market to. You can't do both at the same time, or not particularly well, anyway.

Good Is Not Almost as Good as Great

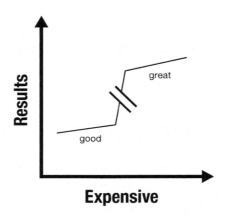

I went to trade in my Jay Porter Prius for an updated Prius today. Well, I meant to do that, but I walked out instead.

I arrived at Westchester Toyota and passed two or three salespeople loitering outside. Inside, there were two or three more, sitting in a line of chairs, waiting for the signal from the headmistress at the counter.

My guess is that even for a thriving brand like Toyota, most of these guys weren't paid so much. They were "good" salespeople, lifers who showed up, did what they were told, and closed a sale here and there.

It soon became clear that the salesperson who was assigned to me wasn't "great." The dealership had messed up: he had no record of my appointment, no file, no history of why I came. But he just punted. He made no effort to engage with me or look me in the eye or empathize with my frustration at the complete waste of time my call yesterday had been. He gave up after about ten seconds, bummed out that he had lost his place in line. So I left.

Driving home, I started to think about the discontinuity in the graph of salespeople. Discontinuities are interesting, because that's where you can see how a system works. In this case, it's obvious that a great salesperson is going to sell far, far more than a good one. Nine women working together can't have a baby in one month, and ten good salespeople still aren't going to close the account that a great one could. That's because it's not a linear scale. The great ones reach out. They work the phones when they're not first in line. They understand what a customer wants. They're not just better than good. They're playing a totally different game.

My best advice: fire half your sales force. Then give the remainder, the top people, a big raise, and use the money left over to steal the best salespeople you can find from other industries or even from your competition. You'll end up with fewer salespeople. But all of them will be great.

And the good guys? Have them go work for the competition.

Lessons from Neil Young

I've been listening to Neil Young's *Live at Massey Hall* and thinking and even crying a bit. It's an awfully powerful piece of work.

Two lessons for marketers: one small, the other bigger. First, it's interesting to note how much more excited and open the crowd is to songs they've heard before. Even some of the songs that ended up becoming classics got a tepid reaction because they were unknown at the time.

Second, on songs that aren't working so well, you will hear Neil try harder, play louder, raise his voice and strain to make an impact. It doesn't work. At all. It's what you say, most of the time, not how you say it.

Stinky Durian

Durian is a fruit from Southeast Asia that can be charitably described as smelling like stale baby vomit. It is also revered by millions and served with pride in many Thai and Malaysian households. Most of all, it's a great way to learn about marketing.

Songpol Somsri, a scientist fascinated by the durian, has spent decades cross-breeding more than 90 varieties of durian and has come up with a stinkless variety. No odor.

This is what most marketers do. They listen to complaints from non-customers ("why don't you buy from us?"), address them, and wait for the market to grow. After all, if the people who don't eat durian don't eat it because of the smell, then removing the smell ought to dramatically increase the size of your market.

Except this almost never works.

Non-durian eaters don't have a "durian problem." They aren't standing by, fruitless, impatiently waiting for Songpol Somsri to figure out how to make a stinkless durian. Nope. They've got cantaloupes and kiwis and all manner of other fruits to keep them busy.

The feedback you get from non-consumers is rarely useful, because the objection they give is the reason they *don't* buy from you, not the thing that will cause them to affirmatively choose you.

Will stinkless durian revolutionize the marketplace? Possibly. I've been wrong before. But if I were a durian farmer, *I'd work hard to make durian stinkier.*

Reaching the Unreachable

Marketing, I think, can be divided into two eras.

The first, the biggest, the baddest, and the most impressive was the era in which marketers were able to reach the unreachable. Ads could be used to interrupt people who weren't intending to hear from you. PR could be used to get a story to show up on *Oprah* or in the paper, reaching people who weren't seeking you out.

Sure, there were exceptions to this model (the Yellow Pages and the classifieds, for example), but generally speaking, the biggest wins for a marketer happened in this arena.

We're watching it die.

The latest example is the hand-wringing about the loss of the book review sections from major newspapers. Book publicists love these sections, because they provide a way of putting your book in front of people who weren't looking for it. Oprah is a superstar because she has the power (the right? the expectation?) of regularly putting new ideas in front of people who weren't looking for that particular thing.

Super Bowl ads? Another example of spending big money to reach the unreachable. This is almost irresistible to marketers.

Notice the almost.

In the last few years, this model has been replaced. Call it permission if you want, or turning the world into the Yellow Pages. The Web is astonishingly bad at reaching the unreachable. Years ago, the home-page banner at Yahoo! was the hottest property on the Web. That's because lazy marketers could buy it and reach everyone.

Thanks to the Long Tail and to competition and to a billion websites and to busy schedules and selfish consumers, the unreachable are now truly unreachable.

If I want a book review, I'll go read one. If I want to learn about turntables, I'll go do that. Mass is still seductive, but mass is now so expensive, marketers are balking at buying it. (Notice how thin *Time* magazine is these days? Nothing compared to *Gourmet*.)

And yet. And yet marketers still start every meeting and every memo with ideas about how to reach the unreachable. It's not in our nature to do what actually works: start making products, services, and stories that appeal to the reachable. Then do your best to build that group ever larger. Not by yelling at them, but by serving them.

One, a Few, Most, or All

There are four kinds of marketing situations, and the approach to each one is radically different. Yet most of the time, we lump them together as just plain "marketing."

If you are trying to sell a house or fill a job, you only need to persuade **one person**.

If you want your book to sell a bunch of copies, your restaurant to be filled on Saturday night, or your coaching practice to have a full schedule, you need to sell to a **few** people.

On the other hand, viral bestsellers, killer websites, and essential conferences hit their stride when **most** people in a marketplace have been converted. You can't get elected president (most years, anyway) without persuading most of the people who vote.

Lastly, when the market is defined right, there are situations in which you need to persuade **all** of the people involved. If you need 51 senators to agree with you on a bill, or if you need the purchasing committee at a big company to buy your software, then you need a unanimous decision.

This four-way distinction is important for two reasons. First, because you often have a choice. You can choose which approach your venture will take on its way to accomplishing its goals. Gandhi didn't need **most** of the people to change India; he instead relied on a smaller **few**, but with more passion than most politicians are able to generate.

You could, for example, plan a business that works when almost everyone adopts it (like eBay), or you could alter the business so it works just fine if a much smaller universe of people embrace it (like Threadless). Worth noting that neither business would work if just a few people showed up. 37signals has done a great job of designing Web products that need to be sold to only a **few** people, and then those people do the hard work of getting **everyone** in their organization to use them.

Here's a quick list of how the four situations differ:

ONE: You're a needle, the market is a haystack. Make your needle as sharp as you can, and put it in as many haystacks as you can afford. Alternatively, you've already decided on your one (the date for the prom or the perfect job). In that case, throw the haystack out and engage in a custom, one-on-one, patient effort to tell your story to the person who needs to hear it.

A FEW: Being exceptional matters most. Stand out, don't fit in. Shun the non-believers.

MOST: Amplify the excitement of the few and make it easy for them to spread the story to the caring majority.

ALL: Compromise. You need to be many things to many people, embraced by the passionate but not offensive to the masses. Sooner or later, the issue for the reluctant part of the buyer community is that it becomes more expensive/risky to stand in the way of the group than it is to go along.

Blogs, for now, are almost always about the **few**. Google and Starbucks and the iPod are exciting stories because they've moved from the few to the **most**. The most important industry trade shows make huge profits because they've transitioned to the **all**.

Choose wisely, and realize that as you succeed, the game will change.

Three Humps and a Stick (On Pricing)

I've been working on a video project and thinking about pricing. That led me to this chart, which is more conceptual than accurate.

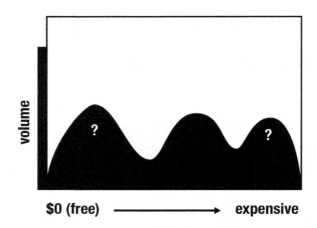

Let's go through it, starting with the stick on the left.

FREE stuff spreads. You don't make any money from the thing you're giving away, but you do get attention, which is worth as much, or more, in many cases.

Charge even a penny, though, and the drop-off is huge.

Jump over to the middle hump, the one without the question mark.

REASONABLE PRICING puts you right in the middle of the market. With reasonable pricing, you can move just a bit to the left or the right to find the sweet spot, the spot where you can balance money for promotion or shelf space or advertising against keeping your price low. Most of us are familiar with the shape of this curve in our industry. For example, hardcover books go for about $21. At $28, you have more money for co-op and ads, but sales go down a bit. At $19, you can't promote much, but sales go up a bit.

Move a bit to the left, to the first hump with a question mark.

REALLY LOW PRICING is a whole new world. That's when something becomes cheap enough to be irresistible to someone who might not consider the category at all. This is what happens when MP3 songs go from

99 cents to 20 cents. This is what happens when you sell a hardcover book for $10. There's no room for big promotion, at least at first, but as Walmart has shown us, you can get scale at the super low end and have plenty of profit left over to hire fancy PR firms and lobbyists and ad agencies.

The last hump, the one on the right, is usually unexplored.

REALLY HIGH PRICING is the domain of specialty markets and superstars. Elton John gets $300,000 to do a bar mitzvah. John Cleese offers training videos that cost $1,000 for one DVD. This is the land of high service and extreme exclusivity.

What's interesting about the four choices is that most organizations are familiar with only one. Ask them to try another and they freak out. They don't even want to consider it.

I think real growth can come when you get out of your comfort hump and create a blend. Understanding how to live in multiple worlds and to balance them isn't obvious, but the opportunities are worth it. Ben Zander's brilliant book, *The Art of Possibility,* costs $10.20 at Amazon in hardcover. The DVD costs $1,495.00.

If he wanted to sell the DVD in large quantities, he'd need to price it differently and sell it in a different channel. But if he wants to work with trainers and the distributors who sell to them, he's exactly in the center of that third hump.

Careful about the Y axis (volume). Units aren't always the goal (that's why I said this chart was conceptual). FREE gets you the most units, REALLY EXPENSIVE the least. But depending on your objectives, units might not be the point.

It's not important to know the right answer, which hump to choose, because there isn't one. It's essential to know the question, because there are four distinct choices, and not choosing is still choosing.

The Opposite

The opposite of up is down.

The opposite of in is out.

Those two are easy. They are one-dimensional.

The opposite of Steve Jobs is Bill Gates.

Sort of. That's because Bill and Steve have a lot in common (outsize personalities, many Google matches, successful tech companies). But it's useful to consider them as opposites because we learn a lot about their approaches, personalities, and yes, brands, by looking at the inverse.

The opposite of Starbucks is Dunkin' Donuts.

Not an independent coffee shop, and not coffee at home.

On the other hand, the opposite of Dunkin' Donuts is not Starbucks. The opposite is "not having coffee out."

That's because when someone considers getting their morning coffee, the choice is usually home or Dunkin'. That person doesn't have Starbucks as part of their choice set. Defining your brand in this way makes it easier to ignore the irrelevant competition and easier to figure out what you are (and aren't).

Bill Clinton and John Edwards aren't the opposite of Rush Limbaugh. Al Franken is.

The BlackBerry isn't the opposite of the iPhone. A plain-Jane Motorola phone is. Apple understands this. BlackBerry doesn't seem to.

The opposite of the Food Network is hours spent poring over cookbooks at a local independent bookstore. Or perhaps it's *Good Housekeeping* magazine. Or *Gourmet*.

One of the hardest things to do is invent a brand with no opposite. You don't have an anchor to play against.

Does your team agree on who your opposite is?

Elephant Math

Darwin pointed out that if you take one pair of breeding elephants and make some conservative estimates about their fertility, you would have more than 15 million elephants in less than 500 years (if none of them died an early death).

It's pretty clear it doesn't work that way. Perfect viral growth, even slow viral growth, rarely happens. If it did, we'd have an elephant problem.

The same thing happens with your idea. If one person told four and the cycle repeated itself for a few generations, everyone would know about it. But they don't. It tails off. One person often tells zero. Or people hear about it but forget.

Real viral growth comes from one of a few likely paths:

- Someone sneezes your idea with amplification. They show up on *Oprah*, or you have $100 million to spend on ads. Great work if you can get it.
- The idea spreads with fidelity. One person really does tell four, and there's not a lot of leakage. Starbucks worked this way, largely because the chain grew at just the right rate and kept its character as it did.
- The idea is particularly "viral" (using a popular understanding of the word). One typical person doesn't tell four; she tells 400. This is the blogger effect—lots of small amplifiers, working in unison.
- The idea lives a very long time and spreads slowly. In our rapid-fire world, this one is pretty rare.

It's possible to combine some of these tactics. When a political candidate starts out, for example, it's almost certainly with a grassroots approach, but then, perhaps, once enthusiasm picks up, he or she shows up on TV. You can organize around this and plan for it, but you certainly can't guarantee it.

Here's the big news: it doesn't matter much how many elephants you start with. In other words, big launches don't necessarily scale. What matters is how fertile your elephants are (number of babies per generation) and how long they live. If Darwin's elephants manage to squeeze in just one more generation, they end up with 30 million.

Seven Tips to Build for Meaning

What happens after I click on your Google ad?

I was thinking about great Squidoo pages (lenses) yesterday, and realized that many of them, along with many blogs, have the same goal: give someone a handle, a sense of meaning—context—so they can go ahead and take action.

You have a blog to turn a browser into a raging fan for your candidate or your product.

You have a lens designed to teach people what they need to know to confidently sign up for your tour.

You have a landing page to convert Google AdWords clickers into buyers.

With that in mind, here are a few tactical tips that might help if that's what you're trying to do online:

1. *Use numbers and bullets.* People don't read online, they scan.
2. *Give people a place to go.* The Web is incredibly efficient when it's a road, much less so when it's a dead end. The best meaning-building delivers the reader to a new place, in context.
3. *Use pictures.* Back to the scanning thing. Pictures, properly chosen, communicate quality as well as large amounts of information. I'm not talking about product shots (which are important) as much as about pictures that tell a story.
4. *Have an opinion.* Guides that bend over backward to be fair rarely impart information. Context is built more quickly if people know where you stand and can plug that into their previous point of view. If you're giving meaning, you're also making an argument—one in favor of your point of view.
5. *Don't be afraid to compare.* Saying this is better than that helps me understand if I already have an understanding of that.
6. *It's a brick wall, not a balloon.* This is a hard one for many people. We try to build something quickly and get it totally complete all in one go. If we can't, we get frustrated and give up. But great blogs and lenses are built brick by brick, a little at a time. You learn what works and do it more.
7. *It's okay to be long, if you're chunky.* The great lesson of direct mail was that long letters always do better than short ones. That's because once you've sold me, I'll stop reading. But if I'm not sold and I get to the end, you lose. The Web is infinitely expandable. So go ahead and tell your story.

Is Viral Marketing the Same as Word of Mouth?

I got a note from a college student last week, explaining that his professor told him he couldn't use the term "viral marketing" in a paper. It doesn't exist; apparently, it's just a newfangled form of word of mouth.

I found the interaction fascinating ("I'm not certain what benefit is gained by arguing with an instructor" is my favorite quote from his teacher), but I got to thinking about whether the instructor had a point.

"Viral marketing" shows up 2,000,000 times in Google; "ideavirus" shows up 200,000 times. Of course, you could argue that just because millions of people are using a term doesn't make it legitimate (though you'd be wrong).

Anyway . . .

Viral marketing [does not equal] word of mouth. Here's why:

Word of mouth is a decaying function. A marketer does something, and a consumer tells five or ten friends. And that's it. Word of mouth amplifies the marketing action and then fades, usually quickly. A lousy flight on United Airlines is word of mouth. A great meal at Momofuku is word of mouth.

Viral marketing is a compounding function. A marketer does something, and then a consumer tells five or ten people. Then they tell five or ten people. And it repeats. And grows and grows. Like a virus spreading through a population. The marketer doesn't have to actually do anything else. (Marketers can help by making it easier for the word to spread, but in the classic examples, the marketer is out of the loop.) The *Mona Lisa* is an ideavirus.

This distinction is vital.

For one thing, it means that constant harassment of the population doesn't increase the chances of something's becoming viral. It means that most organizations should realize that they have a better chance with word of mouth (more likely to occur, more manageable, more flexible) and focus on that. And it means, most of all, that viral marketing is like winning the lottery, and if you've got a shot at an ideavirus, you might as well over-invest and do whatever it takes to create something virus-worthy.

And yes, I happen to think that arguing with the instructor is a very good idea.

Permission Marketing

Permission marketing is the privilege (not the right) of delivering anticipated, personal, and relevant messages to people who actually want to get them.

It recognizes the new power of the best consumers to ignore marketing. It realizes that treating people with respect is the best way to earn their attention.

"Pay attention" is a key phrase here, because permission marketers understand that when someone chooses to pay attention, they are actually paying you with something precious. And there's no way they can get their attention back if they change their mind. Attention becomes an important asset, something to be valued, not wasted.

Real permission is different from presumed or legalistic permission. Just because you somehow get my email address doesn't mean you have permission. Just because I don't complain doesn't mean you have permission. Just because it's in the fine print of your privacy policy doesn't mean it's permission, either.

Real permission works like this: If you stop showing up, people complain; they ask where you went.

I got a note from a Daily Candy reader the other day. He was upset because for three days in a row, his Daily Candy newsletter hadn't come. That's permission.

Permission is like dating. You don't start by asking for the sale at the first impression. You earn the right, over time, bit by bit.

One of the key drivers of permission marketing, in addition to the scarcity of attention, is the extraordinarily low cost of dripping to people who want to hear from you. RSS and email and other techniques mean that you don't have to worry about stamps or network ad buys every time you have something to say. Home delivery is the milkman's revenge—it's the essence of permission.

Permission doesn't have to be formal, but it has to be obvious. My friend has permission to call me if he needs to borrow five dollars, but the person you meet at a trade show has no such ability to pitch you his entire résumé, even though he paid to get in.

Subscriptions are overt acts of permission. That's why home-delivery newspaper readers are so valuable, and why magazine subscribers are worth more than readers who buy the magazine at a newsstand.

In order to get permission, you make a promise. You say, "I will do x, y, and z; I hope you will give me permission by listening." And then—this is the hard part—that's all you do. You don't assume you can do more. You don't sell the list or rent the list or demand more attention. You can promise a newsletter and talk to me for years, you can promise a daily RSS feed and talk to me every three minutes, or you can promise a sales pitch every day (the way Woot does). But the promise is the promise until both sides agree to change it. You don't assume that just because you're running for president or coming to the end of the quarter or launching a new product that you have the right to break the deal. You don't.

Permission doesn't have to be a one-way broadcast medium. The Internet means you can treat different people differently, and it demands that you figure out how to let your permission base choose what they hear and in what format.

When I launched my book that coined this phrase nine years ago, I offered people a third of the book for free in exchange for an email address. And I never, ever did anything with those addresses again. That wasn't part of the deal. No follow-ups, no new products. A deal's a deal.

If it sounds like you need humility and patience to do permission marketing, you're right. That's why so few companies do it properly. The best shortcut, in this case, is no shortcut at all.

Fear, Hope, and Love: The Three Marketing Levers

Where does love come from? Brand love?

The TSA is in the fear business. Every time they get you to take off your shoes, they're using fear (of the unknown or perhaps of missing your plane) to get you to take action.

Chanel is in the hope business. How else to get you to spend $5,000 a gallon for perfume?

Hope can be something as trivial as convenience. I hope that this smaller size of yogurt will save me time or get a smile out of my teenager.

And love? Love gets you to support a candidate even when he screws up or changes his mind on a position or disagrees with you on another one. Love incites you to protest when they change the formula for Coke, or to cry out in delight when you see someone at the market wearing a Google T-shirt.

People take action (mostly) based on one of three emotions:

Fear
Hope
Love

Every successful marketer (including politicians) takes advantage of at least one of these basic needs.

Forbes magazine, for example, is for people who hope to make more money.

Rudy Giuliani was the fear candidate. He tried to turn fear into love but failed.

Few products or services succeed out of love. People are too selfish for an emotion that selfless, most of the time.

It's interesting to think about the way certain categories gravitate to various emotions. Doctors selling checkups, of course, are in the fear business (while oncologists certainly sell hope). Restaurants have had a hard time selling fear (healthy places don't do so well). Singles bars certainly thrive on selling hope.

Google, amazingly quickly, became a beloved brand, something many people see as bigger than themselves, something bigger than hope. Apple lives in this arena as well. I think if you deliver hope for a long time (and deliver on it sometimes), you can graduate to love. Ronald Reagan was beloved, even when he was making significant long-term errors. So was JFK. Hillary may be respected, but Obama is loved.

I don't think love is often a one-way street, either. Brands that are loved usually start the process by loving their customers in advance.

The easiest way to build a brand is to sell fear. The best way, though, may be to deliver on hope while aiming for love.

Which Comes First (Why Stories Matter)

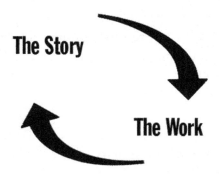

I was brainstorming with my friend Jay today and he put this picture into my head.

Most of the time we do the work. The work comprises our initiative and our reactions and our responses and our output. The work comprises the decisions we make and the people we hire.

The work is what people talk about, because it's what we experience. In other words, the work tells a story.

But what if you haven't figured out a story yet?

Then the work is random. Then the story is confused or bland or indifferent and it doesn't spread.

On the other hand, if you decide what the story is, you can do work that matches the story. Your decisions will match the story. The story will become true because you're living it.

Does Starbucks tell a different story from McDonald's? Of course they do. But look how the work they do matches those stories—from the benefits they offer employees to the decisions they make about packaging or locations.

Same is true for that little consulting firm down the street vs. McKinsey. While the advice may end up being similar, each firm lives a story in whom they hire, how they present themselves, etc.

The story creates the work, and the work creates the story.

Why Word of Mouth Doesn't Happen

Sometimes, what you do is done as well as it can be done. It's a service that people truly love, or a product they can't live without. You're doing everything right, but it's not remarkable, at least not in the sense of "worth making a remark about."

What's up with that?

Here's a smorgasbord of reasons:

1. It's embarrassing to talk about. That's why VD screening, no matter how well done, rarely turns into a viral [ahem] success.

2. There's no easy way to bring it up. This is similar to item number 1 but involves opportunity. It's easy to bring up "hey, where'd you get that ring tone?" because the ring tone just interrupted everyone. It's a lot harder to bring up the fact that you just got a massage.

3. It might not feel cutting edge enough for your crowd. So, it's not the thing that's embarrassing; it's the fact that you just found out about it. Don't bring up your brand-new Tivo with your friends from MIT. They'll sneer at you.

4. On a related front, it might feel too popular to profitably sneeze about. Sometimes bloggers hesitate to post on a popular source or topic because they worry that they'll seem lazy.

5. You might like the exclusivity. If you have no trouble getting into a great restaurant or a wonderful club, perhaps you won't tell the masses because you're selfish.

6. You might want to keep worlds from colliding. Some kids, for example, like the idea of being the only kid from their school at the summer camp they go to. They get to have two personalities, be two people, keep things separate.

7. You might feel manipulated. Plenty of hip kids were happy to talk about Converse, but once big, bad Nike got involved, it felt different. Almost like they were being used.

8. You might worry about your taste. Recommending a wine really strongly takes guts, because maybe, just maybe, your friends will hate the wine and think you tasteless.

9. There are probably ten other big reasons, but they all lead to the same conclusions:

First, understand that people talk about you (or don't talk about you) because of how it makes them feel, not how it makes you feel.

Second, if you're going to build a business around word of mouth, better not have these things working against you.

Third, if you do, it may be a smart strategy to work directly to overcome them. That probably means changing the fundamental DNA of your experience and the story you tell to your users. "If you like us, tell your friends" might feel like a fine start, but it's certainly not going to get you there.

What *will* change the game is actually changing the game. Changing the experience of talking about you so fundamentally that people will choose to do it.

Start with a Classified Ad

Copy gets in the way.

Actually, *thinking* about copy gets in the way. You start writing and then you patch and layer and write and dissemble and defend and write and the next thing you know, you've killed it.

So, try this instead:

Write a classified ad. What's the offer? What do you want me to do? You're paying by the word!

"Lose weight now. Join our gym."

Six words. Promise and offer.

Now, you can make it longer. Of course, if your gym is on the space station and it's the only gym around, and if the people reading your ad are looking at the bulletin board and seeking out what they want, then your ad is now long enough.

But most of the time, in most settings, a little longer is better. So, add a few words or even a sentence. Is it better? More effective? Gently and carefully add words until it's as effective as possible, but as short as possible.

Perhaps you want to make your promise more vivid, or more clear. Perhaps you need a testimonial or two to back up your promise. Perhaps your call to action needs to be more urgent. You can play with all of that, keeping in mind the original classified ad, keeping in mind that you're still paying by the word (because attention is expensive).

And yes, this principle applies to articles in the newspaper, to blog posts, to how-to books, and to direct marketing letters. It applies to the emails you send and the copy on your website, too.

Five Easy Pieces

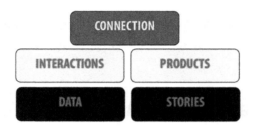

You really don't understand a concept until you know what it's made of. The taxonomy of marketing (filled with a bazillion tactics) is murky at best. The tactics are so numerous, expensive, and sometimes emotional that we easily focus on the urgent instead of the important. Perhaps we could try a different approach.

Never mind the Ps. Marketing has five elements:

Data
Stories
Products (services)
Interactions
Connection

DATA are observational. What do people actually do? Walmart uses data to decide if an end cap is working. Google AdWords advertisers use data to decide which copy delivers clicks and sales. The library can use data to decide which books to buy (and which not to buy). Paco

Underhill uses data to turbo-charge retail. Data are powerful, overlooked, and sometimes mistaken for boring. You don't have to understand the why; you merely need to know the what.

STORIES define everything you say and do. The product has a myth; the service has a legend. Marketing applies to every person, every job, every service, and every organization. That's because all we can work with as humans is stories. I want to argue that data and stories are the two key building blocks of marketing—the other three are built on these two.

PRODUCTS (and services) are physical manifestations of the story. If your story is that you are cutting edge and faster/newer/better, then your products better be. "Average products for average people" is a common story, but not one that spreads. When in doubt, re-imagine the product. Push it to be the story, to live the story, to create a myth.

INTERACTIONS are all the tactics the marketer uses to actually touch the prospect or customer. Interactions range from spam to billboards, from the way you answer the phone to the approach you take to an overdue bill. Interactions are the hero of marketing, because there are so many and most of them are cheap. Unfortunately, all lazy marketers can do is buy ads or spam people. And that creates an interaction that belies your story, right?

CONNECTION is the highest level of enlightenment, the end goal. Connection between you and the customer, surely, but mostly connection between customers. Great marketers create bands of brothers, tribes of people who wish each other well and want to belong. Get the first four steps right and you may get a shot at this one.

Some questions marketers must ask: Does this interaction lead to connections? Do our products support our story? Is the story pulling in numbers that demonstrate that it's working?

In that light, what are you working on? If it's not one of these five, and not going to seriously change the dynamic of your marketing, why exactly are you bothering?

My guess is that your organization spends almost all of its time on the interactions. Once you see the world through the prism of the five pieces, you can get in balance. Or you could be Jack Nicholson.

Scarcity

One day, you may be lucky enough to have a scarcity problem. A product or a service or even a job that's in such high demand that people are clamoring for more than you can make.

We can learn a lot from the abysmal performance of Apple this weekend. They took a hot product and totally botched the launch because of a misunderstanding of the benefits and uses of scarcity.

First, understand that scarcity is a choice. If you raise your price, scarcity goes away. If your product is going to be scarce, it's either because you benefit from that or because your organization is forbidden to use price as a demand-adjustment tool. I'm going to assume the former. (But I riff a bit on the latter toward the end.)

Why be scarce?

- Scarcity creates fashion. People want something that others can't have.
- Lines create demand. People want something that others want.

- Scarcity also creates word of mouth, because people talk about lines and shortages and hot products.
- And finally, scarcity drives your product to the true believers, the ones most likely to spread the word and ignite the ideavirus. Because they expended effort to acquire your product or service, they're not only more likely to talk about it, but they've also self-selected as the sort of person likely to talk about it.

The danger is that you can kill long-term loyalty. You can annoy your best customers. You can spread negative word of mouth. You can train people to hate your scarcity strategy (Apple did all four this weekend).

Take a look at the guy in the photo. That's the goal. He feels great. He's a hero, at least for a moment, all because he stood in line all night. He gets to talk about it, and others (not everyone, but enough) aspire to be him next time. You reward the tribe and you build the tribe at the same time.

The problem is that our knee-jerk way of dealing with scarcity is to treat everyone the same and to have people "pay" by spending time to indicate their desire.

Waiting in line is a very old-school way of dealing with scarcity. And treating new customers like old customers, treating unknown customers the same as high-value customers, is painful and unnecessary.

Principle 1: Use the Internet to form a queue. If you have a scarce product, you almost certainly know in advance that it's scarce. Instead of taxing customers by wasting their time, reward the early shoppers by taking orders online. A month before the sale date, for example, tell them it's coming. If you sell out before the ship date, that's great, because the next time, people will be even quicker to order when they hear about what you've got. (And you can do this in the real world, too—postcards with numbers or even playing cards work just fine.)

A hot band that regularly sells out on the road, for example, could put a VIP serial number inside every CD or T-shirt they sell. People could then use that number to preorder their tickets.

Principle 2: Give the early adopters a reward. In the case of Apple, I would have made the first 100,000 phones a different color. Then, instead of the buyer being a hero for ten seconds, he gets to be a hero for a year.

Principle 3: Treat different customers differently. Apple, for example, knows how to contact every single existing customer. Why not offer VIP status to big spenders? Or to those that make a lot of calls? Let them cut the line. It's not fair? What does fair mean? I can't think of anything more fair than treating the people who treat you well, better.

Principle 4: When things happen in real time, you're way more likely to screw up. One of the giant advantages of the 'Net is that you can fix things before the whole world notices. Try to do your rollout in small sections, so you can fix mistakes before you hurt the very people you're trying to embrace.

Principle 5: Give your early adopters a forum to celebrate. A place to brag or demonstrate or show off or share insights and ideas. Amplify the heroes, which is far better than amplifying the pain of standing in line.

Imagine what the Apple and AT&T stores would have been like this weekend if they had been filled with happy customers who had prepaid and preregistered and were just dropping in for three minutes to pick up their (very coveted) phones, walking up the VIP line, past all the others just waiting for a chance to buy one.

Hot restaurants in New York violate all five of these principles on a regular basis. So do sports teams and stores that have lines out front in the middle of winter. What a waste.

Even colleges do it. They pretend they've got a meritocracy, but in practice, it's a high-pressure lottery with enormous financial and stress overhead involved.

Yes, there are times when scarcity is mandated (the TSA at airports, for example, or food rations at an emergency site). I know that there are plenty of ways to deal with this scarcity as well. Ways to treat your customers (and yes, they are customers) with more respect, to communicate the situation more clearly, and to architect the environment so that people are grateful, not stressed out.

Smart marketers understand that scarcity (intentional or not) is a tool, one that can be used to enhance the story, not detract from it.

The Power of Smart Copywriting

Consider this riff from a professionally printed freestanding sign in front of a Peet's store in San Jose:

"UNLIKE ANY COFFEE YOU'VE EVER TASTED BEFORE."

Wait. Why the capitals?

"UNLIKE ANY COFFEE YOU'VE EVER TASTED BEFORE."

"Before" is redundant.

"UNLIKE ANY COFFEE YOU'VE EVER TASTED."

Too negative. And why is "unlike" a positive trait? I mean, boiled leech guts is also unlike any coffee I've ever tasted, but that doesn't mean I want to drink it. How about:

"THE BEST COFFEE YOU'VE EVER TASTED."

Well, the thing is, the only coffee that matters is coffee I've tasted, right? So we could get shorter still:

"THE BEST COFFEE."

The problem with that is that it's nothing but bragging. Of course you think it's the best coffee. So what? You're lying. And even if you're not lying, how do you know it's the best? Compared to what?

This is where the smart copywriter becomes a marketer.

"BETTER THAN STARBUCKS."

Well, it's still bragging. This is the moment when the marketer becomes a smart marketer and realizes that changing the offer or the product is more important than changing the hype.

**"FREE TASTE TEST
ARE WE BETTER THAN STARBUCKS?"**

Invest $20 in espresso in little cups, and maybe, just maybe, your sign will make some magic.

What Marketers Actually Sell

Not powder or chemicals or rubber or steel or silicon or talk or installations or even sugary water.

What marketers sell is hope.

The reason is simple: people need more. We run out. We need it replenished. Hope is almost always in short supply.

The magical thing about selling hope is that it makes everything else work better, every day get better, every project work better, every relationship feel better. If you can actually deliver on the hope you sell, there will be a line out the door.

Hope cures cynicism. Hope increases productivity. Hope needs no justification.

The Rational Marketer (and the Irrational Customer)

The most common frustration I see, and I see it daily, comes from marketers who can't figure out why more people won't buy their products. This frustration particularly afflicts B2B marketers, who ostensibly have rational customers.

Let's say, for example, that you have a service that can deliver leads for 5% of what it costs to get them via a trade show. Why would any rational business, particularly one that says it wants qualified leads, spend that money on trade shows and not on you?

I mean, I mean, you can PROVE that your system works. You can guarantee it. You can provide testimonials and real-time evidence. And yet, the person you're calling on won't give you money and will spend it on the traditional system, which is a total waste.

You *know* that your car is more aerodynamic. You *know* that your insulation is more effective. You *know* that your insurance has a higher ROI.

You've thought about it a lot because it's your job to think about it. It's your job to make those charts and tables and graphs and brochures. So you know it.

The problem is that your prospect doesn't care about any of those things. He cares about his boss or the story you're telling or the risk or the hassle of making a change. He cares about whom you know and what other people will think when he tells them what he's done after he buys from you.

The opportunity, then, is not to insist that your customers get more rational, but instead to embrace just how irrational they are. Give them what they need. Help them satisfy their needs at the same time they get the measurable, rational results that your product can give them in the long run.

The Panhandler's Secret

When there were old-school parking meters in New York, quarters were precious.

One day, I was walking down the street and a guy came up to me and said, "Do you have a dollar for four quarters?" He held out his hand with four quarters in it.

Curious, I engaged with him. I took out a dollar bill and took the four quarters.

Then he turned to me and said, "Can you spare a quarter?"

What a fascinating interaction.

First, he engaged me. A fair trade, one that perhaps even benefited me, not him.

Now, we have a relationship. Now, he knows I have a quarter (in my hand, even). So his next request is much more difficult to turn down. If he had just walked up to me and said, "Can you spare a quarter?" he would have been invisible.

Too often, we close the sale before we even open it.

Interact first, sell second.

Direct-from-Consumer Marketing

Drug companies have coined an initialism for the marketing they do that bypasses doctors: DTC. Direct to consumer. Think of those happy-face ads you see in *Reader's Digest* and other magazines, or the erectile dysfunction ads you see during the Super Bowl.

What drug companies are totally unprepared for, and what your organization may be unprepared for, is DFC: direct *from* consumer.

If someone takes your medicine and gets sick, do you want to hear from them, or would you rather have them blog about it or make a video?

Most drug company marketers instantly say, "we want to hear from them!"

Really?

When your airline or hotel has a passenger or guest who is so angry he could spit, do you want to hear from him or do you want him to make a long PowerPoint presentation that spreads around the whole Web? Really?

And when your cable company or chiropractic clinic or consulting firm has a disappointed client, what about you? Really?

I think the actions of almost all marketers say, "we'd rather you were happy, but if you can't be happy, please go away."

If you really want me to call you, then put your toll-free number in giant type on the label. (If you run a free service, Google style, I think it's okay to settle for an easy-to-use and responsive Web presence.) Answer the call on the first ring. No phone tree. And give me instant sympathy, maybe a little empathy, too. Don't blame me or evade. Give me a refund. And say "sorry" and "thank you."

"Oh," the powerful marketers say, "we could never do that." Two reasons, apparently. First, they say, because it would encourage people to pretend they were angry in order to take advantage. And second, they say, because it would be too expensive.

Compared to what?

Back when every consumer was alone, you could ignore the few angry ones and use the money you saved to run more ads. But now? Now in the DFC era, do you really have any choice?

Angry phone calls are your friend. They're your friend because the alternative is angry tweets and angry blog posts.

The Difference Between PR and Publicity

Most PR firms do publicity, not PR.

Publicity is the act of getting ink. Publicity is getting unpaid media to pay attention, write you up, point to you, run a picture, make a commotion. Sometimes publicity is helpful, and good publicity is always good for your ego.

But it's not PR.

PR is the strategic crafting of your story. It's the focused examination of your interactions and tactics and products and pricing that, when combined, determine what and how people talk about you.

Regis McKenna was great at PR. Yes, he got Steve Jobs and the Mac on the cover of more than 30 magazines in the year it launched. That was just publicity. The real insight was crafting the story of the Mac (and yes, the story of Steve Jobs).

If you send out a boring press release, your publicity effort will probably fail, but your PR already has failed.

A publicity firm will tell you stories of how they got a client ink. A PR firm will talk about storytelling and being remarkable and spreading the word. They might even suggest that you don't bother getting ink or issuing press releases.

In my experience, a few people have a publicity problem, but almost everyone has a PR problem. You need to solve that one first. And you probably won't accomplish that if you hire a publicity firm and don't even give them the freedom and access they need to work with you on your story.

Is Marketing an Art or a Science?

It's both, and that's the problem.

Some marketers are scientists. They test and measure. They do the math. They understand the impact of that spend in that market at that time with that message. They can understand the analytics and find the truth.

This sort of marketing works when it works, but it usually doesn't. That's because we're dealing with humans, the wild card in the system.

The other marketers are artists. They inspire and challenge and connect. These marketers are starting from scratch, creating movements, telling jokes, and surprising people. Scientists aren't good at that.

The problem is caused by two things:

1. *Outsiders are confused.* Which are we? When we're artists sometimes and scientists other times, we often seem like charlatans, because we're associating scientific results with artistic endeavors.
2. *We're confused.* If you don't know whether you're doing a science project or an art project, you'll probably emphasize the wrong elements. If you go to school to study marketing, and the blowhard professor acts like she's teaching you science, you'll waste a lot of time trying to apply taxonomy and hypotheses to something that is essentially a gut decision. And vice versa.

We need hats. The hat of the scientist and the hat of the artist. You can wear only one hat at a time, which is why I didn't suggest that we need gloves.

Figure out what sort of marketing you're going to do today and go do that.

The Difference Between Marketing and Sales

The people in the marketing department tell a story that spreads.

The folks in sales overcome the natural resistance to saying yes.

If you don't pay the sales force (because you go direct, or you go free), then who is going to do that for you? The only answer that occurs to me is, "your users/fans/customers."

This means that a critical element of any strategy that ditches the sales force is to figure out how you will empower and encourage your customers to take their place. Easier said than done.

Who Spreads Your Word?

In order for an idea to spread, someone has to do the spreading.

In the dark ages (ten years ago), the only way to spread your idea on a large scale was to do it yourself. With lots and lots of ads.

Today, marketers get all sweaty thinking about how this happens *magically*, virally, for free. If it were only that easy.

What's interesting to me is that different products and ideas are spread by different groups of people. *There isn't just one professional association of idea spreaders, with everyone else being passive.*

If your authentic little Welsh restaurant gets hot, it's going to be because the chowhounds, the folks who love to talk about the next great place, are buzzing about it. On the other hand, if your blog gets a lot of traffic, it might just be because a few of the digerati are going on about it, spreading the idea.

This is obvious, of course.

But what are you doing about it? Have you figured out which portions of your user base are the talkers? Is it possible to focus your development efforts on making something that they like? Or are you confusing the people who talk about your competition or about other industries with the people you need to reach? Might not be the same tribe.

The #1 cause of an idea that's not spreading or a business that's not growing is that they don't have a committed group of people spreading the word about them. If you treat everyone the same, you're not increasing the odds that some people will step up on your behalf.

This is the first question to ask someone who is frustrated at the rate their idea is spreading. "Who are you hoping will talk about you?" If you don't know, it's unlikely to happen all by itself. On the other hand, if a marketer is smart about finding, courting, and delighting the group most likely to spread the idea, it's time well spent.

True Believers (and the Truth)

The Internet has amplified the volume of the true believers, the defenders of any faith.

If you're into high-end stereo, it's far easier to find strident voices in defense of $100,000 stereos than ever before. If you have strong views on health care (either side), it's not hard to find the orthodox and articulate believers. It's not just specialty magazines or conferences any longer. The true believers are in our faces every day.

When you lead a tribe, the volume and accessibility of the true believers are good things. The true believers are easy to find, and they maintain order and create a culture for the group you're leading.

The problem is that these loud voices may be loud, but they might not be right.

If you want them to write glowingly about your company's new stereo, you'll make one that's so obscure and expensive that you won't sell very many. If you want them to adore your new restaurant, it might be so edgy and cutting edge that not enough people will actually come, and you'll go under.

Go check out the track record of the loudest believers in your industry. They're wrong far more than they are right. In fact, when they love a new tech product or candidate, it might just be the jinx that guarantees failure.

The truth of the market is that the market you sell to isn't filled with true believers. It's filled with human beings who make compromises, who tell stories, who have competing objectives. And as a result, the truth of the market is that the products and services that win (if win means you can make a good living and make positive change) are rarely the products and services that are beloved without reservation by the true believers.

What's It Like? (The Sad Story of the Hot Pepper)

Can you imagine how difficult it was to sell the jalapeño when it came over from the New World?

"What's it like?" you'd be asked.

Well, it's like a pepper. (Of course, it wasn't. Black pepper is dried and tastes very different.)

Well, it's hot. (No, it's not. Hot is a temperature, spicy is a taste.)

It's not like anything, actually. Capsicum is an experience unto itself, and forcing me to tell you what it's like does neither of us much of a service.

"What's it like?" is actually shorthand for, "I don't trust you enough to just try it, so you better explain in detail what category this item fits into so I can decide in advance how to understand it."

"What's it like?" is a huge impediment to growth and to the spread of new ideas, because forcing a marketer to pigeonhole an idea naturally limits it.

"What's it like?" leads to sequels and high concepts and crossovers, but it doesn't get us 1966 Bob Dylan or even yoga class.

Great marketers take advantage of categories every day. Great marketers understand how to create books or services or products or technologies that are very much like something else, but better. You should do that whenever you can.

If you want a fast start and good sales, be ready to answer the question.

When you have something that's a breakthrough, though, perhaps you need to say instead, "It's not like anything. You need to trust me and just taste it."

Think Like Me, Agree with Me

When you're trying to sell your idea, it's natural to assume that the people you're selling to think the way you do. If you can only show them the facts and stories that led you to believe what you believe, then of course they'll end up where you are: believing.

The problem, of course, is that people don't always think like you.

Go watch some videos of people of different political ideologies talking about why they support a candidate other than your candidate. These people are stupid! They can't conjugate an idea, they have no factual basis for their beliefs, they are clueless, they are ideologues, they are parroting a talking head who knows even less than they do! (And those epithets apply to anyone you disagree with, of course.) In fact, they're saying the same thing about you.

Same goes for die-hard fans of the other brand or, worse, the clueless who should be using your solution but don't even care enough to use your competitor's product.

If they only thought like you, of course, and knew what you know, then there wouldn't be a problem.

The challenge doesn't lie in getting them to know what you know. It won't help. The challenge lies in helping them see your idea through their lens, not yours. If you study the way religions and political movements spread, you can see that this is exactly how it works. Marketers of successful ideas rarely market the facts. Instead, they market stories that match the worldview of the people being marketed to.

[There's an alternative, one that you might want to think hard about: perhaps you should market your idea only to people who already think the way you do. After all, you're not running for president; you don't need a majority. Screen people by their behavior (what they read, what they buy, how they act) and tell your story to only the people who will embrace it. Doing that is a lot easier than it's ever been before.]

What Every Mass Marketer Needs to Learn from Groucho Marx

Perhaps the most plaintive complaint I hear from organizations goes something like this: "We worked really hard to get very good at xyz. We're well regarded, we're talented, and now, all the market cares about is price. How can we get large groups of people to value our craft and buy from us again?"

Apparently, the bulk of your market no longer wants to buy your top-of-the-line furniture, lawn care services, accounting services, tailoring services, consulting . . . all they want is the cheapest. The masses don't want a better PC laptop. They just want the one with the right specs at the right price. It's not because people are selfish (though they are) or shortsighted (though they are). It's because in this market, right now, they're not listening. They've been seduced into believing that all options are the same, and they're only seeing price. In terms of educating the masses to differentiate yourself, the market is broken.

Fixing this is almost always a losing battle. Just because you're good at something doesn't mean the market cares any longer.

The Marx Brothers were great at vaudeville. Live comedy in a theater. And then the market for vaudeville was killed by the movies. Groucho didn't complain about this or argue that people should respect the hard work he and his brothers had put in. No, they went into the movies.

Then the market for movies like the Marx Brothers were making dried up. Groucho didn't start trying to fix the market. Instead, he saw a new medium and went there. His TV work was among his best (and certainly most lucrative).

It's extremely difficult to repair the market.

It's a lot easier to find a market that will respect and pay for the work you can do. Technology companies have been running this race for years. Now, all of us must.

If Walmart or some cultural shift has turned what you do into a commodity, don't argue. Find a new place before the competition does. It's not easy or fair, but it's true. You bet your life.

[Please note that nothing I wrote above applies to niche businesses. In fact, exactly the opposite does. You can make a good living selling bespoke PC laptops or doing vaudeville today, even though the mass market couldn't care a bit. How he got in my pajamas, I'll never know . . .]

In Between Frames

Scott McCloud's classic book on comics, *Understanding Comics*, explains a lot more than comics.

A key part of his thesis is that comic books work because the action takes place between the frames. Our imagination fills in the gaps between what happened in *that* frame and what happened in *this* frame, which means that we're as involved as the illustrator and author are in telling the story.

Marketing, it turns out, works precisely the same way.

Marketing is what happens in between the overt acts of the marketer. Yes, you made a package and yes, you designed a uniform and yes, you ran an ad . . . but the consumer's take on what you did is driven by what happened out of the corner of her eye, in the dead spaces, in the moments when you let your guard down.

Marketing is what happens when you're not trying, when you're being transparent, and when there's no script in place.

It's not marketing when everything goes right on the flight to Chicago. It's marketing when your people don't respond after losing the guitar that got checked.

It's not marketing when I use your product as intended. It's marketing when my friend and I are talking about how the thing we bought from you changed us.

It's not marketing when the smiling waitress appears with the soup. It's marketing when we hear two waiters muttering to each other behind the serving station.

Consumers are too smart for the frames. It's the in-between-frames stuff that matters. And yet we marketers spend 103% of our time on the frames.

Strangers, Critics, Friends, or Fans

The work you do when you spread the word or run an ad or invent a policy is likely aimed at one of these four groups.

- Strangers are customers to be, but not yet.
- Critics are those that would speak ill of you, or need to be converted.
- Friends are those that might have given permission, or might even buy now and then.
- Fans are members of your tribe, supporters, and insiders.

You already know the truth: You can't please all these groups at once. And you also probably realize that each of us with an idea to spread has a knee-jerk default, the one we lean to without thinking. Many marketers are evangelical, focused on strangers at all costs; they'd rather convert a new customer than revisit an old one. A cubicle worker, on the other hand, might focus on no one but the boss, at the expense of broadening her platform.

Before you launch anything, run down the list. How can you optimize for the group you truly care about? How much is that optimization worth? (Hint: a new true fan is worth a thousand times as much as a slightly mollified critic.)

Random Rules for Ideas Worth Spreading

If you've got an idea worth spreading, I hope you'll consider this random assortment of rules. Like all rules, some are made to be broken, but still . . .

- You can name your idea anything you like, but a Google-friendly name is always better than one that isn't.
- Don't plan on appearing on a reality show as the best way to launch your idea.
- Waiting for inspiration is another way of saying that you're stalling. You don't wait for inspiration; you command it to appear.
- Don't poll your friends. It's your art, not an election.
- Never pay a non-lawyer who promises to get you a patent.
- Avoid powerful people. Great ideas aren't anointed; they spread through a groundswell of support.
- Spamming strangers doesn't work. Spamming friends doesn't work so well, either, but it's certainly better than spamming strangers.
- The hard part is finishing, so enjoy the starting part.
- Powerful organizations adore the status quo, so expect no help from them if your idea challenges the very thing they adore.
- Figure out how long your idea will take to spread and multiply by four.
- Be prepared for the Dip.
- Seek out apostles, not partners. People who benefit from spreading your idea, not people who need to own it.

- Keep your overhead low and don't quit your day job until your idea can absorb your time.
- Think big. Bigger than that.
- Are you a serial idea-starting person? If so, what can you change to end that cycle? The goal is to be an idea-shipping person.
- Try not to confuse confidence with delusion.
- Prefer dry, useful, but dull ideas to consumer-friendly "I would buy that" sorts of things. A lot less competition and a lot more upside in the long run.
- Pick a budget. Pick a ship date. Honor both. Don't ignore either. No slippage, no overruns.
- Surround yourself with encouraging voices and incisive critics. It's okay if they're not the same people. Ignore both camps on occasion.
- Be grateful.
- Rise up to the opportunity, and do the idea justice.

Frightened, Clueless, or Uninformed?

In the face of significant change and opportunity, people are often one of the three. If you're going to be of assistance, it helps to know which one.

Uninformed people need information and insight in order to figure out what to do next. They are approaching the problem with optimism and calm, but they need to be taught. Uninformed is not a pejorative term; it's a temporary state.

Clueless people don't know what to do and they don't know that they don't know what to do. They don't know the right questions to ask. Giving them instructions is insufficient. First, they need to be sold on what the platform even looks like.

And frightened people will resist any help you can give them, and they will blame you for the stress the change is causing. Scared people like to shoot the messenger. Duck.

The worst kind of frightened person is one with power. Someone in a mob of other frightened people, someone with a gun, someone who is the CEO. When confronted with a scared CEO, time to run. Before someone can change, they have to learn, and before they learn, they have to cease being scared.

One reason so many big ideas come from small organizations is that there is far less fear of change at the top. One mistake board members and shareholders make is that they reward the scared but hyperconfident CEO, instead of calling him on the carpet as he rages at change.

When I first encountered surfing, I was scared of it. It looks cool, but an old guy like me can get hurt. A patient instructor allayed my fears until I was willing to get started. When you first start out, the things you think are important are actually irrelevant, and it's the stuff that you don't know is important that gets you thrown into the ocean. Finally, and only then, was I smart enough to actually learn.

I'm bad at surfing now, but at least I know why.

Comfort the frightened, coach the clueless, and teach the uninformed.

The Brand, the Package, the Story, and the Worldview

Madécasse has a lot going for it. It's delicious chocolate. It's made in Africa (the only imported chocolate made on the continent with local beans). The guys who make it are doing good work and are nice as well.

The question I asked them was, "does your packaging do its job?"

I don't think the job of packaging is to please your boss. I think you must please the retailer, but most of all, attract and delight and sell to the browsing, uncommitted new customer.

Let me take you through the reasoning, because I think it applies to your packaging as well.

We start with this: if I've already purchased and liked your product, the packaging isn't nearly as important. I'm talking here about packaging as a sales tool for converting browsers into buyers. (If you're already a buyer, all I need to do is remind you what we look like.) If word of mouth or other factors are at work, your package matters a lot less. But for a company this size, in this market, the package matters a lot.

Now, among people who haven't bought, but might, understand that every one of them starts with a worldview. What are the beliefs and expectations and biases they have about the world?

In this case, it's about someone in the market for high-end chocolate. If your worldview is, "Hershey's is the best, it reminds me of my childhood," then I'd argue that this $4 bar isn't for you no matter what they do with the package.

Perhaps you believe, "All that matters is how it tastes, and great chocolate looks a certain way,"

or perhaps, "I care about the origin of what I buy,"

or perhaps, "I want something out of the ordinary, unlike anything I've had before,"

or perhaps, "Chocolate is like wine. I am interested in vintages and varietals,"

or maybe, "Chocolate should be fun. Enough with the seriousness."

As you can see, no package can optimize for all of these people. You can compromise your packaging, try to appeal to everyone, muddy your brand promise, and hide your story. I think that's sort of what the existing packaging does and I'm not sure it's smart.

The alternative is to focus not on ALL the people in the market, but on just a few. Winning hands-down with 25% is plenty in this market, and perhaps in your market, too.

You could figure out how to tell the *delicious* story, by referencing (copying the style of) other products in other categories that are already seen as delicious, at least by this audience.

You could tell the *snobby varietal handmade* story, and that's been done many times as well.

Or you could tell a story that is yours and yours alone.

For example, the Madécasse story about *made by Africans in Africa* is very powerful, at least as powerful as fair trade, if not more. (They keep four times as much money in Africa by selling chocolate bars as they would if they just sold cocoa beans to other companies.)

If that's true, then why not put your workers on the label? Big beautiful pictures that would be an amazing juxtaposition against all the other abstract stuff in the store. Tell me the story of the worker on the back of the package. Make each one different and compelling. Packaging as baseball card. I wouldn't put a word on the front, just the picture. Now

I not only eat something that tastes good, but I feel good. You've made it personal. The story on the back is about a real person, living a better life because I took the time to buy her chocolate instead of someone else's. When I share the chocolate, I have something to say. What do you say when you give someone a chocolate bar? This package gives you something to say.

Or be fun and funny. Make the product itself almost a bumper sticker, something worth buying and talking about.

The two elements that must come together are:

- The story you can confidently tell and
- The worldview the buyer tells herself

When those align, you win.

Good at Talking Vs. Good at Doing

This is the chasm of the new marketing.

The marketing department used to be in charge of talking. Ads are talking. Flyers are talking. Billboards are talking. Trade shows are talking.

Now, of course, marketing can't talk so much, because people can't be easily forced to listen.

So the only option is to be in charge of doing. Which means the product, the service, the interaction, the effluent and other detritus left behind when you're done.

If you're in marketing and you're not in charge of the doing, you're not going to be able to do your job.

If You Want to Learn to Do Marketing . . .

. . . then do marketing.

You can learn finance and accounting and media buying from a book. But the best way to truly learn how to do marketing is to market.

You don't have to quit your job and you don't need your boss's permission. There are plenty of ways to get started.

If you see a band you like coming to town, figure out how to promote them and sell some tickets (posters? Google ads? PR?). Don't ask, just do it.

If you find a book you truly love, buy 30 and figure out how to sell them all (to strangers).

If you're 12, go door to door selling fresh fruit—and figure out which stories work and which don't.

Set up an online business. Get a candidate you believe in elected to the school board.

The best way to learn marketing is to do it.

The Power of Buttons and Being Normal

Taxi drivers in New York were worried about adding the ability to accept credit cards in their cabs. The fee (5% or so) would cost them too much, they said.

It turns out that tips are up, way up. Taxi drivers are actually making far more money now.

Why? Because most of the card-reading machines offer a shortcut for the tip: $2, $3, or $4.

You can decide to be a cheapskate and hit the $2 button. Except . . .

Except that if you had paid cash, you probably would have tipped 75 cents for that $4.25 ride. It takes a few more clicks to type in 75 cents, and hey, $2 is the lowest and it's a more "normal" amount.

It's a three-second decision that happens over and over. People really like cues.

The Market Is Not Seduced by Logic

People are moved by stories and drama and hints and clues and discovery.

Logic is a battering ram, one that might work if your case is overwhelming. Walmart won by logic (cheap!), but you probably won't.

Needs Don't Always Lead to Demand

One of the accepted holy grails of building an organization is that you should fill a need. Fill people's needs, they say, and the rest will take care of itself.

But . . . someone might know that they need to lose some weight, but what they demand is potato chips.

Someone might know that they need to be more concerned about the world, but what they demand is another fake reality show.

As my friend Tricia taught me, this contradiction is brought into sharp relief when you're doing social enterprise work in the developing world. There are things that people vitally need . . . and yet providing it is no guarantee you'll find demand.

Please don't get confused by what the market needs. That's something you decided, not them.

If you want to help people lose weight, you need to sell them something they demand, like belonging or convenience, not lecture them about what they need.

I Spread Your Idea Because . . .

Ideas spread when people choose to spread them. Here are some reasons why:

1. I spread your idea because it makes me feel generous.
2. . . . because I feel smart alerting others to what I discovered.
3. . . . because I care about the outcome and want you (the creator of the idea) to succeed.
4. . . . because I have no choice. Every time I use your product, I spread the idea (Hotmail, iPad, a tattoo).
5. . . . because there's a financial benefit directly for me (Amazon affiliates, MLM).
6. . . . because it's funny and laughing alone is no fun.
7. . . . because I'm lonely and sharing an idea solves that problem, at least for a while.

8. . . . because I'm angry and I want to enlist others in my outrage (or in shutting you down).

9. . . . because both my friend and I will benefit if I share the idea (Groupon).

10. . . . because you asked me to, and it's hard to say no to you.

11. . . . because I can use the idea to introduce people to one another, and making a match is both fun in the short run and community-building.

12. . . . because your service works better if all my friends use it (email, Facebook).

13. . . . because if everyone knew this idea, I'd be happier.

14. . . . because your idea says something that I have trouble saying directly (AA, a blog post, a book).

15. . . . because I care about someone and this idea will make them happier or healthier.

16. . . . because it's fun to make another teen snicker about prurient stuff we're not supposed to see.

17. . . . because the tribe needs to know about this if we're going to avoid an external threat.

18. . . . because the tribe needs to know about this if we're going to maintain internal order.

19. . . . because it's my job.

20. I spread your idea because I'm in awe of your art and the only way I can repay you is to share that art with others.

On Buying Unmeasurable Media

Should you invest in TV, radio, billboards, and other media for which you can't measure whether your ad works? Is an ad in *New York* magazine worth 1,000 times as much as a text link on Google? If you're doing the comparison directly, that's how much extra you're paying if you're only measuring direct Web visits.

One school of thought is to measure everything. If you can't measure it, don't do it. This is the direct marketer's method and there's no doubt it can work.

There's another thought, though: most businesses (including your competitors) are afraid of big investments in unmeasurable media. Therefore, if you have the resources and the guts, it's a home run waiting to be hit.

Ralph Lauren is a billion-dollar brand. Totally unmeasurable. So are Revlon, LVMH, Donald Trump, Andersen Windows, Lady Gaga, and hundreds of other mass-market brands.

There are two things you should never do:

1. Try to measure unmeasurable media and use that result to make decisions. You'll get it wrong. Sure, some sophisticated marketers get good hints from their measurements, but it's still an art, not a science.
2. Compromise on your investment. Small investments in unmeasurable media almost always fail. Go big or stay home.

And if you're selling unmeasurable media? Don't try to sell to people who are obsessed with measuring. You'll waste your time and annoy the prospect at the same time.

Are $300 Headphones Worth It?

A friend wanted to buy Dr. Dre's headphones. They list for about $300.

Any audiophile can tell you that they sound like $39 headphones. Instead, consider a pair of $300 Grado headphones. We can prove they sound better!

But of course, that's not the question. It's not what sounds better, it's what's worth it.

The Dre headphones come with admiring glances at no extra charge. They come with self-esteem built in. You can argue that this is a worthless feature in a device designed to reproduce sound accurately, but you'd be wrong. After all, the whole reason you're listening to music in the first place is to feel good. To be happy. If the Dres make you happy, and your happiness is worth $300, then they're worth it, no?

For others (put me in that category), headphones are evaluated differently. I get more happiness knowing that I didn't fall for a clever marketing ploy, and I buy the headphones that I believe *sound* better. Of course, that's a clever marketing ploy, too—persuading me that better sound is worth this much. But don't tell anyone. That would make me feel manipulated.

Ethical Placebos (Stunning, but Not Actually Surprising)

A recent study found that placebos work even if the patient is told by the doctor that the drug they're taking has no "real" medicine in it.

Huh?

We've come to understand that the placebo effect is real. If we believe we're going to get better, perform better, make the sale, etc., it often happens that we do. That's because the brain is the single best marketing agent when it comes to selling ourselves something. If we think we're going to get better, we're much more likely to actually get better.

So then why do clearly labeled placebos work?

Because of the process. The ritual. The steps we go through to remember to take them, to open the bottle, to get the water, to swallow. Over time, we don't remind ourselves so much about what's in the pill, and we remind ourselves a lot that we're taking significant action.

This is one reason Disney makes you wait in line for a ride even if the park is empty. Why a full restaurant is more fun than an empty one, even if you know the food is precisely the same.

Marketers ostensibly know this, but it seems as though most organizations still act as though they're selling pencils to accountants.

We're complicated. I hope that's okay with you, because like it or not, you're not going to make people simple.

Compared to Perfect: The Price/Value Mismatch in Content

"How's the wine?"

You really can't answer that question out of context. Compared to what? Compared to a hundred-dollar bottle? Not so good. Compared to any other $12 bottle? Great!

"How was the hotel?"

"How's the service at the post office?"

In just about all the decisions we make, we consider the price. A shipper doesn't expect the same level of service quality from a first-class letter delivery that it does from an overnight international courier service. Of course not.

And yet . . .

A quick analysis of the top 100 titles on Amazon (movies, books, music, doesn't matter what) shows *zero* correlation between the price and the reviews. (I didn't do the math, but you're welcome to—might be a good science-fair entry.) Try to imagine a similar disconnect if the subject was cars or clothing.

For any other good or service, the value of a free alternative that was any good would be infinite—free airplane tickets, free dinners at the café. . . When it comes to content, though, we rarely compare the experience with other content at a similar price. We compare it to perfect.

People walking out of the afternoon bargain matinee at the movies don't cut the film any slack because it was half-price. Critics piling on to a music video on YouTube never mention the fact that HEY IT WAS FREE. *There is no thrift store for content.* Sure, we can get an old movie for ninety-nine cents, but if we hate it, it doesn't matter how cheap it was. If we're going to spend time, apparently, it better be perfect, the best there ever was, regardless of price.

This isn't true for cars, potato chips, air travel, worker's comp insurance . . .

Consider people walking out of a concert where tickets might be being scalped for as much as $1,000. That's $40 or more for each song played—are people considering the price when they're evaluating the experience? There's a lot of nuance here . . . I'm certainly not arguing that expensive is always better.

In fact, I do think it's probably true that a low price *increases* the negative feedback. That's because a low price exposes the work to individuals that might not be raving fans.

Free is a valid marketing strategy. In fact, it's almost impossible for an idea to have mass impact without some sort of free element (TV, radio, Web pages, online videos . . . they're all free). At the same time, it's not clear to me that cheaper content outperforms expensive in many areas. As the marginal cost of delivering content drops to zero (all digital content meets this definition), I think there are valid marketing reasons to do the opposite of what economists expect.

Free gets you mass. Free, though, isn't always the price that will help you achieve your goals.

Price is often a signaling mechanism, and perhaps nowhere more so than in the area of content. Free enables your idea to spread, but price signals individuals and often ends up putting your idea in the right place. Mass shouldn't always be the goal. Impact may matter more.

Hungry or Guarded

The hungry person at the all-you-can-eat buffet is happy to take one more item. She doesn't spend a lot of time comparing this to that or saying "no thank you" or avoiding certain items. If it's interesting, "sure I'll try a little bit. I can always come back."

The guarded person walking down the street avoids eye contact with the homeless person, doesn't answer a request from the person looking for petition signatures, and certainly doesn't help a Boy Scout with that old lady.

And this is precisely the dichotomy that every cause, every candidate, and every marketer faces.

Either you're selling to people who are hungry for what you offer, who are open to hearing what you have to say, who are *fans* . . .

Or you're selling to people who are actively protecting themselves, guarding against interruption or a mistake or worse.

How can you possibly have a strategy about what you're going to do next until you determine which mindset you're marketing to?

Here's the key truth: in any given moment, in any given situation, a person is either hungry or guarded. You need to decide which sort of person you'll be telling your story to, because one approach won't work on the other type of person.

PS: The mindset can (and does) change as people go through their day. At the bookstore, she might be hungry for a new idea, and just a few minutes later, at the bus stop, she wants to be alone.

Selling Vs. Inviting

Selling is often misunderstood, largely by people who would be a lot more comfortable merely inviting.

If I invite you to a wedding, or a party, or to buy a $500,000 TV ad for $500, there's no resistance on your part. Either you jump at the chance and say yes, or you have a conflict and say no. It's not my job to help you overcome your fear of commitment, to help you see the ultimate value or, most of all, to work with you as you persuade yourself and others to do something that might just work.

If the marketing and product development team does a great job, selling is a lot easier—so easy it might be called inviting. The guy at the counter in the Apple store selling the iPad 2 isn't really selling them at all. Hey, there's a long line of people with money in their pockets. I'm inviting you to buy this, so if you don't want it, next!

The real estate broker who says that the house would sell if only he could get below-market pricing and a preapproved mortgage is avoiding his job.

The salesperson's job: help people overcome their fear so they can commit to something they'll end up being glad they invested in.

The goal of a marketer ought to be to make it so easy to be a salesperson that you're merely an inviter. The new marketing is largely about this—creating a scenario where you don't even need salespeople. (Until you do.)

Selling is a profession. It's hard work. Ultimately, it's rewarding, because the thing you're selling delivers real value to the purchasers, and your job is to counsel them so they can get the benefit.

But please . . . don't insist that the hard work be removed from your job to allow you to become an inviter. That's great work if you can get it, but it's not a career.

A Marketing Lesson from the Apocalypse

If you're reading this blog, then the world didn't end, at least in my time zone.

How does one market the end of the world? After all, you don't have a big ad budget. Your "product" is something that has been marketed again and again through the ages and it has *never* worked. There's significant peer pressure not to buy it.

And yet, every time, people succumb. They sell their belongings, stop paying into their kid's college fund, and create tension and despair.

Here's the simple lesson:

Sell a story that some people want to believe. In fact, sell a story they *already* believe.

The *story* has to be integrated into your product. The iPad, for example, wasn't something that people were clamoring for, but the story of it, the magic tablet, the universal book, the ticket to the fashion-geek tribe—there was a line out the door for that. The same way that every year, we see a new music sensation, a new fashion superstar. That's not an accident. That story is just waiting for someone to wear it.

And the *some* part is vital. Not everyone wants to believe in the end of the world, but some people (fortunately, just a few) really do. To reach them, you don't need much of a hard sell at all.

Too often, marketers take a product and try to invent a campaign. Much more effective is to find a tribe, find a story, and make a product that resonates, one that makes the story work.

That's the whole thing. A story that resonates and a tribe that's tight and small and eager.

I hope you can dream up something more productive than the end of the world, though.

Selling Nuts to Squirrels

In *All Marketers Tell Stories* I argue that most organizations shouldn't try to change the worldview of the audience they're marketing to.

"Worldview" is a term popularized by George Lakoff. It's the set of expectations and biases that color the way each of us see the world (before the marketer ever arrives on the scene). The worldview of a 45-year-old, wine-loving investment banker is very different from that of a fraternity brother. One might see a $100 bottle of burgundy as both a bargain and a must-have, while the other might see the very same bottle of wine as an insane waste of money.

Worldview changes three things: *attention, bias,* and *vernacular.* Attention, because we choose to pay attention to those things that we've decided matter. Bias, because our worldview alters the way we filter and interpret what we hear. And vernacular, because words and images resonate differently with people based on their worldview.

It's extremely expensive, time-consuming, and difficult to change someone's worldview. The guys at Opus One shouldn't spend a lot of time marketing expensive wine to fraternities because it's not efficient. Sell nuts to squirrels; don't try to persuade dolphins that nuts are delicious.

There's an exception to this rule, and that's the necessity of changing worldviews if you want to become a giant brand, a world changer, a marketer for the ages. Starbucks changed the way a significant part of the world thought about spending $4 for a cup of coffee.

Or consider Facebook. It started by selling nuts to squirrels. At first, Facebook was social crack for lonely (all college students are lonely) college students. Over time, the social pressure it created snuck up on and surrounded those with a different inclination, those that would never have signed up on their own. These folks had a worldview that privacy was valuable and that time was better spent elsewhere. But once a sufficient number of their friends and colleagues were online, they felt they had little choice. Converting those people (often against their short-term wishes) is where Facebook's most recent 300 million users came from.

The interesting truth in both the Starbucks and Facebook examples is that a different worldview was at work. The latecomers to each company were sold a very different story—the story of "you need to be here because all your friends are." That worked because it matched the latecomers' worldview, the one that includes an imperative, "don't be left out." Different nut, same squirrel.

Three Things Clients and Customers Want

Not just the first one.

And not all three.

But you really need at least one.

1. Results. If you can offer a return on investment, an engineering solution, more sales, no tax audits, a cute haircut, the fastest roller-coaster, a pristine beach, reliable insurance payouts at the best price, peace of mind, productive consulting, or any other measurable result, this is a great place to start.

2. Thrills. More difficult to quantify but often as important, partners and customers respond to heroism. We are amazed and drawn to over-the-top effort, incredible risk taking on our behalf, the blood, sweat, and tears that (rarely) come from a great partner. A smart person working harder on your behalf than you'd be willing to work—that's pretty compelling.

3. Ego. Is it nice to feel important? You bet. When you greet us at the door with a glass of white wine, put our name in the lobby of the hotel, actually treat us better than anyone else does (not just promise it, but do it), it feels great. This approach can get old really fast if you industrialize and systemize it, though.

This list explains why the local branch of the big insurance company has trouble growing. It's hard for them to outdeliver the other guys when it comes to the cost-effectiveness of their policy (#1). They are unsuited from a personality and organizational point of view to do #2. And they just can't scale the third.

Put just about any business with partners into this matrix and you see how it works. Book publishing, for sure. Hairdressers. Spas. Even real estate.

The Ritz-Carlton is all about #3, ego, right? And on a good day, there's a perception that the guys at Apple are hell-bent on amazing us yet again, delivering on #2, taking huge career and corporate risks on our behalf. As soon as they stop doing that, the tribe will get bored.

(There's a variation of ego, #3, that comes from being in good company. This is what gets people to sign up for Davos or to choose ICM as their agent. Your ego is stroked by knowing that only people as cool as you are part of this gig. Sort of the anti-Groucho opportunity. Nice position, if you can get it, because it scales.)

It's tempting, particularly for a small business, to obsess about the first factor—results—and to spend all its time trying to prove that the

ROI is higher, the brownies are tastier, and the coaching is more effective. You'd be amazed at how far you can go with the other two, though, if you commit to doing them, not merely talking about them.

When "Minimal Viable Product" Doesn't Work

One of my favorite ideas in the new wave of programming is the notion of a minimal viable product. The thought is that you should spec and build the smallest kernel of your core idea, put it in the world, and see how people react to it, and then improve from there.

For drill bits and other tools, this method makes perfect sense. Put the product out there, get it used, improve it. The definition of "minimal" is obvious.

Often, for software we use in public, this definition leads to failure. Why? Two reasons:

1. Marketing plays by different rules than engineering. Many products depend on community, on adoption within a tribe, on buzz—these products aren't viable when they first launch, precisely because they haven't been adopted. "Being used by my peers" is a key element of what makes something like a fax machine a viable product, and of course, your new tool isn't yet being used.

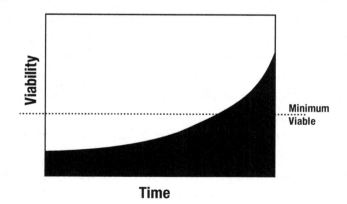

With enough patience and push and consistent enthusiasm, these products have a shot at crossing the threshold. But if the mindset is "see what works and do it more," you'll often discover yourself giving up long before that happens.

2. There's a burst of energy and attention and effort that accompanies a launch, even a minimally viable one. If there's a delay in pickup from the community, though (see #1), it's easy to move on to the next thing, the next launch, the next hoopla, as opposed to doing the insanely hard work of sticking with that thing you already launched.

Inherent in the process of minimal viable product development, then, is building a trusting, large permission base that will eagerly listen to you, try your new work, and let you know what they think. And you don't have the option of building that audience once the product is ready—that's too late.

Moving Beyond Impressions

Internet advertising is so cheap (particularly Facebook and run-of-site network buys) that just about anyone can afford a million impressions, and a billion isn't out of reach.

Pretty soon it turns into noise. An infinite number of impressions is dangerously close to no impressions at all.

The conversation media reps have with advertisers quickly devolves into, "how cheap can I buy a million impressions?" What a waste. That number, out of context, is nothing but a crutch, a poor stand-in for the insightful analysis that media buyers ought to be using.

Far better to focus on two things (both leading to the real goal):

Perception. Does the ad you're running increase the value of your name? Are you perceived as an annoyance, an interrupter—or are you a valued sponsor, a trusted friend, someone who is making things better?

and

Interaction. Not merely a click that leads to a sale. I'm talking about any sort of interaction with you or your organization, whether it's an online chat, a phone call, or the process of navigating your site. Too often, online marketers are focused on pennies per click instead of on long-term value per engagement.

Both perception and interaction lead to permission. Permission to deliver anticipated, personal, and relevant messages over time. Permission to tell a story. Permission to earn attention on an ongoing basis.

Impressions don't automatically get you permission. In fact, they might cost it.

The Pricing Formula (S&S)

Years ago, my bosses and I needed to finalize the pricing for a new line of software I was launching. In the room, we had MBAs from Harvard (two), Stanford, Tuck and, I think, Wharton. We had three prices in mind, and the five of us couldn't agree. So we did the only scientific thing: we flipped a coin (two out of three, just to be sure).

Pricing your product is actually simple, as long as you consider it from the buyer's point of view. How much it costs you to make something is irrelevant. Buyers don't care (of course, you can't price something at a loss and hope to stay in business for long). The two keys to the analysis:

Substitutes: Every purchase is a choice, and that means the buyer can choose to do nothing or to buy something else instead. If there are easy and obvious substitutes for what you sell, that factor has to be built into your pricing. If you make something rare and unique, you still might not be able to charge a lot—because people can always choose to buy nothing. A 42-carat diamond, for example, might be hard to replace, but it's not worth $100 million unless someone actually chooses to buy it.

Part of the work of design and marketing is to help people understand that there are no good substitutes for what you have to offer, meaning, of course, that you can happily charge more.

Story: The other half of the pricing formula is the story the price itself tells. A Prius at $40,000 or a Prius at $10,000 is the same car, but the price becomes a dominant part of the story. You can tell a story of value/cheapness/affordability or a story of luxury. If you price your product or service near the median, you're telling no story at all with the price, giving yourself the chance to tell a story about some other element of what you sell.

If you're not happy with your pricing options, focusing on your costs might not be the right path. Instead, focus on how the design or delivery changes the availability of substitutes, and how the price becomes part of the story of your product.

Horizontal Marketing Isn't a New Idea

But it is the new reality for just about every organization.

Vertical marketing means that the marketer (the one with money) is in charge. Vertical marketing starts at the top and involves running ads, sending out direct mail, and pushing hype through the media. Your money, your plans, your control. It might not work, but generally the worst outcome is that you will be ignored and need to spend more money.

Horizontal marketing, on the other hand, means creating a remarkable product and story and setting it up to spread from person to person. It's out of your control because all the interactions are controlled by passionate outsiders, not paid agents.

Most marketers instinctively want control. We reach for the budget and the ad and the press release, and most of all, the powerful media middleman. We buy Super Bowl ads or schmooze the reporter.

Horizontal marketing, though, requires giving up control. We spend all of our time and money on a great story and a great service and a remarkable offering. The rest is up to the market itself. You can't control this, and you can no longer ignore it, either.

The Essential Question to Ask Before Extending Your Brand

Are we doing this because it's better?

Or because we can?

As organizations grow, they gain an audience, revenue, cash flow, and trust. They add staff and then, soon, they decide it's time to offer something new. Smucker's decides that perhaps it should use its shelf space to offer a peanut butter. A corporate coach wonders if he ought to add HR consulting services. A website decides to clone a product that is made by a smaller company and that they can bring to a larger audience.

If you extend your reach because you can, because you have market power, you will probably be doing your existing customers a small service (centralized support or billing or just one less person to deal with), but your brand doesn't increase in stature. You had a chance to bring some of your original magic to the table (after all, it's that magic that got you started), but all you did was bully the competitors out of the way.

On the other hand, if you extend your brand because the new offering is better, magical in the way you can make it magical, then you've dramatically increased not just your market share but your status as well.

Nike and Apple sometimes fit into the second category—the iPhone and some of Nike's clothing options are clearly different/better. Starbucks did it when they launched their ice cream. On the other hand, there are literally thousands of organizations (including nonprofits) that head down the path of mediocrity by rushing to offer 57 varieties, merely to please today's shareholders, merely because they can.

How Much for a Really Small Slice?

When the hardware store sells you a single screw for a dime, shouldn't they just give it to you? Especially if you're a good customer?

Shouldn't that singer (you bought all her albums) return the love? You're only asking for a few seconds, a hug, a handshake, an autograph . . .

It's easier than ever to break your offering into smaller bits, into pieces that are part of the whole but are tiny on their own.

Add up enough small slices and that's the whole cake. Asymmetry is the rule now, not the exception.

Small slices can't be free in the long run, not if that's the only kind of slice there is.

Either you need to figure out how to sell your small slices, or you need to invent some big slices that are obviously worth what you need to sell them for.

Needs and Wants Are Often Confused

When people have their basic needs met, it's not uncommon for wants to magically become needs. It's our hardwired instinct to seek to fill unmet needs.

That instinct pays off for any marketer that has persuaded his market that they need what he sells. It backfires when those "needs" are seen for what they actually are—luxuries.

When you sell a want, you have to work harder, you must seduce the market, because wants are fickle, picky, and not easily bullied.

The Story of Money Is Not a Straight Line

A Paradoxical Curve of Money and Effort

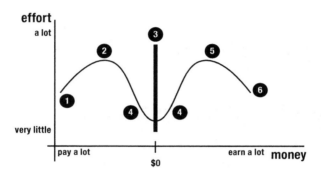

We all tell ourselves different stories about money, but there's no doubt at all that the story we tell ourselves changes our behavior.

Consider this curve of how people react in situations that cost money.

A musician is standing on a street corner, playing really well for free. Most people walk on by (3 in the graph). That same musician playing at a bar with a $5 cover gets a bit more attention. Put him into a concert hall at $40 and suddenly it's an event.

Pay someone minimum wage or a low intern stipend (4) and she treats the work like a job. Don't expect that worker to put in extra effort or conquer her fear—the message is that her effort was bought and paid for and wasn't worth very much to the boss, and so she reciprocates in kind. The same sort of thing can happen in a class that's easy to get into and that doesn't cost much—a Learning Annex sort of thing. Easy to start, cheap to try—not much effort as a result.

It's interesting to me to see what happens to people who pay a lot or get paid well (2, 5). The kids at Harvard Law School, for example, or a third-year associate at a law firm. Here, we see all-nighters, heroic, career-risking efforts, and all sorts of personal investment. And yet as we extend the curve to situations where the rules of rational money are suspended, something happens—people get fearful again. Don't look to Oprah or J. K. Rowling or the Donald to bet it all—the huge amount of money they could earn (or could pay) to play at the next level (1, 6) isn't enough to get them out of their comfort zone. Money ceases to be a motivator for everyone at some point.

Most interesting of all is the long black line at zero (3). The curve goes wild here, like dividing by zero. At zero, at the place where no money changes hands, we see volunteer labor and free exchange. In these situations, sometimes we see extraordinary effort, the stuff that wins Nobel Prizes. *Just about every great, brave, or beautiful thing in our culture was created by someone who didn't do it for money.* We see the local volunteer putting in insane hours even though no one is watching. We hear the magical song or read the amazing poem that no one got paid to write. And sometimes, though, we see very little, just a trolling comment or a halfhearted bit of commentary. Remove money from the story and we're in a whole new category. The most vivid way to think about this is the difference between a mutually agreed-upon romantic date and one in which money changes hands.

All worth thinking about when you consider how much to charge for a gig, what tuition ought to be, what motivates job creators, or whether or not a form of art disappears when the business model for that art goes away.

Seven Marketing Sins

Impatient . . . great marketing takes time. Doing it wrong (and rushed) ten times costs much more and takes longer than does doing it slowly, but right, over the same period of time.

Selfish . . . we have a choice, and if we sense that this is all about you, not us, our choice will be to go somewhere else.

Self-absorbed . . . you don't buy from you, others buy from you. They don't care about your business or your troubles nearly as much as you do.

Deceitful . . . see selfish, above. If you don't tell us the truth, it's probably because you're selfish. How urgent can your needs be that you would sacrifice your future to get something now?

Inconsistent . . . we're not paying that much attention, but when we do, it helps if you are similar to the voice we heard from last time.

Angry . . . at us? Why are you angry at us? It's not something we want to be part of, thanks.

Jealous . . . is someone doing better than you? Of course they are. There's always someone doing better than you. But if you let your jealousy change your products or your attitude or your story, we're going to leave.

Of course, they're not marketing sins, they're human failings.

Humility, empathy, generosity, patience, and kindness, combined with the arrogance of the brilliant inventor, are a potent alternative.

SUCCESS, FAILURE, AND THE SURE THING

Doing the Work. Risk and Fear.

Everybody Stalls

There's no question about whether you are procrastinating about something. The only question is: what?

Knowledge work creates myriad opportunities for stalling. You can stall about making a sales call, stall about redoing a website, stall about reorganizing your department . . . the list of areas is so long, it becomes a stall in itself.

But deep down, you already know where you're stalling. It's that thing that makes you uncomfortable, probably because it involves doing something you might be held accountable for.

The problem with Google AdSense is that it makes marketers accountable. Unlike with Super Bowl ads, you can tell if your Google ads work. And so it's easy to stall.

The problem with inventing a new product that challenges the status quo is that whoever did it is responsible for whatever happens.

The problem with prioritizing your group's tasks and publishing the list is that it makes it really clear what you're on the hook for.

In very tiny, very motivated organizations, new employees are often stunned by how much gets done. That's because of how hard it is to stall.

A Million Little Cuts

Most businesses don't fail dramatically.

They do it slowly.

But you wouldn't know that from sitting in at meetings or listening to speeches. Same is true, of course, for countries, nonprofits, and other organizations.

Human beings respond to emergencies. It's easy to get everyone to take action if we're in the middle of some sort of security crisis . . . but fixing the educational system isn't going to happen.

Faced with the gradual, inexorable decline that faces most organizations, it's just natural to try to fix the problem with a broad stroke. A big ad campaign or a new slogan or a totally redesigned website.

The answer, more likely than not, is to consistently and regularly stop the bleeding. To improve the boring stuff.

Organizations fail slowly. They often succeed fast, though. That's where the remarkable comes in. So, if I had to summarize it: you take a big step up . . . by being bold. But you avoid a slow death by getting every little thing right.

Q: How Can We Get Our Company Funded?

A: Don't.

I'm frequently asked (by friends and, sometimes, aggressive strangers) to help them find someone to fund their company. Often, but not always, these people are happy to hear the following answer.

1. If you fund your company, even a little, you've just sold it. Maybe not today, or tomorrow, but one day. That's because rational investors are funding your company in the expectation that you are going to sell it and make them a profit. (Sure, there are exceptions, but not many.) So, if you don't expect that your company will be easy to sell for a big profit, or you don't ever want to sell your company, it's not a smart idea to raise money for it.

2. Most companies are not appropriate sites for VC money. That's because they're freelance ventures, not entrepreneurial ones. A freelance

venture is one where you work to get paid. An entrepreneurial one is where you can make money while you sleep. Meaning that you work really, really hard and you scale and suddenly you own real estate or media properties or technology or a system or a brand that people pay for without your actually doing any incremental work yourself.

3. One friend ran a very successful specialty school. He decided he wanted to start a division that would sell books about his system. The numbers on the publishing side were terrific (on the spreadsheet). The investors wanted 40% of the existing business in order to put up sufficient money to recapitalize everything and bring big-company thinking, etc., etc. I pointed out that this would not only ruin my friend's life but probably also cripple the economics of both businesses.

The alternative (which might work for you as well) is not to fund the business. It's to fund the *project*. That's how they fund movies. You don't get a piece of the studio. You get a piece of *Rocky XIV*.

If you've got something that works and you're ready to go to the next level, consider funding the expansion, with the payoff being a scaling piece of the project. Maybe 100% of the proceeds until the investment is repaid, then 25% after that, forever. Once *that* project pays off, you'll be able to fund the next project, probably on even better terms. And on and on, with each project having, if you choose, different investors and different payout streams.

4. The real lesson is this: if you absolutely need a lot of money to do a particular business, and the terms you'll need to accept to get that money are unacceptable, find a new business. Nothing wrong with that. The market might be trying to tell you something.

#1 at the Box Office

So, Tom Cruise devoted an entire year of his life to promoting a movie that will be #1 in the U.S. for exactly 14 days.

To be replaced by another movie, even more hyped than Cruise's, that may just triumph for three weeks instead of two.

Lulu.com just released a study of bestselling books. It turns out that in the last forty years, the length of stay of a typical bestseller at #1 is down by more than 85%. In other words, best sellers used to be bestsellers for **seven times** as long as they are now.

That's an awe-inspiring figure.

Why?

Because the base of the pyramid is so much bigger (ten times as many books published every year, at least), you would expect that the winners would win bigger and longer to make it worth the journey. Not so.

And awe-inspiring because the effort necessary to get to #1 is far greater than it used to be. From co-op (bribes) given to retailers for shelf space and advertising, to the extensive touring and cross-promotion that's necessary, it's a lot more work and a lot more risk to get there.

Now, we're seeing authors building permission assets and timing all their promotion so they can be #1 on Amazon for an hour—an hour! Allen Drury had a #1 bestseller for a year.

Of course, it's not just movies and books. Just about any style-based business (and what business is no longer style based?) sees the same phenomenon. The lesson I draw is this:

If your marketing strategy requires you to hit #1 in order to succeed, you probably need a new marketing strategy.

Overnight Success?

What's the opposite of that? An overnight failure?

The idea of an overnight success is relatively new. Joan of Arc, Robin Hood, and Sarah Bernhardt were not overnight successes. It took media (the old kind, like TV and movies, and especially the new kind, like Google video) to create the overnight success. My friends Pomme and Kelly are overnight successes. So are some of the characters on *American Idol*.

Along the way, some people have trained themselves to believe that the only kind of success worth having is overnight success. That if you don't hit #1 the first week, you've failed. That if your interface isn't perfect out of the box, or if you don't get 5,000 people standing in line at the opening of your new store, you've failed.

The *Times* today reports on Kathleen McGowan, easily considered an overnight failure. She spent years researching and writing a novel. She went to the annual book convention on her own nickel last year, trying to pitch it. Day after day was spent slogging her way to any person willing to look at it. This year, of course, she's back with a million-dollar-plus advance, feted by booksellers, the whole drill.

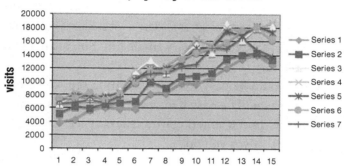

Squidoo is another interesting case. Here's a look at our daily traffic, courtesy of our Google Analytics package, since January (I removed four weeks, from mid-March to mid-April, because of a glitch with searches). Squidoo has more than 27,000 lenses built by 15,000 people in about five months. No, the chart doesn't look like Myspace or Flickr. What it does look like is the early days of Google and Wikipedia and other overnight failures.

The challenge for observers, investors, and partners (like the publisher who took on Kathleen) is to avoid the temptation of buying into the media infatuation with the overnight success story (which rarely happens overnight). The challenge for marketers is to figure out what daily progress looks like and obsess about that.

The goal, I think, is to be an overnight failure, but one that persists. Keeping costs low, building a foundation that leads to the right kind of story, the right kind of organic growth. Kathleen wrote a book that she believes in, one that was worth investing years of her life in. And then she painstakingly made progress until she became the next big thing.

The Thing About the Wind

I just had some great windsurfing lessons. I can tell you that windsurfing is very easy . . . except for the wind.

The wind makes it tricky, of course. It's not particularly difficult to find and rent great equipment, and the techniques are fairly straightforward. What messes up the whole plan is the fact that the wind is unpredictable. It'll change exactly when you don't want it to.

Just the other day I read a riff that reminded me that the same thing is true about customer service (it would be a lot easier if it weren't for the customers). Then I realized that every single function of an organization has a wind problem.

Accounting would be easy if every incoming report were accurate and on time. Sales would be easy if it weren't for the prospects not buying from you all the time. Marketing would be easy if every prospect and customer thought the way you do.

Here's the good news: the fact that it's difficult and unpredictable is the best thing that's happened to you all day. Because if it were any other way, there'd be no profit in it. The reason people bother to go windsurfing is that the challenge makes it interesting. The driving force that gets people to pay a specialist is the fact that their disease is unpredictable or hard to diagnose. *The reason we're here is to solve the hard problems.*

The next time you're tempted to vilify a particularly obnoxious customer or agency or search engine, realize that this failed interaction is the best thing that's happened to you all day long. Without it, you'd be easily replaceable.

Top Ways to Defend the Status Quo

1. "That will never work."
2. ". . . That said, the labor laws make it difficult for us to do a lot of the suggestions [you] put out. And we do live in a lawsuit-oriented society."
3. "Can you show me some research that demonstrates that this will work?"

4. "Well, if you had some real-world experience, then you would understand."

5. "I don't think our customers will go for that, and without them we'd never be able to afford to try this."

6. "It's fantastic, but the sales force won't like it."

7. "The sales force is willing to give it a try, but [major retailer] won't stock it."

8. "There are government regulations and this won't be permitted."

9. "Well, this might work for other people, but I think we'll stick with what we've got."

10. "We'll let someone else prove it works ... it won't take long to catch up."

11. "Our team doesn't have the technical chops to do this."

12. "Maybe in the next budget cycle."

13. "We need to finish this initiative first."

14. "It's been done before."

15. "It's never been done before."

16. "We'll get back to you on this."

17. "We're already doing it."

All quotes actually overheard, or read on blogs/comments about actual good ideas.

The Two Things That Kill Marketing Creativity

The first is fear.

The fear that you'll have to implement whatever you dream up.

The fear that you will fail.

The fear that you will do something stupid and be ridiculed by your peers for decades.

The fear that you'll get fired.

The fear that there will be an unanticipated backlash associated with your idea.

The fear of change.

The fear of missing out on the thing you won't be able to do if you do this.

The second is a lack of imagination.

I believe that every single person I've met in this profession is capable of astounding creativity. That you, and everyone else for that matter, are able to dream up something radical and viral and yes, remarkable. So why doesn't it happen more often? Sure, fear is a big part, but it's also a lack of imagination.

Basically, most people don't believe something better can occur. They believe that the status quo is also the best they can do. So they don't look. They don't push. They don't ask "what else?" and "what now?" They settle.

Fear is an emotion, and it's impossible to counter an emotion with logic. So you need to mount emotional arguments for why your fear of the new is the thing you truly need to fear.

As for the second issue, just knowing it exists ought to be enough. Once you realize you're settling, it may just be enough to get you wondering . . . wondering whether maybe, just maybe, something better is behind curtain number two.

Coloring Inside the Lines

People who want to do a good job are more likely to follow instructions that they know they can successfully complete, while they'll often ignore the "softer" tasks if they can.

If you're marketing a product or an idea to a group of people, and you juxtapose two ideas—one obvious and simple, while the other is challenging and subtle—you can bet that the mass of people will grab the first idea (if they don't ignore you altogether).

Example: It's easy to get people to wake up early on the day after Thanksgiving if you offer them a TV at a discount, the way Walmart does every year. It's a lot trickier to challenge consumers to figure out which one of the eighteen refrigerators you offer is likely to offer the best price/performance ratio.

The first task requires nothing much but effort, and that effort is likely to be rewarded. The second task takes judgment, and the opportunity for failure is much higher.

If you're a teacher and you give your third graders instructions for an essay, the motivated ones will listen. If you ask them for vivid, creative writing, and also let them know it must be five sentences long, in blue ink, and with not one word outside that little red line that marks the margin, guess what sort of work you'll get back? Writing in your format is easy. Being vivid is hard. It's easy to focus on the achievable, the measurable, and the simple.

I thought of this as I braved the insanity of JFK for a quick JetBlue flight. The instructions for the TSA folks probably fill several loose-leaf notebooks, but I imagine that they can be summarized as follows:

Volume 1: Identify suspicious people and be on the lookout for bad people and new and unimagined threats.

Volume 2: Stop anyone with liquid in their bag.

Guess which volume got read?

The guy in front of me got busted (aggressively) for having a four-ounce can of shaving cream. Isn't it OBVIOUS that the limit is three ounces? I could hear the TSA thinking, "What's going on here!!" At the same time that scores of expensive, trained teams of inspectors were focusing on interdicting the forbidden liquids, no one cared very much about ID or travel history or what that item on the X-ray actually was.

The same thing happens on your website every day. Sure, if I work my way through the site map and pay attention to your carefully crafted copy, I'll probably find exactly what I need. But it's way more likely that I'll just click on that cute picture or leave the site altogether.

People want to feel successful, but they're often unwilling to invest the time in doing something that might not pay off. It's not fair, but that's the way it works.

The Cycle of Choice

Most markets are busted open by one successful leader. Burton in snowboards, Henry Ford in cars, the iPod in MP3 players.

It sure seems, for a while, that the leader can do no wrong. Market share is high, the market grows, and then, oof, the leader fades.

It looks a bit like this:

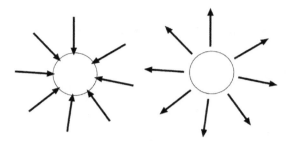

The leader attracts newcomers—both new users and new competitors—to the market. The competitors offer new choices, alternative pricing and distribution models, and just plain old choice. Unless there is a significant external barrier to change (like the iTunes store or the Windows distribution monopoly), then the leader appears to fade. At one point, there were more than 2,000 car companies in the U.S.

There are several lessons available for marketers here. First, if you bust open a market, don't expect to own it forever. Second, if you can, invest heavily in some sort of external effect that creates a natural monopoly and gives people a really good reason to stick (beyond the fact that you're the leader). And third, if you're not the leader, realize that: a) you're not going to replace them, and b) being just like them isn't the way to grow. As a market grows, the "scraps" left over from the leader can add up to a huge piece of market share. And then, over time, a new leader may emerge.

The China Problem

Big markets look sexy. Big markets are a problem.

Sitting at the vet's office today, I saw a brochure for an injectable chip that makes it easier to identify a lost dog. No doubt, the investor meetings all started with, "Well, there are a hundred million dogs in the United States, and if we just make a dollar annual profit on each one . . ."

It sounds reasonable. It's not.

The problem with huge markets is the same problem you'd have with playing squash or racquetball on a court that's too big. The ball doesn't have a wall to bounce off of. Huge horizontal markets have no echo chamber, no niches, no easy entry points. To make a system like this work, everyone has to agree on the technology, and then there has to be a huge push to get millions of people to make the same decision at about the same time. It might work, but it's awfully expensive.

Small markets aren't as sexy, but they're actually a better place to start.

Thrill Seekers

I now firmly believe that there are two polar opposites at work:

Thrill seekers and
Fear avoiders

Notice that I don't use the word "risk" to describe either category.

How do we explain the fact that *Forbes* finds more than 700 billionaires, and virtually none are both young and retired? Why keep working?

How do we explain why so many organizations get big and then just stop? Stop innovating, stop pushing, stop inventing . . .

Why are seminars sometimes exciting, bubbling pots of innovation and energy, while others are drone fests?

I think people come to work with one of two attitudes (though there are plenty of people with a blend that's somewhere in between):

Thrill seekers love growth. They most enjoy a day where they try something that was difficult or—even better—said to be impossible, and then pull it off. Thrill seekers are great salespeople because they view every encounter as a chance to break some sort of record or have an interaction that is memorable.

Fear avoiders hate change. They want the world to stay just the way it is. They're happy being mediocre, because being mediocre means less threat/fear/change. They resent being pushed into the unknown, because the unknown is a scary place.

An interesting side discussion: one of the biggest factors in the success of the U.S. isn't our natural resources or location. It's that so many people in this country came here seeking a thrill.

So why not call them risk seekers and risk avoiders? Well, it used to be true. Seeking thrills was risky. But no longer. Now, of course, safe is risky. The horrible irony is that the fear avoiders are setting themselves up for big changes because they're confused. The safest thing they can do now, it turns out, is to become thrill seekers.

Whom do you work with?

The Realistic Entrepreneur's Guide to Venture Capital

Optimism is a key to success, but it doesn't necessarily work so well when it comes to VC. Because this is a cottage industry with thousands of players, all with different objectives, it's very easy to keep knocking on doors, just waiting to find the right match. It's also easy to spend a year or more adjusting your business to what each VC asks for ("bring me the broomstick of the Wicked Witch!") while you could have been out there building a real organization.

Here are a bunch of conditions that you ought to take seriously before you invest the time and the energy to track down outside money for your great idea:

1. Investors like to invest in categories they've already invested in. If your business is so new that it's never been tested before, or is in a category VCs hate, think twice.
2. Investors want you to sell out. As soon as possible. For as much as possible. They have no desire to own part of your company forever.
3. Investors want to invest in a project that's tested. If you can't make it work in the "small," why do you think it'll work when it's big?
4. Being a little better than the market leader is worthless.
5. Investors don't want you to use their money to cover your losses. They want you to build an asset (a patent, an audience, channel relationships) that's actually worth something.
6. Investors want someone to run your company who has successfully run a company before.
7. Investors want to be able to come to one of your board meetings and still make it home in time for dinner.
8. VCs like curves more than they like cliffs.

9. There are actually very, very few business problems that can be solved with money.

10. You will probably have to replace many of your employees if you raise money from someone.

11. VCs understand that being the best in the world (#1) is the place with the biggest rewards, so it's unlikely they will settle for any performance (even a profitable one) that puts you in second or third place.

12. VCs are very smart and very connected, but they're smart enough to know that their connections and their insights can't fix a broken business.

13. Investors are very focused on the company, not on you. They're not interested in having you take out your original investment or paying you a large salary as profits go up.

14. Business plans are bogus. The act of writing one is critical, but no one is going to read more than three pages of what you write before they make a decision.

15. The companies that VCs most want to invest in are the companies that don't need their investment to survive.

More Perfect

Most people in the U.S. can't cook. So you would think that reaching out to the masses with entry-level cooking instruction would be a smart business move.

In fact, as the Food Network and cookbook publishers have demonstrated over and over again, you're way better off helping the near-perfect improve. You'll also sell a lot more management consulting to well-run companies, more high-end stereos to people with good stereos, and yes, more church services to the already well behaved.

Pundits Are (Nearly) Always Wrong

Here's why:

Because we measure the wrong things.

Talk show bookers, business plan competitions, acquiring book editors, movie critics, tech entrepreneurs who run trade shows that try to predict the future, tech bloggers, marketing bloggers . . . when we're trying to predict whether a new technology or website or book or song is going to hit, we're almost always wrong.

Take a look at some of the picks for past Web 2.0 shows, or see who got hyped on various morning TV programs or see which authors were turned down by five or ten or fifteen publishing houses—"surprise hits," they call them.

The astonishing thing isn't that we're wrong so often, but that given the amplifying power of our platforms, we're unable to yell loud enough to make our predictions self-fulfilling prophecies. In English: You'd think that being featured by a big publisher or at a big conference would be enough in and of itself to make something undeserving a hit. Alas, only Oprah can do that.

So, why are we wrong? Why does your boss/in-law/friend/VC/editor/pundit always get it wrong?

Because they measure "presentation." Not just the PowerPoint presentation, but the way an idea feels. How does it present? Is it catchy? Clever? Familiar? We measure whether or not it agrees with our worldview and our sense of the way the world is.

The problem is that hits change worldviews. Hits change our senses. Hits appeal to people other than the gatekeepers, and then the word spreads.

How? Through persistence and hard work and constant revision. By getting through the Dip.

If I have a skill in developing stuff, it's in ignoring these people. *Purple Cow* was turned down by my old publisher and a few others. Squidoo was dissed by some of the best in the business (the site is about to hit 8 million monthly page views—update, now it's closer to 40 million!). *The Dip* was a hard sell to my agent and my publisher.

No one "pre-predicted" the astonishing success of Flickr or Google or Twitter or Bill Clinton's first run for president. Sure, it was easy to connect the dots after the fact, but that doesn't count.

Of course, there are plenty of failures to go around (I know that I've got more than plenty). Just because everyone hates it doesn't mean it's good. Execution is everything. Execution and persistence and the ability to respond to the market far outweigh a pundit's gut instinct. But the thing to remember is this: if everyone loves it, it is almost certain to have troubles.

In fact, my rule of thumb is this: if the right people like it, I'm not trying hard enough.

How to Make a Million Dollars

One popular method is to make a dollar in profit from each of a million people. Or a penny from a hundred million. This is the China strategy. It almost never works.

It almost never works because the challenge of reaching that many people is just too great. It's too risky and too expensive. Doesn't matter that you're hoping for only a dollar or a penny. The price isn't the challenge; it's the difficulty of spreading your idea.

Far easier to make a thousand dollars from each of a thousand people, or even $10,000 from a hundred organizations. You can focus on a small hive of people, a group that talks to itself. You can push through a smaller dip and reach a level of recommendation and dominance that makes incremental sales far easier.

And you can learn much earlier in the process if you've gotten it right or not. Because you're making more per sale, you can spend the time necessary to figure out what really sells and modify your offering sooner in the process.

The irony is that many products and services that have reached huge masses of people actually have significant margins (Windows, for example, or a cup of Starbucks coffee). They got the best of both worlds because first they focused on winning over small communities and that led to the larger market.

The 80:1 Freakonomics Paradox

The Wall Street Journal reports that there are a slew of *Freakonomics*-like books on the market. Some of them are actually pretty good; few are selling at all. My guess is that the original has outsold its competitors by about 80 to 1.

That's not surprising if you talk to people. A good friend of mine who never, ever reads books about business or economics just picked up a copy last week. She said, "I think it's time I read this, right?" When a product becomes a hit, an entirely new class of people become interested in it, largely because it's a hit.

Which leads to the paradox. The easiest products in the world to develop, option, license, and get to market are copycat products. They are beyond reproach. They feel safe. In actuality, though, most markets aren't big enough for two blockbusters. The first one dominates the little market, which allows it to break through and capture the attention of the big market. The bestseller creates the problem (I haven't read that/tasted that/been there) and then solves that problem. The second (and third and fourth and fifth) iterations are trying to sell a solution to people who no longer have the problem.

You Get to Choose

That's the cool thing about marketing. Unlike most other functions in the organization, marketing lets you choose where and how you do what you do.

If you don't have the money to do a full-scale TV campaign that's going to work, you shouldn't choose TV.

If you don't have the organizational support to engage in a long-term grassroots strategy, don't do it.

I was talking to a journalist about bootstrapping the other day, and he wanted me to share some examples of big, capital-intensive companies that got their start by bootstrapping. My answer was pretty simple, "If you don't have a lot of capital, don't choose a business that requires it."

If you have an organization that is slow and deliberative, don't enter a market that rewards the fleet of foot.

If you have colleagues that love to discuss everything out loud, don't choose a campaign that will fail if the market senses internal discussion and disagreement.

Don't raise VC money for a business that can't possibly pay off for the investors. Don't promote a lunch menu in a neighborhood where no one goes out for lunch. It seems terribly obvious, but bad choices, choices where you're going against the wind instead of with it, are the easiest mistakes to avoid.

Looking for Trouble

Every weekend there's a line out front of the Avis rental car window on the Upper West Side of NYC. Every weekend, ostensibly computer-literate upper-middle-class yuppies waste hours trying to pick up a car when they could just use Zipcar.

For this person, in this moment, a message about Zipcar is not only not spam but is a gift.

Worth wondering why the company doesn't have someone standing out front with fliers.

Along the same lines, why doesn't the local accountant sponsor the business section of the nearby independent bookstore? Slip a bookmark and business card into every personal finance book the store sells; it's the right message at the right time.

Blogs, of course, ought to be the perfect place to find people in trouble. The challenge is in getting past the "I won't click on an ad" mindset that 80% of those online carry around. Guerrilla marketing works best when it takes the form of a sponsorship or some other unexpected combination of advertiser and content. Blogs let you go further than that, though.

The most effective marketing use of blogs seems to occur when the advertiser/marketer uses the blog as an opportunity not to sell a product but to attract people who are in the right mindset. Joel Spolsky rarely writes about his product, but that's fine. The people who read his writing are the very same people who need his product, and his proximity to the valuable ideas (and his reputation) makes it not such a leap to go ahead and buy what he has to sell.

Attract people in trouble ❯ Help solve their problems ❯ Build your reputation ❯ Sales happen.

Sputnik and Roger Bannister

Big marketing lessons here:

1. When you do something that everyone said was impossible, or that they never even considered, you get remembered for a long, long time.
2. Once you demonstrate that the jar actually doesn't have a lid on it, people start jumping out left and right.

There was no space race before Sputnik. We didn't even have something called a space program. Even Arthur C. Clarke, who invented the idea, didn't expect that it would happen.

The other thing to remember: There was a Sputnik 2. There's just about always a sequel, so don't worry about making the first one perfect.

Small-Business Success

Three things you need:

1. The ability to abandon a plan when it doesn't work,
2. The confidence to do the right thing even when it costs you money in the short run, and
3. Enough belief in other people that you don't try to do everything yourself.

Soggy

New organizations and new projects are so crisp.

Things happen with alacrity. Decisions get made. Stuff gets done.

Then, over time, things get soggy. They slow down. Decisions aren't so black and white anymore.

Why?

Here are some things that happen:

1. Every initiative, post-launch, still has a tail of activity associated with it. Launch enough things and, over time, that tail gets bigger and bigger.

2. Most projects either succeed or fail. Successful projects raise the stakes, because the team doesn't want to blow it. There are more people watching, more dollars at stake—things matter more. So things inevitably get more review, get more analysis, and slow down. Projects that fail sap the confidence of the group. People want to be extra sure that they're right this time, so, ironically, they slow down and end up sabotaging the new work.

3. The paper isn't blank anymore. Which means that new decisions often mean overturning old decisions, which means you need to acknowledge that it didn't used to be as good as it was.

4. And the biggest thing is that there is a status quo. Something to compare everything to.

I'm not sure you can eliminate any of these issues. But you can realize that they're there. And you can be really strict about priorities and deadlines. It's so easy to let things slip, rather than confronting the fact that you're stuck and probably afraid. Speak up, call it out . . . and ship!

Write Like a Blogger

You can improve your writing (your business writing, your ad writing, your thank-you notes, and your essays) if you start thinking like a blogger:

1. *Use headlines.* I use them all the time now. Not just boring ones that announce your purpose (like the one on this post) but interesting or puzzling or engaging headlines. Headlines are perfect for engaging busy readers.

2. *Realize that people have choices.* I know that with 80 million other blogs to choose from, you could leave at any moment (see, there goes someone now). So that makes blog writing shorter and faster and more exciting.

3. *Drip, drip, drip.* Bloggers don't have to say everything at once. We can add a new idea every day, piling on a thesis over time.

4. *It's okay if you leave.* Bloggers aren't afraid to include links or distractions in their writing, because we know you'll come back if what we have to say is interesting.

5. *Interactivity is a great shortcut.* Your readers care about someone's opinion even more than yours: their own. So reading your email or your comments or your trackbacks (your choice) makes it easy to stay relevant.

6. *Gimmicks aren't as useful as insight.* If you're going to blog successfully for months or years, sooner or later you need to actually say something. Same goes for your writing.

7. *Don't be afraid of lists.* People like lists.

8. *Show up.* Not writing is not a useful way of expressing your ideas. Waiting for perfect is a lousy strategy.

9. *Say it.* Don't hide, don't embellish.

What would happen if every single high school student had to have a blog? Or every employee in your company? Or every one of your customers?

Proximity to Pain

The closer you are to the point of need, the more you can charge.

Pizza at the airport costs five times more than pizza on the way to the airport.

Tax audit services in the middle of an SEC investigation cost triple what they cost before one.

Scalped tickets cost more than ones bought in advance, by mail.

Emergency towing in a strange town costs more, too.

The single easiest way to increase your fees is to get closer to the pain. It's interesting to note that no large-scale advertising ventures are closer to the pain than the Yellow Pages or Google. Both of which are insanely successful.

The Magic of Low-Hanging Fruit

Imagine that half the cars in the U.S. get 10 miles per gallon. And half get 40 miles per gallon. Further stipulate that all cars are driven the same number of miles per year.

Now, you get one wish. You can give every low-mileage car a new set of spark plugs that will increase fuel efficiency by 5 mpg, up to 15. Or you can replace every 40-mpg car with a car that gets 75 mpg, an increase of 35 miles for every gallon.

Which is better?

It turns out that the 5-mpg increase is far better for overall mileage than the 35-mpg increase, even though it's smaller both as a percentage and absolutely. That's because the 10-mpg hogs use up so much gas. They're the low-hanging fruit, not just easy to fix but worth fixing.

As marketers, we're tempted to tweak the already tweaked, to turn the 100 to 101, to optimize for the peak performances. That long tail is very long, though, and if there's a way you can raise the floor (instead of just focusing on the ceiling), you may be surprised to discover that it can have a huge impact.

Simple example: It's way more profitable to encourage each of your existing customers to spend $3 than it is to get a stranger to spend $300. It's also more effective to get the 80% of your customer service people that are average to be a little better than it is to get the amazing ones to be better still.

The Secret of the Web (Hint: It's a Virtue)

Patience.

Google was a very good search engine for two years before you started using it.

The iPod was a dud.

I wrote *Unleashing the Ideavirus* eight years ago. A few authors tried similar ideas, but they didn't work right away. So those authors gave up. BoingBoing is one of the most popular blogs in the world because they never gave up.

The irony of the Web is that the tactics work really quickly. You friend someone on Facebook and two minutes later, they friend you back. Bang.

But the strategy still takes forever. The strategy is the hard part, not the tactics.

I discovered a lucky secret the hard way about thirty years ago: you can outlast the other guys if you try. If you stick at stuff that bores them, it accrues. Drip, drip, drip, you win.

It still takes ten years to become a success, Web or no Web. The frustrating part is that you see your tactics fail right away. The good news is that over time, you get the satisfaction of watching those tactics succeed right away.

The trap: show up at a new social network, invest two hours, be really aggressive with people, make some noise, and then leave in disgust.

The trap: use all your money to build a fancy website and leave no money or patience for the hundred revisions you'll need to do.

The trap: read the tech blogs and fall in love with the bleeding-edge hip sites and lose focus on the long-term players that deliver real value.

The trap: sprint all day and run out of energy before the marathon even starts.

The media want overnight successes (so they have someone to tear down). Ignore them. Ignore the early-adopter critics that never have enough to play with. Ignore your investors that want proven tactics and predictable instant results. Listen instead to your real customers, to your vision, and make something for the long haul. Because that's how long it's going to take, guys.

The Myth of Launch PR

New start-ups can spend hundreds of thousands of dollars racing after a dream: a giant splash on launch.

Just imagine . . . a big spread in *Time* magazine, a feature on all the relevant blogs, a glowing review in the *Book Review*. Get this part right and everything else takes care of itself.

And yet.

Here are some brands that had no launch at all: Starbucks, Apple, Nike, *Harry Potter*, Google, William Morris, *The Da Vinci Code*, Wikipedia, Snapple, Geico, Linux, Firefox, and yes, Microsoft. (All got plenty of PR, but after the launch, sometimes a lot later.)

I'm as guilty as the next entrepreneur. Great publicity is a treasured gift. But it's hardly necessary, and the search for it is often a significant distraction.

It works for movies; in fact, it's essentially required for movies. But for just about every other product, service, or company, the relentless quest for media validation doesn't really pay. If you get it, congratulations. If you don't, that's fine. But don't break the bank or your timetable in the quest.

Nine Steps to PowerPoint Magic

Perhaps you've experienced it. You do a presentation and it works. It works! That's the reason we keep coming back for more; that's why so many of us spend more time building and giving presentations than almost anything else we do.

Here are some steps to achieve this level of PPT nirvana (your mileage may vary; these are steps, not rules):

1. **Don't use PowerPoint at all.** Most of the time, it's not necessary. It's underkill. PowerPoint distracts you from what you really need to do: look people in the eye, tell a story, tell the truth. Do it in your own words, without artifice and with clarity. There are times PowerPoint is helpful, but choose them carefully.

2. **Use your own font.** Go visit Smashing Magazine (smashingmagazine.com) and buy a font from one of their sponsors or get one of the free ones they offer. Have your tech guy teach you how to install it, and then use it instead of the basic fonts that come with your computer's software. Doing this is like dressing better or having a nicer business card. It's subtle, but it works.

3. **Tell the truth.** By this, I don't mean "don't lie" (that's a given); I mean "don't hide." Be extremely direct in why you are here, what you're going to sell me (you're here to sell me something, right? If not, please don't waste your time or mine). It might be an idea or a budget, but it's still selling. If, at the end, I don't know what you're selling, you've failed.

4. **Pay by the word.** Here's the deal: You should have to put $5 into the coffee fund for every single word on the wordiest slide in your deck.

Four hundred words costs $2,000. If that were true, would you use fewer words? A lot fewer? I've said this before, but I need to try again: words belong in memos. PowerPoint is for ideas. If you have bullets, please, please, please use only one word in each bullet. Two if you have to. Three, never.

5. **Get a remote.** I always use one. Mine went missing a couple of weeks ago, so I had to present without it. I saw myself on video and hated the fact that I lost all that eye contact. It's money well spent.

6. **Use a microphone.** If you are presenting to more than 20 people, a clip-on microphone changes your posture and your impact. And if you're presenting to more than 300 people, use iMag. This is a setup with a camera and projector that puts your face on the screen. You should have a second screen for your slides—the switching back and forth is an incompetent producer's hack that saves a few bucks but is completely and totally not worth it. If 400 people are willing to spend an hour listening to you, someone ought to be willing to spend a few dollars to make the presentation work properly.

7. **Check to make sure you brought your big idea with you.** It's not worth doing a presentation for a small idea or for a budget, or to give a quarterly update. That's what memos are for. Presentations involve putting on a show, standing up and performing. So, what's your big idea? Is it big enough? Really?

8. **Be too breathtaking to allow note taking.** If people are live-blogging, Twittering, or writing down what you're saying, I wonder if your presentation is everything it could be. After all, you could have saved everyone the trouble and just blogged it or note taken it for them, right? We've been trained since youth to replace paying attention with taking notes. That's a shame. Your actions should demand attention. (Hint: bullets demand note-taking. The minute you put bullets on the screen, you are announcing, "write this down, but don't really pay attention now.") People don't take notes when they go to the opera.

9. **Keep it short!** Do you really need an hour for the presentation? Twenty minutes? Most of the time, the right answer is "ten." Ten minutes of breathtaking big ideas with big pictures and big type and few words and scary thoughts and startling insights. And then, and

then, spend the rest of your time just talking to me. Interacting. Answering questions. Leading a discussion.

Most presentations (and I've seen a lot) are absolutely horrible. They're not horrible because they weren't designed by a professional; they're horrible because they are delivered by someone who is hiding what they came to say. The new trend of tweaking your slides with expensive graphic design doesn't solve this problem; it makes it worse. Give me an earnest amateur any day, please.

Too Small to Fail

One secret of being a large financial institution is that you can take huge risks because you're too big to fail. If you hit craps and lose it all, don't worry, because you'll get bailed out.

One secret of "small is the new big" thinking is that you won't fail and you can't fail and you don't need to worry about a bailout. Not because you're small in head count or assets, but because you act small.

A small-acting bank would never have invested in tens of thousands of loans that they hadn't looked at. And a small-acting start-up wouldn't hire dozens of people before they had a business model—and then have to lay off a third of them just because their VC firm showed them a scary PowerPoint presentation.

I've always been frightened by big-firm accounting. The sort of financial legerdemain in which skilled accountants work hard to make the numbers look the way the CEO wants, instead of making them clear. Cash accounting run on a simple bookkeeping system is the small way to do it, even if your company is huge. That's because sooner or later, management has to know what's actually happening as opposed to what they can pretend is happening.

Big-thinking companies lose customers all the time because big-thinking companies isolate the decision makers from the outside world. Angry customers who are leaving don't get heard; that news is heard by the poor schlub reading a script at the call center. Ninety percent of the angry customer mail that people forward to me (I have enough for a lifetime, thanks) is angry because the (former) customer is tired of being ignored.

If you act small and think big, you are too small to fail. You won't need a bailout because your business makes sense each and every day. You won't need a bailout because your flat organization (no matter how large it is) knows about problems long before they're too big to deal with.

The media and the tech blogs glamorize businesses that act big. They write about the big checks VCs hand out and they lionize the organizations that make a splash. The untold story is in the organizations that are close to the customer, close to the product, and close to each other. Acting small always pays off.

(Thanks to Howard for the phrase that inspired this post.)

What Would a Professional Do?

Every day, you do a hundred or a thousand jobs, some of which are occasionally handled by specialists. You make a sales call or give a presentation or answer the phone; you design a slide or create a simple spreadsheet. You get the idea.

When you are busy being a jack-of-all-trades, you're competing against professionals. The recipient of your work doesn't care that you are also capable of doing other things. All she wants is the best she can get.

I'll define a professional as a specialist who does industry-standard work for hire. A professional presenter, for example, could give a presentation on anything, not just on the topic you're passionate about.

When you compete with professionals, you have a problem because, generally speaking, they're better at what they do than you are.

I think there are four valid ways to think your way out of this situation:

1. Hire a professional.
2. Be as good as a professional.
3. Realize that professional-quality work is not required or available, and merely come close.

4. Do work that a professional wouldn't dare do, and use this as an advantage.

The first option requires time and money you might not have, and I'm assuming that's why you didn't do it in the first place.

The second option is smart, particularly if you do the work often and the quality matters. Slide design and selling are two examples that come to mind here. The first step to getting good is admitting that you aren't (yet). Invest the time and become a pro if it's important.

The third option is worth investigation, but it's what you've probably already decided without putting words to it. Is the assumption really true? Does your customer/client/employee *actually believe* that they haven't been shortchanged by your amateur performance? Is it costing you in ways you're not measuring because you're willfully ignoring the consequences? Think of all the sub-pro experiences you've had as a customer, instances when someone was pretending to be a chef or a bartender or a computer jock but came up short. Were you delighted?

The fourth option is really exciting. From personal YouTube videos to particularly poignant and honest presentations or direct and true sales pitches, the humility, freshness, and transparency that come with an honest performance might actually be better than what a professional could do. Harvey Milk was an amateur politician, not a pro. If you're the only person on earth who could have done what you just did, then you're a proud amateur.

You can't skate by when you refuse to mimic a professional. You must connect in a personal, lasting way that matters. That's difficult, but the professionals have no chance to compete with you.

Be an amateur on purpose, not because you have to.

Sprint!

The best way to overcome your fear of creativity, brainstorming, intelligent risk taking, or navigating a tricky situation might be to sprint.

When we sprint, all the internal dialogue falls away and we just go as fast as we possibly can. When you're sprinting, you don't feel that sore knee and you don't worry that the ground isn't perfectly level. You just run.

You can't sprint forever. That's what makes it sprinting. The brevity of the event is a key part of why it works.

"Quick, you have thirty minutes to come up with ten business ideas."

"Hurry, we need to write a new script for our commercial . . . we have fifteen minutes."

My first huge project was launching a major brand of science-fiction computer adventure games (Ray Bradbury, Michael Crichton, etc.). I stopped going to business school classes in order to do the launch.

One day, right after a red-eye flight, the president of the company told me that the company had canceled the project. They didn't have enough resources to launch all the products we had, our progress was too slow, and the packaging wasn't ready yet.

I went to my office and spent the next 20 hours rewriting every word of text, redesigning every package, rebuilding every schedule, and inventing a new promotional strategy. It was probably six weeks of work for a motivated committee, and I did it in one swoop. Like lifting a car off an infant, it was impossible, and I have no recollection at all of the project now.

The board reconsidered and the project was back on again. I didn't get scared until *after* the sprint. You can't sprint every day, but it's probably a good idea to sprint regularly.

Three Things You Need if You Want More Customers

If you want to grow, you need new customers. And if you want new customers, you need three things:

1. A group of possible customers you can identify and reach.
2. A group with a problem they want to solve, using your solution.
3. A group with the desire and ability to spend money to solve that problem.

You'd be amazed at how often new businesses or new ventures have none of these. The first one is critical, because if you don't have permission, or knowledge, or word of mouth, you're invisible.

The Zune didn't have #2.

A service aimed at creating videos for best-selling authors doesn't have #1.

And a counseling service helping people cut back on Big Mac consumption doesn't have #3.

Share of Wallet, Share of Wall, Share of Voice

The first mistake marketers make is that they want more. More customers, more noise, more ads, more shelf space, more customers, more customers, more customers . . .

Almost all of their actions are driven by the search for more customers.

The reason this is a mistake is simple: it's expensive. Attracting a new customer costs far more than keeping an old one happy. Not only that, but an old customer is far more likely to bring you new people via word of mouth than is someone who isn't even a customer yet.

Which is why share of wallet makes so much more sense than share of market. How much does each of your existing customers buy from you? Do they count on you for all the things they buy in this market, or just some? Does Toyota sell me every car my family drives? Does Chubb get to insure every single thing I own? Usually not, because marketers are so focused on more that they forget to take great care of what they've got.

Hugh MacLeod, gifted cartoonist and profane marketing blogger, is now making his living selling limited-edition artwork based on his cartoons. He's a brilliant marketer, of course, so he's not focused on more. He's focused on share of wallet. On selling his dedicated fans a remarkable souvenir that they can keep and display.

So, what's the problem? Share of wall. Unlike with records or shoes, it's hard to buy a lot of art. Pretty soon, you've got no place left to put it, do you? Share of wallet turns into share of wall and you can't grow any more.

That's why you need to be realistic about how much share of wallet you can honestly expect, and why job one is delighting existing customers so much that they can't help but tell their friends. Preferably friends with very big houses.

Circling the Big Domino

Clay taught me a good lesson about making things happen with your brand.

Envision the events that might happen to a brand (shelf space at Walmart, an appearance on *Oprah*, a bestseller, worldwide recognition, a new edition, worldwide rights, chosen by the Queen, whatever) as a series of dominos.

It turns out that if you start with all of them at once, you'll fail.

And if you start with the big one, you'll fail.

But if you line up all the dominos one by one, in the right order, you may just have enough energy to push over the first one. That one, of course, adds momentum so that when you crash into the second one, that one goes, too. All the way to the Queen.

Wait!

Isn't this obvious? Sure it is. So why is it so often ignored?

Brands get stuck constantly. And they always get stuck circling the big domino. They try to launch worldwide and beat Google. They try to get an endorsement from the Prince of Denmark. They try to break out with a feature on a major blog. They try to act like Coca-Cola from the first day. And they try and they try and they try until they get so frustrated, they quit.

A few brands pick out tiny dominos instead. And topple them. And they do it again. They do it so often they create noise, momentum and, most important, a sense of inevitability. That's how you win.

Death Spiral!

You've probably seen it. The fishmonger sees a decline in business, so they have less money to spend on upkeep and inventory, so they keep the fish a bit longer and don't clean up as often, so of course, business declines and then they have even less money . . . Eventually, you have an empty, smelly fish store that's out of business.

The doctor has fewer patients, so he doesn't invest as much in training or staff, and so some other patients choose to leave, which means that there are even fewer patients . . .

The newspaper has fewer advertisers, so the publisher can't invest as much in running stories, so people stop reading the paper, which means that advertisers have less reason to advertise, which leaves less money for stories . . .

As Tom Peters says, "You can't shrink your way to greatness," and yet that's what so many dying businesses try to do. They hunker down and wait for things to get better, but they don't. This isn't a dip, it's a cul-de-sac. It's over.

Right this minute, you still have some cash, some customers, some momentum. Instead of squandering it in a long, slow death spiral, do something else. Buy a new platform. Move. Find new products for the customers that still trust you.

Change is a bear, but it's better than death.

When Tactics Drown Out Strategy

New media creates a blizzard of tactical opportunities for marketers, and many of them cost nothing but time, which means you don't need as much approval and support to launch them.

As a result, marketers are like kids at Rita's Candy Shoppe, gazing at all the pretty opportunities.

Most of us are afraid of strategy, because we don't feel confident outlining one unless we're sure it's going to work. And the "work" part is all tactical, so we focus on that. (Tactics are easy to outline, because we say, "I'm going to post this." If we post it, we succeed. Strategy is scary to outline, because we describe results, not actions, and that means opportunity for failure.)

"Building a permission asset so we can grow our influence with our best customers over time" is a strategy. Using email, Twitter, or RSS, along with sending newsletters, sponsoring contests, and providing a human voice—these are all tactics. *In my experience, people get obsessed about tactical detail before they embrace a strategy,* and as a result, when a tactic fails, they begin to question the strategy that they never really embraced in the first place.

The next time you find yourself spending eight hours on tactics and five minutes refining your strategy, you'll understand what's going on.

Understanding Business Development

Business Development is a mysterious title for a little-discussed function or department in most larger companies. It's also a great way for an entrepreneur or small business to have fun, create value, and make money.

Good business development allows businesses to profit by doing something that is tangential to their core mission. Sometimes the profit is so good, it becomes part of their core mission; other times it supports the brand, and sometimes it just makes money. And often it's a little guy who can be flexible enough to make things happen.

Examples:

- Starbucks licenses their name to a maker of ice cream and generates millions in royalties.
- A rack jobber like Handleman does a deal with a mass marketer like Kmart. Kmart gives them room in the store to sell records and gets a cut; Handleman does all the work.
- AOL buys AIM instant messaging software and integrates it into their service.
- Years ago, I licensed the rights to Isaac Asimov's *Robot* novels from a business development person at his publisher and turned the books into a VCR murder mystery game, which I licensed to a business development person at Kodak, a company that was experimenting with becoming a publisher. (Isaac made more from this project than he did from many of his books.)
- Best Buy offers extended warranties on appliances you buy. They don't provide the warranty, of course; a business development

person did a deal with an insurance/service company to do it, and they share the profits.

- The Princeton Review built a huge test-prep business, but only by licensing their brand to a series of books that did the lion's share of their marketing for them.

You don't see business development, particularly all the potential deals that fail along the way, from the outside. Many companies, though, spend millions of dollars a year looking for deals and then discovering that they pay off many times over. Others, especially smaller competitors, are so focused on their core business that it never occurs to them to consider partnerships, licensing, publishing, acquisition, and other arrangements that might change everything. Harley-Davidson probably makes more money on business development than it makes on motorcycles.

The thing that makes business development fascinating is that *the best deals have never been done before.* There's no template, no cookie-cutter, grind-it-out approach to making it work. This is why most organizations are so astonishingly bad at it. They don't have the confidence to make decisions or believe they have the ability to make mistakes.

Think about the Apple Nike partnership created to make a device that integrates your iPod with your sneakers. This took years and cost millions of dollars to develop. Most companies would just flee, giving up long before a deal was done and a product was shipped.

Here are some tactical tips on how to do business development better:

1. **Process first, ideas second.** If you're going to be bringing new partners and new ideas into your organization, you need a process to do it. Professionals don't "know it when I see it." Instead, professionals think about the abilities of their company and about the strategies necessary to bring ideas in, refine them, and launch them. Great business development people don't waste time in endless meetings with random vendors or hassle about tiny details up front. Instead, they have an agenda and a project manager's understanding of what

it means to get things done. They don't keep the process a secret, either. They share it with anyone who wants to know. Someone needs to say, "here's how we do things around here," and then they have to tell the truth.

2. **Who decides?** Because every great business development project is different, it's incredibly easy to get stuck on who can say *yes* (of course, everyone can say *no*). Professional business development people intentionally limit the number of people who are allowed to weigh in, and they are clear to themselves and their potential partners about exactly who can (and must) give the go-ahead. Don't bother starting a business development deal unless you know in advance who must say yes.

3. **Courtship, negotiation, and marriage.** Every deal has three parts, and keeping them straight is essential. During the courtship phase, you win when you are respectful, diligent, enthusiastic, engaging, outgoing, and relentless in your search to make a connection. Do your homework, research people's backgrounds, learn about their kids, visit them—don't make them visit you. Look people in the eye, ask hard but engaging questions—you know the drill. Basically, treat people as you'd like to be treated, because the people you most want to work with have a choice, and they may just not pick you. Hint: If you skip the courtship part, the other two stages probably won't come up.

4. **Partners, not just buyer and seller.** If you've ever pitched a product or service to a business, you know how soul-deadening it can be. The buyer works hard to make it clear that she's doing you a favor, and you need every dog and every pony available at all times (and you better be the cheapest). But business development doesn't have this dichotomy. Both sides are buying, both sides are selling, right? So talented business development people never act like jaded buyers, arms folded, demanding this and that. Instead, from the start, they seek out partners.

5. **Enthusiasm is underrated.** Business development people are exploring the unknown. That means that there's more than cash on the table; there's bravery and initiative and excitement. The best business development people I've ever worked with are able to capture

the energy in the room and amplify it. They'll build on the ideas being presented, not make them smaller.

6. **Close the open door.** I regularly hear from readers who are frustrated because a big company wasn't willing to hear a great idea they mailed in. Here's the thing: there isn't a shortage of ideas. There's a shortage of execution. That means that successful business development teams look for proven partners and organizations with momentum. A key part of that is the decision to say no early and quickly and respectfully to people who don't meet that threshold.

7. **Call the lawyers later.** A business development deal that never happens is one that's sure to cause no problems. While the legal clarity you need is important, there are plenty of data showing that ten-page NDAs and onerous contracts early in the process don't protect you; they merely waste your time and energy.

8. **Cast a wider net.** The Allen & Co. annual gathering is a dumb place to choose a merger partner. Limiting the number of potential partners to people you've met at a trade show is also silly. Business development (when it works) creates huge value for both sides, so better to be proactive in searching out and soliciting the organizations that can make a difference. Here's a simple way to widen your net: start a blog and go to conferences to speak. Describe your successful business development projects to date and let the world know you're looking for more of them. How many amazing partnerships could the Apple Store launch? How many great books could Starbucks highlight? Not only don't they do this, but they hide. Don't hide.

9. **Talk to the receptionist.** This is huge, and so important. When a great partner shows up at your doorstep, do you know? Here's a test: call your organization (pretending to be from some respected organization), describe a business development opportunity, and ask who can help. If you're not immediately transferred to your office, you've failed, right? Make it easy for the right people to know that you're the right guy.

10. **Hire better.** How do you decide who to put in this job? I'd argue that glibness and charisma aren't as important as strategic thinking, project management, and humility.

11. **Structure deals with the expectation of success.** The only real reason to do business development deals is because when they work, they're so powerful. Andrew Tobias put his name on a piece of software that ended up earning him millions of dollars. It's easy to get hung up on all the bad things that could happen, but keep your focus on how the world looks when you get it right.

12. **End well.** Most of the time, even good business development deals fall down before the end of the negotiation process. If a deal doesn't come together, say so. Acknowledge what went wrong, thank the other party, and end well. If it does come together, track the integration and stay involved enough to learn from what works and what doesn't. I'm still waiting to hear from people who said they'd get back to me "tomorrow" fifteen years ago, but I'm losing hope. Ending well not only teaches you how to do better next time, but it keeps doors open for when you need to come back to someone whom you should have done a deal with in the first place.

Fear of Bad Ideas

A few people are afraid of good ideas, ideas that make a difference or contribute in some way. Good ideas bring change; that's frightening.

But many people are petrified of bad ideas. Ideas that make us look stupid or waste time or money or create some sort of backlash.

The problem is that you can't have good ideas unless you're willing to generate a lot of bad ones.

Painters, musicians, entrepreneurs, writers, chiropractors, accountants—we all fail far more than we succeed. We fail at closing a sale or playing a note. We fail at an idea for a series of paintings or the theme for a trade-show booth.

But we succeed far more often than people who have no ideas at all.

Someone asked me where I get all my good ideas, explaining that it takes him a month or two to come up with one and I seem to have more than that. I asked him how many bad ideas he has every month. He paused and said, "none."

And there, you see, is the problem.

Solving Problems

There are three ways to deal with a problem, I think.

- Lean into it.
- Lean away from it.
- Run away.

You lean *into* a problem, especially a long-term or difficult one, by sitting with it, reveling in it, embracing it, and breathing it in. The problem becomes part of you, at least until you solve it. You try one approach and then another, and when nothing works, you stick with it and work around it as you build your organization and your life. [I don't mean that you just bully the problem, or attack it. I mean that you accept it, live with it, breathe it, and whittle it until you've achieved your goal. Once you start looking forward to your interactions with the problem, you're leaning into it.]

Some people choose to lean *away* from the problems that nag them at home or at work. They avoid them, minimize them, or criticize the cause. Put as little into it as possible and maybe it will go away.

And sometimes, a problem is so nasty or overwhelming that you just run away.

I'm a big fan of the first approach. And sometimes, quitting isn't such a bad idea. The second approach, alas, is the one that many of us end up with by default, and the one that's least likely to pay off.

Making Art

My definition of art contains three elements:

1. Art is made by a human being.
2. Art is created to have an impact, to change someone else.
3. Art is a gift. You can sell the souvenir, the canvas, the recording . . . but the idea itself is free, and the generosity is a critical part of making art.

By my definition, most art has nothing to do with oil paint or marble. Art is what we're doing when we do our best work.

Failure, Success, and Neither

The math is magical: you can pile up lots of failures and still keep rolling, but you need only one juicy success to build a career.

The killer is the category called "neither." If you spend your days avoiding failure by doing not much worth criticizing, you'll never have a shot at success. Avoiding the thing that's easy to survive keeps you from encountering the very thing you're after.

And yet we market and work and connect and create as if just one failure might be the end of us.

Have You Thought About Your Margin?

Gross margin is an often confusing concept but a powerful tool in figuring out how to market your business (and decide what to make, whom to hire, and how to fund it). Few people understand it, while others use a definition I don't find very useful.

I like to think of margin as the money left over after you've paid the direct costs for making an item, the last one of the day.

If you run a pizza place and a large pie costs $10, your gross margin is $10 minus the cost of flour, water, yeast, tomatoes, and cheese. And maybe salt. That's it.

If you're not operating at capacity, the key word here is margin. The marginal profit of one more pizza is high. You've already paid for the rent, the oven, the sign, the ad in the Yellow Pages, the hourly wage, the uniforms, all of it. Whether you sell that last pizza of the day or not, all those costs are fixed. So if your ingredients cost $2, your gross margin is $8.

This concept is vital to understand because it tells you how flexible you can be with a promotional strategy. Some people (like me) prefer businesses with high gross margins, even if we're less busy. Others make billions on companies that run on the tiniest of margins.

If someone offers to run a coupon in the Welcome Wagon envelope that goes to new residents, and the rules are "one per customer, new customers only," and the coupon offers a large pizza for $2, is it worth it for you to run it? That's 80% off! Surely this is too expensive. You can't afford 80% off.

On the margin, of course you can. You got a new customer for free. Unless your store is at capacity, with people waiting in line, one more pizza sold at cost is a great way to build your business (unless there are too many coupons and unless it changes your positioning as a high-end place, but that's a story for a different day).

You probably already guessed this part: for digital goods, the gross margin is 100%. Cell phone calls? The same.

One more customer costs you nothing. That doesn't mean you should price accordingly, but it surely means you should understand how high your margins are.

The Circles (No More Strangers)

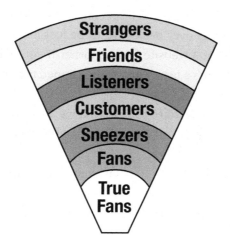

It's so tempting to seek out more strangers.

More strangers to pitch your business, your candidate, your non-profit, your blog. Finding more strangers means more upside and not so much downside. It means growth.

The problem is that strangers are difficult to convert. And the other problem is that they're expensive to reach. And the hardest problem is that we're running out of strangers.

Consider this hierarchy: Strangers, Friends, Listeners, Customers, Sneezers, Fans, and True Fans. One true fan is worth perhaps 10,000 times as much as a stranger. And yet if you're in search of strangers, odds are you're going to mistreat a true fan in order to seduce yet another stranger who probably won't reward you much.

Let's say a marketer has $10,000 to spend. Is it better to acquire new customers at $2,000 each (advertising is expensive) or spend $10 a customer to absolutely delight and overwhelm 1,000 true fans?

Or consider a nonprofit looking to generate more donations. Is it better to embrace the core donor base and work with them to host small parties with their friends to spread the word, or would hiring a PR firm to get a bunch of articles placed pay off more efficiently?

We're the Same, We're the Same, We're . . .

Take a look at just about any industry with many competitors—colleges, hotels, sedans, accounting firms (especially accounting firms).

The websites bend over backward to be just like all the others. You can't identify one hotel website from another if you delete the name of the hotel (unless there's a beach or a snow-capped mountain in the background).

Sometimes, we try so hard to fit in that we give consumers no choice but to seek out the cheapest. After all, if everything is the same, why not buy what's cheap and close?

How about a site that says "here's why we're different"—and means it?

(Easy to read this and nod your head, but what does your résumé look like?)

Six Things About Deadlines

1. People don't like deadlines. They mean a decision, shipping, and risk. They force us to decide.
2. Deadlines work. Products that are about to disappear, auctions that are about to end, tickets that are about to sell out—they create forward motion.

3. Deadlines make people do dumb things. Every time I offer a free digital document or an educational event that has a deadline, I can guarantee that I will hear from several (or dozens of) people with ornate, well-considered, and thoughtful arguments as to why they missed the deadline. Never mind that they had two weeks; the last fifteen minutes are all they are concerned with. If it's important enough to spend an hour complaining about, it's certainly important enough to spend four minutes to just do it in the first place.

4. Deadlines give you the opportunity to beat the rush. Handing in work just a little bit early is a surefire way to tell a positive story and get the attention you seek. The chart below tracks the day (out of ten) that I received each of the more than a thousand applications for the free nano MBA program. Want to guess which day's applications got the most attention from me?

5. When we set ourselves a deadline, we're incredibly lax about sticking to it. So don't (set it for yourself, in your head, informally). Write it down instead. Hand it to someone else. Publicize it. Associate it with an external reward or punishment. If you don't make the deadline, your friend gives the $20 you loaned her to a cause you disagree with.

6. They have a lousy name. Call them live-lines instead. That's what they are.

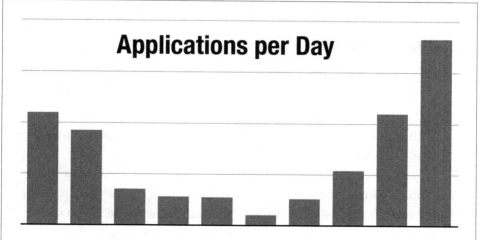

Applications per Day

Actual application rate for a ten-day window. What day would have gotten you the most attention?

Key takeaway: deadlines are a cheap and useful tool to use for yourself (and others) to make a decision and to ship.

Fear of Shipping

Shipping is fraught with risk and danger.

Every time you raise your hand, send an email, launch a product, or make a suggestion, you're exposing yourself to criticism. Not just criticism, but the negative consequences that come with wasting money, annoying someone in power, or making a fool of yourself.

It's no wonder we're afraid to ship.

It's not clear you have much choice, though. A life spent curled in a ball and hiding in the corner might seem less risky, but in fact it's certain to lead to ennui and eventually failure.

Since you're going to ship anyway, then, the question is: Why bother indulging your fear?

In a long-distance race, everyone gets tired. The winner is the runner who figures out *where to put the tired,* figures out how to store it away until after the race is over. Sure, he's tired. Everyone is. That's not the point. The point is to run.

Same thing is true for shipping, I think. Everyone is afraid. Where do you put the fear?

"This Better Work"

. . . is probably the opposite of "this might work."

"This better work" is the thinking of safety, of proven, of beyond blame.

"This might work," on the other hand, is the thinking of art, innovation, and insight.

If you spend all day working on stuff that better work, you back yourself into a corner, because you'll never have the space or resources to throw some "might" stuff into the mix. On the other hand, if you spend all your time on stuff that might work, you'll never need to dream up something that better work, because your art will have paid off long ago.

Getting to Scale: Direct Marketing Vs. Mass-Market Thinking

A mass marketer needs to reach the masses, and to do it in many ways, simultaneously. The mass marketer needs retail outlets and fliers and a website and public relations and TV ads and more, more, more, and then . . . bam . . . critical mass is reached and success occurs.

Best Buy is a mass marketer, but so are Microsoft and the Red Cross. Ubiquity, once achieved, brings them revenue, which advances the cycle, so they reach scale.

The direct marketer, on the other hand, must get it right in the small. That pitch letter can be tested on 100 houses and if it gets a 2% response rate, then it can be mailed to 100,000 houses with confidence. That business-to-business sales pitch can be honed on one or two or three prospects, and then when it works, it can be taught to dozens or hundreds of other salespeople.

The key distinction is *when* you know it's going to work. The mass marketer doesn't know until the end. The direct marketer knows in the beginning.

The mass marketer is betting on thousands of tiny cues, little clues, and unrecorded (but vital) conversations. The direct marketer is measuring conversion rates from the first day.

That's the reason we often default to acting like mass marketers. We're putting off the day of reckoning, betting on the miracle around the corner, spending our time and energy on the early steps without the downside of admitting failure to the boss.

Of course, just because it's our default doesn't mean it's right. Business-to-business marketing is almost always better if you treat it like direct marketing. Most websites that buy Google ads and measure conversion confront the truth every day as well.

Same with nonprofit fund-raising. As well as marketing goods and services to the bottom of the pyramid, to people who live in villages where mass media and mass distribution are difficult and have little impact.

Get it right for ten people before you rush around scaling up to a thousand. It's far less romantic than spending money at the start, but it's the reliable, proven way to get to scale if you care enough to do the work.

15% Changes Everything

When a newspaper loses 15% of its readers or 15% of its advertisers, it goes out of business. There are still people who want to read it, still people who want to advertise, but it's gone.

When a technology company increases its sales by 15%, profits will double. The sales line doesn't have to increase that much for profits to soar.

It's so tempting to head for green fields with a new thing, a new market, a new business. But in fact, 15% right here and right now might be exactly what you need.

Getting Unstuck: Solving the Perfect Problem

The only problems you have left are the perfect ones. The imperfect ones, the ones with clearly evident solutions—well, if they were important, you've solved them already.

It's the perfect problems that keep us stuck.

Perfect because they have constraints, unbendable constraints, constraints that keep us trapped. I hate my job, I need this job, there's no way to quit, to get a promotion, or to get a new boss, no way to move, my family is in town, etc.

We're human, that's what we do—we erect boundaries, constraints we can't ease, and we get trapped.

Or perhaps it's your product or service or brand. Our factory is only organized to make X, but the market doesn't want X as much, or there is regulation, or a new competitor is now offering X at half the price and the board won't do anything, etc.

There's no way to solve the perfect problem because every solution involves breaking an unbreakable constraint.

And there's your solution.

The way to solve the perfect problem is to make it imperfect. Don't just bend one of the constraints, eliminate it. Shut down the factory. Walk away from the job. Change your product completely. Ignore the board.

If the only alternative is slow and painful failure, the way to get unstuck is to blow up a constraint, deal with the pain, and then run forward. Fast.

It's (Always) Too Soon to Know for Sure

The cost of being first is higher than it's ever been.

It's entirely possible that you're racing.

Racing to the market with a new product or a news story or a decision or an innovation. The race keeps getting faster, doesn't it?

If you're racing, you better figure out what to do about the times that you don't know for sure, because more and more of your inputs are going to be tenuous, speculative, and possibly wrong. Day traders have always understood this—all they do is trade on uncertainty. But you, too, if you're racing, are going to have to make decisions on less-than-perfect information.

Given that fact, what are you going to do about it? I think figuring that out is worth a few cycles of your time.

Is it smart to blog on a rumor?

Worth dropping everything and panicking because of a news alert?

Should you hire someone based on information you're not sure of?

What about changing your website (your pricing, your layout . . .) based on analytics that might not be absolutely correct? How long are you willing to wait?

Given that you will never know *everything* for sure (unless you're opting out of the race), some of the issues are:

- What's the cost of waiting one more day?
- Are you waiting (or not waiting) because of the cost of being wrong, or because loud people are yelling at you?

- Is the risk of being wrong unreasonably amplified by part of the market or your team? What if you ignore them and focus on customers that matter?
- And have you thought about the costs of waiting *too* long? If you don't, you'll probably end up last.

Have you noticed how often stock analysts quoted in the news are wrong? Wrong about new products, wrong about management decisions, wrong about the future of a company? In fact, they're almost always first and almost always wrong.

Rule of thumb: being first helps in the short run. Being a little more right than the masses ultimately pays off in the long run. Being last is the worst of all three.

A few people care a lot about scoops. Most of us, though, care about alert people making insightful decisions. Decide whom you're trying to please, and then ship.

Competition

The number-one reason people give me for giving up on something great is, "someone else is already doing that."

Or, parsed another way, "my idea is not brand new." Or even, "Oh, no, now we'll have competition."

Two big pieces of news for you:

1. Competition validates you. It creates a category. It permits the sale to be "this or that," not "yes or no." And "this or that" is a much easier sale to make. Competition also makes decisions about pricing easier because you have someone to compare against and lean on.
2. There are six billion people in the world. Even if your market is handmade spoke shaves for left-handed woodworkers, there are more people in your market than you can ever hope to track down.

There are lots of good reasons to abandon a project. Having a little competition is not one of them. Even if it's Google you're up against.

Efficiency Is Free

Philip Crosby wrote a seminal book (*Quality Is Free*) in which he argued that it's cheaper to build things right the first time than it is to fix them later. Obvious now, but heresy in Detroit in 1980. Quality quickly became not just a better way to manufacture, but a marketing benefit as well. Not only was quality cheaper to make, but it was cheaper to sell.

I'm struck by the thought that we need a new book—call it *Efficiency Is Free*.

It's cheaper to build carpets that don't create poison gas than it is to do the easy thing and let people suffer later. It's cheaper to build an eight-passenger car that gets 30 miles per gallon than it is to suffer the consequences of the 12-mile-per-gallon Suburban. It's cheaper to design smaller, lighter, and recyclable shipping containers *once* than it is to buy and hassle with billions of foam peanuts in the long run.

So why doesn't everyone do this? For the same reason the quality revolution took a full generation to take hold—it costs more *right now*. It takes planning right now. It requires change right now.

Right now will always be difficult. But efficiency is still free.

Living with Doubt

. . . is almost always more profitable than living with certainty.

People don't like doubt, so they pay money and give up opportunities to avoid it. Entrepreneurship is largely about living with doubt, as is creating just about any sort of art.

If you need reassurance, you're giving up quite a bit to get it.

On the other hand, if you can get in the habit of seeking out uncertainty, you'll have developed a great instinct.

Do Elite Trappings Create Success? (Causation Vs. Correlation)

Does a ski trip to Aspen make you a successful bond trader, or do successful bond traders go skiing in Aspen?

It's college acceptance season, and worth considering an often overlooked question:

Do people who are on track to become successful go to elite colleges, buy elite cars, engage in other elite behaviors? (I'm defining elite as something scarce and thus expensive.)

or

Does attending these colleges or engaging in these behaviors make you successful?

It matters, because if you're buying the elite label as a shortcut to success, you might be surprised at what you get.

There are certainly exceptions (for professions that are very focused on a credential, and for the economically disadvantaged), but generally, most elite products, like college, are overrated as life changers.

It turns out that merely getting into Harvard is as good an indicator of future success as actually going. It turns out that being the sort of person that can invest the effort, conquer fear, and/or raise the money to capture some of the elite trappings of visible success is what drives success, not the other way around.

The learning matters a great deal, and especially the focused effort behind it. The brand name of the institution, not so much.

Don't worry so much if some overworked admissions officer or grizzled journalist fails to pick you. It might mean more that you *could* go, not that you do.

Does advertising during the Super Bowl make your brand successful? I think it's more likely that successful brands advertise during the Super Bowl.

A Culture of Testing

Netflix tests everything. They're very proud that they alpha- and beta-test interactions, offerings, pricing, everything. It's almost enough to get you to believe that rigorous testing is the key to success.

Except they didn't test the model of renting DVDs by mail for a monthly fee.

And they didn't test the model of having an innovative corporate culture.

And they didn't test the idea of betting the company on a switch to online delivery.

The three biggest assets of the company weren't tested, because they couldn't be.

Sure, go ahead and test what's testable. But the real victories come when you have the guts to launch the untestable.

On Pricing Power

If you're not getting paid what you're worth, there are only two possible reasons:

1. People don't know what you're worth, or
2. You're not (currently) worth as much as you believe.

The first situation can't happen unless you permit it to. If you're undervalued, then you have a communication problem, one that you can solve by telling accurate stories that resonate.

Far more likely, though, is the second problem. If there are reasonable substitutes for your work, and those substitutes are seen as cheaper, then you're not going to get the work. "Worth," in this case, means "What does it cost to get something like that if something like that is what I want?"

A cheaper substitute might mean buying nothing. Personal coaches, for example, usually sell against this alternative. It's not a matter of finding a *cheaper* coach, it's more about having no coach at all. Same with live music. People don't go to cheaper concerts, they just don't value the concert enough to go at all.

And so we often find ourselves stuck, matching the other guy's price or, worse, racing to the bottom to be cheaper. Cheaper is the last refuge of the marketer unable to invent a better product and tell a better story.

The goal, no matter what you sell, is to be seen as *irreplaceable, essential*, and *priceless*. If you are all three, then you have pricing power. When the price charged is up to you, when you have the power to set the price, there is a line out the door and you can use pricing as a signaling mechanism, not merely as a way to make a living.

Of course, the realization of what it takes to create value might break your heart, because it means you have to specialize, take risks, create art, leave a positive impact, and adopt generosity in all you do. It means that you have to develop extraordinary expertise and that you are almost always hanging way out of the boat, about to fall out.

The pricing-power position in the market is coveted and valuable. The ability to have the power to set a price is at the heart of what it means to do business profitably, so of course there is a never-ending competition for pricing power.

The curse of the Internet is that it provides competitive information, which makes pricing power ever more difficult to exercise. On the other hand, the benefit of the Internet is that once you have pricing power, the list of people who want to pay for your irreplaceable, essential, and priceless contribution will get even longer.

Insist on the Coin Flip

Very often, we're challenged to make decisions with too little information. Sometimes, there's *no* information—merely noise. The question is: How will you decide?

Consider the challenge we faced when setting the pricing for a brand of software we were launching in 1986. It was the biggest project to date of my short career, and it represented more than a year of work by forty people. Should these games cost $29, $34, or $39 each? My bosses and I had one day to finalize our decision for the sales force.

Unlike Harvard case studies, we had no graphs, no history, no data. We were the first in the category and there was nothing significant to go on. The meeting was held late on a Thursday. In addition to my newly minted Stanford MBA, we also had two MBAs from Harvard, one from Tuck, and another, I think from Wharton, in the room.

We talked for an hour and then did the only intelligent thing—we flipped a coin. To be sure we had it right, we double-checked and went with two out of three. The only mistake we made was wasting an hour pontificating and arguing before we flipped.

This is also the way we should settle closely contested elections. We know that the error rate for counting ballots is some percentage—say it's .01%. Whenever the margin is less than the error rate, we should flip. Instead of wasting months and millions in court, we should insist on the flip. Anything else is a waste of time and money.

Or consider the dilemma of the lucky high school student with five colleges to choose from. UVM or Oberlin or Bowdoin or Wesleyan or who knows what famous schools. Once you've narrowed it down and all you're left with is a hunch, once there are no data points to give you a rational way to pick, stop worrying. Stop analyzing. Don't waste $4,000 and a month of anxiety visiting the schools again. The data you'll collect (one lucky meeting, one good day of weather) is just not relevant to making an intelligent decision. Any non-fact-based research is designed to help you feel better about your decision, not to help you make a more effective decision.

One last example: If you know from experience that checking job references in your industry gives you basically random results (some people exaggerate, some lie out of spite), then why are you checking?

When there isn't enough data, when there can't be enough data, *insist on the flip.*

By refusing to lie to yourself, by not telling yourself a fable to make the decision easier, you'll understand quite clearly when you're winging it.

Once you embrace this idea, it's a lot easier not to second-guess your decisions—and if you're applying to college, you'll free up enough time to write a novel before you even matriculate.

How to Fail

There are some significant misunderstandings about failure. A common one, similar to one we seem to have about death, is that if you don't plan for it, it won't happen.

All of us fail. Successful people fail often and, worth noting, learn more from that failure than everyone else does.

Two habits that don't help:

- Getting good at avoiding blame and casting doubt
- Not signing up for visible and important projects

While it may seem like these two choices increase your chances for survival or even promotion, in fact they merely insulate you from worthwhile failures.

I think it's worth noting that my definition of failure does not include being unlucky enough to be involved in a project in which random external events kept you from succeeding. That's the cost of showing up, not the definition of failure.

Identifying these random events, of course, is part of the art of doing ever better. Many of the things we'd like to blame as being out of our control are in fact avoidable or can be planned around.

Here are six random ideas that will help you fail better, more often, and with an inevitably positive upside:

1. Whenever possible, take on specific projects.
2. Make detailed promises about what success looks like and when it will occur.
3. Engage others in your projects. If you fail, they should be involved and know that they will fail with you.
4. Be really clear about what the true risks are. Ignore the vivid, unlikely, and ultimately non-fatal risks that take so much of your focus away.
5. Concentrate your energy and will on the elements of the project that you have influence on, and ignore external events that you can't avoid or change.
6. When you fail (and you will), be clear about it, call it by name, and outline specifically what you learned so you won't make the same mistake twice. People who blame others for failure will never be good at failing, because they've never done it.

If that list frightened you, you might be getting to the nub of the matter. If that list feels like the sort of thing you'd like your freelancers, employees, or even bosses to adopt, then perhaps it's resonating as a plan going forward for you.

Busker's Dilemma (Busker's Delight)

If you play music on the street, with a bucket for donations, every song has to be a showstopper.

No chance for interludes or pauses or moments where you build up for the big finish. If the passerby doesn't stop, it's all for naught.

So your music changes. You're always at level 11, always jamming it, always pushing in the moment.

Online, we're all buskers. For a while, anyway.

Once someone has stopped walking and started to listen, you have a choice. You can take that person on a journey, forgo the next stranger and instead seduce the one you've got . . .

Or you can keep pushing for more attention from more people.

Both options work. The challenge is in making a choice, your choice, a choice based on why you're doing the work in the first place. It's not up to them, it's up to you.

Looking for the Right Excuse

This is the first warning sign that a project is in trouble. Sometimes it even begins before the project does.

Quietly, our subconscious starts looking around for an excuse, deniability, and someone to blame. It gives us confidence and peace of mind. [It's much easier to be calm when the police car appears in your rearview mirror if you have an excuse handy.]

Amazingly, we often look for the excuse before we even accept the project. We say to ourselves, "well, I can start this, and if it doesn't work perfectly, I can point out it was the . . ." Then, as the team ramps up, bosses appear and events occur (or not), we continually add to and refine our excuse list, reminding ourselves of all the factors that were out of our control. Decades ago, when I used to sell by phone, I often found myself describing why I was unable to close this particular sale—and realized that I was articulating these reasons while the phone was still ringing.

People who have a built-in, all-purpose excuse (middle child syndrome, wrong astrology sign, some slight at the hands of the system long ago) often end up failing—they have an excuse ready to go, so it's easier to back off when the going is rough.

Here's an alternative to the excuse-driven life: What happens if you relentlessly avoid looking for excuses at all?

Instead of people seeking excuses, the successful project is filled with people who are obsessed with *avoiding* excuses. If you relentlessly work to avoid opportunities to use your ability to blame, you may never actually need to blame anyone. If you're not pulled over by the cop, no need to blame the speedometer, right?

The Hard Part (One of Them)

A guy asked his friend, the writer David Foster Wallace,

"Say, Dave, how'd y'get t'be so dang smart?"

His answer:

"I did the reading."

No one said the preparation part was fun, but yes, it's important. I wonder why we believe we can skip it and still be so dang smart.

Are You a Scientist?

Scientists make predictions, and predicting the future is far more valuable than explaining the past.

Ask a physicist what will happen if you fire a projectile like *this* in *that* direction, and she'll know. Ask a chemist what happens if you mix x and y, and you'll get the right answer. Even quantum-mechanics mechanics can give you probabilities that work out in the long run.

Analysts who come up with plausible explanations for what just happened don't help us as much, because it's not always easy to turn those explanations into useful action.

Take the layout of Craigslist. Just about any competent Web designer would have predicted that it would fail. Too clunky, undesigned, too many links, not slick or trustworthy. Or consider a new R&B artist, or a brand-new beverage.

After the fact, it's so easy to say, "of course it worked . . ." and then make up a reason for the success of whatever it is that just succeeded.

The practice, then, is to start making predictions. In writing. You don't have to share them in public, but the habit will push you to understand your instincts and to sharpen your ability to see what works (and what doesn't) without the easy out of having to explain what already happened.

Look at start-ups or political campaigns or new products or ad campaigns . . . plenty of places to practice your predicting skills.

I predict you'll learn two things:

1. It's really difficult to make predictions, because success often appears to be random.
2. Based on #1, it's probably smart for you to initiate more projects that aren't guaranteed winners, because most winners aren't guaranteed.

And a bonus: the more you practice your predictions, the better you'll get at discerning where the science is.

The Taskmaster Premium

How much are you paying for the privilege of having someone else tell you what to do?

Example: if you go to your gym and work out for an hour, the cost of that session is zero.

Hire a personal trainer to follow you around and give you instructions and that's $70.

If you take a job as a freelance writer doing short service pieces on assignment to a local paper, you might earn $3 an hour. Which is about 97% less than you'd earn if, like some writers, you dreamed up amazing pieces, wrote them on spec, and turned them into blogs, books, or films. This writer doesn't wait to get hired. He hires himself.

If you do publicity for an agency, working hard and precisely following the VP's and the client's instructions, you might earn $25 an hour. On the other hand, when you do your own PR, when you build a sensation and turn it into a following, you might earn many times that. (And enjoy it more.)

Work for a coal mine and make minimum wage. Discover a coal mine and never need to work again.

We happily give up our freedom and our income in exchange for having someone else take responsibility for telling us what to do next.

How much are you giving up?

How Do You Know When It's Done?

Of course it's not done. It's never done.

That's not the right question.

The question is: When is it good enough?

Good enough, for those that seek perfection, is what we call it when it's sufficient to surpass the standards we've set. Anything beyond good enough is called stalling and a waste of time.

If you don't like your definition of "good enough," then feel free to change that, but the goal before shipping is merely that. Not perfect.

Bypassing the Leap

Every now and then, a creative act comes out of nowhere—a giant leap, a new way of thinking apparently woven out of a brand-new material.

Most of the time, though, creativity is the act of reassembling many elements that are already known. That's why domain knowledge is so critical.

The screenwriter who understands how to take the build that went into the classic Greg Morris episode of *The Dick Van Dyke Show* and integrate it with the Maurice Chevalier riff from the Marx Brothers . . . Or the way Moby took his encyclopedic knowledge of music and turned it into a record that sold millions . . . If you don't have awareness and an analytical understanding of what worked before, you can't build on it.

That's one of the reasons that the recent incarnation of the Palm failed. The fact that the president of the company had never used an iPhone left them only one out: to make a magical leap.

It's not enough to be aware of the domain you're working in—you need to *understand* it. Noticing things and being curious about how they work is the single most common trait I see in creative people. Once you can break the components down, you can put them back together into something brand new.

Run Your Own Race

The rearview mirror is one of the most effective motivational tools ever created.

There's no doubt that many people speed up in the face of competition. We ask, "how'd the rest of the class do?" We listen for someone breathing down our necks. And we discover that competition sometimes brings out our best.

There's a downside, though. Years ago, during my last long-distance swim (across Long Island Sound . . . cold water, jellyfish, the whole nine yards), the competitiveness was pretty thick. On the boat to the starting line, there were hundreds of swimmers, stretching, bragging, prancing, and working themselves up. By the time we hit the water, everyone was swimming someone else's race. The start was an explosion of ego and adrenaline. Twenty minutes later, half the field was exhausted, with three hours left to go.

If you're going to count on the competition to bring out your best work, you've surrendered control over your most important asset. Real achievement comes from racing ahead when no one else sees a path— and holding back when the rush isn't going where you want to go.

If you're dependent on competition, then you're counting on the quality of those that show up to determine how well you'll do. Worse, you've signed up for a career of faux death matches as the only way to do your best work.

Self-motivation is and always will be the most important form of motivation. Driving with your eyes on the rearview mirror is exhausting. It's easier than ever to measure your performance against others, but if it's not helping you with your mission, stop.

First, Make Rice

Fledgling sushi chefs spend months (sometimes years) doing nothing but making the rice for the head chef.

If the rice isn't right, it really doesn't matter what else you do, you're not going to be able to serve great sushi.

Most of the blogging and writing that goes on about marketing assumes that you already know how to make the rice. It assumes that you understand copywriting and graphic design, that you've got experience in measuring direct response rates, that you've made hundreds of sales calls, that you have an innate empathy for what your customers want and think, and that you know how to make a compelling case for what you believe.

Too often, we quickly jump ahead to the new thing, failing to get good enough at the important thing.

Lifetime Value of a Customer/Cost per Customer

Two things every business and nonprofit needs to know:

- How much does it cost you to get one new customer?
- On average, what's that customer worth during the relationship you have with her?

The Internet revolutionizes both sides of the equation.

Facebook and Twitter are marvels because for each company, the cost of a new customer is vanishingly close to zero. When you can get people into a relationship for nothing, you don't need to make much money on each one to be delighted with the outcome.

Note that the ongoing, digital connection with a customer can dramatically increase the lifetime profit as well. Netflix is far more likely to have a higher average lifetime value than the local video store. Musicians are moving from making a dollar per listener from CDs to making hundreds of dollars per true fan from collectibles and concert tickets—things that musicians can deliver only because they know who their best customers are.

On the other hand, legions of unsophisticated marketers are getting both sides of the equation wrong.

They invest a lot in hoopla, spin, and hype to get strangers to notice them (once), making the cost of a connection high, and then, once they borrow a little attention, they put everything into a one-shot transaction, which few people engage in. And those that do engage, create little value because the permission asset is then discarded.

Dates, not singles bars. Subscriptions, not Veg-O-Matics.

Declaring Victory

Whenever you start a project, you should have a plan for finishing it.

One outcome is to declare victory, to find that moment when you have satisfied your objectives and reached a goal.

The other outcome, which feels like a downer but is almost as good, is to declare failure, to realize that you've run out of useful string and it's time to move on. I think the intentional act of declaring becomes an essential moment of learning, a spot in time when you consider inputs and outputs and adjust your strategy for next time.

If you are unable to declare, then you're going to slog, and instead of starting new projects based on what you've learned, you'll merely end up trapped. I'm not suggesting that you flit. A project might last a decade or a generation, but if it is to be a project, it must have an end.

One of the challenges of an open-ended war or the Occupy movement is that they are projects in which failure or victory wasn't understood at the beginning. While you may be tempted to be situational about this, to know it when you see it, to decide as you go, it's far more powerful and effective to define victory or failure in advance.

Declare one or the other, but declare.

Organized Bravery

The purpose of the modern organization is to make it easy and natural and expected for people to take risks. To lean out of the boat. To be human.

Alas, most organizations do the opposite. They institutionalize cowardice. They give their people cover, a place to hide, a chance to say, "that's not my job."

Our organizations are filled with people not only eager to dehumanize those they serve, but apparently instructed to do so. In the name of shareholder value or team play or not rocking the boat . . .

During times of change, the only organizations that thrive are those that are eager to interact and to change as well. And that happens only when individuals take brave steps forward.

Giving your team cover for their cowardice is foolish. Give them a platform for bravery instead.

All Artists Are Self-Taught

Techniques and skill and even a point of view are often handed down, formally or not. It's easier to get started if you're taught, of course.

But art, the new, the ability to connect the dots and to make an impact—sooner or later, that can come only from one who creates, not from a teacher and not from a book.

Volatility and Value

The fine-art market continues to generate headline-making sales. This year, paintings by Warhol and Munch are expected to sell for more than $50 million each.

What makes a painting famous enough to sell for that much money?

Consider the Mona Lisa. The reason that it's the most famous (and arguably the most valuable) painting in the world is that it was stolen in 1911. (Even Pablo Picasso was questioned as a possible suspect.) For two years, it was a media sensation—precisely when newspapers were coming into their own. For two years it was front-page news. As the world media-ized itself, we needed an icon to stand for "famous painting" and the Mona Lisa was it.

Media cycles have gotten shorter and shorter since then, and ironically, it was Andy himself who predicted that one day we'd all be famous for 15 minutes. The thing is, being famous for 15 minutes isn't sufficient to make your painting worth $80 million.

Andy never had his own TV show, wouldn't have had the most viral video on YouTube, and wasn't focused on the fast pump of fame. It turns out that getting big fast (and then fading) doesn't build a reputation that pays.

Media volatility makes more people and more ideas famous for ever shorter periods of time. What the fine-art market shows us, though, is that real value isn't created by this volatile fame. Consistently showing up on the radar of the right audience is more highly prized than is reaching the masses once, then done. This strategy works for every career, even if you've never touched a brush.

Avoiding False Metrics

At the local gym, it's not unusual to see hardcore members contorting themselves to fool the StairMaster machine into giving them good numbers. If you use your arms, you can lift yourself off the machine and trick it into thinking you're working yourself really hard.

Of course, you end up with cramped shoulders and a lousy workout, but who cares, the machine said you burned 600 calories . . .

The same thing happens with authors who put themselves and their readers through the wringer to get a spot on the *New York Times* bestseller list. Danielle LaPorte built a huge campaign around putting her book, *The Fire Starter Sessions*, on the list. She succeeded in selling a huge number of hardcover copies in a week (far more than most other books), but she didn't make the list because of a secret editorial decision that she's not privy to. At the same time, other authors who do a better job of decoding the secrets end up on the list with far fewer books sold.

The point isn't that the list is crooked and unfair (though it is). It measures how good you are at getting on the list, not how many copies of the book your readers buy. The reason to avoid the false metric is that it messes with your shoulders, with the way you approach the work, with the real reason you did the project in the first place.

A third example: many car brands now go to obsessive lengths to contact recent car buyers and ask them to rate their buying experience on a scale of one to five. The car manufacturers use these rankings to allocate cars to dealers, ostensibly to reward the good dealerships. Of course, the dealers are in on the game, and instead of doing the intended thing—providing a great experience—all they do is work hard to get people to give them a five when a drone in a call center makes the call. Many of them will clearly state to a customer, "If anything has happened today that would prevent you from giving us a five when they call, please tell us right now."

The system of false metrics doesn't create a better buying experience, it creates a threatened customer with pressure to give a five.

And my last example: the Arbitron radio rating system used to rely on diaries in which it asked radio listeners to write down which station they had listened to during the day. Several consultants came along with a service that they guaranteed would raise the ratings of any station that hired them. The secret? Repeat the station's call letters twice as often. It turned out that more repetition led to better recall, which led to more people writing down the call letters, which led to "better" ratings.

A useful metric is both accurate (in that it measures what it says it measures) and aligned with your goals. Making your numbers go up (any numbers—your BMI, your blood sugar, your customer service ratings) is pointless if the numbers aren't related to why you went to work this morning.

The Flipping Point

When people talk about "the tipping point," they often misunderstand the concept in Malcolm [Gladwell's] book. They're actually talking about the flipping point.

The tipping point is the sum total of many individuals buzzing about something (or, slightly more accurately, the point at which everything can change, all at once, because of the sheer number of individuals buzzing). But for an individual to start buzzing, something has to change in that person's mind. Something flips from boredom or ignorance to excitement or anger.

It starts when the story of a brand or a person or a store or an experience flips in your head and it goes from good to bad, or from ignored to beloved. The flipping point doesn't represent the sum of public conversations; it's the outcome of an activated *internal* conversation.

It's easy to wish and hope for your project to tip, for it to magically become the hot thing. But that won't happen if you can't seduce and entrance an individual and then another.

Before we can reach the tipping point, someone has to flip. And then someone else. And then a hundred more someones.

We resist incremental improvement in our offerings and our stories because it just doesn't seem likely that one good interaction or one tiny alteration can possibly lead to a significant amount of flipping. And we're right—it won't. The flipping point (for an individual) is almost always achieved after a consistent series of almost invisible actions that create a brand-new whole.

And the reason it's so difficult? Because you're operating on faith. You need to invest and apparently overinvest (time and money and effort) until you see the results. And most of your competitors (lucky for you) give up long before they reach the point where it pays off.

How to Make Money Online

1. The first step is to stop Googling things like "how to make money online." Not because you shouldn't want to make money online, but because the stuff you're going to find by doing that is going to help you lose money online. Sort of like asking a casino owner how to make money in Vegas.

2. Don't pay anyone for simple and proven instructions on how to achieve this goal. In particular, don't pay anyone to teach you how to write or sell manuals or ebooks about how to make money online.

3. Get rich slow.

4. Focus on the scarce resource online: attention. If you try to invent a way to take cheap attention and turn it into cash, you will fail. The attention you want isn't cheap, it's difficult to get via SEO, and it rarely scales. Instead, figure out how to earn expensive attention.

5. In addition to attention, focus on trust. Trust is even more scarce than attention.

6. Don't worry so much about the "online" part. Instead, figure out how to create value. The online part will take care of itself.

7. Don't quit your day job. Start evenings and weekends and figure it out with small failures.

8. Build a public reputation, a good one, and be sure that you deserve it and that it will hold up to scrutiny.

9. Obsessively specialize. No niche is too small if it's yours.

10. Connect the disconnected.

11. Lead.

12. Build an online legacy that increases in value daily.

13. Make money offline. If you can figure out how to create value face-to-face, it's a lot easier to figure out how to do the same digitally. The Web isn't magic, it's merely efficient.

14. Become the best in the world at something that people value. Easier said than done, but worth more than you might think.

15. Hang out with people who aren't looking for shortcuts. Learn from them.

16. Fail. Fail often and fail cheaply. This is the very best gift the Web has given to people who want to bootstrap their way into a new business.

17. Make money in the small and then relentlessly scale.

18. Don't chase yesterday's online fad.

19. Think big, act with intention, and don't get bogged down in personalities. If it's not on your agenda, why are you wasting time on it?

20. Learn. Ceaselessly. Learn to code, to write persuasively, to understand new technologies, to bring out the best in your team, to find underused resources, and to spot patterns.

21. This is not a zero-sum game. The more you add to your community, the bigger your piece gets.

The Unforgiving Arithmetic of the Funnel

One percent.

That's how many you get if you're lucky. One percent of the subscribers to the *Times* read an article and take action. One percent of the visitors to a website click a button to find out more. One percent of the people in a classroom are sparked by an idea and go do something about it.

And then!

And then, of that 1%, perhaps 1% go ahead and take more action, or recruit others, or write a book or volunteer. One percent of one percent.

No wonder advertisers have to run so many ads. Most of us ignore most of them. No wonder it's so hard to convert a digital browsing audience into a real-world paying one—most people are in too much of a hurry to read and think and pause and then do.

The common mistake is to reflexively come to the conclusion that the only option is to make more noise, to put more attention into the top of the funnel. The thinking goes that if a big audience is getting you mediocre results, a huge audience is the answer. Alas, getting a huge audience is more difficult than the alternatives.

A few ways to deal with the funnel:

- Acknowledge that it's there. Don't assume that a big audience is going to easily convert to action.
- Work to measure your losses. Figure out where in the process you're losing interest and clicks or the other behaviors you seek.
- If you can, remove steps. Each step costs you dearly.
- Treat different people differently. If you alter the funnel to maximize interest by the wandering masses, you may very well miss the chance to convert the focused few.

How to Succeed

You don't need all of these, and some are mutually exclusive (while others are not). And most don't work, don't scale, or can't be arranged:

1. Be very focused on your goal and work on it daily.
2. Go to college with someone who makes it big and then hires you.
3. Be born with significant and unique talent.
4. Practice every day.
5. Network your way to the top by inviting yourself from one lunch to another, trading favors as you go.
6. Quietly do your job day in and day out until someone notices you and gives you the promotion you deserve.
7. Do the emotional labor of working on things that others fear.
8. Notice things, turn them into insights, and then relentlessly turn those insights into projects that resonate.
9. Hire a great PR firm and get a lot of publicity.

10. Work the informational interview angle.
11. Perform outrageous acts and say obnoxious things.
12. Inherit.
13. Redefine your version of success as: whatever I have right now.
14. Flit from project to project until you alight on something that works out very quickly and well.
15. Be the best-looking person in the room.
16. Flirt.
17. Tell stories that people care about and spread.
18. Contribute more than is expected.
19. Give credit to others.
20. Take responsibility.
21. Aggrandize, preferably self.
22. Be a jerk and win through intimidation.
23. Be a doormat and refuse to speak up or stand up.
24. Never hesitate to share a kind word when it's deserved.
25. Sue people.
26. Treat every gig as an opportunity to create art.
27. Cut corners.
28. Focus on defeating the competition.
29. When dealing with employees, act like Steve. It worked for him, apparently.
30. Persist, always surviving to ship something tomorrow.
31. When in doubt, throw a tantrum.
32. Have the ability to work harder and more directly than anyone else when the situation demands it.
33. Don't rock the boat.
34. Rock the boat.
35. Don't rock the boat, baby.
36. Resort to black-hat tactics to get more than your share.
37. Work to pay more taxes.
38. Work to evade taxes.
39. Find typos.

STANDING OUT AND FITTING IN

Being Remarkable.

Will You Be Missed?

Tower Records is gone. I used to go there almost every day when I lived in Greenwich Village. I haven't been in more than five years—pretty much since I started buying just about everything at Amazon. Obviously, I won't miss it.

I haven't been inside a bank in nearly as long. Why would I? The ATM is closer, faster, and easier.

I haven't read the classified ads in the paper in five years, either.

None of these three activities were ever particularly emotionally heartwarming. And now that they're gone, I don't miss them.

So, here's the question: When you're gone, will they miss what *you* do? It's not too late to change the answer . . .

The T-shirt Rule

It's a simple test of whether you've created a remarkable experience:

"Would I buy the T-shirt?"

A T-shirt for your blog or your accounting firm or your bug-fighting software.

If you're not T-shirt worthy, what would it take?

The Last Time

This might be the last time you see me in your hotel.

It might be the last time you get to give me support on the $3,000-a-month Web hosting I'm buying from you.

It might be my last blog post (unlikely, but possible).

With so many choices, every business lives right on the edge. When you were the only florist in my town, storming off in a huff cost me as much as it cost you. Now, it's sort of trivial to just type a few different letters into my browser.

Yes, switching costs make some people hesitate before moving to Firefox or KPMG or National Car Rental. But when customers have been trained to no longer tolerate imperfection, they can go (forever) at any moment.

I try to give every speech I do as if it might be the last chance I ever get to give one. I still remember the last canoe lesson I gave, the last time I walked out the door at my one real job, and the last time I talked to my mom. Sometimes you get advance warning; sometimes you get to cherish the moment or try a bit harder. Other times, though, it just—stops.

If you know that tomorrow is your last chance, is it going to go differently?

Edges and Clusters

Most organizations have a sweet spot. That's the product or service that leads to the highest profit, retention, customer satisfaction, and word of mouth. If you walk into a certain bar and order a draft beer, you're more likely in that sweet spot than if you ordered, say, a Coke. A different bar might discover that the customer who orders a top-shelf martini is most likely to lead to the best outcome.

Over time, you'll start to develop slight variations on your sweet spot. If one kind of martini is good, then a few are even better. Pancake houses start selling Swedish, German, and even Brazilian pancakes. Insurance companies start selling a dozen different variations on whole life.

Clusters work because people are likely to be drawn to a crowd. They also work because making a good, better, best comparison gives us the confidence to go ahead and buy something. It's not an accident that profitable products like cars come in so many variations—having a choice makes it easier to choose (at least for a while). When Heinz comes in four colors, you don't have to decide whether or not to buy ketchup; you merely have to decide which color, and they win every time.

Clusters have a few problems. The first is that you inevitably leave people out. If your restaurant serves nothing but spicy food, then the odd duck who came with a group and doesn't like spicy food is going to go away unhappy.

Clusters get boring. If all you've got is another variation of the same fund-raising tool that's worked so well for you, it's hard to get a meeting with me (again).

And most of all, clusters make it hard to develop new sweet spots. First-class long-haul travel was a great sweet spot for Pan Am, but when the world changed, they got hammered.

So, consider this: not just clusters, but edges, too.

Maybe your bar ought to start selling amazing hot chocolate.

It's hard to make outliers, because it's so tempting to gradually work your way over, making each new product an extension of your sweet spot. That doesn't work. It just adds SKUs to your life.

An edge needs to be sharp and abrupt and distinct in order to generate the light it needs to thrive.

Your Best Stuff

Just got my monthly issue of *Relix* magazine. It comes with a free CD, with about a dozen songs from bands ranging from Frank Zappa to Keller Williams.

Each band gets exactly one song as a showcase.

So, the question: Should you put your best song on the free CD?

If it's your best song, and it's free, then no one will pay to get it from iTunes. And if it's the best song on the album, maybe no one will buy the album since they already have the song.

It's easy to argue that you should hold back the best song, make people pay for that.

Until you realize that the >>> button on my CD player works great.

So, eight beats into your "not really my best because, hey, it's free" song, I skip you, and you are gone forever.

Hint: this riff applies to a lot more than just the music business.

Black Suits

I was giving a speech at a hotel in Philly this week and found myself completely engulfed in a sea of black suits. Literally hundreds of eager-beaver college kids, all milling about, preparing themselves for a competition. Sife.org runs a nationwide tournament where students compete with business and community projects.

The thing is: there's no rule that says you have to wear a black suit when you present.

Everyone is so focused on not messing up, on not blowing it, on *not standing out* that they all blend together instead. I talked to a few of the competitors. Amazing kids. Focused, smart, dedicated. I wish, though, that they could realize (before it's too late) that standing out is better than being invisible.

Plussing

Here's a great Walt Disney phrase, new to me, which is similar to edgecraft:

Plussing.

Taking your work a little farther. Going closer to an edge, whichever edge.

Is there anything you can't *plus*? Anything you can't make simpler, more luxurious, cheaper, more extreme? Anything you can't make more remarkable?

The trade-off, of course, is in the time and money it takes.

But not really. I was tricking you. The trade-off is in the perceived risk it takes. Pushing your team a little harder in one direction means you're going away from the center, abandoning "everyone" to really appeal to "someone." And that's the secret of edgecrafting. Plussing yourself all the way to the edge, whatever that edge is.

Fresh Fish Here

My health club has a huge sign designed to go by the heavily traveled railroad tracks next to my office.

EXCLUSIVE CHARTER MEMBERSHIPS AVAILABLE.

Well, of course they're not that exclusive, given that they're on a billboard.

And does it matter that they're "charter"?

Of course they're memberships. All health clubs have memberships.

Which leaves "available," and the fact that they've got a sign pretty much makes that clear.

It's like the apocryphal story about the fish store. "Well, of course the fish is fresh. You're not going to sell me old fish, are you?" and "Of course it's 'here.' Where else would you be selling the fish?" and finally, "We know it's fish. We can smell it!"

The worst thing you can do is be boring and vague.

The second worst thing you can do is be boring and verbose and obvious.

The first goal of copy is to get you to read more copy.

The second goal is to tell a story that spreads.

And then, finally, to have that story get people to take action.

Dial 300 for Harry

You should go mattress shopping.

I did, today.

I admit, I don't think I've ever been mattress shopping before. What an astonishing experience. If you don't believe the "storytelling" riffs in *All Marketers Are Liars*, this will convert you. It's an entire room filled with virtually identical objects, varying in price by as much as 2,000%. And while you can lie down on any of them, lying down on a mattress is totally different from sleeping on one over a decade.

All you can buy is the story.

However, this isn't a post about the story. It's a post about the phone on the Sleepy's salesman's desk. Our sales guy, who was outstanding by the way, explained that all 400 stores in the chain are owned by one guy, and that the instructions are clear: if there's anything in the store, anything important, that's broken and not fixed within 72 hours (including policies, prices, inventory, whatever), his job is to pick up the phone and dial 300.

And Harry Acker, the owner, the billionaire, answers. "This is Harry." And you tell him and he fixes it.

I love that.

Even better . . . every once in a while, the phone rings. It's Harry. "What's up?" he asks. And if you tell him good news, he hangs up on you.

I think I'm glad I don't have Harry's job. But I was (amazingly, surprisingly, shockingly) glad I shopped there today.

But the Focus Group Loved It

John writes in and wants to know why I don't think much of focus groups.

A properly run focus group is great. The purpose? To help you focus.

Not to find out if an idea is any good. Not to get the data you need to sell your boss on an idea.

No!

Focus groups are very bad at that. Groupthink is a problem, for one. Second, you've got a weird cross-section of largely self-selected people, the kind of people willing to sit in a room with bad lighting to make a few bucks.

What focus groups can do for you is give you a visceral, personal, unscientific reaction to little brainstorms. They can help you push something further and further to see what grabs people. But the goal isn't to do a vote or a census. Any time your focus group results include percentages, you've wasted an afternoon.

The Long Trail

(Not a typo.)

Want to guess what these musical acts have in common?

The Rolling Stones
The Eagles
Elton John
U2
Paul McCartney

They each made more than $50 million last year, according to *Forbes*. They accounted for 40% of the top 10 acts. The long trail is what happened.

Same with products like Quicken, websites like eBay, and chefs like Wolfgang Puck.

We're so busy celebrating the hit of the moment that we forget that the real profit often comes from the long trail.

It's easy to persuade yourself to shortchange the design of a product or your investment in its engineering, or to manipulate the launch to maximize the short-term box office appeal of opening weekend. But the long trail proves you wrong.

The Web compounds long-trail thinking. A website might spike with short-term traffic hits, but a great website builds on its traffic, rises in its search rankings, and continues to bring in traffic, year after year.

The long trail explains why so many unprofitable movies turn a profit when the DVD comes out. *The Shawshank Redemption* got seven Academy Award nominations when it was released but disappointed at the box office. Now, after more than 1.3 million reviews at NetFlix, it is one of the most enduring DVD hits ever.

The long trail is a reminder to invest like your product might just be around in ten years.

Lessons Learned from Trader Joe's

I was talking with a colleague today about the magic of Trader Joe's. Here's how they make billions:

1. They target consumers who care a great deal about what they buy at the supermarket. As a result, their customers are more loyal and, more important, are willing to drive farther to get there. This means that Trader Joe's can have smaller, lower-rent locations (and fewer of them), which drives up sales per square foot and profits.

2. These customers are big mouths. They sneeze. When they serve something from Trader's they brag about, they tell the story of the store. This drives down advertising costs.

3. Most of what they sell is private label. Now that they have scale, they are able to negotiate great prices from their suppliers, and more important, encourage/force their suppliers to make unique items, or organic foods, or foods of higher quality for the money. All of this is a virtuous cycle. The key mantra is that *Trader's finds foods for its customers, NOT customers for its foods.*

I think these three steps are viable for a wide range of businesses and sectors. One example to stretch your thinking: the TED conference. It's in a remote location, one that's probably a bit cheaper than some other locations. People who care are happy to schlep there. And they love to talk about it. And because the audience is so focused, the speakers come for free, further enhancing the cycle. If it works for supermarkets and high-end business conferences, where else does it work?

Belief

People don't believe what you tell them.
They rarely believe what you show them.
They often believe what their friends tell them.
They always believe what they tell themselves.

What's Expected

It's expected that you'll tip the masseuse (masseur) at the spa. But not the acupuncturist down the street.

It's expected that the CEO of a public company will hire a hotshot consultant to help her do her job. The CFO gets to do that, too. But not the receptionist.

It's expected that coffee in a fancy restaurant will cost more than it does at a café.

It's expected that Wi-Fi in a business hotel ought to be free. But it didn't used to be that way.

It's expected that the TV in the gym will be on, always. It's expected, though, that you'll wear headphones to listen to Marley.

It's expected that you take a family vacation to Florida. It's not expected, though, to take the kids to Topeka.

It's expected that a child-care facility will run ads with lots of rainbows. A Freudian psychiatrist, on the other hand, is expected not to advertise at all.

Faced with expectations, you've got three really big options:

1. *Embrace* expectations and build a product or service that fits what people are looking for. No change of behavior necessary. Be in the right place at the right time with the right thing priced appropriately, and hope the competition doesn't show up.
2. *Change* the expectations. No one expected to be able to buy digital music for 99 cents a song and have it show up on their iPod. Now, that's the default expectation in some communities. Changing an expectation builds a huge barrier to those that might follow. Change is time consuming and expensive and rarely happens on schedule.
3. *Defy* the expectations. Do the unexpected. This is tempting but often leads to nothing but noise.

Before you start marketing something, it helps to be able to describe which combination of the three you're setting out to accomplish.

Discovery

I was talking with someone the other night, and he said, "I was one of the first to use Wikipedia." When pressed, he confirmed, "Right at the beginning."

He's 13.

It's pretty obvious that he wasn't one of the first to use Wikipedia. He was one of the first people he knew who had used Wikipedia. Big difference.

Nope.

Same thing.

People make their own realities. If Bill thought he was first, then in his mind, he was. When he started using it, it began to exist. When he stops going back, it will disappear.

Every person who encounters your organization for the first time comes with beginner's mind. She knows nothing about yesterday or how hard you worked or your financing or what it took to build it. She's here now, she's first, let's go.

50:1

Every month, the Bureau of Labor Statistics tracks "mass layoffs." That's the term for more than 50 people losing their jobs at once. In August of this year, the total number of people hit by a mass layoff was 127,944. The number has been more than 100,000 every month except for one in the last decade.

And that doesn't count small companies, smaller layoffs, nonprofits, and other ventures that don't show up on the radar. The actual number has to be at least ten times as big—at least a million a month is my guess.

Compare that to the tiny number of people who get fired for attempting to do something great.

Sure, Carly got fired. But thousands at HP got laid off. She lost her job for challenging the status quo. They got canned for embracing it.

Sure, that crazy copywriter on the 11th floor got fired for attempting a viral blog-based campaign that backfired, but it's nothing compared to the entire department that lost their jobs because there just wasn't enough business.

At least once a day, I get mail from people worrying that if they are too remarkable, too edgy, too willing to cause change and growth, they're risking getting fired. I almost never get mail from people who figure that if they keep doing the same boring thing day in and day out at their fading company, they're going to lose their jobs in a layoff.

50 ad agencies lose accounts for being boring, static, and unprofitable, for every one agency that gets fired for being remarkable.

50 churchgoers switch to a new congregation because of a boring or uncaring leader, for every one who leaves because she was offended by a new way of thinking.

50 employees lose their jobs because the business just faded away, for every one who is singled out and fired for violating a silly policy and taking care of a customer first.

50 readers stop visiting your blog (or your site or your magazine or your TV show) because you're stuck in a rut and scared, for every one who leaves because you have the guts to change the format or challenge the conventional wisdom.

50:1.

Brand as Mythology

Just under the wire, L. Frank Baum's heirs have no copyright protection on *The Wizard of Oz*. As a result, there are Broadway musicals, concordances, prequels, sequels, and more. All of which creates a rich, emotional universe (and makes the copyrighted movie even more valuable).

Most of us remember the mythology stories they taught us in school (Zeus and Thor and the rest of the comic-like heroes). Myths allow us to project ourselves into their stories, to imagine interactions that never took place, to take what's important to us and live it out through the myths.

There are dozens, if not hundreds, of entertainment mythological brands. James Bond and Barbie, for example.

But it goes far beyond that.

There's clearly a Google mythology and a Starbucks one as well. We feel different about brands like these than we do about, say, Maxwell House or Random House.

Why do Santa and Ronald McDonald have a mythology but not Dave at Wendy's or the Burger King?

Let's try Wikipedia: *Myths are narratives about divine or heroic beings, arranged in a coherent system, passed down traditionally, and linked to the spiritual or religious life of a community, endorsed by rulers or priests.*

So, if I were trying to invent a mythic brand, I'd want to be sure that there was a story, not just a product or a pile of facts. That story would promise (and deliver) a heroic outcome. And there needs to be growth and mystery as well, so the user can fill in her own blanks. Endorsement by a respected ruler or priest helps as well.

The key word, I think, is *spiritual*. Mythological brands make a spiritual connection with the user, delivering something that we can't find on our own . . . or, at the very least, giving us a slate we can use to write our own mythology on.

People use a Dell. They are an Apple.

This can happen accidentally, but it often occurs on purpose. A brand can be deliberately mythological, created to intentionally deliver the benefits of myth. Casinos in Las Vegas have been trying to do this for decades (and usually failing). But talk to a Vegas cab driver about Steve Wynn and you can see that it's been done at least once.

There's a mythology about Digg and about Wikipedia, but not about About.com. The mysterious nature of rankings and scores and community ensures that we'll be paying attention to them. It doesn't hurt that Digg and Wikipedia both have public figures—heroes—at the helm.

It's easy to confuse publicity with mythology, but it doesn't work that way; there's no Zune mythology, for example. It's also easy to assume that mythology will guarantee financial success, but it didn't work for General Magic, a company that successfully leveraged the heroic reputations of its founders, created a very hot IPO, but failed to match the needs of the larger market.

It did, on the other hand, work for Anderson's, an ice cream stand in Buffalo (!?) that has a line every single day, even in January.

Hard to explain, difficult to bottle, probably worth the effort to pursue.

We Tried Everything

I just got a spectacularly insightful and honest email from Scott. Here's the money quote:

We've "tried everything," by which we mean we've tried a few things that everybody else has done, as long as they didn't involve doing anything different from what we normally do.

Out of the Corner of Your Eye

Juxtaposition matters. And so does surprise.

Most marketing is intentional. In this ad I will advertise this product.

So is most writing. A knitting blog writes about . . . wait for it . . . knitting.

Our minds are prepared for what we are about to receive. If it's a sales pitch, we're ready to ignore it. If it's on a familiar blog, we're ready for it to be familiar.

Real memories are created by surprises.

Real change is created by unexpected juxtapositions.

Time magazine used to work (when it worked) because an irrelevant and slightly loopy article about some unusual idea was right between an article on Israel and one on welfare.

And New York City works, when it works, because the zoning is so mixed up. Right in the middle of the meat market district, there's a high-end clothing store.

Most marketers, probably you, are busy putting your round pegs in the round holes that have been given to you. What if you did the opposite?

How to Succeed in Business (to Business)

The secrets might surprise you. The most successful B2B organizations, in my opinion, understand the value of:

- Patience
- Promises
- Being centered

We worked very closely with Brian and his team at Viget for many months, building the initial architecture of Squidoo. There are plenty of shops that can do Web programming, plenty that claim they can do UI work, and plenty that are even hipper than you. There are very few that manage to pull off the kind of work that Viget does. They were on time and on budget, and most important, they didn't cause anyone to lose sleep.

The very things that I look for as a consumer (surprise, fashion, edginess) were in short supply here. Instead, Viget went out of their way to never overpromise. They pushed the hard decisions early in the process so that the thrashing was early, not late. In fact, the end of the process was the most delightful part. Because they know who they are and are clear about it to themselves and to their clients, the chances of making an honest connection with their clients are much higher than they would be with someone who is trying to be all things to all people.

Drew Dusebout, a broker/financial planner I know at UBS, is the same way. Drew doesn't make vague promises about financial returns, and he doesn't get all excited at the latest gimmick. Instead, he's honest with himself and his colleagues about the world he works in, and his clients always get exactly what they expect. Sure, this is a more difficult way to grow (at first) because you can't seduce the people who are the most likely to jump ship. You can't promise some shortcut that gets you the quick clients. But in the long run, I don't know of any other way to market a service like his.

Here's the hard part about this: if you're very good at what you do, you won't grow. Because *lots* of people are good at what you do. No one is going to be busy referring you and sending you business just because you're very good. Sorry.

The only way to consistently grow in B2B is to be better than very good. In fact, the only way is to find something that organizations need and be the very best in the world at it. Hopefully, that thing is something that organizations in your sphere are eager to talk about among themselves. If it is, you win. There's a line at your door for years to come.

Do You Have to Be Anti-Change to Be Pro-Business?

A few months ago, I heard an interview with one of the leading metal-baseball-bat manufacturers. They were lobbying hard against regulations that would require Little League players to use wood bats.

Today, Chris points us to a Reuters article, "Automakers Challenge Vermont Emissions Law." The car makers continue to lobby hard, or even sue, over emission rules. Wendy's, as previously discussed, is working hard against a rule in New York requiring that they post calorie counts. It's common wisdom that government regulation is bad for business, and especially bad is regulation that requires change.

I don't get it.

A few years ago, the FTC changed the law about how wide apart the bars in cribs for children had to be. Cribs with wide spaces between bars end up strangling kids and breaking arms. The law applied only to home cribs, which meant that hospital cribs weren't covered. Hard Manufacturing, my favorite hospital crib company, took the regulation to heart and alerted every hospital in the country that the cribs they were using weren't deemed safe for home use—so why use them in a hospital? What do you think happened to crib sales? It was a huge few years as the cribs were replaced (and the kids ended up safer).

Wendy's did the best when they were growing with the launch of salads. Not when they were copying McDonald's over burgers. Change is their friend.

If I were a leading bat company, I'd formulate a "slower" metal bat that would be just as safe as wood—and unbreakable, too. What a marketing coup! Then I'd lobby like crazy for change.

If I were Ford Motor, I'd lobby as hard as possible for the strictest emissions regime in the world. If you're losing the game, change the rules. Start over. Be the only major car company to produce 100% pzev (partial zero-emissions vehicles) or hybrid cars.

Business as usual is almost always lousy marketing, because there isn't a lot of room for growth. The opportunities kick in when an external force requires a brand new story, when consumers are choosing to pay attention because they've got no other choice.

It's easy to argue against change. It disheartens shareholders and even employees. But external change is the most likely lever of growth, because it puts you back on the agenda of attention.

The Brand Formula

What's a brand?

I think it is the product of two things:

[Prediction of what to expect] times [emotional power of that expectation]

If I encounter a brand and I don't know what it means or does, it has zero power. If I have an expectation of what an organization will do for me, but I don't care about that, no power.

FedEx is a powerful brand because you always get what you expect, and the relief you get from their consistency is high.

AT&T is a weak brand because you almost never get what you expect, because they do so many different things, and because the value of what they create has little emotional resonance (it sure used to, though, when they did one thing, they did it perfectly, and they were the only ones who could connect you).

The dangers of brand ubiquity are then obvious. When your brand is lots of things (like AOL became), then the expectations are all over the place and the emotional resonance starts to fade. If the predictability of your brand starts to erode its emotional power (a restaurant that becomes boring), then you need to become predictable in your joyous unpredictability!

If you want to grow a valuable brand, my advice is to keep awareness close to zero among the people you're not ready for yet, and build the most predictable, emotional experience you can among those that care about you.

How to Be a Great Receptionist

Being a pretty good receptionist is easy. You're basically a low-tech security guard in nice clothes. Sit at the desk and make sure that visitors don't steal the furniture or go behind the magic door unescorted.

But what if you wanted to be a great receptionist?

I'd start with understanding that in addition to keeping unescorted guests away from the magic door, a receptionist can have a huge impact on the marketing of an organization. If someone is visiting your office, they've come for a reason. To sell something, to buy something, to interview or be interviewed. No matter what, there's some sort of negotiation involved. If the receptionist can change the mindset of the guest, good things happen (or if it goes poorly, bad things).

Think the job acceptance rate goes up if the first impression is a memorable one? Think the tax auditor might be a little more friendly if her greeting was cheerful?

So, a great receptionist starts by acting like Vice President, Reception. I'd argue for a small budget to be spent on a bowl of M&M's or the occasional Heath Bar for a grumpy visitor. If you wanted to be really amazing, how about baking a batch of cookies every few days? I'd ask the entire organization for updates as to who is coming in each day. "Welcome, Mr. Mitchell. How was your flight in from Tucson?"

Is there a TV in reception? Why not hook up some old Three Stooges DVDs?

Why do I need to ask where to find the men's room? Perhaps you could have a little sign.

And in the downtime between visitors, what a great chance to surf the Web for recent positive news about your company. You can print it out in a little binder that I can read while I'm waiting. Or consider the idea of creating a collage of local organizations that your fellow employees have helped with their volunteer work.

One amazing receptionist I met specialized in giving sotto voce commentary on the person you were going to meet. She'd tell you inside dope that would make you feel prepared before you walked in. "Did you know that Don had a new grandchild enter the family last week? She's adorable. Her name is Betty."

In addition to greeting guests, internal marketing can be a focus as well. Every single employee who passes your desk on the way in can learn something about a fellow worker—if you're willing to spend the time to do it, they'll spend the time to read it.

Either that, or you could just work on being grumpy and barking "name and ID please."

Price

Maybe the reason it seems that price is all your customers care about is . . .

. . . that you haven't given them anything else to care about.

The Promiscuity Paradox

Marketers of all stripes are discovering that acquiring a reputation and permission to market to people isn't as expandable as they might have hoped.

A PR firm, for example, might have some terrific clients. These clients give them credibility to talk to the media. Over time, the firm gains a reputation with bloggers and other media outlets. Emails get answered, press releases get read. The clients get ink, new clients show up.

The temptation is to grow the business. To take on new clients. To do the PR magic for an ever larger group of people.

Here's the problem: the people who most want to be your clients are the people you should least want to represent. As you promote the un-promotable, the permission you have to talk to the media doesn't go up, it goes down. Better to be the agency that represents only best-selling authors than to be the biggest agency.

In the long run, the pickier you are, the better you do. Same thing goes for online merchants, brokers, church groups, and just about any-one else who markets with permission.

The Marine Iguana

Marine iguanas swim. They eat stuff in shallow water, which is surprising behavior for an iguana.

How is it possible for there to be marine iguanas?

Ordinary iguanas washed onshore of some of the Galapagos Islands a few millennia ago and quickly discovered that eating the way they were used to wasn't going to work, because there wasn't anything to eat. Most of them starved to death. A few, though, were lucky enough that they could tolerate foraging around on the edge of the ocean. Over generations, iguanas with this trait thrived, while those that were born without it died out. A new species evolved.

The interesting lesson for marketers is this: if iguanas had had predators and competition while this was going on, they never would have survived. The barren nature of their marketplace gave them the time they needed to evolve (or, as marketers with egos would say, "figure out") a strategy that worked.

Too often, marketers are drawn to the hot market. The problem with the hot market is that if you don't get it right quickly, you get crushed. Really big ideas tend to get perfected in the Siberian outposts, the little niches that get ignored (until they get really big). It takes a lot of confidence to walk into a hyper-competitive market with something new. Quieter markets may just give you the cover you need to work out what it's going to take to make those marketers grow.

Just in Time for Fall

I just got a case of socks from littlemissmatched.com. You may remember them from *Purple Cow*. Hundreds of styles of socks; none match. Three to a sleeve, $10 or so.

Why bother with mismatched socks? Because most people don't want them. The few that do, love to talk about them. It makes us happy. Ten dollars for 40 days' worth of joy, repeated over a few years, is a bargain. The obvious market was 12-year-old girls, the sort of people who love having people notice their socks. The company is now branching out into more adult (I use the term advisedly) styles. I hope they don't get too popular! (Not that you care, but I've been wearing their socks every day for three years or so.)

The key lessons:

- The product *is* the marketing.
- Choose a hive of people who seek out products like yours and then talk about them.
- Be true to what you stand for.
- It's okay not to be serious, especially if you're selling a want, not a need.
- Be patient. The market will find you.

How to Create a Great Website

Here are principles I think you can't avoid:

1. Fire the committee. No great website in history has been conceived of by more than three people. Not one. This principle is a deal breaker.
2. Change the interaction. What makes great websites great is that they are simultaneously effortless and new at the same time. That means that the site teaches you a new thing or new interaction or new connection, but you know how to use it right away. (Hey, if doing this were easy, everyone would do it.)
3. Less. Fewer words, fewer pages, less fine print.
4. What works, works. Theory is irrelevant.
5. Patience. Some sites test great and work great from the start. (Great if you can find one.) Others need people to use them and adjust to them. At some point, your gut tells you to launch. Then stick with it, despite the critics, as you gain traction.
6. Measure. If you're not improving, if the yield is negative . . . kill it.
7. Insight is good, clever is bad. Many websites say, "look at me." Your goal ought to be to say, "here's what you were looking for."
8. If you hire a professional, hire a great one. The best one. Let her do her job. Ten mediocre website consultants working in perfect harmony can't do the work of one rock star.

9. One voice, one vision.

10. Don't settle.

Radiohead and the Mediocre Middle

I got a ton of email this week about the Radiohead rollout. The short version: Radiohead (a million-album-selling rock band) launched their new album as a pay-what-you-want MP3 combined with an expensive boxed set. This is the sort of thing that I've been talking about for seven years and that many unknown bands have been doing for at least that long.

A lot of pundits have jumped in and talked about how this is the next big thing. That the music industry is finally waking up and realizing that they can't change the world . . . that the world is changing them.

But that's not the really useful insight here. The question is: Why did it take so long, and why did we see it from Prince (CD in the newspaper), Madonna ($120 million to leave her label and go to a concert promoter), and Radiohead?

Most industries innovate from both ends:

- The outsiders go first because they have nothing to lose.
- The winners go next because they can afford to and they want to stay winners.
- It's the mediocre middle that sits and waits and watches.

The mediocre record companies, mediocre A&R guys, and mediocre acts are struggling to stay in place. They're nervous that it all might fall apart. So they wait. They wait for "proof" that this new idea is going to work, or at least won't prove fatal. (It's the impulse to wait that made them mediocre in the first place, of course.)

So, in every industry, the middle waits. And watches. And then, once they realize they can survive the switch (or once they're persuaded that their current model is truly fading away), they jump in.

The irony, of course, is that by jumping in last, they're condemning themselves to more mediocrity.

That Doesn't Make Sense

Ben has a post about a beer made by an order of monks in Belgium. These monks, who have taken vows of silence, sell the beer only by appointment, don't label the bottles, and severely limit the supply they create. As you can imagine for a beer that some call the best in the world, it has quite a cult following.

There are two ingredients to this remarkability. The first, as Ben points out, is the idea of ritual. By changing the way the product is created and distributed, they add a religious and spiritual element to the process (and this element would be present even if they weren't monks). Second, they're not trying to sell the most. That's critical.

When you try to maximize anything, you work to be efficient, to fit in, to appeal to the average person, since that's where the numbers are. Every time Budweiser makes a decision, it seems to make sense, since they're trying to sell the most beer. "Most" embraces systems and policies that make sense. But "most" rarely succeeds.

Exclusion

When I was in college, the dean tried to put together an advisory group of students. Nobody he invited joined—it wasn't worth the time. Then he named it "the Group of 100," and in just a few days, it was filled. The easiest way to have insiders is to have outsiders.

Credit card companies have made billions by selling a card that others can't get.

Politicians stand up and talk about their (exclusive) religion, or pit one special-interest group against another.

And of course, the best nightclubs have the biggest velvet ropes and the pickiest doormen.

Limiting the supply of your service, or limiting the quantity of your product, or being aggressive in whom you sell to (and whom you don't) are all time-tested ways to build a killer brand. Humans like being insiders, and will work hard to create their own imaginary demarcations to demonstrate that they've made it inside.

Populism is almost always a hard sell, it seems.

When Tiffany's lowered prices and quality and tried to reach out to the masses, they almost went bankrupt.

The 'Net seems to be turning some of this upside down. Twitter and Yahoo! Mail and eBay are completely populist. HotorNot, Flickr, and other websites have embraced this idea as well. (Worth noting that Gmail started as a totally insider service, with a limited number of invites, shared person to person.)

It's interesting to take a second to look at Wikipedia. It started with the most populist, inclusionary point of view of all, but over time, people being people, a hierarchy and an inner circle were created. The exclusion is based on effort and skill, not race or income, but it's still exclusionary. And at its best, it makes the site work. When it fails, it limits discussion, reinforces small thinking, and enrages the outsiders.

The first thing I'd ask myself before launching a product, a service, or a candidate is "who are we leaving out?" If the answer is "no one," be prepared for uncharted waters. The future of marketing (at least the big successes) is going to be fueled by those with the guts to embrace the masses. The profits, at least in the short run, may well be found by those that embrace exclusion.

One last thing: while people are delighted to be included (and seem to enjoy excluding others), the benefits they feel are dwarfed by the anger and disappointment of those excluded. It's something that people remember for their entire lives.

Nickel and Diming

If you run a business that's "all inclusive" (like a buffet, a resort, a membership organization, or even a consulting practice), you really have only two ways to increase your profits.

The first way is to figure out how to get more money out of each customer. That means adding a surcharge on the special lobster appetizer or a small extra fee for better service. It means coming up with ways to not actually be "all inclusive," to give the customers less unless they pay you more.

The goal of this method is to come up with goods and services that have a low marginal cost (your cost of getting or delivering one more) and a high marginal value (what it's worth to the customer). So, if you can charge the best members of your club a $500 fee for attending a networking event that costs you only $3 a person to host, you're going to see a large increase in profit.

The second way is to figure out how to give your customers more. To be even more "all inclusive" than the competition. To find countless items of low marginal cost and just include them. Why? Because it creates return visits from your existing base and, even better, is a significant investment in word of mouth, the most effective marketing tool available to you.

The Beaches resort in Jamaica prides itself on great people (true) and on being totally all inclusive (not so true). I was there for a few days for a family reunion, and it was pretty clear to me that an MBA on a mission was at work. The nickel-and-diming adds up. He had scoured the place to find ways to charge just a little (or a lot) more as often as possible.

Wi-Fi is a great example. The marginal cost of hosting one more person on a Wi-Fi network is as close to zero as something can be. Charge people more than $10 a day and suddenly you're making hundreds or thousands of dollars of extra profit. Or promise free scuba, but charge people $70 for a checkout course before you let them dive—low marginal cost, high incremental profit.

I have no doubt that this scheme works in the short run. It might even work out to be a viable marketing strategy in some markets. However, the alternative is worth considering. *Not only do everything you say you're going to do, but do more.*

Offering low-marginal-cost items for free is a shortcut to generating word of mouth, which is a lot cheaper than buying ads.

Editors

Turns out that for the last twenty-seven years, every single movie that managed to win the Oscar for best picture was also nominated for best editing.

Great products, amazing services, and stories worth talking about get edited along the way. Most of the time, the editing makes them pallid, mediocre, and boring. Sometimes, a great editor will push the remarkable stuff. That's his job.

The easy thing for an editor to do is make things safe. You avoid trouble that way. Alas, it also means you avoid success.

Who's doing your editing?

The Problem with Perfect

When was the last time you excitedly told someone about FedEx?

They're perfect. The only time we notice them is when they screw up.

And that fancy restaurant with the four-star reviews? They've got the fine linen and the coordinated presentation of dishes. It costs hundreds of dollars to eat there, but it's okay, because they're perfect.

Which is a problem, because dinner consists of not much except noticing how imperfect they are. The second course came five minutes later than it should have (ten, even!). The salad was really good, but not as perfect as it was last time. And the valet parking . . . you had to wait in the cold for at least ninety seconds before your car came. What a letdown.

A letdown?

The place is a gift, a positive bit of karma in a world filled with compromise. And all you can do is notice that it's not perfect.

As the quality of things goes up, and competition increases, it's so easy to sell people on perfect. But perfect rarely leads to great word of mouth, merely because expectations are so hard to meet.

I think it's more helpful to focus on texture, on interpersonal interaction, on *interesting*. Interesting is attainable, and interesting is remarkable. Interesting is fresh every day, and interesting leads to word of mouth.

I think our FedEx delivery person is interesting. I like her. I talk to her. And yes, it changes my decision about whom to ship with. I also think that Spicy Mina is an interesting restaurant. So far from perfect, it's ridiculous. But I talk about it.

Why Bother Having a Résumé?

In the last few days, I've heard from top students at Cornell and other universities about my internship.

It must have been posted in some office or on a website, because each of the applications is just a résumé. No real cover letter, no attempt at self-marketing. Sort of, "here are the facts about me, please put me in the pile."

This is controversial, but here goes: *I think if you're remarkable, amazing, or just plain spectacular, you probably shouldn't have a résumé at all.*

Not just for my little internship, but in general. Great people shouldn't have a résumé.

Here's why: a résumé is an excuse to reject you. Once you send me your résumé, I can say, "oh, they're missing this or they're missing that," and boom, you're out.

Having a résumé begs for you to go into that big machine that looks for relevant key words, and begs for you to get a job as a cog in a giant machine. Just more fodder for the corporate behemoth. That might be fine for average folks looking for an average job, but is that what you deserve?

If you don't have a résumé, what do you have?

How about three extraordinary letters of recommendation from people the employer knows or respects?

Or a sophisticated project they can see or touch?

Or a reputation that precedes you?

Or a blog that is so compelling and insightful that they have no choice but to follow up?

Some say, "well, that's fine, but I don't have those."

Yeah, that's my point. If you don't have those, why do you think you are remarkable, amazing, or just plain spectacular? It sounds to me like if you don't have those, you've been brainwashed into acting like you're sort of ordinary.

Great jobs, world-class jobs, jobs people kill for . . . those jobs don't get filled by people emailing in résumés. Ever.

The Pope Is Coming

Whether you run a hotel or a retail store or a parts supply store, things change when you find out the Pope is coming for a visit.

The fresh flowers get delivered, the beds are made a little tighter, and your best staff are waiting out front. Everything is a little bit cleaner and shinier. Maybe a few staff bring in their kids to sing a song or two.

The thing is, everyone enjoys this extra work. It's fun to stretch a bit. It doesn't feel quite as much like work when you're doing something special.

You probably guessed the punch line: The Pope isn't coming to your place of business this trip. He won't be reading your blog or calling your customer service line, either. Sorry for the confusion. Go ahead and rent out that room or give away that table you were saving.

But since it's so much fun, why not do it for someone who isn't the Pope? Like your next customer?

Silly Traffic

This is a truth of the Internet: when traffic comes to your site without focused intent, it bounces.

Seventy-five percent of all unfocused visitors leave within three seconds.

Any site, anywhere, anytime: 75% bounce rate within three seconds.

By unfocused, I mean people who visit via Digg or StumbleUpon or even a typical Google search. If your site is spammy or clearly selling something, the number is certainly higher. If you're getting traffic because you have a clever domain name, it might be even higher. I don't know of many examples where it is lower.

Big traffic numbers are good for your ego, that's certain. You can brag about hits, or page views or visits, if you can get away with it. But the bounce rate is still that scary 75%.

So, what should you do about silly traffic?

The tempting thing to do is to obsess over it. If you could convert just 10% of the bouncers, you'd be increasing your conversion rate by almost a third! (The math: 7.5% is about a third of the 25% who don't bounce.) There are a million things you can do to focus on this, and almost none of them will show you much improvement.

One other thing you can do is to get hooked on the traffic, focus on building your top-line number. Keep working on sensational controversies or clever images, robust controversies, or other link bait that keeps the silly traffic coming back.

I think it's more productive to worry about two other things instead.

1. Engage your existing users far more deeply. Increase their participation, their devotion, their interconnection, and their value.
2. Turn those existing users into ambassadors, charged with the idea of bringing you traffic that is focused, traffic with intent.

"I'm just looking" is no fun for most retailers. Yet they continue to pay high rent for high-traffic locations, and invest time and money in window displays. Very few retailers lament all the traffic that walks by the front door without ever walking in. A long time ago, they realized that the shoppers with focused intent are far more valuable. *Smart retailers work hard to get focused people to walk in the door and to keep the riffraff walking on down the sidewalk.*

Your website can do the same thing. In fact, you might want to make it *more* likely that bouncers bounce, not less, but only if those changes increase the results you get from the visitors you truly care about.

Four Words

Make big promises; overdeliver.

If you can define great marketing in fewer words than that, you win.

"Big promises": treating people with respect, improving self-esteem, delivering results, contacting as often as you say you will but not more, including side effects in your planning, delivering joy, meeting spec, being on time, connecting people to one another, delivering consistency, offering value, and on and on. Caring. The stories involved in your promises matter. Those are often what people are buying.

This is the first place where the equation breaks down. Marketers often make big promises that appear to be unrealistic or are delivered in ways that don't match the worldview of the prospect. Marketers get carried away with themselves and get focused on their greatness and forget to tell a story that people enjoy believing.

And sometimes, they make promises that are too small to get our attention. Boring promises are hardly worth making.

"Overdeliver" means doing more than you said you would, which is the secret to word of mouth.

Here, of course, the pitfall is obvious. You made too big a promise and you did your best, but no, you didn't overdeliver, not really. You didn't amaze and delight and yes, stun me with the incredible results of your offering.

Just because it's only four words doesn't mean it's easy!

Thinking About Danny Devito

George Clooney is a movie star. He looks like one. He makes tens of millions of dollars a year, hangs out at Cannes, and has starlets falling at his feet.

Danny DeVito is exactly five feet tall. He was perfectly cast as the Penguin.

Can you imagine the career advice Danny got? The well-meaning people who explained to him (as if he didn't know) that he didn't look like George Clooney? That perhaps, maybe, he should consider a job as a personal trainer or short-order cook?

The math, however, tells us something different.

(Number of people resembling George Clooney)/(Number of jobs for people resembling George Clooney) is a much bigger number than the ratio available to Danny. For the math challenged: because everyone in Hollywood is trying to be George, there are a lot more opportunities for the few Dannys willing to show up. Invest in Danny. The edges usually pay off.

No Such Thing as Price Pressure

Your sales force and your customers may scream that you need to lower your price.

It's not true.

You need to increase your value. If people don't want to pay, it's because you're not delivering enough value for the money you're charging.

You're not selling a commodity unless you want to.

Bravery and WALL•E

At every turn, Pixar messed up the marketing of their new movie. It has a hard-to-spell name, no furry characters, not nearly enough dialogue (the first 45 minutes are almost silent), no nasty (but ultimately ridiculous) bad guy, hardly any violence, and very little slapstick. WALL•E didn't get a huge Hollywood PR campaign or even a lot of promotion, it doesn't feature any hot stars, and as far as I can tell, the merchandising options are quite limited.

Can you imagine the meetings?

Can you imagine the yelling?

Pixar, recently purchased by Disney, could crank out multibillion-dollar confections. They know all the moves; they have the chops to create merchandising powerhouses. And with just one movie a year, Pixar certainly must have been under huge pressure to do just that.

And yet, instead, they made a great movie. A movie for the ages. A film, not 90 minutes of commerce.

The irony, of course, is that they'll make plenty of money. Bravery often pays off, even if paying off is not your goal. *Especially* if that's not your goal.

Marketing isn't always about pandering to the masses and shooting for the quick payoff. Often, the best marketing doesn't feel like marketing at all.

I Need to Build a House;
What Kind of Hammer Should I Buy?

I want to write a novel. What word processor do you recommend?

Yesterday on the radio, Jimmy Wales was talking about the Wikipedia movement. A caller who identified himself as a strategist at Amnesty International asked: "We're going to build a website to promote freedom and democracy and human rights. What software should we use?"

Really.

If you want to do something worth doing, you'll need two things: passion and architecture. The tools will take care of themselves. (Knowledge of tools matters, of course, but it pales in comparison to the other two.)

Sure, picking the wrong tools will really cripple your launch. Picking the wrong software (or the wrong hammer) is a hassle. But nothing great gets built just because you have the right tools.

My approach is to make an assertion about tools early in the process, and then move on to a solid draft of the good stuff. "Given: that we can make a computer do what xyz.com makes it do." Or "given: we can make a piece of titanium do what Frank Gehry makes it do." Then, go design something, imagine it, spec it, flesh it out, and fall in love with it. *Now* you can ask Jimmy Wales what sort of software to use.

The Intangibles

Let's say your service costs more than the commodity-oriented competition (I hope it does!).

Where do you find repeat business or even new business? How do you make a sale (to another business or to a consumer) when you cost more?

The answer, of course, is in the intangibles. The things that have no price. Things that customers value more than it costs you to provide them.

If you don't have that, all you can do is beg. And begging is not a scalable strategy.

If you find yourself saying, "the boss won't let me lower the price," or "we're more expensive, but that's because our cost structure is higher," then you're selling the intangibles too short. The stuff people can't buy at any price, from anyone else, but that they really value.

Here are some random ways you can embrace some intangibles:

- Call the person **before** you get the RFP, before they know they need you. Brainstorm with them about how you can work together to create the thing they need. *Participation* is priceless. After all, if all you're doing is meeting my spec, why exactly should you be rewarded?
- You'd be amazed at how much people value *enthusiasm*. Genuine, transparent enthusiasm about the project they're working on. Are you a framer? How do you respond to someone who brings something in to be framed? (Hint: if it involves a tape measure, you're missing the point.)
- Don't forget *speed*. If you are overwhelmingly faster than the alternatives, what's that worth? For some people, more than you can imagine.
- *Focus* and personal service are obvious (but priceless) intangibles.
- *Generosity* is remembered for a long time. People remember what you did for them when you didn't have to do a thing, when you weren't looking for new business, when it was expensive or costly for you to do it. Did you know that the movie studio bought Robert Downey Jr. a Bentley when *Iron Man* hit it big? He didn't ask; they didn't want anything (at least right then).
- How do you respond when you make an error? This is actually a huge opportunity to deliver an intangible, especially in a business-to-business setting. The last thing a client wants is to have to explain a snafu to her boss.
- *Peer pressure* is another silent intangible. What will my friends and colleagues think if I choose you? What if I don't choose you? Is it fashionable to pay a lot? How hard are you working at establishing a connection across your market so that choosing you is the right thing to do, regardless of the price?
- The last one is probably the biggest. *Hope.* Do you offer hope for something really big in the future? Maybe just around the corner,

but perhaps in the long run. What does it look and feel like? Are you drawing a vivid picture?

Simple example: IDEO. Check them on each one of these criteria and you'll see why they have a waiting list.

When providers are stressed or scared or pressured, they instinctively resort to price. It feels real and reliable. It's a trap, I'm afraid. All of the non-commodity decisions are driven by the intangibles, and your job is to build remarkable ones and tell stories about them.

The Dead Zone of Slick

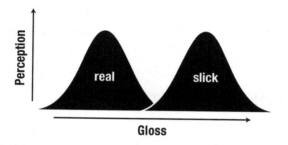

There was a terrific duo playing live music at the farmer's market the other day. They were well rehearsed, enthusiastic, and really good. Being a patron of the arts, I bought a CD.

I hated it.

I've thought a lot about what turned me off, and I think it's the curve above.

Faced with the excitement of making a CD and playing with all the knobs and dials, the musicians overproduced the record. They went from being two real guys playing authentic music, live and for free, and became a multitracked quartet in search of a professional sound. And they ended up in the dead zone. Not enough gloss to be slick, too much to be real.

This happens at restaurants all the time. Give me a handmade huarache, and it's fine if it's on a paper plate. Or give me something from Thomas Keller. But I have no patience for the stuff in the dead zone, the items that are too slick to be real, but not slick enough to be a marvel.

Who, exactly, wants an industrial tuna sandwich wrapped in plastic wrap?

You can send me a handwritten note (but don't write it in crayon with words spelled wrong), and I'll read it. And you can send me a beautifully typeset FedEx package. But if you send me mass-produced junk with a dot matrix printer, out it goes. The dead zone again.

That's why really-well-done HTML email works, as does unique, hand-typed text email. It's the banal stuff in the middle that people don't read. And yet, 95% of what I see is precisely in the dead spot of the middle zone.

The Blair Witch Project and *Pi* both felt authentic. *The Matrix* was perfectly slick. The new *Star Wars* cartoon is just dumb.

That's why a personalized letter works better than a generic résumé. We crave handmade authenticity and we adore perfectly professional slickness.

Thinking Bigger

"How do you like the draft of the new brochure?" asks the boss.

There are several responses available to you, in order of wonderfulness:

1. It's great.
2. There's a typo here on page two.
3. What if we changed the size of the headline?
4. Are you open to considering different typefaces and colors?
5. Where are you going to distribute this?
6. Why use a brochure? Couldn't we spend the same money more effectively?

Where are you on this scale?

You could hire a brilliant graphic designer to take your bullet-filled PowerPoint presentation and fix the fonts and clean it up. But would it change the game?

When in doubt, challenge the strategy, not the tactics.

Simple example of thinking bigger: What if you hired Jill Greenberg to Photoshop well-known people in your industry to turn them into memorable images instead?

Every day you have the chance to completely reimagine what it is to communicate via PowerPoint. What Marc Andreessen has done is to completely reimagine what it is to be online. That's where the win lies, when you reinvent.

The bigger point is that **none of us are doing enough to challenge the assignment.** Every day, I spend at least an hour of my time looking at my work and what I've chosen to do next and wonder, "is this big enough?"

Yesterday, I was sitting with a friend who runs a small training company. He asked, "I need better promotion. How do I get more people to take the professional type design course I offer at my office?" My answer was a question, as it usually is. "Why is the course at your office?" and then, "why is it a course and not accreditation, or why not turn it into a guild for job seekers, where you could train people and use part of the tuition to hire someone to organize a private job board? You could guarantee clients well-trained students (no bozos), and you could guarantee students better jobs—everyone wins."

I have no idea if my idea for the training company is a good one, but I know it's a *bigger* one. That's when marketing pays for itself. Not when we find a typo or redesign a logo, but when we reconsider the question and turn the answer into something bigger than we ever expected.

What Does This Remind You Of?

Every time you visit a new website, enter a new airport, visit a new store, examine a new book, the question you ask first is, "what's this like?"

At a strange airport, if it's "like" your airport, you know just what to do. It's easy. If it's totally different, you have to stop, regroup, and start to understand what's involved.

If a book has cheap color separations, the wrong sort of gloss on the cover, and the wrong hue to the paper, it just feels cheap and self-published and unlikely to be the real deal. It doesn't matter a bit what's inside, who wrote it, anything. You've already decided because this book reminds you of untrustworthy books you've encountered before.

Visit a website with a brown-on-brown color scheme, a stock photo of a nautilus, some flashing graphics, a bunch of widgets, and a typeface that's not quite right, and you've already decided how you feel. Entirely based on the fact that *this* site is like *those* sites, and you didn't like those sites.

Meet someone at a conference who is dressed perfectly, with shined shoes and a great suit (but not trying too hard), and you're inclined to trust and respect him, because he reminds you of someone in a similar situation who was trustworthy.

Obvious, right?

So why do marketers so often miss this shortcut? Before you make what you're going to make, find something you want people to be reminded of. Feel free to discard this model if you want to make a point (the iPod did not remind you of a Sony CD player), but discard it on purpose. If you're writing a book, for example, your goal (probably) isn't to reinvent what it means to be a book. You're merely trying to reinvent the words and ideas. So when it comes to the jacket and the type, steal relentlessly. Your audience will thank you, because it's one less thing to process.

When in doubt, ask your colleagues, "what does this remind you of?"

Is That It?

- How long after getting a big promotion does it take for an executive to get antsy?
- Why does a powerful senator take small bribes and risk his entire career?
- Why do Amazon customers, with a choice of every book, delivered overnight, for free, whine about Amazon's customer service going downhill?
- Why do customers at a truly great four-star restaurant often feel a little bit of a letdown after the last course is served?
- Why do users of Facebook (a free service that they used to love) complain so vehemently about a change in layout?
- Why do the very same Apple lovers who waited in line for days now scoff at incremental (free) improvements in their iPhones?

"IS THAT IT?"

This state of ennui explains why we'll never run out of remarkable, why consumers are restless, why successful people keep working and taking risks. It explains the self-centered, whiny attitude of some bloggers who can never get enough from the world, and it explains why a rich country like the U.S. could almost bankrupt itself in search of ever more.

I'm not saying that consumers don't deserve respect and quality in exchange for their attention. I'm pointing out that we make ourselves unhappy just for the sport of it.

Marketers have played into this attitude and certainly amplified it. It helps them to gain share, of course, but it also raises the bar on what they're going to have to do next.

As a marketer or a leader, it helps to see two things about your work:

The first is to realize that people will never, ever be satisfied with you; they'll even whine when you give away something for free. Embrace the whining and realize that this attitude gives you an opportunity to answer the question with, "no! Wait, there's more!"

The second is to understand that a hug and a smile from a true friend *is* it. Along the way, marketers of stuff have tried to offer that stuff as a replacement for the thing that children/consumers/employees/customers/spouses really seek, which is connection and meaning and belonging and love.

You're Boring

If the marketplace isn't talking about you, there's a reason.

If people aren't discussing your products, your services, your cause, your movement, or your career, there's a reason.

The reason is that you're boring. (I guess that's what boring means, right?) And you're probably boring on purpose. You have boring pricing because that's safer. You have a boring location because to do otherwise would be nuts. You have boring products because that's what the market wants. That boring staff? They're perfectly well qualified.

You don't get unboring for free. Remarkable costs time and money and effort, but most of all, remarkable costs a willingness to be wrong.

Remarkable is a choice.

Love (and Annoying)

The goal is to create a product that people love. If people love it, they'll forgive a lot. They'll talk about it. They'll promote it. They'll come back. They'll be less price sensitive. They'll bring their friends. They'll work with you to make it better.

If you can't do that, though, perhaps you can make your service or product less annoying.

I understand that "love" and "annoying" are rarely two ends of the spectrum, but in this case, I think they are.

I think smart marketers at Apple work to make products that people love. Smart marketers at American Airlines ought to work at making an airline that isn't annoying.

Firefox used to be a product that people loved. Compared to the alternatives, it was magical. You could go on a quest to promote it and improve it.

At that point, a few years ago, the Firefox movement had a choice. Either continue to make Firefox ever more quirky and lovable (engaging a small audience, but with more passion), or work to make it less annoying (and allow it to reach more people). Today, people *like* (not love) Firefox, they continue to use it, and the idea spreads, but slowly. The goal has been chosen by the Firefox folks: to continue to make it less annoying. That's disappointing to the passionate, but it's a strategy.

Another example: I use iCal to keep track of my schedule. It defaults new appointments to 9 A.M., and if the appointment isn't at 9 A.M., I have to manually change it. Makes sense. Problem: if the appointment is at 4 P.M., and I change the 9 to a 4, iCal sets the alarm to go off at 4 A.M. Hey, wait a minute. I have never, ever had an appointment at 4 A.M. Doesn't iCal know this? Why is it so annoying! No one is ever going to love iCal as it stands, or even with some simple improvements, so why don't the engineers spend time making it less annoying instead?

What could Apple do to make the product something you would love? Really love? Clearly, that would require an overhaul. What could they do to make it less annoying? 100 little things, easy to do.

Example: Momofuku was a New York restaurant beloved by many people. People loved it because (not in spite of) how annoying the place could be. They were annoyingly inflexible. They didn't have particularly comfortable seating or great waiters. And the flagship restaurant made getting a reservation almost impossible. The quirkiness was part of the deal. Something to talk about when you brought a friend.

If all they did was think of ways to be less annoying, the restaurant wouldn't get better for the people who loved it; it would get worse. Unfortunately, they got really popular, forgot what made them lovable, and crossed a line. The annoying parts got really annoying, and they forgot to dream up new ways to be beloved. I gave up. It flipped and I hate it now. It's unloved *and* annoying. Boy, are customers like me fickle.

Think of the ordinary things you do or places you go. Could they be less annoying? What if the marketers there spent time and money to eliminate annoying? No, it's not the sort of big-time stuff that leads to love, but they're probably not going to get to love anyway. I'm not going to love my dry cleaner or the post office. But if they made those places less annoying, I'd spend more money and go more often. Face it, you use FedEx because it's less annoying than the post office, not because you love them.

I think there's a chasm here. You don't go for love and end up with less annoying. You need to do one or the other. There are products and services I love that are annoying, but that's okay, because that's part of being in love. And there are products and services that are annoyance-free, but I don't love them. That's okay, too. I like them just fine.

Put a sign on your office door, or send a memo to the team. It should say either, "Everything we do needs to make our product less annoying" or "Everything we do should be idiosyncratic and engage people and invite them to fall in love with us. That's not easy, which is why it's worth it." Can't have both. Must do one.

What Is School For?

Seems like a simple question, but given how much time and money we spend on it, it has a wide range of answers, many unexplored, some contradictory. I have a few thoughts about education, about how we use it to market ourselves and compete, and I realized that without a common place to start, it's hard to figure out what to do.

So, a starter list. The purpose of school is to:

1. Become an informed citizen
2. Be able to read for pleasure
3. Be trained in the rudimentary skills necessary for employment
4. Do well on standardized tests
5. Homogenize society, at least a bit
6. Pasteurize out the dangerous ideas
7. Give kids something to do while parents work
8. Teach future citizens how to conform
9. Teach future consumers how to desire
10. Build a social fabric
11. Create leaders who help us compete on a world stage
12. Generate future scientists who will advance medicine and technology
13. Learn for the sake of learning
14. Help people become interesting and productive
15. Defang the proletariat
16. Establish a floor below which a typical person is unlikely to fall
17. Find and celebrate prodigies, geniuses, and the gifted
18. Make sure kids learn to exercise, eat right, and avoid common health problems
19. Teach future citizens to obey authority
20. Teach future employees to do the same
21. Increase appreciation for art and culture
22. Teach creativity and problem solving
23. Minimize public spelling mistakes
24. Increase emotional intelligence
25. Decrease crime by teaching civics and ethics

26. Increase understanding of a life well lived

27. Make sure the sports teams have enough players

If you have the email address of the school board or principals, perhaps you'll forward this list to them (and I hope you *are* in communication with them regardless, since it's a big chunk of your future and your taxes!). Should make an interesting starting point for a discussion.

Like a Dream Come True

That's the way Derek Sivers (founder of CD Baby) described his mission statement in building the company. "What could I build that would be like a dream come true for independent musicians?"

What an extraordinarily universal way to construct a product, a service, or a business. Notice that dreams are rarely "within reason" or "under the circumstances." No, dreams are dreams. If your business is a dream come true for customers, you win. Game over.

Too often, I hear about businesses that just might be a dream come true for their owners, but hardly for the people they seek to recruit or the customers they hope to snare. What do your prospects dream of? What would get them to wait in line?

Return on Design

Return on investment is easy to measure. You put money in, you measure money out, divide, and prosper.

But return on design? (Design: graphics, system engineering, user interfaces, etc.)

Design can take money and time and guts, and what do you get in return? It turns out that the sort of return you're getting (and hoping for) will drive the decisions you make about design.

I think there are four zones of return that are interesting to think about. I find it's more useful to look at them as distinct states as opposed to a graduated line, because it's easy to spend a lot of time and money on design but not move up in benefits the way you might expect. Crest might have a better package than Colgate (or the other way around, I can't remember), but it doesn't sell any more units.

Negative return. The local store with the boarded-up window, the drooping sign, and the peeling paint is watching their business suffer because they have a design that actually hurts them. Software products suffer from this ailment often. If the design actively gets in the way of the story you tell or the utility you deliver, you lose money and share.

No impact. Most design falls into this category. While aesthetically important, design in this case is just a matter of taste, not measurable revenue. You might not like the way the liquor store looks, or the label on that bottle of wine, but it's not having any effect on sales. It's good enough.

Positive return. We're seeing a dramatic increase in this category. Everything from a bag of potato chips to a Web-based service can generate incremental sales and better utility as a result of smart design.

The whole thing. There are a few products where smart design *is* the product (or at least the product's reason for being). If you're not in love with the design of a Porsche 911, you would never consider buying it—same with an OXO peeler. The challenge of building your product around breakthrough design is that the design has to, in fact, be a breakthrough. And that means spending far more time or money than your competitors, who are merely seeking a positive return.

Knowing where you stand and where you're headed is critical. If you have a negative return on design, go ahead and spend enough money to get neutral, ASAP. But don't spend so much that you're overinvesting just to get to neutral. If a local store builds an expensive but not stellar custom building, that is a perfect example of this mismatch.

If you're betting the whole thing, building your service launch on design first, skimping on design is plain foolish. The Guggenheim in Bilbao would be empty if they'd merely hired a very good architect.

Two Halves of the Value Fraction

In a down economy, marketers fret a lot about price. We think that since times are tough, people care about price and nothing but price.

Of course, people actually care more about *value*. They care about value more than they used to because they can't afford to overpay; they don't want to make a mistake with their money.

Value = benefit/price. That means that one way to make value go up is to lower price, right?

The thing is, there's another way to make the value go up. Increase what you give. Increase quality and quantity and the unmeasurable pieces that bring confidence and joy to an interaction.

When all of your competitors are busy increasing value by cutting prices, you can actually increase market share by increasing value and raising benefits.

When You Buy Zappos, What Do You Buy?

Amazon just announced that they're spending $800,000,000.00 (looks better that way) to buy Zappos.com.

But wait.

Amazon already has plenty of shoes.

Amazon already has great technology.

Amazon already has relationships with FedEx and UPS.

What you buy when you spend that kind of money is what matters now. And what matters is:

- A corporate culture that's not the same (and where great people choose to work)
- A tight relationship with customers who give you permission to talk with them
- A business model that's remarkable and worth talking about
- A story that spreads
- Leadership

These things are available to organizations of every size. If you want them and choose to work for them.

Trolls

Lots of things about work are hard. Dealing with trolls is one of them. Trolls are critics who gain perverse pleasure in relentlessly tearing you and your ideas down. Here's the thing(s):

1. Trolls will always be trolling.
2. Critics rarely create.
3. They live in a tiny echo chamber, ignored by everyone except the trolled and the other trolls.
4. Professionals (that's you) get paid to ignore them. It's part of your job.

"Can't please everyone" isn't just an aphorism; it's the secret of being remarkable.

Upside Vs. Downside

How much time, staffing, and money does your organization spend on creating incredible experiences (vs. avoiding bad outcomes)?

At the hospital, it's probably 5% on the upside (the doctor who puts in the stitches, say) and 95% on the downside (all the avoidance of infection or lawsuits, records to keep, forms to sign). Most of the people you interact with in a hospital aren't there to help you get what you came for (to get better); they're there to help you avoid getting worse. At an avant-garde art show, on the other hand, perhaps 95% of the effort goes into creating and presenting shocking ideas, with just 5% devoted to keeping the place warm or avoiding falls and spills as you walk in.

Which is probably as it should be.

But what about you and your organization? As you get bigger and older, are you busy ensuring that a bad thing won't happen that might upset your day, or are you aggressively investing in having a remarkable thing happen that will delight or move a customer?

A new restaurant might rely on fresh vegetables and whatever they can get at the market. The bigger, more established fast-food chain starts shipping in processed canned food. One restaurant is less reliable with a bigger upside; the other is more dependable with less downside.

Here's a rule that's so inevitable that it's almost a law: *as an organization grows and succeeds, it sows the seeds of its own demise by getting boring.* With more to lose and more people to lose it, meetings and policies become more about avoiding risk than about providing joy.

The Why Imperative

Successful organizations spend a lot of time saying, "that's not what we do."

It's a requirement, because if you do everything, in every way, you're sunk. You got to where you are by standing for something, by approaching markets and situations in a certain way. Sure, Nike could make money in the short run by licensing their name to a line of wines and spirits, but that's not what they do.

"That's not what we do" is the backbone of strategy; it determines who you are and where you're going.

Except in times of change. Except when opportunities come along. Except when people in the organization forget to ask, "why?"

If the only reason you don't do something is because you never did, that's not a good reason. If the environment has changed dramatically and you are feeling pain because of it, this is a great reason to question yourself, to ask why.

The why factor is really clear online. Simon & Schuster or the *Encyclopedia Britannica* could have become Google (organizing the world's information), but they didn't build a search engine because that's not what they do. Struggling newspapers could have become thriving networks of long-tail content, but they chose not to, because that's not what they do.

Why?

That's the key question, one that organizations large and small need to ask a lot more often now that the economy is officially playing by new rules.

Choose Your Customers, Choose Your Future

Marketers rarely think about choosing customers. Like a sailor on shore leave, we're not so picky. Huge mistake.

Your customers define what you make, how you make it, where you sell it, what you charge, who you hire, and even how you fund your business. If your customer base changes over time but you fail to make changes in the rest of your organization, stress and failure will follow.

Sell to angry cheapskates and your business will reflect that. On the other hand, when you find great customers, they will eagerly co-create with you. They will engage and invent and spread the word.

It takes vision and guts to turn someone down and focus on a different segment, on people who might be more difficult to sell to at first, but who will lead you where you want to go over time.

Can't Top This

Getting someone to switch is really difficult.

Getting someone to switch because you offer more of what they were looking for when they chose the one they have now is essentially impossible. For starters, they're probably not looking for more. And beyond that, they'd need to admit that they were wrong for not choosing you in the first place.

So, you don't get someone to switch because you're cheaper than Walmart. You don't get someone to switch because you serve bigger portions than the big-portion steakhouse down the street. You don't get someone to switch because your hospital is more famous than the Mayo Clinic.

The chances that you can top a trusted provider on the very thing the provider is trusted for are slim indeed.

Instead, you gain converts by winning at something that the existing provider didn't think was so important.

Represent

The great brands of our time are not about what they are. They are about what they represent.

Apple, Sarah Palin, Harley-Davidson, TOMS Shoes . . . In each case, the reality of the product means far less than what the brand represents.

The facts of iPod battery life, knowledge of world affairs, gas mileage, and foot comfort are almost irrelevant. What matters is the Jungian rush these brands connote, their ability to allow us to identify ourselves and fellow tribe members, the sense of belonging and labeling and the journey we're on (or not, our choice).

Great brands represent something bigger than themselves. You can create this accidentally if you're lucky, but you can create it on purpose if you try.

The Lesson from Two Lemonade Stands

The first stand is run by two kids. They use Country Time lemonade, paper cups, and a bridge table. It's a decent lemonade stand, one in the long tradition of standard lemonade stands. It costs a dollar to buy a cup, which is a pretty good price, considering that you get both the lemonade and the satisfaction of knowing you supported two kids.

The other stand is different. The lemonade is free, but there's a big tip jar. When you pull up, the owner of the stand beams as only a proud eleven-year-old girl can beam. She takes her time and reaches into a pail filled with ice and lemons. She pulls out a lemon. Slices it. Then she squeezes it with a clever little hand juicer.

The whole time that she's squeezing, she's also talking to you, sharing her insights (and yes, her joy) about the power of lemonade to change your day. It's a beautiful day and she's in no real hurry. Lemonade doesn't hurry, she says. It gets made the right way or not at all. Then she urges you to take a bit less sugar, because it tastes better that way.

While you're talking, a dozen people who might have become customers drive on by because it appears to take too long. You don't mind, though, because you're engaged, almost entranced. A few people pull over and wait in line behind you.

Finally, once she's done, you put $5 in the jar, because your free lemonade was worth at least twice that. Well, maybe the lemonade itself was worth $3, but you'd happily pay again for the transaction. It touched you. In fact, it changed you.

Which entrepreneur do you think has a brighter future?

[PS: A few hours after I posted this, Elizabeth sent in this photo of her daughter doing exactly what I imagined. She said, "she made a fortune."]

The Ubiquity of Competition

Sure, there are playoffs in football, but competition is everywhere; we just forget to notice it.

There are 300 photographers looking for work in a particular specialty. One photographer puts a Creative Commons license on his shots in Flickr and they start showing up in many places, from presentations to brochures. Which of the 300 photographers has won the competition for attention? Which one of the 300 has shared his ideas enough to be noticed?

There are twenty towns you can choose for your family's new home. One town invests in its schools and has a focus on inquiry, AP courses, and community, while the others are muddling through, arguing about their future. Which one commands a higher premium for its houses?

There are a hundred new kinds of snacks and energy bars at the supermarket checkout. One bar is a little bigger, a little more exciting, and a little closer to eye level. Which one of the hundred wins the battle for your impulse buy?

There are fifty people applying for a job. Forty-nine have great credentials and beautifully standard layouts on their résumés. One résumé was hand-delivered to the CEO by his best friend, together with a glowing recommendation about a project the applicant did for the friend's nonprofit. Who gets the interview?

There are ten great jobs for the superstar programmer who is looking for a new challenge. One job offers offices (not cubicles), free lunch, great customer support, and the freedom to work on interesting projects. Where does she choose to apply?

There are thirty places that sell bumper stickers. One place shows up first in the Google ads when I do a search. Which one gets my business?

There are seventy houses for sale in town. One of them is represented by a broker who is a pillar of the community, a friend of many, and a role model for the industry. Which broker gets more people to the open house?

[There are 80 million blogs to choose from. Thanks for picking mine to read today.]

You don't have to like competition in order to understand that it exists. Your fair share isn't going to be yours unless you give the public a reason to pick you.

What's Expected Vs. What's Amazing

I visited a favorite restaurant last week, a place that, alas, I hadn't been to in months. The waiter remembered that I don't like cilantro. Unasked, she brought it up. Incredible. This was uncalled for, unnecessary, and totally delightful.

Scott Adams writes about the cyborg tool that is coming momentarily, a device that will remember names, find connections, bring all sorts of external data to us the moment we meet someone. "Oh, Bob, sure, that's the guy who's friends with Tracy . . . and Tim just tweeted about him a few minutes ago."

The first time someone does this to you in conversation (no matter how subtly), you're going to be blown away and flabbergasted. The tenth time, it'll be ordinary, and the twentieth time, boring.

Hotels used to get a lot of mileage out of remembering what you liked, but it was merely a database trick, not emotional labor on the part of the staff.

Today, if you go to an important meeting and the other people haven't bothered to Google you and your company, it's practically an offense. We're about to spend an hour together and you couldn't be bothered to look me up? *It's expected, no longer amazing.*

On the other hand, consider Dolores, a clerk at a 7-Eleven, who broke all sorts of coffee sales records because she remembered the name of every customer who came in every morning. Unexpected and amazing.

You can raise the bar or you can wait for others to raise it, but it's getting raised regardless.

[Irrelevant aside: *Linchpin* made the *New York Times* bestseller list yesterday. The list is hand tweaked, unreliable, and often wrong, but it's still a great thing to have happen the first week a book is out. Thank you to each of you who pitched in and spread the word. Unexpected and amazing, both.]

Pulitzer Prizefighting

People are drawn to existing competitions like moths to a flame.

It's precisely the wrong way to succeed.

Lots of journalists take significant detours in their careers and their writing in order to win a Pulitzer. Maybe not to actually win one, but to be in that class, to have peers that have won one. Mystery novelists stick to the center of the road, because that's where the road is. Movies are written and released in order to win an Oscar. Once there's a category, a ranking, a place to battle for supremacy, we run for it.

Do you go to trade shows or enter markets or submit RFPs or push for a GPA or even gross ratings points because there's a list of winners or because it's what you actually want to do? Most bestseller lists and prizes measure popularity, not effectiveness.

I wonder if real art comes when you build the thing that they don't have a prize for yet.

How to Use Clichés

I love this definition from Wikipedia:

> In printing, a cliché was a printing plate cast from movable type. This is also called a stereotype. When letters were set one at a time, it made sense to cast a phrase used repeatedly as a single slug of metal. "Cliché" came to mean such a ready-made phrase. The French word "cliché" comes from the sound made when the matrix is dropped into molten metal to make a printing plate.

To save time and money, then, printers took common phrases and re-used the type.

Along the way, they trained us to understand the image, the analogy, the story. Hear it often enough and you remember it. That training has a useful purpose. Now, you can say "Festivus" or "There is no I in team . . ." or "that took real courage" when describing a golf shot, and we immediately get it. Monty Python took a cliché about the Spanish Inquisition and made it funny by making it real. The comfy chair!

The effective way to use a cliché is to point to it and then do precisely the opposite. Juxtapose the cliché with the unexpected truth of what you have to offer. Apple does this all the time. They point out the cliché of a laptop or a desktop or an MP3 player and then they turn it upside down. Richard Branson takes the expected boredom of a CEO and turns it upside down by doing things you don't expect.

I often use the *Encyclopedia of Clichés* to find clichés that then inspire opposites. It's a secret weapon and it's all yours now. Have fun.

Finding Your Brand Essence

I got an email from someone who had hired a consulting firm to help his company find its true brand self. They failed. He failed. He asked me if I could recommend a better consulting firm.

My answer: the problem isn't the consultant; it's the fact that if you have to search for a brand essence, you're unlikely to find one.

Standing for something means giving up a lot of other things and opening yourself to criticism. Most people in the financial services industry (or any industry, actually) aren't willing to do that, which is why there are so few Charles Schwabs in the world.

First, decide that it's okay to fail and to make a ruckus while failing. THEN go searching for the way to capture that energy and share it with the world.

Clothes don't make the man; the man makes the man. Clothes (and the brand) just amplify that.

Hardly Worth the Effort

In most fields, there's an awful lot of work put into the last 10% of quality.

Getting your golf score from 77 to 70 is far more difficult than getting it from 120 to 113 or even from 84 to 77.

Answering the phone on the first ring costs twice as much as letting the call go into the queue.

Making pastries the way they do at a fancy restaurant is a lot more work than making brownies at home.

Laying out the design of a page or a flyer so it looks like a pro did it takes about ten times as much work as merely using the template Microsoft builds in for free, and the message is almost the same.

Except it's not. Of course not. The message is not the same.

The last 10% is the signal we look for, the way we communicate care and expertise and professionalism. If all you're doing is the standard amount, all you're going to get is the standard compensation. The hard part is the last 10%, sure, or even the last 1%, but it's the hard part because everyone is busy doing the easy part already.

The secret is to seek out the work that most people believe isn't worth the effort. That's what you get paid for.

But You're Not Saying Anything

And this is the problem with just about every lame speech, every overlooked memo, every worthless bit of boilerplate foisted on the world: you write and write and talk and talk and bullet and bullet, but no, you're not really saying anything.

It took me two minutes to find a million examples. Here's one: "The firm will remain competitive in the constantly changing market for defense legal services by creating and implementing innovative and effective methods of providing cost-effective, quality representation and services for our clients."

Write nothing instead. It's shorter.

Most people work hard to find artful ways to say very little. Instead of polishing that turd, why not work harder to think of something remarkable or important to say in the first place?

Hourly Work Vs. Linchpin Work

There's a gulf between hourly work and linchpin work.

You should pay people by the hour when there are available substitutes. When you rely on freelancers, you can put a value on their time based on what the market is paying. If there are six podiatrists in town and all can heal your foot, the going rate is based on their time and effort, not on the lifetime use of your foot.

On the other hand, if there are no short-term substitutes, then you don't pay what the market will bear; instead, you pay what someone is worth. Big difference.

Consider, for example, someone putting together a series of concerts for which they intend to sell subscriptions, or even have the musicians sell tickets.

They could seek out pretty good musicians and imagine that paying them $500 or more per hour is very fair compensation. After all, that's more than a podiatrist gets, and she gives you back the use of your foot.

But when they find a linchpin, someone who either will make it easier for them to sell subscriptions or will bring an audience with them, the question isn't how much time it took for the musician to do her set; the question is "what did she bring in terms of value," right? An indispensable person, someone with a rare asset, has few substitutes, and an hourly rate makes a lot less sense.

So, if a musician is going to sell 300 subscriptions for you and you earn $200 a subscription from that effort, that person just added $60,000 worth of value. Who cares if it took a minute or a day? What's on the table is who gets what portion of the value added.

I had a college professor who did engineering consulting. A brand-new office tower in Boston had a serious problem—there was a brown stain coming through the drywall (all of the drywall), no matter how much stain killer they used. In a forty-story building, if you have to rip out all the drywall, this is a multimillion-dollar disaster. They had exhausted all possibilities and were a day away from tearing out everything and taking a loss. They hired Henry in a last-ditch effort to solve the problem. He looked at the walls and said, "I think I can work out a solution, but it will cost you $45,000 if I succeed." They instantly signed on because if he succeeded, the project would be saved.

Henry asked for a pencil and paper and wrote the name of a common hardware-store chemical and handed it to them. "Here, this will work." And then he billed them $45,000. That's quite an hourly wage. It's also quite a bargain.

Lula's Logic

When Blythe and her partners started Lula's Sweet Apothecary, the best vegan ice cream stand in this hemisphere, they didn't have enough money to afford the letters to put "dairy free" on the sign in their window. They couldn't even afford "vegan." So the signage says nothing about what they *don't* put in their ice cream.

What they discovered was that word among the tribe of vegans in the East Village of New York City (an even bigger group than you might imagine) spread fast. The product was remarkable enough that just a few happy customers were enough to spread the word.

The other thing they discovered is that non-vegans were willing to walk on in if the place looked cool enough. In fact, the lack of ingredient declaration on their window actually helped them reach out to people who might have been scared away at the lack of milk.

Ink on the website is free, so they use the v-word there, but even though they can now afford lettering, the window is still proudly mute on their rigor regarding ingredients. No sense scaring away customers who don't care (and the customers who do care probably heard the news from their friends in advance).

Betting on Smarter (or Betting on Dumber)

Marketers fall into one of two categories:

A few marketers benefit when they make their customers *smarter*.

The more the people they sell to know, the more informed, inquisitive, freethinking, and alert they are, the better these marketers do.

And most marketers benefit when they work to make their customers *dumber*. The less they know about options, the easier they are to manipulate, the more helpless they are, the better these marketers do.

Tim O'Reilly doesn't sell books. He sells smarts. The smarter the world gets, the better he does.

The vast majority of marketers, though, take the opposite tack. Ask them for advice about their competitors, and they turn away and say, "I really wouldn't know." Ask them for details about their suppliers, and they don't want to tell you. Ask them to show you a recipe for how to make what they make on your own, and "it's a trade secret." Their perfect customer is someone in a hurry, with plenty of money and not a lot of knowledge about their options.

You've already guessed the punch line—if just one player enters the field and works to make people smarter, the competition has a hard time responding with a dumbness offensive. They can obfuscate and run confusing ads, but sooner or later, the inevitability of information spreading works in favor of those that bet on it.

The Market Has No Taste

When it comes to art, to human work that changes people, the mass market is a fool. A dolt. Stupid.

If you wait for the market to tell you that you're great, you'll merely end up wasting time. Or perhaps instead you will persuade yourself to ship the merely good, and settle for the tepid embrace of the uninvolved.

Great work is always shunned at first.

Would we (the market) benefit from more pandering by marketers churning out average stuff that gets a quick glance, or would we all be better off with passionate renegades on a mission to fulfill their vision?

The Paradox of Promises in the Age of Word of Mouth

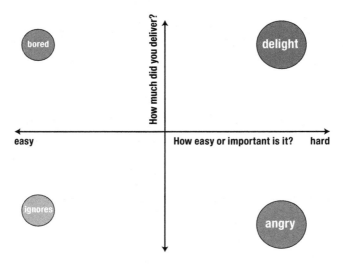

Word of mouth is generated by surprise and delight (or anger). This is a function of the difference between what you promise and what you deliver (see clever MBA chart above).

The thing is, if you promise very little, you don't get a chance to deliver because I'll ignore you. And if you promise too much, you don't get a chance to deliver, because I won't believe you.

Hence the paradox. The more you promise, the less likely you are to achieve delight and the less likely you are to earn the trust to get the gig in the first place. Salespeople often want you to allow them to overpromise, because it gets them through the RFP. Marketers, if they're smart, will push you (the CEO) to underpromise, since that's where the word of mouth is going to come from.

I have worked with someone who is very good at the promising part. She enjoys it. And when the promises don't work out, she's always ready with the perfect excuse. This is a great strategy if you have a regular job and the excuses are really terrific, but if you need internal or external clients, it gets old pretty fast. It certainly doesn't lead to the sort of word of mouth one is eager to encounter.

Surgeons have this problem all the time. They promise a complete, pain-free recovery and work hard to build up a positive expectation, particularly for elective surgery. And the entire time you're in bed, in pain, unable to pee, all you can do is hate on the doctor.

This is one reason why recovering from failure is such a great opportunity. If you or your organization fail and then you pull out all the stops to recover or make good, the expectation/delivery gap is huge. You don't win because you did a good job; you win because you so dramatically exceeded expectations.

Foundation Elements for Modern Businesses

When you sit down to dream up a new business, you can imagine a world without constraints. Or you can choose to build in fundamental pieces that will make it more likely that your idea will pay off.

Here are some fundamental pieces of most new successful businesses. The goal is to build these elements into the very nature of the business itself, not just to tack them on. For example, the Scotch Tape people at 3M can't do item #5 in the list below because of the structure of retail distribution and the way they mass-produce and can't track who is buying what.

You can live without some of these pieces, but go in with your eyes open if you do:

1. Build in virality. Consider: Groupon.
2. Don't sell a product that can be purchased cheaper at Amazon.
3. Subscriptions beat one-off sales.
4. Try to create an environment where your customers are happier when there are other customers doing business with you (see #1).
5. Treat different customers differently.
6. Generate joy; don't just satisfy a need for a commodity.
7. Rely on unique individuals, not an easily copied system.
8. Plan on remarkable experiences, not remarkable ads.
9. Don't build a fortress of secrets; bet on open.
10. Unless there's a differentiating business reason, use off-the-shelf software and cheap cloud storage.
11. The asset of the future is the embrace of a tribe, not a cheaper widget.

12. Match expenses to cash flow—don't run out of money, because it's no longer 1999.
13. Create scarcity, but act with abundance. Free samples create demand for the valuable (but not unlimited) tier you offer.
14. Tell a story, erect a mythology, walk the walk.
15. Plan on obsolescence (of your products, not your customers).

Notes:

3. The cost of selling a subscription to your product or service is not a lot higher than the cost of selling just one instance, but you benefit by having sales you can count on at low cost. Your customers benefit because you depend on them more and they save time.
5. Everyone has different needs and expectations and resources. The Internet lets you tell people apart and give them what they need.
7. AKA as linchpins.
9. If you're building a business based on trade secrets or lack of information among your customers, you're trying to fill a leaky bucket. Far easier to bet on the idea that the more people know, the better you do.
10. Cheap software and the cloud are going to continue to get cheaper, and custom work that's worth anything is going to continue to get more expensive.
12. The best people to fund your growth are your customers.
13. When the marginal cost of an interaction approaches zero, you benefit by creating plenty of interactions.
14. We can tell.

Alienating the 2%

When a popular rock group comes to town, some of their fans won't get great tickets. Not enough room in the front row. Now they're annoyed. Two percent of them are angry enough to speak up or bad-mouth or write an angry letter.

When Disney changes a policy and offers a great new feature or benefit to the most dedicated fans, 2% of them won't be able to use it, because of timing or transport or resources or whatever. They're angry and they let the brand know it.

Do the math. Every time Apple delights 10,000 people, they hear from 200 angry customers, people who don't like the change or the opportunity or the risk it represents.

If you have fans or followers or customers, no matter what you do, you'll annoy or disappoint 2% of them. And you'll probably hear a lot more from the unhappy 2% than from the delighted 98%.

It seems as though there are only two ways to deal with this: stop innovating and just stagnate; or go ahead and delight the vast majority.

Sure, you can try to minimize the cost of change, and you might even get the number down to 1%. But if you try to delight everyone, all the time, you'll just make yourself crazy. Or become boring.

The One Who Isn't Easily Replaced

The law of the Internet is simple: either you do something I can't do myself (or get from someone else), or I pay you less than you'd like.

Why else would it be any other way?

Twenty years ago, self-publishing a record was difficult and expensive. A big label could get you shelf space at Tower easily; you couldn't. A big label could pay for a recording session with available capital, but it was difficult for you to find the money or take the risk. A big label could reach the dozens of music reviewers, and do it with credibility. Hard for you to do that yourself.

Now?

Now when someone comes to a successful musician and says, "we'll take 90% and you do all the work," they're opening the door to an uncomfortable conversation. The label has no assets, just desire. That's great, but that's exactly what the musician has, and giving up so much pie (and control over his destiny) hardly seems like a fair trade.

Multiply this by a thousand industries and a billion freelancers and you come to one inescapable conclusion: be better, be different, or be cheaper. And the last is no fun.

Everyone and No One

Two things are always not true:

Everyone likes this.

No one likes this.

Sorry.

If you try to please everyone, the few you don't delight will either ruin your day or ruin your sense of what sort of product you should make.

And if you believe the critic who insists that no one is going to like what you made, you will walk away from a useful niche.

One other thing: sometimes it's easy to confuse "the small cadre of people I want to impress because my ego demands that this 'in' group is important" with "everyone." They're not the same.

Unreasonable

It's unreasonable to get out of bed on a snow day, when school has been cancelled, and turn the downtime into six hours of work on an extra-credit physics lab.

It's unreasonable to launch a technology product that jumps the development curve by nine months, bringing the next generation out much earlier than more reasonable competitors would.

It's unreasonable for a trucking company to answer the phone on the first ring.

It's unreasonable to start a new company without the reassurance that venture capital funding can bring.

It's unreasonable to expect a doctor's office to have a pleasant and helpful front-desk staff.

It's unreasonable to walk away from a good gig in today's economy, even if you want to do something brave and original.

It's unreasonable for teachers to expect that we can enable disadvantaged inner-city kids to do well in high school.

It's unreasonable to treat your colleagues and competitors with respect, given the pressure you're under.

It's unreasonable to expect that anyone but a great woman, someone with both drive and advantages, could do anything important in a world where the deck is stacked against ordinary folks.

It's unreasonable to devote years of your life to making a product that most people will never appreciate.

Fortunately, the world is filled with unreasonable people. Unfortunately, you need to compete with them.

Pleasing

A motto for those doing work that matters:

"We can't please everyone—in fact, we're not even going to try."

Or perhaps:

"Pleasing everyone with our work is impossible. It wastes the time of our best customers and annoys our staff. Forgive us for focusing on those we're trying to delight."

The math here is simple. As soon as you work hard to please everyone, you have no choice but to sand off the edges, pleasing some people *less* in order to please others a bit more. And it drives you crazy at the same time.

Who Will Say "Go"?

Here's a little-spoken truth learned via crowdsourcing:

Most people don't believe they are capable of initiative.

Initiating a project, a blog, a Wikipedia article, a family journey. Initiating something even when you're not putatively in charge.

At the same time, almost all people believe they are capable of editing, giving feedback, or merely criticizing.

So finding people to fix your typos is easy.

A few people are vandals, happy to anonymously attack or add graffiti or useless noise.

If your project depends on having individuals step up and say, "This is what I believe, here is my plan, here is my original thought, here is my tribe," then you need to expect that most people will see that offer and decline to take it.

Most of the edits on Wikipedia are tiny. Most of the tweets among the billions that go by are reactions or possibly responses, not initiatives. Q&A sites flourish because everyone knows how to ask a question, and many people feel empowered to answer it, if it's specific enough. Little tiny steps, not intellectual leaps or risks.

I have a controversial belief about this: I don't think the problem has much to do with the innate ability to initiate. I think it has to do with believing that it's possible and acceptable for you to do it. We've had these doors wide open for only a decade or so, and most people have been brainwashed into believing that their job is to copyedit the world, not to design it.

There's a huge shortage . . . a shortage of people who will say "go."

Jumping the Line Vs. Opening the Door

Every morning, the line of cars waiting to get onto the Hutchinson River Parkway exceeds 40. Of course, you don't have to patiently wait—you can drive down the center lane, passing all the civilized suckers, and then, at the last moment, cut over.

Drivers hate this, and for good reason. The road is narrow, and your aggressive act didn't help anyone but you. You slowed down the cars in the lane behind you, and your selfish behavior merely made 40 other people wait.

This is a different act than the contribution someone makes when she sees that everyone is patiently waiting to enter a building through a single door. She walks past everyone and opens a second door. Now, with two doors open, things start moving again, and she's certainly earned her place at the front of that second entrance.

Too often, we're persuaded that initiative and innovation and by-passing the status quo constitute some sort of line jumping, a selfish gaming of the zero-sum game. Most of the time it's not. In fact, what you do when you solve an interesting problem is that you open a new door. Not only is that okay, but I think it's actually a moral act.

Don't wait your turn if waiting your turn is leaving doors unopened.

Seven Questions for Leaders

Do you let the facts get in the way of a good story?

What do you do with people who disagree with you? Do you call them names in order to shut them down?

Are you open to multiple points of view, or do you demand compliance and uniformity? [Bonus: Are you willing to walk away from a project or customer or employee who has values that don't match yours?]

Is it okay if someone else gets the credit?

How often are you able to change your position?

Do you have a goal that can be reached in multiple ways?

If someone else can get us there faster, are you willing to let them?

No textbook answers . . . It's easy to get tripped up by these. In fact, most leaders I know, do.

Are You Doing a Good Job?

One way to approach your work: "I come in on time, even a little early. I do what the boss asks, a bit faster than she expects. I stay on time and on budget, and I'm hardworking and loyal."

The other way: "What aren't they asking me to do that I can do, learn from, make an impact on, and possibly fail (yet survive)? What's not on my agenda that I can fight to put there? Whom can I frighten, what can I learn, how can I go faster, what sort of legacy am I creating?"

You might very well be doing a good job. But that doesn't mean you're a linchpin, the one we'll miss. For that, you have to stop thinking about the job and start thinking about your platform, your point of view, and your mission.

It's entirely possible that you work somewhere that gives you no option but to merely do a job. If that's actually true, I wonder why someone with your potential would stay.

In the post-industrial revolution, the very nature of a job is out-moded. Doing a good job is no guarantee of security, advancement, or delight.

Kraft Singles

Here's a ubiquitous food that succeeds because it's precisely in the center, perfectly normal, exactly the regular kind. No kid whines about how weird Kraft Singles are.

If you're Kraft, this is a good place to be. Singles mint money. My friend Nancy worked on this brand. It's a miracle.

If you're anyone else, forget about becoming more normal than they are, more regular than the regular kind. That slot is taken.

Most mature markets have their own version of Kraft Singles. The challenge for an insurgent is not to try to battle the incumbent for the slot of normal. The challenge is to be edgy and remarkable and to have the market move its center to you.

Perfect Vs. Interesting

There are two jobs available to most of us:

You can be the person or the organization that's perfect. The one that always ships on time, without typos, that delivers flawlessly and dots every *i*. You can be the hosting company or the doctor that might be boring but is always right.

Or you can be the person or the organization that's interesting. The thing about being interesting, making a ruckus, creating remarkable products, and being magnetic is that you have to be that way only once in a while. No one is expected to be interesting all the time.

FedEx vs. Playwrights Horizons.

When an interesting person is momentarily not-interesting, I wait patiently. When a perfect organization, the boring one that's constantly using its policies to dumb things down, is imperfect, I get annoyed. Because perfect has to be perfect all the time.

Economies of Small

Economies of scale are well understood. Bigger factories are more efficient, bigger distribution networks are more efficient, bigger ad campaigns can be more efficient. It's often hard to defeat a major competitor, particularly if the market is looking for security and the status quo.

But what about the economies of small? Is being bigger an intrinsic benefit in and of itself?

If your goal is to make a profit, it's entirely possible that less overhead and a more focused product line will increase it.

If your goal is to make more art, it's entirely possible that ridding yourself of obligations and scale will help you do that.

If your goal is to have more fun, it's certainly likely that avoiding the high stakes of more debt, more financing, and more stuff will help with that.

I think we embraced scale as a goal when the economies of that scale were so obvious that we didn't even need to mention them. Now that it's so much easier to produce a product in the small and to market a product in the small, and now that it's so beneficial to offer a service to just a few, with focus and attention, perhaps we need to rethink the very goal of scale.

Don't be small because you can't figure out how to get big. Consider being small because it might be better.

What's the Point of Popular?

You'd think that it's the most important thing in the world. Homecoming queen, student-body president, the most Facebook friends, Oscar winner, how many people are waiting in line at the book signing . . .

Popular is almost never a measure of impact, or genius, or art, though. Popular rarely correlates with guts, hard work, or a willingness to lead (and to be wrong along the way).

I'll grant you that being popular (at least on one day in November) is a great way to get elected president. But in general, the search for popular is wildly overrated, because it corrupts our work, eats away at our art, and makes it likely that we'll compromise to please the anonymous masses.

Worth considering is the value of losing school elections and other popularity contests. Losing reminds you that the opinion of unaffiliated strangers is worthless. They don't know you, they're not interested in what you have to offer, and you can discover that their rejection actually means nothing. It will empower you to do even bigger things in the future.

When you focus on delighting an audience you care about, you strip the masses of their power.

Brand Exceptionalism

Your brand is your favorite. After all, it's yours. You understand it, you helped build it, you're obsessed with the nuance behind it. Your organization's actions make sense to you, you sat in the room as they were being argued about . . . you might even have helped make some of the decisions.

So, your brand doesn't do anything wrong. What it does is the best it could do under the circumstances. Someone who knew what you know would make the very same decision, because under the circumstances it was the only/best option.

Of course we should buy from you. You're better!

When your brand starts falling behind a competitor (Dell vs. Apple, Microsoft vs. Google, Washington Mutual vs. Everyone, and then Apple vs. Android, Google vs. Facebook), you say it's not fair, or expected.

The problem with brand exceptionalism is that once you believe it, it's almost impossible to innovate. Innovation involves failure, which an exceptional brand shouldn't meet with, and the only reason to endure failure is to get ahead, which you don't need to do. Because you're exceptional.

In the battle for attention or market share, the market makes new decisions every day. And the market tends to be selfish. Often, it will pick the arrogant market leader (because the market also tends to be lazy), but upstarts and new competitors always have an incentive to change the game or the story.

Brand humility is the only response to a fast-changing and competitive marketplace. The humble brand understands that it needs to re-earn attention, re-earn loyalty, and reconnect with its audience as if every day is the first day.

How to Be Interviewed

The explosion of media channels and public events means that more people are being interviewed about more topics than ever before. It might even happen to you . . . and soon.

1. They call it *giving* an interview, not taking one, and for good reason. If you're not eager to share your perspective, don't bother showing up.

2. Questions shouldn't be taken literally. The purpose of the question is to give you a chance to talk about something you care about. The audience wants to hear what you have to say, and if the question isn't right on point, answer a different one instead.

3. In all but the most formal media settings, it's totally appropriate to talk with the interviewer in advance, to give her some clues about what you're interested in discussing. It makes you both look good.

4. The interviewer is not your friend, and everything you say is on the record. If you don't want it to be in print, don't say it.

5. If you get asked the same question from interview to interview, there's probably a good reason. Saying, "I get asked that question all the time," and then grimacing in pain, is disrespectful to the interviewer and the audience. See rule #1.

6. If your answers aren't interesting, exciting, or engaging, that's your fault, not the interviewer's. See rule #2.

The Grateful Dead and the Top 40

I wonder if Jerry ever got jealous of acts that were able to put songs on the radio. (The Dead had exactly one hit record.)

I hope not. Jerry was in a different business. Sure, he played music. Elton John also plays music. But they were in different businesses, performing for different audiences, generating revenue in different ways, creating different sorts of art.

In a world filled with metrics and bestseller lists, it's easy to decide that everyone is your competitor, and easier still to worry about your rank. Worry all you want, but if it gets in the way of your art or starts changing your mission, it's probably a mistake.

It used to be that the non-customers, passersby, and quiet critics of your venture were totally invisible to you. They drove by, or muttered under their breath, or simply went to someone else. Now, all is visible. Just because you're vividly aware of your shortcomings in market share doesn't mean it's important.

The next time you have a choice between chasing the charts (whichever charts you keep track of) and doing the work your customers crave, do the work instead.

Are You Wow Blind?

Kevin asked me: "Do 'great ideas' possess universally some sort of Wow Factor?"

The problems with this question: What does "great" mean? And who decides what "wow" is?

The challenge is this: lots of people think they know what both words mean in their area of endeavor, and many of them are wrong.

Consider the case of Web 2.0 companies. People like Brad Feld and Fred Wilson are brilliant at understanding what wow means from an investor's point of view. They have great taste about what's going to pay off. They have a sense for which teams and which ideas will actually turn into great businesses.

The peanut galleries at tech sites, though, don't have such great abilities (if they did, they'd be Brad, not anonymous voters). As a result, they mistake consumer wow for investor wow, and they often focus on the wrong attributes when they're criticizing or congratulating a company.

This tendency is endemic in the book business, which resolutely refuses to understand the actual P&L of most of the books it publishes. As a result, there are plenty of editors who continue to overpay for the wrong books, because their wow isn't the market's wow.

In his book *Moneyball*, Michael Lewis wrote about how virtually every single scout and manager in baseball was wrong about what makes a great baseball player. They had the wrong radar, the wrong wow. When statistics taught a few teams what the real wow was, the balance of power shifted.

By definition, just about every great idea resonates early with those who have better radar than with those who don't. The skill, then, is to expose yourself often enough, learn enough, and fail enough that you get to say wow before the competition does.

Unbetterable

The two best ways to break through a rut and to make an impact:

- Find things that others have accepted as the status quo and make them significantly, noticeably, and remarkably better.
- Find things that you're attached to that are slowing you down, realize that they are broken beyond repair, and eliminate them. Toss them away and refuse to use them any longer.

When a not-so-good software tool or a habit or an agency or a policy has too much inertia to be fixed, when it's unbetterable, you're better off without it. Eliminating it will create a void, fertile territory for something much better to arrive.

Defining Quality

Given how much we talk about it, it's surprising that there's a lot of confusion about what quality is.

Which is a higher-quality car: a one-year-old Honda Civic or a brand-new, top-of-the-line Bentley?

It turns out that there are at least two useful ways to describe quality, and the conflict between them leads to the confusion:

Quality of design: Thoughtfulness and processes that lead to user delight, that make it likely that someone will seek out a product, pay extra for it, or tell a friend.

Quality of manufacture: Removing any variation in tolerances that a user will notice or care about.

In the case of the Civic, the quality of manufacture is clearly higher by any measure. The manufacturing is more exact, so the likelihood is tiny that the car will perform (or not perform) in a way you don't expect.

On the other hand, we can probably agree that the design of the Bentley is more bespoke, luxurious, and worthy of comment.

Let's think about manufacturing variations for a second: FedEx promises overnight delivery. Delivery at 10:20 vs. delivery at 10:15 is not something the recipient cares about. Tomorrow vs. Thursday, they care about a lot. The goal of the manufacturing process isn't to reach the perfection of infinity. It's to drive tolerances so hard that the consumer doesn't care about the variation. Spending an extra million dollars to get five minutes faster isn't as important to the FedEx brand as is spending a million dollars to make the website delightful.

Dropbox is a company that got both right. The design of the service is so useful that it now seems obvious. At the same time, though, and most critically, the manufacture of the service is to a very high tolerance. Great design in a backup service would be useless if one in a thousand files were corrupted.

Microsoft struggles (when they struggle) because sometimes they get both wrong. Software that has a user interface that's a pain to use rarely leads to delight, and bugs represent significant manufacturing defects, because sometimes (usually just before a presentation), the software doesn't work as expected—a *noticed* variation.

The Shake Shack, many New York burger fans would argue, is a higher-quality fast-food experience than McDonald's, as evidenced by lines out the door and higher prices. Except from a production point of view. The factory that is McDonald's far outperforms the small chain in terms of efficient production of the designed goods within certain tolerances. It's faster and more reliable. And yet, many people choose to pay extra to eat at Shake Shack. Because it's "better." Faster doesn't matter as much to the Shake Shack customer.

The balance, then, is to understand that marketers want both. A shortsighted CFO might want neither.

Deming defined quality as: (result of work effort)/(total costs). Unless you understand both parts of that fraction, you'll have a hard time allocating your resources.

Consider what Philip Crosby realized a generation ago: quality is free.

It's cheaper to design marketing quality into the product than it is to advertise the product.

It's cheaper to design manufacturing quality into a factory than it is to inspect it after the product has already been built.

These quality definitions go hand in hand. Don't tell me about server uptime if your interface is lame or the attitude of the people answering the phone is obnoxious. Don't promise me a brilliant new service if you're unable to show up for the meeting. Don't show me a boring manuscript with no typos in it, and don't try to sell me a brilliant book so filled with errors that I'm too distracted to finish it.

There are two reasons that quality of manufacture is diminishing in importance as a competitive tool:

A. Incremental advances in this sort of quality get increasingly more expensive. Going from one defect in a thousand to one in a million is relatively cheap. Going from one in a million to one in a billion, though, costs a fortune.

B. As manufacturing skills increase (and information about them is exchanged), it means that your competition has as much ability to manufacture with quality as you do.

On the other hand, quality of design remains a fast-moving, judgment-based process in which supremacy is hard to reach and harder to maintain.

And yet organizations often focus obsessively on manufacturing quality. Easier to describe, easier to measure, easier to take on as a group. It's essential, it's just not as important as it used to be.

The Trap of Social Media Noise

If we put a number on it, people will try to make the number go up.

Now that everyone is a marketer, many people are looking for a louder megaphone, a chance to talk about their work, their career, their product . . . and social media looks like the ideal soapbox, a free opportunity to shout to the masses.

But first, we're told to make that number go up. Increase the number of fans, friends, and followers, so your shouts will be heard. The problem, of course, is that *more noise is not better noise.*

In Corey's words, the conventional, broken wisdom is:

- Follow a ton of people to get people to follow back.
- Focus on the number of followers, not on the interests of followers or your relationship with them.
- Pump links through the social platform (take your pick, or do them all!).
- Offer nothing of value, and no context. *This is a megaphone, not a telephone.*
- Think you're winning, because you're playing video games (highest follower count wins!).

This activity looks like winning (the numbers are going up!), but it's actually a double-edged form of losing. First, you're polluting a powerful space, turning signals into noise and bringing down the level of discourse for everyone. And second, you're wasting your time when you could be building a tribe instead, could be earning permission, could be creating a channel where your voice is welcomed.

Leadership (even idea leadership) scares many people, because it requires you to own your words, to do work that matters. The alternative is to be a junk dealer.

Game theory pushes us in one of two directions:

Either be better at pump-and-dump than anyone else, get your numbers into the millions, outmass those that choose to use mass, and always dance at the edge of spam (in which the number of those you offend or turn off forever keeps increasing), *or*

Relentlessly focus. Prune your message and your list, and build a reputation that's worth owning and an audience that cares.

Only one of these strategies builds an asset of value.

The Simple First Rule of Branding and Marketing Anything (Even Yourself)

Not a secret, often overlooked:

"Keep your promises."

If you say you'll show up every day at 8 A.M., do so. Every day.

If you say your service is excellent, make it so.

If circumstances or priorities change, well then, invest to change them back. Or tell the truth, and mean it.

If traffic might be bad, plan for it.

Is there *actually* unusually heavy call volume? Really?

Want a bigger brand? Make bigger promises. And keep them.

No One Ever Bought Anything in an Elevator

The purpose of an elevator pitch isn't to close the sale.

The goal isn't even to give a short, accurate, Wikipedia-standard description of you or your project.

And the idea of using vacuous, vague words to craft a bland mission statement is dumb.

No, the purpose of an elevator pitch is to describe a situation or solution so compelling that the person you're with wants to hear more even after the elevator ride is over.

Time Doesn't Scale

But bravery does.

The challenge of maintaining work/life balance is a relatively new one, and it is an artifact of a world where you get paid for showing up, paid for hours spent, paid for working.

In that world, it's clearly an advantage to have a team that spends more time than the competition does. One way to get ahead as a freelancer or a factory worker of any kind (even a consultant at Deloitte) is simply to put in more hours. After all, that makes you more productive, if we define productivity as output per dollar spent.

But people have discovered that after hour 24, there are no more hours left. Suddenly, you can't get ahead by outworking the other guy, because both of you are already working as hard as Newtonian physics will permit.

Just in time, the economy is now rewarding art and innovation and guts. It's rewarding brilliant ideas executed with singular direction by aligned teams on behalf of truly motivated customers. None of which is measured on the clock.

John Cage doesn't work more hours than you. Neither does Carole Greider. Work/life balance is a silly idea, just as work/food balance or work/breathing balance is. It's not really up to you after a certain point. Instead of sneaking around the edges, you might find that it pays to cut your hours in half but take the intellectual risks and do the emotional labor you're capable of.

Speaking When They Care (Reorganizing the Economics and Attitude of Customer Service)

Advertisers struggle to be heard through the noise. Customer service reps, on the other hand, can whisper.

A few organizations have figured out how to turn customer service into a marketing opportunity and thus a profit center. They figure that if they've got your attention, if they're talking to you at a moment when you care a great deal, they can turn that into an opportunity to delight. And being delighted is remarkable and worth talking about.

That means that if your organization has a "stall, deny, and avoid" policy when it comes to customer interaction, you will almost certainly be defeated if a competitor comes up with a scalable way to delight.

Overseas call centers and online chats handled by untrained workers with no incentives seem like clever ways to cut costs during stressful times. What they actually are, are *scalable engines of annoyance*, time-sucking processes that raise expectations and then totally dash them. Better to not even have a phone number. (You can't call Google, but you don't *want* to call Adobe. Which one generates more animus—the inability to call, or the unfulfilled promise of respect and thoughtful help?)

Or consider: some airlines are starting to realize that a delayed or cancelled flight is actually a chance to earn some remarkability. In the two hours that someone is stranded, he is paying very careful attention to your brand. What are you (the airlines) doing? Notifying stranded customers by email that the flight is late, offering them free Wi-Fi, even giving them a link to a free book or movie online—none of that costs more than caring. All of those actions are important opportunities to be heard and remembered.

Investing in delight via customer service is cheap to experiment with and easy to prove. Just siphon off 1% of your calls to a trained person who actually cares and wants to help—and see what happens to customer satisfaction and word of mouth. Cancel a few TV ads and you can pay for it—soon it will pay for itself.

On Making a Ruckus in Your Industry

Bring forward a new idea or technology that disrupts business as usual and demands a response.

Change pricing dramatically.

Redefine a service as a product (or vice versa).

Organize the disorganized, connect the disconnected.

Radically alter the speed to market.

Change the infrastructure, the rules, or the flow of information.

Give away what used to be expensive and charge for something else.

Cater to the weird, bypassing the masses.

Take the lead on ethics.

(Or you could just wait for someone to tell you what they want you to do.)

Multiplying or Dividing?

If you have a list of 1,000 subscribers or 5,000 fans or 10,000 supporters, you have a choice to make.

You can create stories and options and benefits that naturally spread from this group to their friends, and your core group can multiply, with 5,000 growing to 10,000 and then 100,000.

Or you can put the group through a sales funnel, weed out the free riders, and monetize the rest. A 5% conversion rate means you just turned 5,000 interested people into 250 paying customers.

Multiplying scales. Dividing helps you make this quarter's numbers.

Do We Have to Pander?

The road to the bottom is paved with good intentions or, at the very least, clever rationalizations.

National Geographic goes into a cable TV partnership and ends up broadcasting shameless (shameful? same thing) reality shows, then justifies it as a way to make money to pay for the good stuff.

Restaurants serve chicken fingers to their guests' kids, because it's the only thing they'll eat.

Some comedians give up their best work in exchange for jokes that everyone will get.

Brands extend their products or dumb down their offerings or slap their names on inferior substitutes, all in the name of reaching the masses.

And that's the problem with the shortcut. You trade in your reputation (another word for brand) in exchange for a short-term boost of awareness or profit, but then you have neither. Yes, you can have a blog that follows every rule of blogging and SEO, but no, it won't be a blog we'll miss if it's gone.

Should Harley-Davidson make a scooter?

Yes, you can pander, and if you're a public company and have promised an infinite growth curve, you may very well have to. But if you want to build a reputation that lasts, if you want to be the voice that some (not all!) in the market seek out, the opportunity to appeal to everyone is nothing but a trap, a test to see if you can resist short-term greed long enough to build something that matters.

NEW WORLD ORDER

Change. Connection. Tactics.

The End of the Job Interview

Let's assert that there are two kinds of jobs you need to fill.

The first kind of job is a cog job. A job where you need someone to perform a measurable task and to follow instructions. This can range from stuffing envelopes to performing blood tests. It's a profitable task if the person is productive, and you need to find a reliable, skilled person to do what you need.

The second kind of job requires insight and creativity. This job relies on someone doing something you could never imagine in advance, producing outcomes better than you had hoped for. This might include a sales job, or someone rearranging the factory floor to increase productivity. It could also include a skilled craftsperson or even a particularly skilled receptionist.

If you're hiring for the first kind of job, exactly why are you sitting a nervous candidate down in your office and asking her to put on some sort of demonstration of her ability to interact with strangers under pressure? Why do you care what his suit looks like or whether or not he can look you in the eye?

Years ago, in order to keep the ethnic balance at Harvard the way some trustees felt was correct, the school created interviews and essays as a not-so-subtle way to weed out the undesirables. This practice spread to just about every college in the country, and persists to this day, even though it's a largely discredited way to determine anything. Your company is probably doing exactly the same thing. If someone can do the cog job, what other information are you looking for? Why?

And if you're hiring for the second kind of job, the question becomes even more interesting. Would you marry someone based on a one-hour interview in a singles bar? And how does repeating the forced awkwardness of an interview across your entire team help you choose which people are going to do the extraordinary work you're banking on?

I've been to thousands of job interviews (thankfully as an interviewer mostly) and I have come to the conclusion that the entire effort is a waste of time.

At least half the interview finds the interviewer giving an unplanned and not very good overview of what the applicant should expect from this job. Unlike most of the marketing communications the organization does, this spiel is unvetted, unnatural, and unmeasured. No one has ever sat down and said, "When we say X, is it likely that the applicant understands what we mean? Are we putting our best foot forward? Does it make it more likely that the right people will want to work here, for the right reasons?" [Tell the truth: Do you test your job interview spiel the same way you test your Web results or even your direct mail?]

The other half of the interview is dedicated to figuring out whether the applicant is good at job interviews or not.

I should have learned this lesson in 1981, when my partner and I (and three of our managers) hired Susan, who was perhaps the best interviewer I have ever met. And one of the worst employees we ever hired. Too bad we didn't have a division that sold interviews.

Let me be clear about what I'm recommending: the next time someone asks you to "sit in" on an interview, just say no. Don't do it. Don't waste your time or theirs.

So, what should you do instead?

Glad you asked!

First, none of this will work if you're not offering a great job at a great company for fair pay. These techniques will not succeed if you are the employer of last resort. Assuming that's not the case, how about this:

Every applicant gets a guided tour of your story. Maybe from a website or lens or DVD. Maybe from one person in your organization who is really good at this. It might mean a plant tour or watching an interview with the CEO. It might involve spending an hour sitting in one of your stores or following one of your doctors around on her rounds. But it's a measurable event, something you can evaluate after the process is over. If you're hiring more than a few people a week, clearly it's worth having a full-time person to do this task and do it well.

There are no *one-on-one-sit-in-my-office-and-let's-talk* interviews. Boom, you just saved seven hours per interview. Instead, spend those seven hours actually doing the work. Put the person on a team and have a brainstorming session, or design a widget or make some espressos together. If you want to hire a copywriter, do some copywriting. Send back some edits and see how they're received.

If the person is really great, hire them. For a weekend. Pay them to spend another 20 hours pushing their way through something. Get them involved with the people they'll actually be working with and find out how it goes. Not just the outcomes but the process. Do their behavior and insight change the game for the better? If they want to be in sales, go on a sales call with them. Not a trial run, but a real one. If they want to be a rabbi, have them give a sermon or visit a hospital.

Yes, people change after you hire them. They always do. But do they change more after an unrealistic office interview or after you've actually watched them get in the cage and tame a lion?

When Culture Gets Stuck

Classical music wasn't always "classical."

Geeks spend a lot of time worrying about the cutting edge, focusing on creating Digg bait, reaching the early adopters, making something cool enough and fresh enough to capture attention and to spread.

We spend very little time thinking about the other end of the curve.

That's where culture gets stuck.

Once something makes its way to the mass market, the mass market doesn't want it to change. And once it moves from that big hump in the middle of the market to become a classic, the market doesn't just want it to not change, but insists that it not change.

So classical music gets stuck because the new stuff isn't like the regular kind, the classics. French food got stuck, because no restaurant could risk its three stars to try something new. A convention can't change cities or formats. Schools can't start their curriculum over. The culture gets stuck because the masses want it be stuck.

That's because the late adopters and the laggards have plenty of money and influence—while the early adopters have a short attention span and rank low in persistence.

Inside most fields, we see pitched battles between a few people who want serious change to reinvigorate the genre they love—and the masses, who won't tolerate change of any kind. Hey, there are still people arguing vehemently about whether Mass should be in Latin or not.

History has shown us that the answer is crystal clear: if you want change, you've got to leave. Change comes, almost always, from the outside. The people who reinvented music, food, technology, and politics have always gone outside the existing dominant channels to create something new and vital and important.

Understanding the Super Bowl

It's hard to remember back 23 years ago, but back then, when dinosaurs walked the earth, a few things were true:

1. Commercials were commercials—they sold stuff.
2. Content was content—it wasn't filled with commercials.

The famous 1984 Apple ad changed everything. It was now commercial as content, commercial as event. The Apple ad was seen by more people *after* the game, via free media, than saw it during the game itself.

So, as you waste an evening watching television, understand that the media game you're watching (as opposed to the football game) is not about selling anything per se. Instead, it's about creating a short little movie that spreads. Yes, it's permission marketing. Permission marketing because viewers are asking for the ads, they want the ads, they look forward to them. BUT we're not watching them because we want to buy or even to learn (the way, say, Google ads work). We're watching because we want to be in on the joke, to have something to share. It's big enough that there are entire Web pages about the commercials. I'll be contributing to the one at *Adweek*. At least until I get too bored with the game . . .

The commercial aspect of this is fascinating as well. Who wins? Probably not the shareholders. Someone at Frito Lay told me that they can prove that enough people buy chips during halftime (they leave their house and race out to the store) that the ads pay for themselves. But insurance?

The winners, I think, are the agencies and the pundits and those that would like advertising to be more than it actually is.

No-Impact-Man Makes an Impact

Since he was written up in the *Times* last week, No Impact Man has been causing shockwaves. Here's a guy who, with his family, is going without; he's restricting his intake to local foods, and his output to a tiny fraction of the typical American's.

I was at the Union Square Market last week, buying some local eggs. A well-dressed woman marched up and handed two empty cardboard egg trays to the farmer, for reusing (a step better than recycling).

Suddenly, $40 an ounce for raspberries flown in from Chile isn't so sexy anymore.

Now, people look at someone driving a Chevy Suburban the same way they look at a fit person parking in a handicapped space. "Why," they wonder, "do you need to do that?" It's sort of a mix of suspicion and pity.

The richest and best-educated people in our economy are shifting, and pretty quickly. They're just as willing to spend money as they always were, but now it's not focused on fancy organic stuff at the Whole Foods Market or giant bulletproof cars from Germany or private jet travel. Instead, the market is trying as hard as it can to spend time and money without leaving much of a trace.

I think this story has legs and is going to be around for a long time. Zero is the new black.

I'd Ignore Him Too

I got more mail about the *Washington Post* story of violinist Joshua Bell playing in a DC Metro station than about any other non-blog topic ever. I saw it when it first came out but didn't blog it because I thought the lesson was pretty obvious to my readers. World-class violinist plays for hours in a subway station; almost no one stops to listen. The experiment just proved what we already know about context, permission, and worldview. If your worldview is that music in the subway isn't worth your time, you're not going to notice when the music is better than usual (or when a famous violinist is playing). It doesn't match the story you tell yourself, so you ignore it. Without permission to get through to you, the marketer/violinist is invisible.

But why all the mail? (And the *Post* got plenty too.) Answer: I think it's because people realized that if they had been there, they would have done the same thing. And it bothers us.

It bothers us that we're so overwhelmed by the din of our lives that we've created a worldview that requires us to ignore the outside world most of the time, even when we suffer because of it. It made me feel a little smaller, knowing that something so beautiful was ignored because the marketers among us have created so much noise and so little trust.

I don't think the answer is to yell louder. Instead, I think we have an opportunity to create beauty and genius and insight and to offer it in ways that train people to maybe, just maybe, loosen up those worldviews and begin to trust.

Meetings

I had breakfast today with a senior executive who estimates that she spends more than 30% of her time in internal meetings.

My guess is that many marketers (who seem to go to more meetings than most people) might envy a number that low.

Despite the time spent, most people don't seem particularly happy with the results the meetings create. In that spirit, I want to share some radical thoughts on how you could completely change the meeting dynamic in your organization.

DIFFERENT TYPES OF MEETINGS. It's a huge mistake to just show up in a conference room and have a meeting. If the expectation is "yet another meeting," then the odds are, you'll have yet another meeting.

Here are a few very distinct types of meetings:

- *Just so everyone knows:* This is a meeting in which one person or small group tells other people what's already been decided and is about to happen. These meetings should always have a written piece to go with them, and in many cases, it should be distributed a day before the meeting. The meeting should be very short, take place in an auditorium-type setting, not a circle, and have focused Q&A at the end. Even a quiz. It's the football huddle, and the running back isn't supposed to challenge the very premises the quarterback is using to call the play.

- *What are you up to:* This is a meeting in which every participant needs to present the state of their situation. It probably happens on a regular basis and each person should have a strict time limit. Like two minutes (with an egg timer). After presenting the situation, each attendee can send their summary in an email to one person, who can sum it up and send it out to everyone.

- *What does everyone think?* In third place, a meeting where anyone can speak up. People who don't speak up on a regular basis should not be invited back. It's obvious that they are good at some other function in the office, so you're wasting their time if they sit there.

- *We need a decision right now:* These are ad hoc meetings that have a specific agenda and should end with a decision. A final decision that doesn't get reviewed.

- *Hanging-out meetings:* These are meetings with no real agenda, lots of side conversations, bored people, people instant messaging and just sort of hanging out. Sometimes these are fun, but I wouldn't know, because I haven't been to one in three years.

- *To-hear-myself-talk meetings:* You get the idea.

There are more, of course, and your situation is special, but in general, you ought to be able to clearly delineate what an ideal meeting is like, and then make it happen.

TIPS: I think most of the time, most meetings should be held without chairs. People standing up think more quickly and get distracted less often. And the meetings don't last as long.

All-day meetings should be banned. Meetings that attempt to accomplish more than one of the tasks above should be banned.

Bonus tip: Last person to walk in the door pays $10 to the coffee fund.

Extra bonus tip: Hire someone to come in and videotape a few of your standard meetings. Watch what happens.

Last tip: If there's someone senior in the group who comes to meetings, spouts off, and then either changes his mind or doesn't take action, start asking people to sign in to meetings (with a pen) and then, when the meeting is over, sign out (with a pen) on a document that you create in the meeting that says what you did and what's going to happen next.

If it's not worth doing this stuff, then you've just signed up to keep wasting 30% of your day.

The Marketer's Guide to Personal Finance

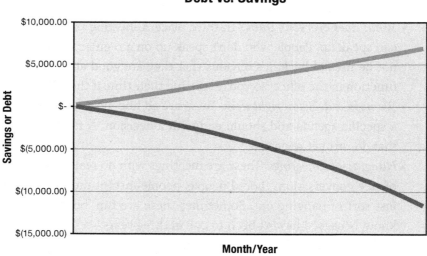

Debt vs. Savings

Even in the Web 2.0 world, marketers need money. We need money to create remarkable products and to tell stories that spread. We need it to hire the best people and, most of all, to stick it out until our ideas spread.

Which is why all but the largest companies need to learn a key lesson of personal finance.

The chart opposite shows what happens to two people. The smart person, we'll call him Gallant, manages to save $100 a month for five years.

The other one, we'll call him Doofus, spends $100 more than he has every month.

After five years, Gallant has almost $7,000 in the bank. Even with only 5% interest, he's building an asset that keeps him out of trouble with his mother-in-law and gives him the freedom to invest in the next part of his business.

In the same period of time, Doofus has used his credit cards to finance his debt of $100 a month. That tiny nut has now added up to about $13,000 in 24%-interest credit card debt. And every single month it gets a lot bigger.

If this isn't interesting to you, consider the company that spends $10,000 or $100,000 extra every month.

A lot of organizations decide to skip the "rice and beans and studio apartment" step. They decide to "go big or stay home." More often than not, they end up going home.

I spent many years window-shopping restaurant menus and driving all night to get to meetings where the plane ride cost just a bit too much. I thought at the time that I had no choice, but now I realize that I could have borrowed money on my credit cards and lived a little easier. I'm glad I didn't.

When I talk to people who want to become marketers, I almost always tell them to go start something and go market something. The same advice for 15-year-olds and seniors. Turning off the TV and building a CafePress store is not only free but starts to build a professional-skills asset for the long haul. Pay as much as you need to for things that matter, and as little as you can for things that don't. And never borrow money to pay for something that goes down in value.

Learning from Bananas

It turns out that it's a lot easier to peel a banana if you start from the "wrong" end.

You don't even have to use your teeth.

Here's the thing: I know this. I've tried it. It's true.

I still peel a banana the hard way. It feels like the right thing to do.

Selling change is much harder than you think.

[More] or (Less)

Many people are arguing for a fundamental change in the way humans interact with the world. This isn't a post about whether or not we need smaller cars, local produce, smaller footprints, and less consumption. It's a post about how deeply entrenched the desire for more is.

More has been around for thousands of years. Kings ate more than peasants. Winning armies had more weapons than losing ones. Elizabeth Taylor had more husbands than you.

Car dealers are temples of more. The local Ford dealership lists four different models, by decreasing horsepower. Car magazines feature Bugattis, not Priuses, on the cover. Restaurants usually serve more food (and more calories) than a normal person could and should eat.

Is this some sort of character flaw? A defective meme in the system of mankind? Or is it an evil plot dreamed up by marketers?

There's no doubt that marketers amplify this desire, but I'm certain it's been around a lot longer than Jell-O.

One reason that the litter campaign of the 1960s worked so well is that "not littering" didn't require doing less; it just required enough self-control to hold on to your garbage for an hour or two. The Achilles heel of the movement to limit carbon is the word "limit."

It's a campaign about less, not more. Even worse, there's no orthodoxy. There's argument about whether x or y is a better approach. Argument about how much is enough. As long as there's wiggle room, our desire for more will trump peer pressure to do less. "Fight global warming" is a fine slogan, except it's meaningless. That's like dieters everywhere shouting "eat less" while they stand in line to get blue cheese dressing from the salad bar.

From a marketing standpoint, my best advice is this: let's figure out how to turn this into a battle to do more, not less. Example one: require all new cars to have, right next to the speedometer, a mileage meter. And put the same number on an LCD display on the rear bumper. Once there's an arms race to see who can have the highest number, we're on the right track.

The Haystack

It's easy to be wowed by what a magical job the search engines do in finding you just the right needle in the haystack.

The fact is that search engines are very good at fairly simple searches, and very good at finding information about single products, services, people, and ideas.

But they're terrible at connections, at rankings, at horizontal results. They can't help me find the 25 most important up-and-coming artists in the United States. They can't help me find six products that are viable alternatives to something that was just discontinued. They can't help me rank the service of four accounting firms.

There's a giant opportunity. (Many opportunities, actually.) It's to collate and slice and dice and rank domain-specific knowledge and surface it. There are some areas where this is done extremely well (restaurants, for example), but in most cases, it's not done at all.

Organizing the world's information is a laudable goal. But we're only an inch down the road.

Meatball Mondae (#1)

What's a meatball sundae?

Maybe this is familiar. It is to me, anyway:

You go to a marketing meeting. There's a presentation from the new Internet marketing guy. He's brought a fancy (and expensive) blogging consultant with him. She starts talking about how blogs and the "Web 2.0 social media infrastructure" are just waiting for your company to dive in. "Try this stuff," she seems to be saying, "and the rest of your competitive/structural/profit issues will disappear."

In the last ten years, the Internet and radical changes in media have provided marketers everywhere with a toolbox that allows them to capture attention with seemingly little effort, planning, or cash. Six years after the dot-com boom, there are more websites, more email users, and more viral ideas, online and offline, than ever before. There are hundreds of cable TV networks and thousands of online radio stations. Not to mention street marketing, email marketing, and Myspace.

Corporations, political parties, nonprofits, job seekers, and yes, even people looking for love are all scrambling around, trying to exploit the power of these new tools. People treat the New Marketing like a kid with a twenty-dollar bill at an ice cream parlor. They keep wanting to add more stuff—more candy bits and sprinkles and cream and cherries. The dream is simple: "If we can just add enough of [today's hot topping], everything will take care of itself."

Most of the time, despite all the hype, organizations fail when they try to use this scattershot approach. They fail to get buzz or traffic or noise or sales. Organizations don't fail because the Web and the New Marketing don't work. They fail because the Web and the New Marketing work only when applied to the right organization. New Media makes a promise to the consumer. If the organization is unable to keep that promise, then it fails.

New Marketing—whipped cream and a cherry on top—isn't magical. What's magical is what happens when an organization uses the New Marketing to become something it didn't used to be—it's not just the marketing that's transformed, but the entire organization. Just as technology propelled certain organizations through the Industrial Revolution, this new kind of marketing is driving the right organizations through the digital revolution.

You can become the right organization. You can align your organization from the bottom up to sync with New Marketing, and you can transform your organization into one that thrives on the new rules.

Meatball Mondae (#2)

Talking 'bout a revolution . . .

Everyone studies the Industrial Revolution in school, but most of us don't really understand it. The basic idea, it seems, is that Henry Ford, Eli Whitney, and some guy with rifles invented the assembly line, and the whole world changed in about a week.

Actually, we've had several industrial revolutions over the last 250 years. While the assembly line, the invention of the corporation, and improvements in transport appear to be the obvious causes, it's easy to forget that in just a few generations, we saw changes in every element of what it meant to be in business. Standardized quality control, innovative product design for utilitarian products, employees (!), branding, investment, advertising, insurance, product development . . . the list is miles long.

Why care?

Because just sixty years ago, there was another revolution. This one was caused by the triumph of mass marketing. General Foods, General Motors, and the rest of the consumer-focused *Fortune* 500 are organized around a single idea: that efficient factories making average stuff for average people could triumph.

GM had a great run. So did tons of other companies. They figured out how to make stuff in large quantities. Run big factories. Hire and manage large numbers of people. The age of advertising ushered in a revolution that had more impact on organizations (and the planet) than any age that came before it.

The Meatball Sundae is an idea that's possibly even bigger than that one. When mass marketing dies, the future of the companies that embrace this approach dies, too. We're living through a wholesale change, but all most of us can do is worry about the color of the links on our blogs.

The Meatball Sundae has a subtle but subversive lesson: change the media, and the organizations change, too. Kiva instead of the American Heart Association, Amazon instead of the local bookstore, MoveOn instead of the DNC.

We're spending a ton of time arguing about tactics, social networks, and AdWords. Behind the scenes, an even bigger revolution is brewing. It's the one where entire organizations change in response to the lever of the change in marketing. Henry Ford could have said, "we're all manufacturers" and been right. Today, we can say, "we're all marketers," and we will be just as right.

Every time the deck is reshuffled, the early players profit. You and I don't have the chance to build a mass-media company ever again. But every organization has the chance to reinvent and grow in the face of the huge opportunity today's shift brings.

This sounds hard. It's not. Once you understand the key forces at work (I figure there are about 14 of them), it's actually easier to go with the flow than it is to fight it.

This is way too conceptual for a blog post or even a useful book, so I guess I'll ask the question this way: If you were alive in 1947 and knew what you know now about the last sixty years of mass marketing, what would you have done? What would you have built? Was it just about making better TV commercials?

Meatball Mondae (#3): Columbus Day Edition

Google and Discovery

Google and the other search engines have broken the world into little tiny bits. No one visits a website's home page anymore—they walk in the back door, to just the place Google sent them. By atomizing the world, Google destroys the end-to-end solution offered by most organizations, replacing it with a pick-and-choose, component-based solution.

Columbus is the center of a popular fable about discovery. He set out to find something, got lost along the way, and instead gets credit for an even bigger find. The analogy of the Web is pretty much a stretch, but here goes: people don't always find you the way you want to be found.

Not only are there literally a million ways to discover you and your offerings, but rarely do people hear your story the way you want it to be heard. The idea of a home page and a site map and a considered, well-lit entryway to your brand is quaint but unrealistic.

I can clone a frog from one skin cell—and get the whole frog.

Can I clone your brand from one interaction, from one Web page, from one referral? Whether I can or not, I will.

That means that bundling is harder than ever.

Bundling was the glue that held together almost every business and organization.

Bundle donations and parcel them out to charities that deserve them. (That's the United Way.)

Bundle TV shows and present them, with ads, on your TV network.

Bundle the items in your industrial-supplies catalog and hand it to the business buyer.

Bundle 30 businesses and house them in one big office tower.

The Yellow Pages is a multibillion-dollar business that consists of nothing but bundled ads for local businesses. No one wants to keep a flyer for every business in town, but everyone has a copy of the Yellow Pages.

Book publishers bundle authors and share the expertise of their staff, their sales force, and their capital in order to bring books to readers.

We've been doing the bundling so long, we forgot we were doing it.

The world just got unbundled. Like it or not, there you are.

Meatball Mondae (#4): No Middlemen, No Insulation

Perhaps the biggest change the New Marketing brings is the easiest to overlook, mostly because it's so obvious.

Every organization now has the ability (and probably the responsibility) to deal directly with the world. With customers, with prospects, and with those affected by their actions. No middlemen.

The president of the bank isn't used to hearing from a customer about to lose her house. A retailer in Tucson isn't used to hearing from a potential customer in Nebraska. A rock star is used to being entertained by A&R guys, not by maintaining a permission list of 100,000 customers and 55,000 Myspace friends.

This direct connection is an asset or a risk, depending on how you look at it.

The asset (the only asset, pretty much) that can be built online is permission. The privilege of marketing to people who want to be marketed to. This asset is big enough and valuable enough to build an entire business around (witness Scott Adams and Amazon), and it upsets traditional power structures in just about every industry.

More important, it leads to the idea of "no insulation."

Sonos makes a device that would have been inconceivable only ten years ago. The Sonos system is a remote control (with an LCD screen), a hard drive, and a box. The box hooks up to your stereo speakers, and the hard drive holds all your MP3 files. You can use the remote to review your entire music collection and play it anywhere in your house. Add more boxes, add more rooms. One hard drive can be used to let your daughter play Mahler in her room while you listen to Coldplay in the kitchen.

While the idea is simple, and installation is a snap, the products Sonos replaces weren't simple or easy. As a result, multi-room speaker systems were sold by consultants—the sort of private services that cater to multimillionaires and their homes. At a recent CEDIA show (the conference for installers), one of the categories was "Best Installation over £100,000."

If you were in that business (as companies like Runco and Stewart Filmscreen were), you catered to the CEDIA installers. You let them be the middlemen, the service and support people, the installers, and yes, the folks that made most of the profit. The installers guided many of the decisions that their clients made, and you were at their mercy.

Sonos sells a product for about a thousand dollars. That's less than the gratuity on most custom installations. As a result, Sonos decided to use the Web to allow consumers to interact with them directly.

In addition to creating a well-designed discussion board, Sonos invested in motivated, well-trained online staff members, who are seemingly everywhere, answering questions within a few minutes of their being asked. Sonos has pleasant technicians answering the phone on weekends. They not only publish their email address, but actually answer queries (and helpfully) in a matter of hours.

Of course, Sonos is still happy to work with the CEDIA crowd. But by embracing the ideas of accessibility and speed, they have made their product appealing to people who could easily afford to spend ten times as much.

How will their competition catch up? How can their competition simultaneously jettison their entire sales force, dramatically increase the quality of their customer service, lower their end pricing by 70%, and make the product consumer friendly? They can't.

When everyone was playing by the same rules, when all suppliers relied on insulation in order to maintain margins and keep throughput efficient, it was a terrific system. But as soon as one player in the industry can use a direct connection to the end consumer, the rules change for everyone.

Meatball Mondae (#5): Joanne Is Coming!

Everyone is a critic.

One of my dearest friends is Joanne Kates, the restaurant critic for *The Globe and Mail*, the most important newspaper in Toronto. Joanne carries a credit card with someone else's name on it (I promised I wouldn't say whose). Despite her precautions, her picture is posted in the kitchen of dozens of top restaurants. Why? Because once a restaurant knows that Joanne is wearing a wig and sitting in the dining room, the staff can influence the review.

Once a server knows it's her, he can make sure the service is perfect, the food is hot, and the check is calculated properly. Once he knows it's her, he can guarantee that the staff will do their best.

You've already guessed the problem with this strategy. The problem is *Zagat* (and Chowhound.com, and a thousand other restaurant blogs). There isn't just one Joanne Kates in Toronto anymore. Now there are thousands.

You can no longer be on the lookout for Joanne. Now you have to be on the lookout for everyone.

Meatball Mondae (#6): Short

Attention spans are getting shorter, thanks to clutter.

In 1960, the typical stay for a book on the *New York Times* bestseller list was 22 weeks. In 2006, it was two. Forty years ago, it was typical for three novels a year to reach #1. Last year, it was 23.

Advise and Consent won the Pulitzer Prize in 1960. It's 640 pages long. *On Bullshit* was a bestseller in 2005; it's 68 pages long.

Commercials used to be a minute long, sometimes two. Then someone came up with the brilliant idea of running two per minute, then four. Now there are radio ads that are less than three seconds long.

It's not an accident that things are moving faster and getting smaller. There's just too much to choose from. With a million or more books available at a click, why should I invest the time to read all 640 pages of *Advise and Consent* when I can get the idea after 50 pages?

Audible.com offers more than 30,000 titles. If an audiobook isn't spectacular, minute to minute, it's easier to ditch it and get another one than it is to slog through it. After all, it's just bits on my iPod.

Of course, this phenomenon isn't limited to intellectual property. Craigslist.org is a free classified-ad listing service. A glance at their San Francisco listings shows more than 33,000 ads for housing. That means that if an apartment doesn't sound perfect after just a sentence or two, it's easy to glance down at the next ad.

If you're exhausted, it's no wonder. You've been running around all day.

The end.

Meatball Sundae (#7): Election Day Edition

In the new transparent age, it's really difficult to tell two stories simultaneously.

Why George Allen won't be running for president:

It was a great Web moment. George Allen was the Republican Party's next star, anointed as a potential candidate for president in 2008. But first he had to win the Senate race in Virginia, considered by many to be a layup for him.

The traditional way to run a political campaign is to control your message. Control what you say and when you say it. Control who hears it.

Tell one story to your raving fans, and a more moderate story to people in the center.

As voters have seen again and again, politicians are good at this. Some people call it lying. But in general, politicians have gotten away with it.

The top-down, control-the-message strategy worked in the past for a few reasons:

- Media companies were complicit in not embarrassing the people they counted on to appear on their shows and authorize their licenses.

- Politicians could decide where and when to show up and could choose whether or not they wanted to engage.
- Bad news didn't spread far unless it was exceptionally juicy.

But George Allen discovered that the rules have fundamentally changed. Allen's challenger asked S. R. Sidarth, a senior at the University of Virginia, to trail Allen with a video camera. The idea was to document Allen's travels and speeches. During a speech in Breaks, Virginia, Allen turned to Sidarth and said, "Let's give a welcome to Macaca, here. Welcome to America and the real world of Virginia," said Allen. As I write this, YouTube reports that Allen's slur has been watched on YouTube more than 318,000 times. Add to that the pickup from the broadcast media (which picked it up because it was popular, not because it was "important"), and you see why George Allen lost the election.

The ironic part of the appearance is that the first words out of Allen's mouth on the tape are, "Ladies and gentlemen, we're going to run a positive campaign." The story didn't match the facts, and the facts showed up on YouTube.

Summary for non-politicians: you can't tell two stories at the same time. Not for long.

Meatball Mondae (#8): The Wealthy Are Like Us

The democratization of wealth

Rich people used to all be the same, just different from the rest of us. Now they're not just different from the rest of us, but different from each other.

Rich people used to do similar jobs, wear similar clothes, live in similar neighborhoods, and read similar magazines. As a result, marketing to rich people was pretty easy. No longer. As the gulf between rich and poor continues to widen, the number of people considered rich increases daily, and the diversity of the rich increases as well.

It turns out that not only are the wealthy like us, but they are us. Despite the widening gulf, there are more wealthy people than ever before. In fact, you're probably one of them. Michael Silverstein and Neil

Fiske of BCG talked about this in their book *Trading Up*, and the trend has only become more pervasive.

That means there are rich NASCAR fans, rich porn stars, rich entrepreneurs in Kenya, and rich teenagers. Every silo is discovering that it can create a top tier.

Meatball Mondae (#9): The Long Tail

(Almost) everyone wants choice

Choice makes some people stressed and unhappy. But it also makes lots of people happy. And now people have the choice.

By itself, a bias for choice is interesting but not particularly surprising. What's surprising is the magnitude of this desire. My favorite example is the comparison of a typical Barnes & Noble store with Amazon. If you examine the sales of the 150,000 titles in a big store, you'll see that they account for perhaps half of Amazon's book sales. In other words, if you aggregate the millions of poorly selling titles on Amazon, they add up to the total sales of all the best-selling books in the physical world put together.

Another way of looking at it: more people watched more video on YouTube last week than watched the top ten shows on network television.

Another way: a quick look at your grocer's beverage aisle will prove to you that Coca-Cola is no longer the most popular soft drink in the country. The most popular soft drink is "other": none of the above.

The mass of choices defeats the biggest hit.

This curve shows up over and over. It describes travel habits, DVD rentals, and book sales. Give people a choice and the tail always gets longer. Always.

The Long Tail has been around forever, but only now does it really matter. That's because of several trends working together:

A. Online shopping gives the retailer the ability to carry a hundred times the inventory of a typical retail store.

B. Google means that a user can find something if it's out there.

C. Permission marketing gives sellers the freedom to find products for their customers, instead of the other way around.

D. Digital products are easy to store and easy to customize.

E. Digital technology makes it easy to customize nondigital goods.

The question isn't, "is this real?" The question is: "What are you doing about it?"

Meatball Mondae (#10): Big Ideas

In a factory-based organization, little ideas are the key to success. Small improvements in efficiency or design can improve productivity and make a product just a bit more appealing. New Marketing, which exists in the noisy marketplace, demands something bigger. It demands ideas that force people to sit up and take notice.

At the same time that we see how game-changing ideas (like the iPhone) can trump little improvements, we're also noting the end of the "big idea" in advertising.

There's a difference between a big idea that comes from a product or service and a big idea that comes from the world of advertising.

The secret of big-time advertising during the 1960s and '70s was the "big idea." In *A Big Life in Advertising*, ad legend Mary Wells Lawrence writes, ". . . our goal was to have big, breakthrough ideas, not just to do good advertising. I wanted to create miracles." A big idea could build a brand, a career, or an entire agency.

Charlie the Tuna was a big idea. So was "Plop, plop, fizz, fizz."

Big ideas in advertising worked great when advertising was in charge. With a limited amount of spectrum and a lot of hungry consumers, the stage was set to put on a show. And the better the show, the bigger the punch line, the more profit could be made.

Today, the advertiser's big idea doesn't travel very well. Instead, the idea must be embedded into the experience of the product itself. Once again, what we used to think of as advertising or marketing is pushed deeper into the organization. Let the brilliant ad guys hang out with your R&D team and watch what happens.

Yes, there are big ideas. They're just not advertising-based.

We Accidentally Marketed Ourselves into a Corner

What if I told you about an industry that:

- Indebts most of its customers, sometimes for twenty or more years per person
- Not only consumes most of four years of its customers' time, but affects its prospects for years before even interacting with them
- Enjoys extremely strong brand preferences between competitors and has virtually no successful generic substitutes
- Dramatically alters relations within a family, often for generations
- Doesn't do it on purpose

. . . and . . .

. . . according to most of the studies I've seen, shows very little or no difference in the efficacy of one competitor vs. another.

Of course, I'm talking about undergraduate colleges in the U.S.

The most competitive colleges are as competitive as ever—in most cases, more so. Many admit only one in ten students. According to two senior officials at Swarthmore, the differences among the "good enough" applicants are basically zero. Rather than putting tens of thousands of kids through insane anxiety, these officials wonder, why not just put all the "good enough" students in a pool and pick the winners randomly?

Here's the amazing part: according to *The Chosen*, an exhaustive study of college admissions, there's no measurable difference between the outcomes of education with the most exclusive schools and the next few tiers. Graduates don't end up happier. They don't end up with better-paying jobs. They don't end up richer or even healthier. The whole thing is a sham (which costs a quarter of a million dollars a person at the top end).

There's no question that a Harvard degree helps (or is even required) in a few fields. There's also no doubt that spending four years at Yale is a mind-changing experience. The question isn't, "are they wonderful?" The question is, "is it worth it?"

It's almost as if every single high school student and her parents insisted on having a $200,000 stereo because it was better than the $1,000 stereo. Sure, it might be a bit better, but is it better *enough*?

Boomer parents have bought into the marketing hype at a level rarely seen in any other form of marketing. They push school districts, teachers, and kids to perform pointless tasks at extreme levels just to be admitted to the "right" school, even though there's hardly any evidence that the right school does anything but boost their egos.

Schools respond by spending a fortune on facilities that will increase their rankings in various faux polls, even though there's no evidence at all that a better gym or a bigger library matters one bit to an undergraduate's long-term success in life.

If it weren't so expensive (in terms of time and money), it would make a marvelous marketing case study. Add in the tears and wasted anxiety and it's really a shame. Very few people are pointing out that the emperor is barely clothed, and those that do (like me, I guess) get yelled at.

I'm not criticizing a college education per se. No, it's clear that that's a smart investment. I'm talking about the incremental cost (and anxiety) separating consumers of the "top" 500 schools from students at the "top" 50. It appears to be pure storytelling, a story that so appeals to the worldview of baby boomers with teens that they are absolutely unable to resist the story, despite the facts.

High school students are thrust into a Dip, in some cases the biggest one of their lives. The Dip extracts significant costs along the way, and then ends with a giant spin of the roulette wheel. I wonder if we're marketing ourselves to a dead end.

I guess I'd do two things. First, I'd figure out how to teach parents to understand what really matters and what doesn't about time spent in high school and the choice of a college. Second, I'd push for every selective college to share one application and do a draft similar to the one they do for medical residencies. Every applicant ranks the schools they'd like to attend, in order. Every school considers all the applications, grabs the students they'd love to have in priority order, puts the rest into the "good enough" pile, and lets a computer sort 'em all out as Pareto optimally as possible. At least kids will go into their twenties correctly blaming a computer instead of mistakenly blaming themselves.

Music Lessons

Things you can learn from the music business (as it falls apart).

The first rule is so important, it's rule 0:

0. *The new thing is never as good as the old thing, at least right now.*

Soon, the new thing will be better than the old thing. But if you wait until then, it's going to be too late. Feel free to wax nostalgic about the old thing, but don't fool yourself into believing that it's going to be here forever. It won't.

1. *Past performance is no guarantee of future success.*

Every single industry changes and, eventually, fades. Just because you made money doing something a certain way yesterday, there's no reason to believe that you'll succeed at it tomorrow.

The music business had a spectacular run alongside the baby boomers. Starting with the Beatles and Dylan, they just kept minting money. The coincidence of expanding purchasing power of teens along with the birth of rock, the invention of the transistor, and changing social mores meant a long, long growth curve.

As a result, the music business built huge systems. They created top-heavy organizations, dedicated superstores, a loss-leader touring industry, extraordinarily high profit margins, MTV, and more. It was a well-greased system, but the key question is: Why did it deserve to last forever?

It didn't. Yours doesn't, either.

2. *Copy protection in a digital age is a pipe dream.*

If the product you make becomes digital, expect that the product you make will be copied.

There's a paradox in the music business that is mirrored in many industries: you want ubiquity, not obscurity, yet digital distribution devalues your core product.

Remember, the music business is the one that got in trouble for bribing disc jockeys to play their music on the radio. Music execs are the ones that spent millions to make (free) videos for MTV. And yet once the transmission became digital, they understood that there's not a lot of reason to buy a digital version (via a cumbersome, expensive process) when the peer-shared or pirated digital version of the same song is free (and easier to get).

Most items of value derive that value from scarcity. Digital changes that, and you can derive value from ubiquity now.

The solution isn't to somehow try to become obscure, to get your song off the (digital) radio. The solution is to change your business.

You used to sell plastic and vinyl. Now, you can sell interactivity and souvenirs.

3. *Interactivity can't be copied.*

Products that are digital and also include interaction thrive on centralization and do better and better as the market grows (consider Facebook or Basecamp).

Music is social. Music is current and ever changing. And most of all, music requires musicians. The winners in the music business of tomorrow are individuals and organizations that create communities, connect people, spread ideas, and act as the hub of the wheel—indispensable and well compensated.

4. *Permission is the asset of the future.*

For generations, businesses had no idea who their end users were. No ability to reach through the record store and figure out who was buying that Rolling Stones album, no way to know who bought this book or that vase.

Today, of course, permission is an asset to be earned: the ability (not the right, but the privilege) to deliver anticipated, personal, and relevant messages to people who want to get them. For ten years, the music business has been steadfastly avoiding this opportunity.

It's interesting, though, because many musicians have NOT been avoiding it. Many musicians have understood that all they need to make a (very good) living is to have 10,000 fans. Ten thousand people who look forward to the next record, who are willing to trek out to the next concert. Add seven fans a day and you're done in five years. Set for life. A life making music for your fans, not finding fans for your music.

The opportunity of digital distribution is this:

When you can distribute something digitally, for free, it will spread (if it's good). If it spreads, you can use it as a vehicle to allow people to come back to you and register, to sign up, to give you permission to interact and to keep them in the loop.

Many authors (I'm on that list) have managed to build an entire career around this idea. So have management consultants and yes, insurance salespeople. Not by viewing the spread of digital artifacts as an inconvenient tactic but by viewing it as the core of their new businesses.

5. *A frightened consumer is not a happy consumer.*

I shouldn't have to say this, but here goes: suing people is like going to war. If you're going to go to war with tens of thousands of your customers every year, don't be surprised if they start treating you like the enemy.

6. *This is a big one: the best time to change your business model is while you still have momentum.*

It's not so easy for an unknown artist to start from scratch and build a career self-publishing. Not so easy for her to find fans, one at a time, and build an audience. Very, very easy for a record label or a top artist to do so. So, the time to jump was yesterday. Too late. Okay, how about today?

The sooner you do it, the more assets and momentum you have to put to work.

7. *Remember the Bob Dylan rule: it's not just a record, it's a movement.*

Bob and his handlers have a long track record of finding movements. Anti-war movements, sure, but also rock movies, the Grateful Dead,

SACDs, Christian rock, and Apple fanboys. What Bob has done (and I think he's done it sincerely, not as a calculated maneuver) is to seek out groups that want to be connected, and he works to become the connecting point.

By being open to choices of format, to points of view, to moments in time, Bob Dylan never has a reason to say, "I make vinyl records that cost money to listen to." He understands at some level that music is often the soundtrack for something else.

I think the same thing can be true for chefs and churches and charities and politicians and makers of medical devices. People pay a premium for a story, every time.

8. *Don't panic when the new business model isn't as "clean" as the old one.*

It's not easy to give up the idea of manufacturing CDs with a 90% gross margin and switch to a blended model of concerts and souvenirs, of communities and greeting cards and special events and what feels like gimmicks. I know.

Get over it. It's the only option if you want to stay in this business. You're just not going to sell a lot of CDs in five years, are you?

If there's a business here, the first few in will find it; the rest lose everything.

9. *Read the writing on the wall.*

Hey, guys, I'm not in the music business and even I've been writing about this for years. I even started a record label five years ago to make the point. Industries don't die by surprise. It's not like you didn't know it was coming. It's not like you didn't know whom to call (or hire).

This isn't about having a great idea (it almost never is). The great ideas are out there, for free, on your neighborhood blog. Nope; this is about taking initiative and making things happen.

The last person to leave the current record business won't be the smartest and he won't be the most successful, either. Getting out first and staking out the new territory almost always pays off.

10. *Don't abandon the Long Tail.*

Everyone in the hit business thinks they understand the secret: just make hits. After all, if you do the math, it shows that if you just made hits, you'd be in fat city.

Of course, the harder you try to just make hits, the less likely you are to make any hits at all. Movies, records, books—the blockbusters always seem to be surprises. Surprise hit cookbooks, even.

Instead, in an age when it's cheaper than ever to design something, to make something, to bring something to market, the smart strategy is to have a dumb strategy. Keep your costs low and go with your instincts, even when everyone says you're wrong. Do a great job, not a perfect one. Bring things to market, the right market, and let them find their audience.

"Stick to the knitting" has never been more wrong. Instead, find products your customers want. Don't underestimate them. They're more catholic in their tastes than you give them credit for.

11. *Understand the power of digital.*

Try to imagine something like this happening ten years ago: an eleven-year-old kid wakes up on a Saturday morning, gets his allowance, and then, standing in his pajamas, buys a Bon Jovi song for a buck.

Compare this to hassling for a ride, driving to the mall, finding the album in question, finding the $14 to pay for it, and then driving home.

You may believe that your business doesn't lend itself to digital transactions. Many people do. If you've got a business that doesn't thrive on digital, it might not grow as fast as you like. Maybe you need to find a business that does thrive on digital.

12. *Celebrity is underrated.*

The music business has always created celebrities. And each celebrity has profited for decades from that fame. Frank Sinatra is dead and he's still profiting. Elvis is still alive and he's certainly still profiting.

The music business has done a poor job of leveraging that celebrity and catching the value it creates. Many businesses now have the power to create their own micro-celebrities. These individuals capture attention and generate trust, two critical elements in growing profits.

13. *Value is created when you go from many to few, and vice versa.*

The music business has thousands of labels and tens of thousands of copyright holders. It's a mess.

And there's just one iTunes music store. Consolidation pays.

At the same time, there are other industries where there are just a few major players, and the way to profit is to create splinters and niches.

14. *Whenever possible, sell subscriptions.*

Few businesses can successfully sell subscriptions (magazines being the very best example), but when you can, the whole world changes. HBO, for example, is able to spend its money making shows for its viewers, rather than working to find viewers for every show.

The biggest opportunity for the music business is to combine permission with subscription. The possibilities are endless. And I know it's hard to believe, but the good old days are yet to happen.

Encyclopedia Salesmen Hate Wikipedia . . .

And CNET hates Google.

And newspapers hate Craigslist.

And music labels hate Napster.

And used-books stores hate Amazon.

And so do independent bookstores.

Dating services hate Plenty of Fish.

And the local shoe store hates Zappos.

And courier services hate fax machines.

And monks hate Gutenberg.

Apparently, technology doesn't care whom you hate.

Workaholics

A workaholic lives on fear. It's fear that drives him to show up all the time. The best defense, apparently, is a good attendance record.

A new class of jobs (and workers) is creating a different sort of worker, though. This is the person who works out of passion and curiosity, not fear.

The passionate worker doesn't show up because she's afraid of getting in trouble; she shows up because it's a hobby that pays. The passionate worker is busy blogging on vacation, because posting that thought and seeing the feedback it generates is actually more fun than sitting on the beach for another hour. The passionate worker tweaks a site design after dinner because, hey, it's a lot more fun than watching TV.

It was hard to imagine someone being passionate about mining coal or scrubbing dishes. But the new face of work, at least for some people, opens up the possibility that work is the thing (much of the time) that you'd most like to do. Designing jobs like that is obviously smart. Finding one is brilliant.

Tribe Management

Brand management is so 1999.

Brand management was top down, internally focused, political, and money based. It involved an MBA managing the brand, the ads, the shelf space, etc. The MBA argued with product development and manufacturing to get decent stuff, and argued with the CFO to get more cash to spend on ads.

Tribe management is a whole different way of looking at the world.

It starts with permission, the understanding that the real asset most organizations can build isn't an amorphous brand but is in fact the privilege of delivering anticipated, personal, and relevant messages to people who want to get them.

It adds to that the fact that what people really want is the ability to connect to each other, not to companies. So the permission is used to build a tribe, to build a group of people who want to hear from the company because it helps them connect, it helps them find each other, and it gives them a story to tell and something to talk about.

And of course, since this is so important, product development and manufacturing and the CFO *work* for the tribal manager. Everything the organization does is to feed and grow and satisfy the tribe.

Instead of looking for customers for your products, you seek out products (and services) for the tribe. Jerry Garcia understood this. Do you?

Whom does this work for? Try record companies and bloggers, real estate agents and recruiters, book publishers and insurance companies. It works for Andrew Weil and for Rickie Lee Jones and for Rupert at the *WSJ.* But it also works for a small Web development firm or a venture capitalist.

People form tribes with or without us. The challenge is to work for the tribe and make it something even better.

Sorting Out

Gavin Potter says in *Wired*, "The 20th century was about sorting out supply, the 21st is going to be about sorting out demand."

Think about that one for a second. Not about maximizing demand, but about *sorting it out.* When your messages reach the right people at the right time in the right way, magic happens. It's not about forcing or pushing or attacking or targeting or closing.

This is a huge step forward in how you can think about your customers and how they act.

Henry Ford and the Source of Our Fear

Henry Ford left us much more than cars and the highway system we built for them. He changed the world's expectations for work. While Ford gets credit for inventing the assembly line, his great insight was that he understood the power of productivity.

Ford was a pioneer in highly leveraged, repetitive work, done by relatively untrained workers. A farmer, with little training, could walk into Ford's factory and become extraordinarily productive in a day or two.

This is the cornerstone of our way of life. The backbone of our economy does not lie in brain surgeons and master violinists. It's in fairly average people doing fairly average work.

The focus on productivity wouldn't be relevant to this discussion except for the second thing Ford did. He decided to pay his workers based on productivity, not on replacement value. This was an astonishing breakthrough. When Ford announced the $5 day (more than double the typical salary paid for this level of skill), more than 10,000 people applied for work at Ford the very next day.

Instead of paying people the lowest amount he'd need to find enough competent workers to fill the plant, he paid them more than he needed to because his systems made them so productive. He challenged his workers to be more productive so that they'd get paid more.

It meant that nearly every factory worker at Ford was dramatically overpaid! When there's a line out the door of people waiting to take your job, weird things happen to your head. The combination of repetitive factory work plus high pay for standardized performance led to a very obedient factory floor. People were conditioned to do as they were told, and they traded autonomy and craftsmanship for high pay and stability.

All of a sudden, we got used to being paid based on our output. We came, over time, to expect to get paid more and more, regardless of how long the line of people eager to take our job was. If productivity went up, profits went up. And the productive workers expected (and got) higher pay, even if there were plenty of replacement workers, eager to work for less.

This is the central conceit of our economy. People in productive industries get paid a lot even though they could likely be replaced by someone else working for less money.

This is why we're insecure.

Obedience works fine on the well-organized, standardized factory floor. But what happens when we start using our heads, not our hands, and when our collars change from blue to white?

Email Checklist

Before you hit Send on that next email, perhaps you should run down this list, just to be sure:

1. Is it going to just one person? (If yes, jump to #10.)
2. Since it's going to a group, have I thought about who is on my list?
3. Are they blind copied?
4. Did every person on the list really and truly opt in? Not like sort of, but really ask for it?
5. So that means that if I *didn't* send it to them, they'd complain about not getting it?
6. See #5. If they wouldn't complain, take them off!
7. That means, for example, that sending bulk email to a list of bloggers just 'cause they have blogs is not okay.
8. Aside: the definition of permission marketing—anticipated, personal, and relevant messages delivered to people who actually want to get them. Nowhere does it say anything about you and your needs as a sender. Probably none of my business, but I'm just letting you know how I feel. (And how your prospects feel.)
9. Is the email from a real person? If it is, will hitting Reply get a note back to that person? (If not, change it, please.)
10. Have I corresponded with this person before?
11. Really? They've written back? (If not, reconsider email.)
12. If it is a cold-call email, and I'm sure it's welcome, and I'm sure it's not spam, then don't apologize. If I need to apologize, then yes, it's spam, and I'll get the brand-hurt I deserve.
13. Am I angry? (If so, save it as a draft and come back to the note in one hour.)
14. Could I do this note better with a phone call?
15. Am I blind-CCing my boss? If so, what will happen if the recipient finds out?
16. Is there anything in this email that I don't want the attorney general, the media, or my boss seeing? (If so, hit Delete.)
17. Is any portion of the email in all caps? (If so, consider changing it.)

18. Is it in black type at a normal size?
19. Do I have my contact info at the bottom? (If not, consider adding it.)
20. Have I included the line "Please save the planet. Don't print this email"? (If so, please delete the line and consider a job as a forest ranger or flight attendant.)
21. Could this email be shorter?
22. Is there anyone copied on this email who could be left off the list?
23. Have I attached any files that are very big? (If so, Google something like "send big files" and consider your options.)
24. Have I attached any files that would work better in PDF format?
25. Are there any :-) or other emoticons involved? (If so, reconsider.)
26. Am I forwarding someone else's mail? (If so, will they be happy when they find out?)
27. Am I forwarding something about religion (mine or someone else's)? (If so, delete.)
28. Am I forwarding something about a virus or worldwide charity effort or other potential hoax? (If so, visit Snopes.com and check to see if it's true.)
29. Did I hit Reply All? If so, am I glad I did? Does every person on the list need to see it?
30. Am I quoting back the original text in a helpful way? (Sending an email that says, in its entirety, "yes" is not helpful.)
31. If this email is to someone like Seth, did I check to make sure I know the difference between *its* and *it's*? Just wondering.
32. If this is a press release, am I really sure that the recipient is going to be delighted to get it? Or am I taking advantage of the asymmetrical nature of email—free to send, expensive investment of time to read or delete?
33. Are there any little animated creatures in the footer of this email? Adorable kittens? Endangered species of any kind?
34. Bonus: Is there a long legal disclaimer at the bottom of my email? Why?
35. Bonus: Does the subject line make it easy to understand what's to come and likely that it will get filed properly?
36. If I had to pay 42 cents to send this email, would I?

The Economy, the Press, and the Paradox

Wealth is not created by financial manipulation, the trading of equities, or the financing of banks. They just enable it.

Wealth is created by productivity. Productive communities generate more of value.

Productivity comes from innovation.

Innovation comes from investment and change.

The media lemmings, the same ones that encouraged you to get a second mortgage, buy a McMansion, and spend, spend, spend, are now falling all over themselves to out-mourn the others. They are telling everyone to batten down, to cut back, to freeze and panic. They're looking for stories about this, advice about this, hooks about this.

And of course, the paradox. If, in the middle of some sensible budgeting and waste trimming, we stop investing in the future, stop innovating, stop finding the breakthrough that leads to the next round of productivity gain, then in fact they're right; the recession does last forever.

I believe that we're on the verge of some exponential increases in productivity. Productivity in marketing, as the waste of reaching the masses goes away. Productivity in energy, as we figure out how to make a renewable process that gives us incremental units of power for free (think about the impact of that for a moment), and productivity in group work and management, as we allow the network to do more than let us watch stupid YouTube videos at work. The three biggest expenses of most endeavors (the energy to make it, the people who create it, and the marketing that spreads the idea) are about to be overhauled.

What a tragedy it will be if we let defensive thinking hold us back.

When Newspapers Are Gone, What Will You Miss?

Years and years after some pundits began predicting the end of newspapers, the newspapers themselves are finally realizing that it's over. Huge debt, high costs, declining subscription rates, plummeting ad base—will the last one out please turn off the lights?

On their way out, though, we're hearing a lot of "you'll miss us when we're gone . . ." laments. I got to thinking about this. It's never good to watch people lose their livelihoods or have to move on to something new, even if it might be better. I respect and honor the hard work that so many people have put into newspapers along the way. If we make a list of newspaper attributes and features, which ones would you miss?

Wood pulp, printing presses, typesetting machines, delivery trucks, those stands on the street and the newsstand . . . I think we're okay without them.

The sports section? No, that's better online, and in no danger of going away; in fact, overwritten commentary by the masses is burgeoning.

The weather? Ditto. Comics are even better online, and I don't think we'll run out of those.

Book and theater and restaurant reviews? In fact, there are more of these online, often better, definitely more personal and relevant, and also in no danger of going away.

The full-page ads for local department stores? The freestanding inserts on Sunday? The supermarket coupons? Easily replaced.

How about the editorials and op-eds? Again, I think we're not going to see opinion go away; in fact, the Web amplifies the good stuff.

What's left is local news, investigative journalism, and intelligent coverage of national news. Perhaps 2% of the cost of a typical paper. I worry about the quality of a democracy when the state government or the local government can do what it wants without intelligent coverage. I worry about the abuse of power when the only thing a corrupt official needs to worry about is the TV news. I worry about the quality of legislation when there isn't a passionate, unbiased reporter there to explain it to us.

But then I see the in-depth stories about the gowns to be worn to the inauguration or the selection of the White House dog, and I wonder if newspapers are the most efficient way to do this, anyway.

The Web has excelled at breaking the world into the tiniest independent parts. We don't use *this* to support *that* online. Things support themselves. The food blog isn't a loss leader for the gardening blog. They're separate, usually run by separate people or organizations.

Punch line: if we really care about the investigation and the analysis, we'll pay for it one way or another. Maybe it's a public good, a nonprofit function. Maybe a philanthropist puts up money for prizes. Maybe the Woodward and Bernstein of 2017 make so much money from breaking a story that it leads to a whole new generation of journalists.

The reality is that this sort of journalism is relatively cheap (compared to everything else the newspaper had to do in order to bring it to us). Newspapers took two cents' worth of journalism and wrapped it in ninety-eight cents' worth of overhead and distraction. The magic of the Web, the reason you should care about this even if you don't care about the news, is that when the marginal cost of something is free and when the time to deliver it is zero, the economics become magical. It's like 6 divided by zero. Infinity.

I'm not worried about how muckrakers will make a living. Tree farmers, on the other hand, need to find a new use for newsprint.

Pivots for Change

When industry norms start to die, people panic. It's difficult to change when you think that you must change everything in order to succeed. Changing everything is too difficult.

Consider for a minute the pivot points available to you:

- Keep the machines in your factory, but change what they make.
- Keep your customers, but change what you sell to them.
- Keep your providers, but change the profit structure.
- Keep your industry, but change where the money comes from.
- Keep your staff, but change what you do.
- Keep your mission, but change your scale.
- Keep your products, but change the way you market them.
- Keep your customers, but change how much you sell each one.
- Keep your technology, but use it to do something else.
- Keep your reputation, but apply it to a different industry or problem.

Simple examples:

- Keep the musicians, but change how you make money (sell concerts, not CDs).

- Keep making guitars, but make bespoke expensive ones, not the mass-market ones that overseas competition has made obsolete.
- Keep the punch press and the lathe, but make large-scale art installations, not car parts.
- Keep your wealthy travel clients, but sell them personal services instead of trips to Europe.
- Keep the factory that makes missiles, but figure out how to make high-efficiency turbines instead.

The Pillars of Social-Media-Site Success

Why people choose to visit online social sites:

- Who likes me?
- Is everything okay?
- How can I become more popular?
- What's new?
- I'm bored; let's make some noise.

None of these are new, but in the digital world, they're still magnetic.

If you want to understand why Twitter is so hot, look at those five attributes. They deliver all five instantly.

Pick Anything—the Calculus of Change

Remember WordPerfect? This word processor dominated the world until Word wiped them out. How did that happen?

WordPerfect was the default word processor in every law firm, big company, and organization in the land. If you had the DOS operating system, it was likely you were using WordPerfect. And if the operating system in the office hadn't changed to Windows, it's likely you'd still be using it now.

What happened was that the change in operating system created a moment when people had to pick. They had to either switch to Word or wait for a new version of WordPerfect. In that moment, "do nothing" was not an option.

Do nothing is the choice of people who are afraid. Do nothing is what you do if too many people have to agree. Do nothing is what happens if one person with no upside has to accept downside responsibility for a change. What's in it for them to do anything? So they do nothing.

The key moment for an insurgent, then, is the time of "pick anything." That's why these are such good times for iPhone apps. That's why the beginning of an administration is a good time to lobby. When people *have* to pick, they have to confront some of the fear and organizational barriers that led to the status quo.

It seems to me, then, that the best time for a marketer to grow is when clients have to pick something. Seeking these moments out is inexpensive and productive.

Thinking About Business Models

A business model is the architecture of a business or project. It has four elements:

1. What compelling reason exists for people to give you money (or votes or donations)?
2. How do you acquire what you're selling for less than it costs to sell it?
3. What structural insulation do you have from relentless commoditization and a price war?
4. How will strangers find out about the business and decide to become customers?

The Internet 1.0 was a fascinating place because business models were in flux. Suddenly, it was possible to have costless transactions, which meant that doing something on a huge scale was very cheap. That means that #2 was really cheap, so #1 didn't have to be very big at all.

Some people got way out of hand and decided that costs were so low, they didn't have to worry about revenue at all. There are still some Internet hotshot companies that are operating under this scenario, which means that it's fair to say that they don't actually have a business model.

The idea of connecting people, of building tribes, of the natural monopoly provided by online communities means that the Internet is the best friend of people focusing on the third element, insulation from competition. Once you build a network, it's extremely difficult for someone else to disrupt it.

As the Internet has spread into all aspects of our culture, it is affecting business models offline as well. Your T-shirt shop or consulting firm or political campaign has a different business model than it did ten years ago, largely because viral marketing and the growth of cash-free marketing means that you can spread an idea farther and faster than ever before. It also makes it far cheaper for a competitor to enter the market (#3), putting existing players under significant pressure from newcomers.

This business model revolution is just getting started. It's not too late to invent a better one.

Malcolm Is Wrong

I've never written those three words before, but he's never disagreed with Chris Anderson before, so there you go.

Free is the name of Chris's new book, and it's going to be wildly misunderstood and widely argued about.

The first argument that makes no sense is, "should we want free to be the future?"

Who cares if we want it? It is.

The second argument that makes no sense is, "how will this new business model support the world as we know it today?"

Who cares if it does? It is. It's happening. The world will change around it, because the world has no choice. I'm sorry if that's inconvenient, but it's true.

As I see "free," there are two forces at work:

In an attention economy (like this one), marketers struggle for attention, and if you don't have it, you lose. Free is a relatively cheap way to get attention (both at the start and then through viral techniques).

Second, in a digital economy with lots of players and lower barriers to entry, it's quite natural that the price will be lowered until it meets the incremental cost of making one more unit. If a brand can gain share by charging less, a rational player will.

Condé Nast (publisher of *Wired*, Chris's magazine, and yes, *The New*

Yorker, Malcolm's magazine) is going to go out of business long before you get sick, never mind die. So will newspapers printed on paper. They're going to disappear before you do. I'm not wishing for this to happen, but by refusing to build new digital assets that matter, traditional publishers are forfeiting their future.

Magazines and newspapers were perfect businesses for a moment of time, but they wouldn't have worked in 1784, and they're not going to work very soon in the future, either.

We're always going to need writers, but the business model of their platform is going to change.

People will pay for content *if* it is so unique that they can't get it anywhere else, so fast that they benefit from getting it before anyone else, or so related to their tribe that paying for it brings them closer to other people. We'll always be willing to pay for souvenirs of news, as well— things to go on a shelf or badges of honor to share.

People will not pay for by-the-book rewrites of news that belongs to all of us. People will not pay for yesterday's news, driven to our house, delivered a day late, static, without connections or comments or relevance. Why should we? A good book review on Amazon is more reliable and easier to find than a paid-for professional review that used to run in your local newspaper, isn't it?

Like all dying industries, the old perfect businesses will whine, criticize, demonize and, most of all, lobby for relief. It won't work. The big reason is simple:

In a world of free, everyone can play.

This is huge. When there are thousands of people writing about something, many will be willing to do it for free (like poets), and some of them might even be really good (like some poets). There is no poetry shortage.

The reason that we needed paid contributors before was that there was only economic room for a few magazines, a few TV channels, a few pottery stores, a few of everything. In a world where there is room for anyone to present their work, anyone will present their work. Editors become ever more powerful and valued, while the need for attention grows so acute that free may even be considered expensive.

Of course, it's ironic that sometimes people pay money for my books

(I view them as souvenirs of content you could get less conveniently and less organized for free online if you chose to). And it's ironic that I read Malcolm's review for free. And ironic that you can read Chris's arguments the most cogently by paying for them.

Neatness is for historians. For a long time, all the markets for attention-based goods are going to be messy, which means that there are going to be huge opportunities for people (like you?) who are able to get that most precious asset (our attention) for free. At least for a while.

The Massive Attention Surplus

There was an attention drought for the longest time. Marketers paid a fortune for TV ads (and in fact, network ads sold out months in advance) because it was so difficult to find enough attention. Ads worked, so the more ads you bought, the more money you made, thus marketers took all they could get.

This attention shortage drove our economy.

The Internet has done something wacky to this situation. It has created a surplus of attention. Ads go unsold. People are spending hours on YouTube or Twitter or Facebook or other sites and not spending their attention on ads, because the ads are either absent or not worth watching.

When people talk about the problem with free online, they're missing the point. Free is creating lots of attention, but marketers haven't gotten smart enough to do something profitable with that attention.

Hint: funny commercials with chimps won't be the answer.

It turns out that the almost infinitely long tail of attention varieties is what will kick open the monetization of online attention. *Yes*, I will give my attention to an ad, but only if it's anticipated, personal, and relevant. We still give permission to marketers that earn it, but so few marketers do.

Simple example: ten years ago, there was nowhere for a company like Best Made Axe to advertise. Today, with billions of tiny micro-markets, it's not hard to imagine many audiences of one or two or three or ten that would be delighted to know about their products. Right now, there's no easy way for a marketer to conceptualize that effort, never mind execute it, though it's surely coming.

Big companies, nonprofits, and even candidates will discover hyperlocal, hyperspecialized, hyperrelevant—this is where we are going, and it turns out that this time, the media are way ahead of the marketers.

Competing with the Single-Minded

I was talking with a few executives from one of the biggest technology companies in Europe, and they were explaining how their hands were tied in moving forward on the Internet. They were doing the best they could under the circumstances, of course, but there were units in their organization that needed to be protected, prices that needed to be supported, sacred cows that couldn't be touched. After all, they argued, how could they wipe out their current business just to succeed online?

This conversation happens every single day at organizations large and small. You want to do the new thing, but of course you must do it in a measured, rational way.

Which is great, unless your competition doesn't agree.

When you have someone who is willing to accomplish A without worrying about B and C, they will almost always defeat you in accomplishing A. Online, of course, this scenario often leads to doom, since there are many organizations that are willing to get big at the expense of revenue, or writers willing to be noticed at the expense of ethics or reputation. But in the short run, the single-minded have a fantastic advantage. And sometimes, their single-minded focus on accomplishing just that one thing (whatever it is) pushes them through the Dip far ahead of you, and then yes, they make a ton of money and you've lost forever.

Newspapers, magazines, TV stations, hardware companies, real estate brokers, travel agents, bookstores, insurance agents, art galleries, and five hundred other industries need to think hard about this before it's too late.

Clout

The Web knows something, but it's not telling us, at least not yet.

The Web knows how many followers you have on Twitter, how many friends you have on Facebook, how many people read your blog.

It also knows how often those people retweet, amplify, and spread your ideas.

It also knows how many followers your followers have.

So, what if, Google-style, someone took all this data and figured out who has clout? Which of your readers is the one capable of making an idea break through the noise and spread? Bloggers don't have impact because they have a lot of readers; they have a lot of impact because of who their readers are (my readers, of course, are the most sophisticated and cloutful on the entire Web).

If you knew which of your followers had clout, you could invest more time and energy in providing personal attention. If we knew where big ideas were starting, that would be neat, and even more useful would be understanding who the key people were in bringing those new ideas to the rest of the world.

Back in the old days, we had no idea, so we defaulted to big newspapers or magazines or the TV networks. But now we know. We just need to surface the data in a way that is useful.

The Platform Vs. the Eyeballs

This might be the most subtle yet important shift that marketers face as they deal with the reality of new media. Marketers aren't renters; now they own.

For generations, marketers were trained to buy (actually rent) eyeballs.

A media company assembled a large amount of attention. A TV network or a magazine or even a billboard company found a place you could put an ad, and they sold you a shot at reaching their audience.

You, the marketer, don't care about the long-term value of this audience. It's like a rental car. You want it to be clean and shiny when you get it, you want to avoid getting in trouble when you return it, but hey, it's a rental.

And so when we buy ads, we ask "how big an audience?" and then we design an ad with our brand in mind, not with the well-being of the media company or its audience in mind. And if we get a 0.1% or even a 1% response rate, we celebrate.

A trade-show booth is an example of eyeball thinking. The trade-show organizer assembles attendees, and your job at the booth is to grab as many as you can.

Old media was not the same as old branding. Media companies built audiences, and then brands rented those audiences.

Suddenly the new media comes along and the rules are different. You're not renting an audience; you're building one. You're not exhibiting at a trade show; you're starting your own trade show.

If you still ask "how much traffic is there?" or "what's the CPM?" you're not getting it. Are you buying momentary attention or are you investing in a long-term asset?

Now, when you buy something (that thing you used to call "media"), you're not paying for eyeballs, you're paying for a platform. A platform you can use to build your own audience, one that you can nurture, educate, and ultimately convert. You'll take care of this audience differently, measure them differently, and have a different sales cycle. This isn't natural, but it works.

Two steps: buy a platform and then fill it with people. Some examples:

Authors have traditionally relied on publishers to bring them readers. The author gives up the majority of the income, and the publisher brings them the readers. But then you see someone like Frank at PostSecret, who builds his own audience for his (sometimes NSFW) content. He owns a platform; it's not something he rents. Now, using a publisher is a choice, not a necessity. Just about every successful author going forward (except for the lucky exceptions like Dan Brown) will own her own media channel. And not just authors, of course.

Consider the local real estate agent. She can spend money to run ads every week in the local paper, or she can use the same money to start a legitimate media channel, a digital magazine, say, one that cheers on the school and gives the local paper a run for its money. And oh, yes, the only houses listed for sale are hers. It might take a lot of work and even some money. But what does she get? A platform forever.

Traditionally, a clothing brand has to give up income and control to a retailer, since the retailer has the eyeballs. The Web allows a brand like LittleMissMatched to build their own platform and their own audience and thus bypass all those gatekeepers. LittleMissMatched invested in a product that told a story, instead of investing in giving Walmart a cut. Boring products can't do this.

Or consider the local chiropractor. He can spend money on a Yellow Pages ad, or he can invest in a platform, creating a local running club and coaching its members.

(Compare these examples with McDonald's, a company that continues to rent eyeballs for a high price and has no real platform to speak of.)

Or consider the acquisition of Omniture by Adobe. What did Adobe pay for? I'd argue it was direct access to the right people at the leading advertisers and websites around the world. Technology isn't so hard to copy. Permission to connect is almost impossible to achieve.

Compared to the cost of renting eyeballs, buying a platform is cheap. Filling it with people eager to hear from you—that's the expensive part. But if you don't invest in the platform, you'll be at a disadvantage, now and forever. The smart way to build a brand today is to invest in the elements of the platform: the product, the technology, the websites (plural), and the systems you need to make it easy for people to show up at your very own trade show. And then embrace these people and shoot for 90% conversion, not 0.5%.

Like most good investments, it's expensive and worth more than it costs.

Dunbar's Number Isn't Just a Number, It's the Law

Dunbar's Number is 150.

And he's not compromising, no matter how much you whine about it.

Dunbar postulated that the typical human being can have only 150 friends. One hundred fifty people in the tribe. After that, we just aren't cognitively organized to handle and track new people easily. That's why, without external forces, human tribes tend to split in two after they reach this size. It's why W. L. Gore limits the size of their offices to 150 (when they grow, they build a whole new building).

Facebook and Twitter and blogs fly in the face of Dunbar's Number. They put hundreds or thousands of friendlies in front of us, people we would have lost touch with (why? because of Dunbar!), except that they keep digitally reappearing.

Reunions are a great example of Dunbar's Number at work. You might like a dozen people you meet at that reunion, but you can't keep up, because you're full.

Some people online are trying to flout Dunbar's Number, to become connected and actual friends with tens of thousands of people at once. And guess what? It doesn't scale. You might be able to stretch to 200 or 400, but no, you can't effectively engage at a tribal level with a thousand people. You get the politician's glassy-eyed gaze or the celebrity's empty stare. And then the nature of the relationship is changed.

I can tell when this happens. I'm guessing you can, too.

Hammer Time

So if it's true that to a person with a hammer, every problem looks like a nail, the really useful question is, "what sort of hammer do you have?"

At big TV networks, they have a TV hammer. At a surgeon's office, they have the scalpel hammer. A drug counselor has the talk hammer, while a judge probably has the jail hammer.

Maybe it's time for a new hammer . . .

One study found that when confronted with a patient with back pain, surgeons prescribed surgery, physical therapists thought that therapy was indicated, and yes, acupuncturists were sure that needles were the answer. Across the entire universe of patients, the single largest indicator of treatment wasn't symptoms or patient background; it was the background of the doctor.

When the market changes, you may be seeing all the new opportunities and problems the wrong way because of the solutions you're used to. The reason so many organizations have trouble using social media is that they are using precisely the wrong hammer. *And odds are, they will continue to do so until their organization fails.* PR firms try to use the new tools to send press releases because, you guessed it, that's their hammer.

It's not just about new vs. old. Inveterate community-focused social media mavens often bring that particular hammer to other venues. So they crowdsource keynote speeches or restaurants or board meetings and can't figure out why they don't have the impact others do.

The best way to find the right tool for the job is to learn to be good at switching hammers.

How to Protect Your Ideas in the Digital Age

If we're in the idea business, how to protect those ideas?

One way is to misuse **trademark** law. With the help of search engines, greedy lawyers who charge by the letter are busy sending claim letters to anyone who even comes close to using a word or phrase they believe their client "owns." News flash: trademark law is designed to make it clear who *makes* a good or a service. It's a mark we put on something we create to indicate the source of the thing, not the inventor of a word or even a symbol. They didn't invent trademark law to prevent me from putting a picture of your cricket team's logo on my blog. They invented it to make it clear who was selling you something (a mark for trade = trademark).

I'm now officially trademarking thank-you™. From now on, whenever you use this word, please be sure to send me a royalty check.

Another way to protect your ideas is to (mis)use copyright law. You might think that this is a federal law designed to allow you to sue people who steal your ideas. It's not. Ideas are free. Anyone can use them. **Copyright** protects the *expression* of ideas, the particular arrangement of words or sounds or images. Bob Marley's estate can't sue anyone who records a reggae song; they can sue only the people who use his precise expression of words or music. Sure, get very good at expressing yourself (like Dylan or Sarah Jones) and then no one can copy your expression. But your ideas? They're up for grabs, and it's a good thing, too.

The challenge for people who create content isn't to spend all their time looking for pirates. It's to build a platform for commerce, a way and a place to get paid for what they create. Without that, you've got no revenue stream and pirates are irrelevant anyway. Newspapers aren't in trouble because people are copying the news. They're in trouble because they forgot to build a scalable, profitable online model for commerce.

Patents are an option, except they're really expensive and do nothing but give you the right to sue. And they're best when used to protect a particular physical manifestation of an idea. It's a real crap-shoot to spend tens of thousands of dollars to patent an idea you thought up in the shower one day.

So, how to protect your ideas in a world where ideas spread?

Don't.

Instead, spread them. Build a reputation as someone who creates great ideas, sometimes on demand. Or as someone who can manipulate or build on your ideas better than a copycat can. Or use your ideas to earn a permission asset so you can build a relationship with people who are interested. Focus on being the best tailor with the sharpest scissors, not the litigant who sues any tailor who deigns to use a pair of scissors.

The Reason Using Social Media Is So Difficult for Most Organizations

It's a process, not an event.

Dating is a process. So is losing weight, being a public company, and building a brand.

On the other hand, putting up a trade-show booth is an event. So is going public or having surgery.

Events are easier to manage, pay for, and get excited about. Processes build results for the long haul.

You Don't Have the Power

A friend is building a skating rink. Unfortunately, he started with un-even ground and the water keeps ending up on one side of the rink. Water's like that, and you need a lot of time and power and money if you want to change it. One person, working as hard as he can, has little chance of persuading water to change.

Consider this quote from a high-ranking book publisher who should know better: "We must do everything in our power to uphold the value of our content against the downward pressures exerted by the market-place and the perception that 'digital' means 'cheap' . . ."

Hello?

You don't have the power. Maybe if every person who has ever published a book or is ever considering publishing a book got together and made a pact, then they'd have enough power to fight the market. But solo? Exhort all you want; it's not going to do anything but make you hoarse.

Movie execs thought they had the power to fight TV. Record execs thought they had the power to fight iTunes. Magazine execs thought they had the power to fight the Web. Newspaper execs thought they had the power to fight Craigslist.

Here's a way to think about it, inspired by Merlin Mann: imagine that next year your company is going to make ten million dollars instead of a hundred million dollars in profit. What would you do, knowing that your profits were going to be far less than they are today? Because that's exactly what the upstart with nothing to lose is going to do. Ten million in profit is a lot to someone starting with zero and trying to gain share. They don't care that you made a hundred million last year from the old model.

If I'm an upstart publisher or a little-known author, you can bet I'm happy to sell my work at $5 and earn 70 cents a copy if I can sell a million copies.

Smart businesspeople focus on the things they have the power to change, not on whining about the things they don't.

Existing publishers have the power to change the form of what they do, increase the value, increase the speed, segment the audience, create communities, lead tribes, generate breakthroughs that make us gasp. They don't have the power to demand that we pay more for the same stuff that others will sell for much less.

And if you think this is a post about the publishing business, I hope you'll reread it and think about how digital will change your industry, too.

Competition and the market are like water. They go where they want.

First, Organize 1,000

Kevin Kelly really changed our thinking with his post about 1,000 true fans.

But what if you're not an artist or a musician? Is there a business case for this?

I think the ability to find and organize 1,000 people is a breakthrough opportunity. One thousand people coordinating their actions is enough to change your world (and make a living).

A thousand people each spending $1,000 on a special-interest cruise equals a million dollars.

A thousand people willing to spend $250 to attend a day-long seminar gives you the leverage to invite just about anyone you can imagine to fly in and speak.

A thousand people voting as a bloc can change local politics forever.

A thousand people willing to try a new restaurant you find for them gives you the ability to make an entrepreneur successful and change the landscape of your town.

Even better, coordinating the learning and connections of this tribe of 1,000 is not just profitable, it's rewarding. If you can take them where they want to go, you become indispensable (and respected).

What's difficult? What's difficult is changing your attitude. Instead of speed dating your way to interruption, instead of yelling at strangers all day trying to make a living, coordinating a tribe of 1,000 requires patience, consistency, and a focus on long-term relationships and lifetime value. You don't find customers for your products. You find products for your customers.

It's Not the Rats You Need to Worry About

If you want to know if a ship is going to sink, watch what the richest passengers do.

iTunes and file sharing killed Tower Records. The key symptom: the best customers switched. Of course people who were buying 200 records a year would switch. They had the most incentive. The alternatives were cheaper and faster mostly for the heavy users.

Amazon and the Kindle have killed the bookstore. Why? Because people who buy 100 or 300 books a year are gone forever. The typical American buys just one book a year for pleasure. Those people are meaningless to a bookstore. It's the heavy users that matter, and now officially, as 2009 ends, they have abandoned the bookstore. It's over.

When law firms started switching to fax machines, FedEx realized that the cash-cow part of their business (100 or 1000 or more envelopes per firm per day) was over and they switched fast to packages. Good for them.

If your ship is sinking, get out now. By the time the rats start packing, it's way too late.

Hunters and Farmers

Ten thousand years ago, civilization forked. Farming was invented, and the way many people spent their time was changed forever.

Clearly, farming is a very different activity from hunting. Farmers spend time sweating the details, worrying about the weather, making smart choices about seeds and breeding, and working hard to avoid a bad crop. Hunters, on the other hand, have long periods of distracted noticing, interrupted by brief moments of frenzied panic.

It's not crazy to imagine that some people are better at one activity than another. There might even be a gulf between people who are good at each of the two skills. Thom Hartmann has written extensively on this. He points out that it doesn't make a lot of sense to medicate kids who might be better at hunting so that they can sit quietly in a school designed to teach farming.

A kid who has innate hunting skills is easily distracted, because noticing small movements in the brush is exactly what you'd need to do if you were hunting. Scan and scan and pounce. That same kid is able to drop everything and focus like a laser—for a while—if it's urgent. The farming kid, on the other hand, is particularly good at tilling the fields of endless homework problems, each a bit like the other. Just don't ask him to change gears instantly.

Marketers confuse the two groups. Are you selling a product that helps farmers . . . and hoping that hunters will buy it? How do you expect that people will discover your product or believe that it will help them? The woman who reads each issue of *Vogue*, hurrying through the pages and then clicking over to Zappos to overnight order the latest styles—she's hunting. Contrast this to the CTO who spends six months issuing RFPs to buy a PBX that was last updated three years ago—she's farming.

Both groups are worthy; both groups are profitable. But each group is very different from the other, and I think we need to consider teaching, hiring, and marketing to these groups in completely different ways. I'm not sure if there's a genetic component or if this is merely a convenient grouping of people's personas. All I know is that it often explains a lot about behavior (including mine).

Some ways to think about this:

- George Clooney (in *Up in the Air*) and James Bond are both fictional hunters. Give them a desk job and they freak out.
- Farmers don't dislike technology. They dislike failure. Technology that works is a boon.
- Hunters are in sync with Google, a hunting site; farmers like Facebook.
- When you promote a first-rate hunting salesperson to internal sales management, be prepared for failure.
- Farmers prefer productive meetings; hunters want to simply try stuff and see what happens.
- Warren Buffet is a farmer. So is Bill Gates. Mark Cuban is a hunter.
- Hunters want a high-stakes mission; farmers want to avoid epic failure.
- Trade shows are designed to entrance hunters, yet all too often, the booths are staffed with farmers.
- The last hundred years of our economy favored smart farmers. It seems as though the next hundred are going to belong to the persistent hunters who are able to stick with it for the long haul.
- A hunter will often buy something merely because it is difficult to acquire.
- One of the paradoxes of venture capital is that it takes a hunter to get the investment, and a farmer to patiently make the business work.
- A farmer often relies on other farmers in her peer group to be sure a purchase is riskless.

Whom are you hiring? Competing against? Teaching?

No More Big Events

Here are things that you can now avoid:

- The annual review
- The annual sales conference
- The big product launch
- The grand opening of a new branch
- Drop-dead, one-shot negotiation events

The reasons? Well, they don't work. They don't work because big events leave little room for iteration, for trial and error, for earning rapport. And the biggest reason: frequent cheap communication is easier than ever, and if you use it, you'll discover that the process creates far more gains than events ever can.

It's Easier to Teach Compliance Than Initiative

Compliance is simple to measure, simple to test for, and simple to teach. Punish non-compliance, reward obedience, and repeat.

Initiative is very difficult to teach to 28 students in a quiet classroom. It's difficult to brag about in a school board meeting. And it's a huge pain in the neck to do reliably.

Schools like teaching compliance. They're pretty good at it.

To top it off, until recently the customers of a school or training program (the companies that hire workers) were buying compliance by the bushel. Initiative was a red flag, not an asset.

Of course, now that's all changed. The economy has rewritten the rules, and smart organizations seek out intelligent problem solvers. Everything is different now. Except the part about how much easier it is to teach compliance.

The Factory in the Center

Old-time factories had a linear layout because there was just one steam engine driving one drive shaft. Every machine in the shop had to line up under the shaft (connected by a pulley) in order to get power.

That metaphor extended to the people working in the factory. Each person was hired and trained and arranged to maximize output. The goal was to engage the factory, to feed it, maintain it, and have it produce efficiently.

Distribution was designed in sync with the factory. You wanted to have the right number of trucks and drivers to handle whatever the factory produced and to get it where it needed to go.

Marketing was driven by the factory as well. The goal of marketing was to sell whatever the factory could produce in a given month, for as much money and with as little overhead as possible.

And things like customer service and community relations were expenses, things you did in order to keep the factory out of trouble.

So . . .

What happens when the factory goes away?

What if the organization has no engine in the center that makes something? What if that's outsourced? What if you produce a service or traffic in ideas? What happens when the revolution comes along (the post-industrial revolution) and now all the value lies in the stuff you used to do because you had to, not because you wanted to?

Now it doesn't matter where you sit. Now it doesn't matter whether or not you're adding to the efficiency or productivity of the machine. Now you don't market to sell what you made; you make things to satisfy the market. Now, the market and the consumer and the idea trump the system.

Suddenly, the power is in a different place, and the organization must change or else the doughnut collapses.

Drive-By Culture and the Endless Search for Wow

The 'Net has spawned two new ways to create and consume culture.

The first way is the wide-open door for amateurs who want to create. This is blogging and online art, Wikipedia, and the maker movement. These guys get a lot of press, and deservedly so, because they're changing everything.

The second way, though, is distracting and ultimately a waste. We're creating a culture of clickers, stumblers, and jaded spectators who decide in the space of a moment whether to watch and participate (or not).

Imagine if people went to the theater or the movies and stood up and walked out after the first six seconds. Imagine if people went to the senior prom and bailed on their date three seconds after the car pulled away from the curb.

The majority of people who sign up for a new online service rarely or never use it. The majority of YouTube videos are watched for just a few seconds. Chatroulette institutionalizes the glance-and-click mentality. I'm guessing that more than half the people who started reading this post never finished it.

This is all easy to measure. And it drives people with something to accomplish crazy, because they want visits to go up, clicks to go up, eyeballs to go up.

Should I write blog posts that increase my traffic or that help change the way (a few) people think?

Should a charity focus on instant donations by texting from a million people, or is it better to seek dedicated attention and support from a few who understand the mission and are there for the long haul?

More and more often, we're seeing products and services coming to market designed to appeal to the momentary attention of the clickers. *The Huffington Post* has downgraded itself, pushing thoughtful stories down the page in exchange for link bait and sensational celebrity riffs. This strategy gets page views, but does it generate thought or change?

If you create (or market), should you be chasing the people who click and leave? Or is it like trying to turn a cheetah into a house pet? Is manipulating the high-voltage attention stream of millions of caffeinated Web surfers a viable long-term strategy?

Mass marketing used to be able to have it both ways. Money bought you an audience. Now, the only things that buy you a mass market are wow and speed. Wow keeps getting harder to achieve and dives for the lowest common denominator at the same time.

Time magazine started manipulating the cover and then the contents in order to boost newsstand sales. They may have found a short-term solution, but the magazine is doomed precisely because the people they are pandering to don't really pay attention and aren't attractive to advertisers.

My fear is that the endless search for wow further coarsens our culture at the same time it encourages marketers to get ever more shallow. That's where the first trend comes in: the artists, idea merchants, and marketers that are having the most success are ignoring those that would rubberneck and drive on, and are focusing instead on cadres of fans that matter. Fans that will give permission, fans that will return tomorrow, fans that will spread the word to others that can also take action.

Culture has been getting faster and shallower for hundreds of years, and I'm not the first crusty pundit to decry the demise of thoughtful inquiry and deep experiences. The interesting question here, though, is not how fast is too fast, but what works? What works to change mindsets, to spread important ideas, and to create an audience for work that matters? What's worth your effort and investment as a marketer or creator?

The difference this time is that drive-by culture is both fast *and* free. When there's no commitment of money or time in the interaction, can change or commerce really happen? Just because you can measure eyeballs and page views doesn't mean you should.

In the race between "who" and "how many," *who* usually wins—if action is your goal. Find the right people, those that are willing to listen to what you have to say, and ignore the masses that are just going to race on, unchanged.

First and Never

I met a new addition to the family the other day. She was eleven days old.

It was the warmest day of her whole life the day I was there. And she had just eaten her biggest meal ever.

Firsts are fun and exciting, and it's neat to keep topping ourselves.

I've also come to grips with the fact that I'm never going to eat tuna ever again, and that I'm never going to be able to easily walk onto a shuttle flight at the last minute and just show up in Boston. *Never* is a lot harder than *first*, but I guess you get used to it.

The Internet is like Ice-Nine. It changes what it touches, probably forever. We keep discovering firsts—the biggest viral video ever, the most Twitter followers ever, the fastest bestseller ever. And we constantly discover nevers as well. There's never going to be a mass-market TV show that rivals the ones that came before. There's never going to be a worldwide brand built by advertising ever again, either. And Michael Jackson's record deal is the last one of its kind. And there may never be a job like that job you used to have, either.

Revolutions are like that. They invent and destroy and they go only one way. It's like watching a confused person in a revolving door for the first time. They push backward, try to slow it down, fight the rotation . . . and then they embrace the process and just walk and it works.

The Modern Business Plan

It's not clear to me why business plans are the way they are, but they're often misused to obfuscate, bore, and show an ability to comply with expectations. If I want the real truth about a business and where it's going, I'd rather see something else. I'd divide the modern business plan into five sections:

- Truth
- Assertions
- Alternatives
- People
- Money

The **Truth** section describes the world as it is. Footnote if you want to, but tell me about the market you are entering, the needs that already exist, the competitors in your space, the technology standards, the ways that others have succeeded and failed in the past. The more specific, the better. The more ground knowledge, the better. The more visceral the stories, the better. The point of this section is to be sure that you're clear about the way you see the world, and that you and I agree on your assumptions. This section isn't partisan, it takes no positions, it just states how things are.

Truth can take as long as you need to tell it. It can include spreadsheets, market share analysis, and anything I need to know about how the world works.

The **Assertions** section is your chance to describe how you're going to change things. We will do X, and then Y will happen. We will build Z with this much money in this much time. We will present Q to the market and the market will respond by taking this action.

This is the heart of the modern business plan. The only reason to launch a project is to change something, and I want to know what you're going to do and what impact it's going to have.

Of course, this section will be incorrect. You will make assertions that won't pan out. You'll miss budgets and deadlines and sales. So the **Alternatives** section tells me what you'll do if that happens. How much flexibility does your product or team have? If your assertions don't pan out, is it over?

The People section rightly highlights the key element: who is on your team, who is going to join your team. "Who" doesn't mean their résumés; "who" means their attitudes and abilities and track records in shipping.

And the last section is all about money. How much you'll need, how you'll spend it, what cash flow will look like, P&Ls, balance sheets, margins, and exit strategies.

Your local VC might not like this format, but I'm betting it will help your team think through the hard issues more clearly.

Goodbye to the Office

Factories used to be arranged in a straight line. That's because there was one steam engine, and it turned a shaft. All the machines were set up along the shaft, with a belt giving each of them power. The office needed to be right next to this building, so management could monitor what was going on.

A hundred and fifty years later, why go to work in an office/plant/factory?

1. That's where the machines are.
2. That's where the items I need to work on are.

3. The boss needs to keep tabs on my productivity.

4. There are important meetings to go to.

5. It's a source of energy.

6. The people I collaborate with all day are there.

7. I need someplace to go.

But . . .

1. If you have a laptop, you probably have the machine already, in your house.

2. If you do work with a keyboard and a mouse, the items you need to work on are on your laptop, not in the office.

3. The boss can easily keep tabs on productivity digitally.

4. How many meetings are important? If you didn't go, what would happen?

5. You can get energy from people other than those in the same company.

6. Of the 100 people in your office, how many do you collaborate with daily?

7. So go someplace. But it doesn't have to be to your office.

If we were starting this whole office thing today, it's inconceivable that we'd pay the rent/time/commuting cost to get what we get. I think that in ten years the TV show *The Office* will be seen as a quaint antique.

When you need to have a meeting, have a meeting. When you need to collaborate, collaborate. The rest of the time, do the work, wherever you like.

The gain in speed, productivity, and happiness is massive. What's missing is #7—someplace to go. Once someone figures that part out, the office is dead.

Information About Information

The first revolution hit when people who made stuff started to discover that information was often as valuable as the stuff itself. Knowing where something was or how it performed or how it interacted with you could be worth more than the item itself.

Frito Lay dominates the snack business because of the information infrastructure they built on top of their delivery model. 7-Eleven in Japan dominated for a decade or more because they used information to change their inventory. Zara in Europe is an information business that happens to sell clothes.

You've probably already guessed what's important now: information about information. That's what Facebook and Google and Bloomberg do for a living. They create a meta layer, a world of information about the information itself.

And why is this so valuable? Because it compounds. A tiny head start in access to this information gives you a huge advantage in the stock market. Or in marketing. Or in fund-raising.

Many people and organizations are contributing to this mass of data, but few are taking advantage of the opportunity to collate it and present it to people who desperately need it. Think about how much information needs to be sorted, compared, updated, and presented to people who want to choose or learn or trade on it.

The race to deliver this essential scalable asset isn't over; it's just beginning.

A Post-Industrial A-to-Z Digital Battledore

New times demand new words, because the old words don't help us see the world differently.

Along the way, I've invented a few, and it occurs to me that sometimes I use them as if you know what I'm talking about. Here, with plenty of links, are 26 of my favorite neologisms (the longest post of the year, probably):

A is for Artist: an artist is someone who brings humanity to a problem, who changes someone else for the better, who does work that can't be written down in a manual. Art is not about oil painting; it's about bringing creativity and insight to work, instead of choosing to be a compliant cog. (From *Linchpin*)

B is for Bootstrapper: a bootstrapper is someone who starts a business with no money and *funds growth through growth.* The Internet has made bootstrapping much easier than ever, because the costs of creating and marketing remarkable things are lower than ever. It's really important not to act like you're well-funded if you're intent on bootstrapping (and vice versa). You can read the *Bootstrapper's Bible* for free.

C is for Choice: I didn't coin the term the Long Tail, but I wish I had. It describes a simple law: given the choice, people will take the choice. That means that digital commerce enables niches. The practice of aggregating and enabling the long tail accounts for the success of eBay, iTunes, Amazon, Craigslist, Google, and even Match.com.

D is for Darwin: things evolve. But evolution is speeding up (and yes, evolving). While it used to take a hundred thousand years for significant changes to happen to our physical culture, the nature of information and a connected society means that "everything" might change in just a few months. Ideas that spread, win, and organizations that learn from their mistakes lead the rest of us. (From *Survival Is Not Enough*)

E is for Edgecraft: brainstorming doesn't work so well, because most people are bad at it. They're bad at it because their lizard brain takes over moments before a big idea is uttered. "Oh, no!" it says; "I better not say that because if I do, then I'll have to do it." And so brainstorming quickly becomes clever stalling and time-wasting. Far better is to practice edgecraft. Someone announces a direction ("we'll be really convenient; we'll offer our menu by fax") and then the next person goes closer to that edge, topping it ("we'll offer it by email!"), and so on, each topping the other in any particular direction. (From the book *Free Prize Inside*)

F is for the Free Prize: people often don't buy the obvious or measured solution to their problem; they buy the extra, the bonus, the feeling, and the story. The free prize is the layout of Google—the search results are the same, but the way the search feels is why you choose to search there. If engineers thought more about the free prize, we'd need fewer marketers.

G is for Go go go™: I just trademarked this one, but you have my permission to use it all you like. Go go go is the mantra of someone who has committed to defeating their anxiety and ignoring their lizard brain.

Not a good strategy for airline pilots, but for the rest of us, a little Go go go might be just the ticket.

H is for broken: Isn't it just like a marketer to compromise when he should have organized better in the first place? There's a lot in our consumer society that's broken, but try to avoid getting obsessed with it. Far better to ship your own stuff that's not broken instead.

I is for Ideavirus: a decade ago, I wrote a book that was free. [It still is.] It argues that ideas that spread, win, and you can architect and arrange and manipulate your ideas to make them more likely to spread. Note that I'm not saying you can add gimmicks and spam and networking to spread your idea. I'm saying that the idea itself is more or less likely to spread based on how you design it.

J is for Just looking: When there are plenty of choices and everything is a click away, I'm very unlikely to take action, certainly unlikely to actually buy something from you. I'll do it tomorrow. Or the day after. Which means the only way you create action is to produce an emergency. Why now? Why not later . . .

K is for kindle: No, not the ebook reader. Kindle as in patiently starting a fire. The TV era demanded blockbuster launches of blockbuster products aimed at the masses. The Internet responds better to bonfires that are kindled over time, to ideas that spread because the idea itself, not the hype or the promotion, is the engine.

L is for Lizard Brain: this is a huge impediment to getting what you want, finding your calling, and satisfying your customers. The lizard brain is near your brain stem, including your amygdala. It's the part of your brain responsible for anger, revenge, fear, anxiety, and reproduction. It's the original brain, the one that wild animals possess. Steve Pressfield has named the voice of the lizard: it's the Resistance. The Resistance rationalizes, hides, and sabotages your best work.

M is for Meatball Sundae: this is the unfortunate combination of traditional products and services (designed for low price and good quality) with the high-growth nature of the idea-driven Internet. When your boss tells you to build a viral campaign about some lame product gathering dust in the warehouse, she's asking you to build a meatball sundae and you should flee.

N is for NOBS: otherwise known as the *new-order business school.* My rant about this points out that for most people, a traditional MBA is a waste of both time and money. The two biggest benefits—the selection process of getting in and the social process of networking—could be accomplished, in a Swiftian fashion, without any classes at all.

O is for Orangutan: I could have used the word *monkey,* but I already had an M listing, plus I love the way you spell orangutan. Anyway, the primate is the best way to think about how people interact with websites. They're like monkeys in a psychology experiment, looking for the banana. Where's the banana? they ask. Of course, I don't know the monkey word for banana, so I'm paraphrasing. If your website offers a banana, people are going to click on it. If it doesn't, they'll leave. My argument for banana design is in *The Big Red Fez.*

P is for Permission: anticipated, personal, and relevant messages will always outperform spam. Obvious, but true. So then why do you persist in spamming people? Billboards, TV ads, phone calls—they all are defeated soundly by delivering your offers with permission. In fact, the biggest asset a company can build online is this privilege, the list of people who would miss you if you didn't show up. The original interview appeared (12 years ago!) in *Fast Company.*

Q is for Quitting: sticking things out is overrated, particularly if you stick out the wrong things. In fact, I think you'd be much better off quitting most of what you do so you have the resources to get through the hard slog I call the Dip. The challenge, then, is to not quit in the Dip, but instead to quit everything else so you have the focus to get through the slog of what matters.

R is for Remarkable: a purple cow is remarkable because it's worth talking about. Not because you, the marketer, said it was, but because I, the consumer, did. And in a world without effective, scalable advertising, remarkable products and services are the single best way to succeed.

S is for Sneezer: What do we call someone who spreads an idea the way some people spread a virus? Seek them out, cater to them, organize them.

T is for Tribe: human beings evolved to be attracted to tribes. Groups of like-minded people who share a culture, a connection, and, perhaps, a goal. And each of these tribes seeks leadership. The opportunity for marketers today isn't to sell more average stuff to more average people. The opportunity is to find and connect and lead tribes of people, taking them somewhere they want to go.

U is for Ululate: not because it's relevant, just because it's the single best word in the English language. Can I sneak an extra C? The cliff business.

V is for Very good: no one cares about very good. I can get very good from just about anyone, and certainly cheaper than I can get it from you. We don't have a competence shortage, not anymore. No, I'm going to pay extra only for the personal, the magical, the artistic, and the work of the linchpin.

W is for Worldview: I first encountered this term via George Lakoff. Your worldview is the set of expectations and biases you bring to a situation before any new data appear. Some people hear a politician say something and hate it, while others are thrilled by it. Is it the thing that was said or the person who said it? Some people hear that Apple is about to launch a new product and they get out their wallets; others flee— before they even know what it is. If you don't understand the worldview of the people you're selling to, you *will* fail.

X is for Xebec: I hate it when A-to-Z list makers cheap out on the X. Hey, a xebec is a three-masted schooner. And it's obsolete. Just like CDs, newspapers, and a whole host of interesting but dated business models. Sorry. Imagine someone saying: "he's a nice guy, but that company he works for is a xebec."

Y is for You: you, the artist. You, the one who makes a difference. You, the one who stands for something and now has the leverage (and access to the market) to actually ship. Go go go.™

Z is for Zoometry: originally a term from zoology (pronounced zo-ology, in case you were curious), zoometry is the science of instigating and learning from change. This is the revolution of our time, the biggest one in history, and it's not just about silly videos on YouTube. One by one, industry by industry, the world is being remade again and again, and the agents of change are the winners.

Accept All Substitutes

Commerce is about pricing, and pricing is about scarcity. Scarcity, of course, demands no easy substitutes.

Some news websites are foolishly putting up pay walls, requiring readers to pay by the day or the year to see what's there. This is foolish because substitutes are so easy to find. If I can't get to the *Times of London* or *Time* magazine, no problem; I'll find the same news (or almost the same news) somewhere else.

This is the mistake that book publishers are making on the Kindle. I was mildly interested in the new biography of Henry Luce. But it's $19 on the Kindle. That's outrageous in a world where there are plenty (more than I can ever read) of great biographies for less than $10 on this very same device. (In fact, I can buy *The Man Time Forgot*, the biography of his forgotten partner, the actual founder of *Time*, for $4 in paperback or $10 on the Kindle.) Is a biography about someone else a perfect substitute? Not if you're writing your dissertation about Luce, no, it's not. But the publishers seek a broader audience than that, don't they?

The Internet has dramatically widened the number of available substitutes. You don't have to like it, but it's true. That means you have to work far harder to create work that can't easily be replaced.

A Little Out of Sync

All those devices in your bag make it easier than ever to stay in sync.

You can reap what you sow in FarmVille, keep up with your email, know what's going on in every important blog, be in the right room at the right time earning badges, etc. You can be synchronized at all times.

And if you get a little out of sync, just a little, it's painful. One more reason you might want to stop reading this and check your feeds.

Building your success on being more in sync than everyone else is a sharp edge to walk on. You'll always be near the edge of perfect sync, but never there.

The alternative is to be a *lot* out of sync.

People who are way out of sync with the digital maelstrom of the moment aren't always bad followers. They might be great leaders.

Marketing to the Bottom of the Pyramid

PART 1: THE BOTTOM IS IMPORTANT

Almost a third of the world's population earns $2.50 or less a day. The enormity of this disparity takes my breath away, but there's an interesting flip side to it: that's a market of more than $5 billion *a day*. Add the next segment ($5 a day) and it's easy to see that every single day, the poorest people in the world spend more than $10 billion to live their lives.

Most of that money is spent on traditional items purchased in traditional ways. Kerosene. Rice. Basic medicines if you can afford them, or if death is the only alternative. And almost all of these purchases are inefficient. There's lack of information, there are high costs because of a lack of choice, and most of all, there is a lack of innovation.

There are two significant impacts here: first, the inefficiency is a tax on the people who can least afford it. Second, the side effects of poor products are dangerous. Kerosene kills, and so does dirty water.

PART 2: THE BOTTOM IS AN OPPORTUNITY (FOR BOTH BUYER AND SELLER)

If a business can offer a better product—one that's more efficient, provides better information, increases productivity, is safer, cleaner, faster, or otherwise improved—it has the ability to change the world.

Change the world? Sure. Because capitalism and markets scale. If you can make money selling someone a safer item, you'll make more. And more. Until you've sold all you can. At the same time, you've enriched the purchaser, who bought something of her own free will because it made things better.

Not only that, but engaging in the marketplace empowers the purchaser. If you've got a wagon full of rice as food aid, you can just dump it in the town square and drive away. You have all the power. But if you have to sell something in order to succeed, it moves the power from the seller to the buyer. Quality and service and engagement have to continually improve, or the buyer moves on.

The cell phone, for example, has revolutionized the lives of billions in the developing world. If you have a cell phone, you can determine the best price for the wheat you want to sell. You can find out if the part for your tractor has come in, without spending two days to walk to town to find out. And you can be alerted to weather, and so on. Productivity booms. There's no way the cell phone could have taken off as quickly or efficiently as a form of aid, but once someone started engaging with this market, the volume was so huge it just scaled. And the market now competes to be ever more efficient.

PART 3: IT'S NOT AS EASY AS IT LOOKS

And here's the kicker: if you're a tenth-generation subsistence farmer, your point of view is different from that of someone working in an R&D lab in Palo Alto. *The Moral Economy of the Peasant* makes this argument quite clearly. Imagine standing in water up to your chin. The only thing you're prepared to focus on is whether the water is going to rise four more inches. Your penchant for risk is close to zero. One mistake and the game is over.

As a result, it's extremely difficult to sell innovation to this consumer. The line around the block to get into the Apple Store is an insane concept in this community. A promise from a marketer is meaningless because the marketer isn't part of the town, the marketer will move away, and the marketer is, of course, a liar.

Let me add one more easily overlooked point: Western-style consumers have been taught from birth the power of the package. We see the new iPod nano or the new Porsche or the new convertible note on a venture deal, and we can easily do the math: [new thing] + [me] = [happier]. We've been taught that an object can make our lives better, that a purchase can make us happier, that the color of the Tiffany's box or the ringing of a phone might/will bring us joy.

That's not true for someone who hasn't bought a new kind of consumer good in a year or two or three or maybe ever. As a result, stores in the developing world tend to be stocked with the classic, the tried and true, because people buy refills of previous purchases, not the new.

No subsistence farmer walks into a store or stall, saying, "I wonder what's new today. I wonder if there's a new way for me to solve my problems." Every day, people in the West say that very thing as they engage in shopping as a hobby.

You can't simply put something new in front of people in this market and expect them to buy it, no matter how great, no matter how well packaged, no matter how well sold.

So you see the paradox. A new product and approach and innovation could dramatically improve the life and income of a billion people, but those people have been conditioned to ignore the very tools that are a reflex of marketers that might sell it to them. Fear of loss is greater than fear of gain. Advertising is inefficient and ineffective. And the worldview of the shoppers is that they're not shoppers. They're in search of refills.

The answer, it turns out, is in connecting and leading tribes. It lies in engaging directly and experientially with individuals, not in getting distribution in front of markets. Figure out how to use direct selling in just one village, and then do it in ten, and then in a hundred. The broad, mass-market approach of a Western marketer is foolish because there is no mass market in places where villages *are* the market.

THE (EVENTUAL) POWER OF THE EARLY ADOPTER

On a trip to Berelli, India, I met this man. He is a swami, a leader in his village. He owns a d.light lantern—he purchased it from his savings and uses it to replace the dangerous, expensive kerosene lantern he used to use. Why did he take the risk and buy a new technology? He could fit all

his worldly positions into a Rollaboard, and yet he owns a solar lantern, and he's the first man in his village to buy one.

For him, at least this one time, he liked the way it felt to be seen as a leader, to go first, to do an experiment. Perhaps his followers contributed enough that the purchase didn't feel risky. Perhaps the person he bought it from was a friend or was somehow trusted. It doesn't really matter, other than understanding that he's rare.

After he got the lantern, he set it up in front of his house. Every night for six months, his followers would meet in his front yard to talk, to connect and, yes, to wonder how long it would be before the lantern would burn out. Six months later, the jury is still out.

One day, months or years from now, the lantern will be seen as obvious and trusted and a safe purchase. But it won't happen as fast as it would happen in Buffalo or Paris. The imperative is simple: find the early adopters, embrace them, adore them, support them, don't go away, don't let them down. And then be patient and persistent. Mass-market acceptance is rare. Viral connections based on experience are the only reliable way to spread new ideas in communities that aren't traditionally focused on the cult of the new.

This situation raises the bar for customer service and for exceptional longevity, value, and design. It means that the only way to successfully engage this market is with relentless focus on the conversations that tribe leaders and early adopters choose to have with their peers. All the tools of the Western mass market are useless here.

Just because it is going to take longer than it should doesn't mean we should walk away. There are big opportunities here, for all of us. It's going to take some time, but it's worth it. [More info: acumenfund.org]

The Inevitable Decline Due to Clutter

Digital media expand. Digital isn't like paper; it can get bigger.

As digital marketers seek to increase profits, they almost always make the same mistake. They continue to add more clutter, messaging, and offers because hey, it's free.

One more link, one more banner, one more side deal on the Groupon page.

Economics tells us that the right thing to do is run the factory until the last item produced is being sold at marginal cost. In other words, keep adding until it doesn't work anymore.

In fact, human behavior tells us that this is a more permanent effect than we realize. Once you overload the users, you train them not to pay attention. More clutter isn't free. In fact, more clutter is a permanent shift, a desensitization to *all* the information, not just to the last bit.

And it's hard to go backward.

More is not always better. In fact, more is almost never better.

Asymmetrical Mass Favors, a Tragedy of Our Commons

If the farmer and the baker make a trade, both win. The farmer benefits from having someone turn his wheat into flour and bake it, and the baker gets money from the bread he sells that he can use to buy things he needs (like food).

This sample math of the transaction (Pareto, et al) created the world we live in. It also is connected to the idea of a favor.

A favor is the first half of a transaction. I ask you to do something for me today, something where I will probably benefit a lot in exchange for a small effort on your part. Inherent in the idea of a favor, though, is that one day soon, the transaction will be completed. One day, I will do something for you that gives you a benefit.

As Pareto and any economist will tell you, we willfully engage in this transaction because we'll benefit. Maybe not right now, but soon.

By spreading the idea of the trade over time, the favor makes trades more likely to occur, and also makes sure that they are even more efficient. If I'm already holding open the heavy door, holding it two more seconds for you is easy for me. And then, the next time you're holding open the door, you'll be more likely to hold it for me.

If I recommend you for a job, it doesn't take much effort on my part, but you might get three years of gainful employment out of it. And of course, you're happy to complete that transaction as soon as you can, because no one wants to walk around owing favors.

The efficiency caused by this sort of exchange is so extraordinary that we built it into the social contract. I'm not just selfish if I let the door slam as you walk toward the elevator—I'm rude. I'm risking becoming an outcast.

Favors are so ingrained that the next step was inevitable: mass symmetrical favors. Halloween is a great example: how else to explain a hundred million people buying half a billion Snickers bars? We give away the candy because it's expected, and because people gave us candy when we were kids, and because people are giving our kids candy as well. To opt out is uncivilized.

School taxes create a similar obligation. If you don't pay when you're childless, there will be no one to pay when your kids are in school. (And you have to live in a world with uneducated people.) And so the transactions are spread out over time, with everyone giving and taking, not so much keeping score as knowing that a key part of civil society is to participate in these mass fungible favors.

But!

There's a big "but." The Internet and other connecting tools now make it easy to create the asymmetrical mass favor—in which one person can ask a *large* number of people, some of them strangers, some friendlies, some friends—for an accommodation that may very well never be repaid.

The simple example is the person running for the Metro North commuter train that leaves at 5:20. She's only 2 minutes late. If she misses it, she's delayed half an hour. Surely the people on the train can wait 120 seconds.

Not really. Not if there are 300 people on the train. That's a ten-hour penalty on the passengers, and if there's no reasonable expectation of each of them somehow finishing the transaction one day in the future, the entire system will fall apart. No, in the abstract, we WANT the conductor to say "sorry."

It gets far more dramatic when we think about spamming 10,000 or 100,000 people with your résumé or plea for help.

The problem is that under the cover of the social contract, under the guise of doing what's civilized, what some people are doing is beginning exchanges that they and those they engage with *know* will never be consummated. She's not transacting, she's taking.

And people resent her for it. "It can't hurt to ask" is almost never true, but here, especially, it hurts a lot. The person looking for the favor is undoing the tacit agreement we all live by, by seeking a favor when the recipient has no real (social) choice in the matter.

The favor is too important to be discarded, but the Internet is making things that look like favors (but are actually asymmetrical takings) more and more common. It's putting pressure on people who are usually open to a favor to do the difficult thing and just say no.

A Flip Side: The Asymmetrical Gift

Worth a thought: the alternative, the good news that comes with the bad, is the **massive asymmetrical gift**.

A gift is not a favor, because no recompense is implied or expected. A gift is just from me to you, that's it.

The Internet makes it easy to give gifts to large numbers of people at very, very low cost. Editing a Wikipedia article, for example, is a gift for the ages, one that might be seen by a million people over three years.

This kind of gift leads to a new clause in the social contract. In this environment, we expect that civilized participants will give. Just because. Because they can. Because the gift makes all of it work better.

While mass favors have to fade (too easy to ask for, too unfair at scale), mass gifts show up to change the equation. Gifts are easy to scale, so now the more generous, the better. For all of us.

The Realization Is Now

New polling out this week shows that Americans are frustrated with the world and pessimistic about the future. They're losing patience with the economy, with their prospects, with their leaders (of both parties).

What's actually happening is this: we're realizing that the Industrial Revolution is fading. The 80-year-long run that brought ever-increasing productivity (and, along with it, well-paying jobs for an ever-expanding middle class) is ending.

It's one thing to read about the changes the Internet brought and it's another to experience them. People who thought they had a valuable skill or degree have discovered that being an anonymous middleman doesn't guarantee job security. Individuals who were trained to comply and follow instructions have discovered that the deal is over . . . and it isn't their fault, because they've always done what they were told.

This isn't fair, of course. It's not fair to train for years, to pay your dues, to invest in a house or a career and then suddenly see it fade.

For a while, politicians and organizations promised that things would get back to normal. Those promises aren't enough, though, and it's clear to many people that this might be the new normal. In fact, it *is* the new normal.

I regularly hear from people who say, "enough with this conceptual stuff, tell me how to get my factory moving, my day job replaced, my consistent paycheck restored . . ." There's an idea that somehow, if we just do things with more effort or skill, we can go back to the *Brady Bunch* era and mass markets and mediocre products that pay off for years. It's not an idea, though; it's a myth.

Some people insist that if we focus on "business fundamentals" and get "back to basics," all will return. Not so. The promise that you can get paid really well to do precisely what your boss instructs you to do is now a dream, no longer a reality.

It takes a long time for a generation to come around to significant revolutionary change. The newspaper business, the steel business, law firms, the car business, the record business, even computers . . . one by one, our industries are being turned upside down, and so quickly that it requires us to change faster than we'd like.

It's unpleasant, it's not fair, but it's all we've got. The sooner we realize that the world has changed, the sooner we can accept it and make something of what we've got. Whining isn't a scalable solution.

The Opportunity Is Here

At the same time that our economic engines are faltering, something else is happening. Like all revolutions, it happens in fits and starts, without perfection, but it's clearly happening.

The mass market is being replaced by multiple micro-markets and the long tail of choice.

Google is connecting buyers and sellers over vaster distances, more efficiently and more cheaply than ever before.

Manufacturing is more of a conceptual hurdle than a practical one.

The exchange of information creates ever more value, while commodity products are ever cheaper. It takes fewer employees to generate more value, make more noise, and affect more people.

Most of all is this: every individual, self-employed or with a boss, is now more in charge of her destiny than ever before. The notion of a company town or a stagnant industry with little choice is fading fast.

Right before your eyes, a fundamentally different economy, with different players and different ways to add value, is being built. What used to be an essential asset (for a person or for a company) is worth far less, while new attributes are both scarce and valuable.

Are there dislocations? There's no doubt about it. Pain and uncertainty and risk, for sure.

The opportunity, though, is the biggest of our generation (or the last one, for that matter). The opportunity is there for anyone (with or without a job) smart enough to take it—to develop a best-in-class skill, to tell a story, to spread the word, to be in demand, to satisfy real needs, to run from the mediocre middle, and to change everything.

Note! Like all revolutions, this is an opportunity, not a solution, not a guarantee. It's an opportunity to poke and experiment and fail and discover dead ends on the way to making a difference. The old economy offered a guarantee—time plus education plus obedience = stability. The new one, not so much. The new one offers a chance for you to take a chance and make an impact.

Note! If you're looking for "how," if you're looking for a map, for a way to industrialize the new era, you've totally missed the point and you will end up disappointed. The nature of the last era was that repetition and management of results increased profits. The nature of this one is the opposite: if someone can tell you precisely what to do, it's too late. Art and novelty and innovation cannot be reliably and successfully industrialized.

In 1924, Walt Disney wrote a letter to Ub Iwerks. Walt was already in Hollywood and he wanted his old friend Ubbe to leave Kansas City and come join him to build an animation studio. The last line of the letter said, "PS I wouldn't live in KC now if you gave me the place—yep—you bet—Hooray for Hollywood." And, just above, in larger letters, he scrawled, "Don't hesitate—Do it now."

It's not 1924, and this isn't Hollywood, but it is a revolution, and there's a spot for you (and your boss if you push) if you realize that you're capable of making a difference. Or you could be frustrated. Up to you.

All Economics Is Local

The media try to report on the world economy or the national economy, or even the economy in Detroit or LA. This subject is easy to talk about, statistically driven, and apparently important to everyone.

Alas, this report has virtually nothing to do with your day, your job, and your approach to the market. That's because geography isn't as important as it used to be, but more than that, it has to do with the fact that you don't sell to everyone, and the economy is unevenly distributed.

If the unemployment rate in your industry doesn't match the national numbers, the national numbers don't matter so much.

At the largest Lexus dealer in New Jersey, they're sold out of many models, with a waiting list. In some towns in Missouri, the unemployment rate is twice what it is in your town. In the tech industry, the rate you can charge for developing killer social apps on a tablet is high and going up.

Economics used to be stuck in town. Now, as markets and industries transcend location, useful economic stats describe the state of the people you're working with and selling to.

If your segment is stuck, it might make sense to stick it out. It also might be worth thinking about the cost of moving to a different economy.

The Game Theory of Discovery and the Birth of the Free Gap

It all started because of the discovery problem.

Too many things to choose from, and more every day. No efficient way to alert the world about your service, your music, your book. How about giving it away to help the idea spread?

The simplest old-school examples are radio (songs to hear for free, in the hope that someone will buy them) and Oprah's show (give away all the secrets in your book in the hope that many people will buy).

There's a line out the door of people eager to spread their ideas, because in a crowded marketplace, being ignored is the same as failing.

Most people, most of the time, don't buy things if there's a free substitute available. A hundred million people hear a pop song on the radio, and less than 1% will buy a copy. Millions will walk by a painting in a museum, but very few have prints, posters, or even inexpensive original art in their homes. (In the former case, the purchased music is better—in quality and convenience—than the free version. In the latter case, the print is merely more accessible, but the math is the same—lots of visits, not a lot of conversion.)

We don't hesitate to ask a consultant or doctor or writer for free advice, but often hesitate when it involves a payment. ("Oh, I'm not asking for consulting, I just wanted you to answer a question . . .") And yes, I'm told that some people cut their own hair instead of paying someone a few bucks to do it.

None of this is news. Two things have changed, though:

1. As more commercial activity involves digital goods (websites, ebooks, music, etc.), the temptation to spread the idea for free (to aid discovery) is actually economically possible—if you believe that the free spread will lead to more revenue in the long run. The cost of a single copy is zero, so you can choose to set the digital item loose without bankrupting yourself.
2. A culture of free digital consumption has evolved and is being adopted by a huge segment of the most coveted consumers (teenagers, the educated, the upper-middle class).

The bet a creator makes, then, is that when she gives away something for free, it will be discovered, attract attention, spread, and then, as we saw with radio in 1969, lead to some portion of the masses actually buying something.

What's easy to overlook is that a *leap* is necessary for the last step to occur. As we've made it easier for ideas to spread digitally, we've amplified the gap between free and paid. It turns out that there's a huge cohort that's just not going to pay for anything if they can possibly avoid it.

Radio thirty years ago was simple: everyone hears it for free and a few buy it.

For a time, one could use *free* to promote an idea and to have leverage to turn that attention into paid sales of a similar item (either because free went away or because the similar item offered convenience or souvenir value).

I think that might be changing. As the free-only cohort grows, people start to feel foolish when they pay for something when the free substitute is easily available and perhaps more convenient.

Think about that—buying things now makes some people feel foolish. Few felt foolish buying a Creedence Clearwater Revival album in the 1970s. They felt good about it, not stupid.

This new default to free means that people with something to sell are going to have to push ever harder to invent things that can't possibly have a free substitute. Patronage, live events, membership, the benefits of connection—all of these things are outside the scope we used to associate with the creative business model, but that's changing, fast.

Lady Gaga's music is basically free. It's the concerts that cost money. McKinsey's consulting philosophy is free in the library; it's the bespoke work that costs money. Watching a movie on Netflix is free—once you pay to belong. Playing golf at the local public course is pretty cheap; it's membership in the fancy club that costs money.

There's a growing disconnect between making something worthwhile and getting paid for it. The digital artifact is heading toward free faster and faster, and the inevitable leap to a paid version of the same item is going to get more difficult.

Creators don't have to like it, but free culture is here and it's getting more pervasive. The brutal economics of discovery combined with no marginal cost create a relentless path toward free, which deepens the gap. Going forward, many things that can be free, will be.

BEFORE: Pay was a subset of free.   NOW: There is a widening gap and these are different products or services.

[Worth a side note to talk about the "should." Some commentators have argued quite forcibly that things shouldn't be free, that creators should always be paid, that 47% of our economy is based on intellectual property.

Of course, free has *always* been part of the equation. These commentators, the ones arguing in interviews or in blog posts, are already sharing their ideas for free. The best-selling book of all time has no copyright and has been shared freely for thousands of years. Musicians gladly show up to play for virtually free on *American Bandstand* or *The Tonight Show.*

Most ideas have never been something one could monetize. The inventor of the knock-knock joke, for example, and the two college kids who coined Six Degrees of Kevin Bacon have put ideas into the idea stream, and they spread without much thought for cash compensation.

I'm certainly not arguing that content *should* be free—it's clear that the argument on either side isn't absolute. My argument is that the line for using free as a discovery tool is shifting, and the best (and perhaps only) way to monetize in the future is for the idea to be encased in something that could never realistically be free. Products and services with a marginal cost of more than zero, for example.

Should consumers be willing to pay for great content? You bet. In fact, paying for content is a great way to ensure that more of it gets made.

Does the game theory of the market make it likely that those in search of discovery will accelerate the use of free to get attention? Of course.

Creators have trained the most coveted, biggest-spending, and intelligent portion of the market to expect that many digital items will be free. Now it's up to us to wrap those items in such a way that they're worth paying for again.]

Paying Attention to the Attention Economy

Most of us are happily obsessed with the economy of money. We earn it and we spend it and we generally pay attention to what things cost.

Certainly, salespeople and marketers are truly focused on the price of things, on commissions and shelving allowances and net margin and the cost of goods sold.

With all of this easily measured activity, it's easy to overlook the fast-growing and ever more important economy based around attention.

"If I alert my entire customer base, how much will this cost me in permission?"

"How much time do we save our customers with a better-written manual?"

"When we fail to ask for (and reward) the privilege of following up, are we wasting permission?"

"Does launching this product to an audience of strangers waste the attention we're going to have to buy?"

Attention is a bit like real estate, in that they're not making any more of it. Unlike real estate, though, it keeps going up in value.

Consumers and Creators

Fifty years ago, the ratio was a million to one.

For every person on the news or on primetime, there were a million viewers.

The explosion of magazines brought the ratio to 100,000:1. If you wrote for a major magazine, you were going to affect a lot of people. Most of us were consumers, not creators.

Cable TV and 'zines made the ratio 10,000:1. You could have a show about underwater spear fishing, or you could teach people how to make hamburgers with doughnuts for rolls. The little star was born.

And now of course, when it's easy to have a blog or a YouTube account, or to push your ideas to the world through social media, the ratio might be 100:1. For every person who sells on Etsy, there are 100 buyers. For every person who actively tweets, there are 100 people who mostly consume those tweets. For every 100 visitors to Squidoo, there is one new person building pages.

What does the world look like when we get to the next zero?

When Ideas Become Powerful

Why are we surprised that governments and organizations are lining up to control ideas and the way they spread?

When power resided in property, governments and corporations became focused on the ownership, regulation, and control of property.

When power shifted to machines and interstate commerce, no surprise, the attention shifted as well.

Now, we see that the predictions have come true, and it's ideas and connections and permission and data that truly matter.

So gifted inventors shift gears and become patent trolls, suing instead of merely creating. So government agencies rush to turn off cell phone towers. So corporations work to extend and reinvent the very notion of copyright protection.

Here's what we need to think about:

Are copyright rules being played with as a way to encourage the creation of art (which was the original intent), or are they now a tool for maximizing corporate profit?

Are patents (particularly software patents) being used to encourage new inventions, or have they turned into a tax that all of us have to pay whenever we use a computer or a phone? (Hint: if you can draw your patent on an index card, it's an idea, not a patentable process worthy of protection.)

Is disconnecting a cell phone or a social network any different from trashing a printing press?

When organizations seek to control widgets and hammers and land, it seems right—that property is clearly private, and sharing it doesn't scale. When two people both try to eat a marshmallow, there's less for both.

Controlling ideas and connections and data—that's a fundamentally different deal, partly because it's so personal (that idea in your head might or might not have been inspired by the idea I wrote down, but it feels wrong for me to tell you that you can't have your idea) and partly because shared ideas do scale; they don't usually diminish.

Ideas are going to continue to become more valuable, which means that the urge to control and patrol them is going to increase.

- Ideas that spread, win.
- Networks in which ideas flow are worth more than networks without ideas.
- Great ideas are amplified when others build on them.
- Just because an idea spreads doesn't mean it's good for us.
- Locking down ideas makes them worth less.
- Those in power will try to keep outsiders from bringing new ideas forward.

[Rick asked for my distinction between an idea and an invention. Here goes:

I think an idea is something you can write about in a science-fiction book.

An invention is the thing you build that was deemed impossible by the people who read about it in the science-fiction book.]

The Forever Recession (and the Coming Revolution)

There are actually two recessions:

The first is the cyclical one, the one that inevitably comes and then inevitably goes. There's plenty of evidence that intervention can shorten it, and there are indications that overdoing a response to it is a waste or even harmful.

The other recession, though, the one with the loss of "good factory jobs" and systemic unemployment—I fear that this recession is here forever.

Why do we believe that traditional jobs—jobs where we are paid really good money to do work that can be systemized, written in a manual, and/or exported—are going to come back *ever*? The Internet has squeezed inefficiencies out of many systems, and the ability to move work around, coordinate activity, and digitize data all combine to eliminate a wide swath of the jobs the industrial age created.

There's a race to the bottom, one in which communities fight to suspend labor and environmental rules in order to become the world's cheapest supplier. The problem with the race to the bottom is that you might win.

Factories were at the center of the industrial age. Buildings where workers came together to efficiently craft cars, pottery, and insurance policies—these are job-centric activities, places where local inefficiencies are trumped by the gains from mass production and interchangeable parts. If local labor costs the industrialist more, he has to pay it, because what choice does he have?

No longer. If it can be systemized, it will be. If the pressured middleman can find a cheaper source, she will. If the unaffiliated consumer can save a nickel by clicking over here or over there, then that's what's going to happen.

It was the inefficiency caused by geography that permitted local workers to earn a better wage, and it was the inefficiency of imperfect communication that allowed companies to charge higher prices.

The industrial age, the one that started with the Industrial Revolution, is fading away. It is no longer the growth engine of the economy, and it seems absurd to imagine that great pay for replaceable work is on the horizon.

This state of affairs represents a significant discontinuity, a life-changing disappointment for hardworking people who are hoping for stability but are unlikely to get it. It's a recession, the recession of a hundred years of the growth of the industrial complex.

I'm not a pessimist, though, because the new revolution, the revolution of connection, creates all sorts of new productivity and new opportunities. Not for repetitive factory work, though, not for the sort of thing that ADP measures. Most of the wealth created by this revolution doesn't look like a job, or not a full-time one, anyway.

When everyone has a laptop and a connection to the world, then everyone owns a factory. Instead of coming together physically, we have the ability to come together virtually, to earn attention, to connect labor and resources, to deliver value.

Stressful? Of course it is. No one is trained in how to do this, in how to initiate, to visualize, to solve interesting problems and then deliver. Some people see the new work as a hodgepodge of little projects, a pale imitation of a "real" job. Others realize that this is a platform for a kind of art, a far more level playing field in which owning a factory isn't a birthright for a tiny minority but is something that hundreds of millions of people have the chance to do.

Gears are going to be shifted regardless. In one direction is lowered expectations and plenty of burger flipping. In the other is a race to the top, in which individuals who are awaiting instructions begin to give them instead.

The future feels a lot more like marketing—it's impromptu, it's based on innovation and inspiration, and it involves connections between and among people—and a lot less like factory work, in which you do what you did yesterday, but faster and cheaper.

This means we may need to change our expectations, change our training, and change how we engage with the future. Still, it's better than fighting for a status quo that is no longer. The good news is clear: every forever recession is followed by a lifetime of growth from the next thing.

Job creation is a false idol. The future is about gigs and assets and art and an ever-shifting series of partnerships and projects. It will change the fabric of our society along the way. No one is demanding that we *like* the change, but the sooner we see it and set out to become an irreplaceable linchpin, the faster the pain will fade, as we get down to the work that needs to be (and now can be) done.

This revolution is at least as big as the last one, and the last one changed everything.

The Erosion in the Paid-Media Pyramid

Since the invention of media (the book, the record, the movie . . .), there's been a pyramid of value and pricing delivered by those that create the media:

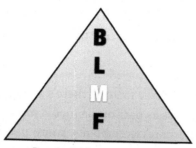

Bespoke, Limited, Mass, and Free

Starting from the bottom:

Free content is delivered to anyone who is willing to consume it, usually as a way of engaging attention and leading to sales of content down the road. This is the movie trailer, the guest on *Oprah*, the free chapter, the tweets highlighting big ideas.

Mass content is the inevitable result of a medium for which the cost of making copies is low. So you get books for $20, movie tickets for $8, and newspapers for pocket change. Mass content has been the engine of popular culture for a century.

Limited content is something rare, and thus more expensive. It's the ticket that not everyone can afford to buy. This is a seat in a Broadway theater, attendance at a small seminar, or a signed lithograph.

And finally, there's bespoke content. This is the truly expensive, truly limited performance. A unique painting, or hiring a singer to appear at an event.

Three things just happened:

A. Almost anyone can now publish almost anything. You can publish a book without a publisher, record a song without a label, host a seminar without a seminar company, sell your art without a gallery. This freedom leads to an explosion of choice. (Or from the point of view of the media producer, an explosion of clutter and competition.)

B. Because of A, attention is worth more than ever before. The single gating factor for almost all success in media is, "do people know enough about it to choose to buy something?"

C. The marginal cost of one more copy in the digital world is precisely zero. One more viewer on YouTube, one more listener to your MP3, one more blog reader—they cost the producer nothing to produce or deliver.

As a result of these three factors, there's a huge sucking sound, and that's the erosion of mass as part of the media model. Fewer people buying movie tickets and hardcover books, more people engaging in free media.

Overlooked in all the hand-wringing is a rise in the willingness of some consumers (true fans) to move up the pyramid and engage with limited works. Is this enough to replace the money that's not being spent on mass? Of course not. But no one said it was fair.

By head count, just about everyone who works in the media industry is in the business of formalizing, reproducing, distributing, marketing, and selling copies of the original creative work to the masses. The creators aren't going to go away—they have no choice but to create. What's in for a radical shift, though, is the infrastructure built around monetizing work that used to have a marginal cost but no longer does.

Media projects of the future will be cheaper to build, faster to market, less staffed with expensive marketers, and more focused on creating free media that earns enough attention to pay for itself with limited patronage.

Spout and Scout

Social media has amplified two basic human needs so much that they have been transformed into entirely new behaviors.

Sites have encouraged and rewarded us to *spout*, to talk about what we're up to and what we care about.

And they've mirrored that by making it easy to *scout*, to see what others are spouting about.

Please understand that just a decade ago, both behaviors were private, non-commercial activities. Now, they represent the future of media, and thus the future of what we do all day.

You're probably doing one, the other, or both. Are you making it easy for your peers and customers to do it about and for you?

The Map Has Been Replaced by the Compass

The map keeps getting redrawn, because it's cheaper than ever to go off-road, to develop and innovate and remake what we thought was going to be next. Technology keeps changing the routes we take to get our projects from here to there. It doesn't pay to memorize the route, because it's going to change soon.

The compass, on the other hand, is more important than ever. If you don't know in which direction you're going, how will you know when you're off course?

And yet . . .

And yet we spend most of our time learning (or teaching) the map, yesterday's map, while we're anxious and afraid to spend any time at all calibrating our compass.

The TripAdvisor Tail Wagging the Real-World Dog

More than 50 years ago, Duncan Hines (a real person, unlike Betty Crocker) turned the restaurant business upside down. He began certifying restaurants as clean and safe, offering a sign for roadside diners that wished to welcome travelers from out of town.

The existence of his certification changed the way restaurants did their job.

Today, it's sites like TripAdvisor and Yelp (among many others) that are transforming the way service businesses operate. Here's how it works: at first, a business might try to ignore the system, but then they notice their customers talking about the reviews and their competitors. So some businesses stoop so low as to attempt to game the system, sending sock puppets and friends to post reviews. But that tactic doesn't scale and the sites are getting smart about weeding this stuff out.

The only alternative? Amazing service. Working with customers in such an extraordinary way that people feel compelled to talk about it, post about it, and yes, review it. It's not an accident that Hotel Amira is one of the highest-rated hotels in all of Turkey. They didn't do it with the perfect building or sumptuous suites. They did it by intentionally being remarkable at service. And yes, the Holiday Inn in Oakland has the same story. They took what they had and then they deliberately went over the top in delivering on something that never would have paid off for them in the past.

Amplifying stories causes the stories that are built to change. Outliers are rewarded (or punished), and the weird and the wonderful are reinforced. Once people see what others are doing, it opens the door for them to do it, but with more flair.

The Web changes everything it touches, sometimes in significant ways. Travelers ranted about poor service for a generation, but now that the Internet makes it easy to rank and sort and connect, the service has no choice but to change. Some businesses see Yelp and others as a tax, a burden they have to pay attention to in order to stay relevant, and they grumble about it. Other businesses see these sites as the opportunity of a lifetime, a chance to deliver service (which takes guts and care, more than money) to get ahead.

"Too Long"

You're going to hear that more and more often.

The movie, the book, the meeting, the memo—few people will tell you that they ran short.

(Shorter, though, doesn't mean less responsibility, less insight, or less power. It means less fluff and less hiding.)

The Coalition of No

It's easy to join.

There are a million reasons to say no, but few reasons to stand up and say yes.

No requires just one objection, one defensible reason to avoid change. No has many allies—anyone who fears the future or stands to benefit from the status quo. And no is easy to say, because you actually don't even need a reason.

No is an easy way to grab power, because with yes comes responsibility, but no is the easy way to block action, to exert the privilege of your position to slow things down.

No comes from fear and greed and, most of all, a shortage of openness and attention. You don't have to pay attention or do the math or role-play the outcomes in order to join the coalition that would rather have things stay as they are (because these people have chosen not to do the hard work of imagining how things might be).

And yet the coalition of No keeps losing. We live in a world of yes, where possibility and innovation and the willingness to care often triumph over the masses that would rather it all just quieted down and went back to normal.

Yes is the new normal. And just in time.

Bandits and Philanthropists

The Web is minting both, in quantity.

Bandits want something for nothing. They take. They take free content where they can find it. They fight for anonymity, for less community involvement. They want more than their fair share, and they walk past the busker, because they can hear him playing real good, for free.

The spammer is a bandit, stealing your attention because he can get away with it, and leaving nothing in return.

Philanthropists see a platform for giving. They support the tip jar. They argue for community standards and yes, for taxes that are more fair to the community. They support artists online, and when they can, they buy the book.

The artist who creates a video that touches you, or an infographic that informs you—she's giving more than she gets, leaving the community better than it was before she got there.

Both types have been around forever, of course. But the Web

magnifies the edges. It's easier than ever to be a free rider, to make your world smaller and to take. And easier than ever to be a big-time contributor, even if you don't have any money. You can contribute your links or your attention or your energy.

The fascinating thing for me is how much more successful and happy the philanthropists are. It turns out that when you make the world smaller, you get to keep more of what you've got, but you end up earning a lot less (respect, connections, revenue) at the same time.

Ranking for Signal-to-Noise Ratio

A whisper in a quiet room is all you need. There's so little noise, so few distractions, that the energy of the whisper is enough to make a dent.

On the other hand, it's basically impossible to have a conversation (at any volume) in a nightclub.

The signal-to-noise ratio is a measurement of the relationship between the stuff you want to hear and the stuff you don't. And here's the thing: Twitter and email and Facebook all have a bad ratio, and it's getting worse.

The click-through rates on tweets is getting closer and closer to zero. Not because there aren't links worth clicking on, but because there's so much junk you don't have the attention span or time to sort it all out.

Spam (and worse, spamlike messages from organizations and people that ought to treasure your attention and permission) is turning a medium (email) that used to be incredibly rich into one that's becoming very noisy as well.

And you really can't do much to fix these media and still use them the way you're used to using them.

The alternative, which is well worth it, is to find new channels you can trust. An RSS feed with only bloggers who respect your time. Relentless editing of whom you follow and whom you listen to and what gets on the top of the pile.

Until you remove the noise, you're going to miss a lot of signal.

Dancing on the Edge of Finished

Before, when your shift was done, you were finished. When the inbox was empty, when the forms were processed, you could stop.

Now, of course, there's always one more tweet to make, post to write, Words With Friends move to complete. There's one more email message you can send, one more lens you can construct, one more comment you can respond to. If you want to, you can be never finished.

And that's the dance. Facing a sea of infinity, it's easy to despair, sure that you will never reach dry land, never have the sense of accomplishment of saying, "I'm done." At the same time, to be finished, done, complete—this is a bit like being dead. The silence and the feeling that maybe that's all.

For the marketer, the freelancer, and the entrepreneur, the challenge is to redefine what makes you feel safe, to be comfortable with the undone, with the cycle of never-ending. We were trained to finish our homework, our peas, and our chores. Today, we're never finished, and that's okay.

It's a dance, not an endless grind.

THE FUTURE IS ARRIVING

Publishing. Paper. Platforms and Gatekeepers.

Compared to What?

It's not unusual for a book publisher to look at Kindle books and get nervous about the pricing. After all, if the Kindle version of a book has the same words, available just as soon as the hardcover, why should it cost half as much (or less)?

Eighty years ago, if you wanted to read a book, your choice was a hardcover. The price was the price. All hardcovers, all new books in a category, cost just about the same.

Decades later, paperbacks gave you an alternative, but the thing was, you had to wait a year for the book to come out in paperback. Bargain-seeking readers could read older books, but *within* each format, there was parity.

The ebook presents a conundrum. It is cheaper than a hardcover for the same content. The real puzzle, though, has nothing to do with hardcovers, and this is what publishers are missing:

The competition for a Kindle book isn't the hardcover. The competition is a game on the iPad or a movie from Netflix or a song playing on your Sonos. Pricing is about substitutions, and if we want books to avoid becoming a tiny niche, we need to price accordingly. There are more substitutes, and they are cheaper than ever before.

An ebook might be faster to get and easier to carry around, but it doesn't offer the prestige or interior-decorating benefits of a hardcover. We don't devalue the book when we price it lower as an ebook, because we're actually not selling the souvenir/lendable element that we sell with the hardcover. *They're different products for different readers.*

The market is clearly willing to buy ebooks, and now our job is to price them in a way that makes them an irresistible habit.

Picked Vs. Spread

Most nonfiction book publishing focuses on solving a problem for the bookstore and the bookstore visitor. The problem is something like this:

I need a book about Marx.

Can you help me find a great book about knitting?

I'm traveling tomorrow . . . got a good junky novel?

This focus explains, for example, the fabulous series of "for beginners" books from Pantheon. If you have a problem like this, they can solve it. Pick this book, they say to the seeker. If there are four picks to choose from and enough people choosing, you can do okay this way, solving information problems for those on a search.

The problem is that Google can probably solve it better.

Which leads to the alternative. Instead of books that seek to be one of many to be chosen by the shopper with a problem, there's the opportunity to publish books that spread, spread from someone who is in love with an idea to someone who *didn't even know they had the problem.*

And in every endeavor, there are far more people who don't know they need help.

The Internet amplifies this behavior. The 'Net makes it easier than ever to spread solutions that touch you, books that matter, ideas that make a difference.

The implication for publishers and readers is this: I think the glory days of publishing to fill a niche are gone. There's just no reason for it; we have enough books in the world to solve most of these book problems. The new frontier is to publish books that spread.

Books, Notes, Tweets, and the Change (Your Change)

My friend Fred Wilson (one of the great VCs of all time) did a talk at Harvard Business School. In his post on it, he said that he was thrilled that the professor encouraged the class to tweet their notes.

I confess to being fascinated, mystified, and horrified by people who tweet lecture notes in real time. I mean, here is one of the giants of his industry, and the best the students can do with their attention is tweet short sentences, out of context, to an unknown audience of busy people who are reading hundreds of other out-of-context, abbreviated notes at the same time? What a wasted opportunity.

From the point of view of the person reading these tweets, it's hard to see how you're actually going to learn enough and be moved enough to change your point of view about something.

From the sender's point of view (the student in that room with Fred), what if you sat quietly and actually gulped in all that was being said and displayed and communicated? What if you were there, *right there*, not halfway there and halfway (mentally) across the world? What if you were interrupting Fred with questions, preparing counterarguments, and actually engaging with him?

I get the flux, the flow, the connective power of social media. It's incredible to be able to widen your circle, to be aware of so many people and so many inputs. I wonder, though: Is one status update enough to get you to alter a habit or make a better decision?

This is why books matter. Books, used properly, immerse us in a single idea. Books bring a voice into our head, create a different brain chemistry, open doors to a more powerful lever, a learning that can change us. Dozens (perhaps hundreds) of times in my life, a book has changed my mind. So have some powerful lectures or direct engagements with teachers or mentors. These are the moments of true change, times when we are in sync with the message, when we feel the learning happening in real time.

Yes, tweet. Yes, stay in sync. Yes, absorb the lessons that come from many inputs, over time.

The quiet enjoyment that books (and great teachers) bring, the uncomfortable place they bring us to when we're open enough to let them in and to be honest with ourselves—these are precious.

The Paradox of the Paid-For PDF Ebook

No one wants to pay for a PDF if they don't know who wrote it and what's in it. Without the filter and imprimatur of a publishing house, we assume the worst.

Once someone *knows* what's in it, they probably don't want to pay for it. (Why should they? They already know what it says.)

If you have a huge audience already (as Jason & Co. did when they launched their PDF at 37signals), then you will inevitably do just fine, as you need only a small fraction of your fans to step up and support you.

If you are marketing a get-rich-quick (or -slow) product, you can possibly make enough promises to entice the reader, but this genre is a tiny slice of all the books in the world.

For the rest of the world, though, if you're trying to break into the market, the purchased PDF is hard to share, hard to talk about, and hard to monetize.

The secret is to write something brilliant, share it far and wide and for free, and then wait until you have enough fans to monetize the *next* one you do.

The Audience for Your Book . . .

Are you publishing for your fans? If so, do you have enough to justify the effort? Do you have a way of reaching them? Is there a better vehicle than a book for reaching your goal?

Are you publishing so your fans will have something to recommend to their friends? Is it in a form that they'll happily recommend? What's the half-life of this cycle—will friends recommend to friends and to friends to infinity? If not, how big an audience do you imagine reaching?

Are you publishing for strangers? How will they discover you? Or are you playing the lottery, figuring that *someone* has to come out of nowhere with a big bestseller, so it might as well be you?

Or are you publishing to make a point, to wave your book in front of a particular audience like a red flag in front of a bull?

Are you publishing to win an award or become a critic's darling? Good luck with that.

Are you publishing for your clients, with the intent of mailing the book directly to them? This is both easy and effective, but it isn't publishing, it's mailing them a book.

Are you publishing this book to make a living? Good luck with that. (Less than 3% of newly published authors make enough in royalties and advances to be happy to live on.)

What you write is directly related to whom you are writing for, and deciding to publish has nothing at all to do with deciding to write. Publishing is a business decision, a financial risk, and a marketing project. If your goal is to generate reach, to share your gifts and your point of view, you can skip all of those aspects of publishing and just give your work away.

There are people who should publish, who I hope will publish, and who will create books we can't wait to read. And there are important books still unwritten, books that should be created and shared. Too often, though, we seek to follow a path where there isn't a sensible business model, and all that happens is nothing. Go, write. But think twice (or three times or six) about publishing the traditional way.

1,500:1

A publisher can produce 1,500 different books, great books, important books, groundbreaking books that could change the world for what it cost to make the *Green Lantern* movie. The publisher could pay each author a $75,000 advance and produce the titles (enough to fill several bookshelves in thousands of homes) for the cost of one summertime clunker.

Some people are saying that the future of books is in the direction of apps, videos, and other multimedia productions, entire experiences that express an idea.

The problem: none of these can be created by a single individual.

The magic of a book is that it is largely the work of one person. Yes, she'll need some help from editors and distributors, etc., but they sometimes come and go, while the author remains.

It's entirely possible that a new art form (one that's smaller than a movie and involves text) may come along, but I'm betting we'll see more of a flourishing on the ebook side, a place where the individual voice remains the key building block.

Dr. Seuss Never Took an Advance

For the last fifty years, the driving economic force of the book business has been the advance against royalties.

Virtually all books aimed at a mass audience earn precisely the same royalty per book. Stephen King, the unknown first-time author, and I get paid exactly the same royalty per book by Penguin.

What changes is the advance. This is a non-refundable earnest payment the publisher puts up to entice the author (and her agent) to sign on, to choose them. When everything else is equal (and it often is), the advance is the thing that gets looked for and reported on.

As you can imagine, the advance affects the rest of the process. The royalties earn out against the advance and in fact are rarely paid at all (if the advance is bigger than the royalties, the author gets no new money). Most publishers don't associate an advance paid four years ago with a royalty statement that comes in today. (And if they do pay attention, they're likely to make a non-economic decision—"let's promote this book even though it's not selling, because we have a big advance at stake.")

If there are two publishers, one with a great marketing and publishing program, and the other with an advance that's three times as big, guess who wins the author? A publisher with a big checkbook is able to land famous authors, a feat which excites the sales force, which gets more shelf space in the store, which, perhaps, leads to a self-fulfilling prophecy.

Of course, for the last half-century, in a static publishing environment, all of this was very good news for authors. Not only did it remove risk for a profession that could ill afford to take risks, but big advances focused the attention of the publisher. You (the author) were getting paid a lot and it bought you a better publishing experience at the same time.

(Dr. Seuss rejected this convention and refused to take an advance from his publisher. He wanted his publisher to have the same incentives he did.)

The advance makes it very clear who's in charge. The publisher pays, so the publisher calls the shots. The author has a scarce asset and sells it to the publisher, who exploits it. The friction comes when the author/ tribe leader/impresario believes that risks and new technologies can help get her work into the world, and the publisher demurs.

As the underpinnings of traditional publishing start to shift, the pressures to change the culture of the advance are sure to mount. Of course, as long as there are two publishers willing to spend freely, advances will stick around.

Having been paid advances for years, I'm not arguing that they should be abolished even if they could be. For those curious about the future of the book business, though, it's impossible to talk about [digital, the long tail, free editions, and sub rights] without acknowledging that they drive the decisions in the heart of the industry.

Strangers and Friends: Understanding Publishing

The bookstore and the publisher keep more than 85% of what a reader pays for a book.

And that money is well earned. Why? Because book publishing is the act of taking a financial risk to bring an idea to an unknown reader.

The key word is "unknown." Before the book is purchased, neither the bookstore nor the publisher knows the identity of the reader.

This is fundamentally different from the core readership of a magazine or a newspaper (they have subscribers).

Reaching strangers is a risky business. Penguin is left with $40 million in debt from Borders as they go bankrupt. Penguin had to advance them that money because otherwise, no bookstore would be able to take the risk of having all those books standing by, just hoping that the right stranger would find the right book on the right day.

Authors, then, have a choice. They can give up more and more free-dom and cash to publishers in exchange for the publishers' taking the risk of finding, alerting, and selling to strangers, or they can start to organize a tribe, to build permission, to engage with readers before the book exists, and to sell those friends on their work.

Selling to friends (people who know you, trust you, are aware of what you can offer) is orders of magnitude more efficient than seeking out strangers. Sure, it's time consuming and frightening to earn those friend-ships, but they are the transformative element of the new publishing.

Once you have a base of friends, then, publishing is reduced to a much simpler set of tasks—the hard work of editing, designing, printing, and fulfilling. Hard, but not financially difficult. Not just that, but the speed, freedom, and control will transform the way you write as well as how you engage with your audience.

It's very seductive for an author to believe that a fairy godmother will introduce her fabulous idea to legions of strangers. Seductive, yes, but rarely something that actually happens.

[There are dozens of businesses that, like book publishing, focus on strangers. What happens to your business when you switch gears and focus on your friends instead?]

The Evolution of Pop Culture

Here's the question: *Does pop culture change from the top down, or do people always get what they want/deserve?*

Do car companies push a style upon the market, or does the market choose a style?

Can influencers (like Ellen or the *NYT*) make a book a mass sensa-tion, or do they merely make a bunch of noise, and the market then reads and recommends and embraces what it wants?

The question matters because we hand over plenty of money and respect to those who say that they can push something onto the culture. The question matters because when it comes to taking responsibility, those very same people often claim that all they can do is make a small ruckus—it's the market that gets what it deserves.

Is banal TV banal because viewers demand it or because it's cheap to make and easy to sell?

Are powerful cars powerful because car guys like to make guzzlers, or does the market insist on them?

Do some newspapers misbehave and cross ethical lines because it's the only way to survive in a world where consumers are hungry for a no-holds-barred race to the bottom, or . . . you get the idea.

Here's my thought: both sides are right. Marketers get too much credit but also take too little responsibility.

A portion of the population is very responsive to the latest buzz, the latest big push. Part of the media (the part that wants to reach that market) is most likely to write about whatever is being hyped right now, and a fraction of the population is a sucker for what this part of the media is writing about.

But, and it's a big but, much of the population isn't even aware of this nonsense. They're oblivious to the hype machine and the cycle of endless promo.

They are more likely to consume media because "everyone else" is already doing it. They're following a trial or reading a book or watching a movie because it's mainstream, safe, approved, the it moment, etc.

They are more likely to demand a big "American-style" car because they've been trained to fit in and to buy what the neighbors think they should buy.

It's impossible to hype your product to this spot in the middle of the market. You can get it started, sure, but only some (a handful) of the things that are adopted by the early adopters actually move through the curve and reach the middle.

We love big cars because car guys loved them and loved making them, and early-adopter car guys liked to buy them, setting a century-long standard that the rest of the consumers in the market try to emulate.

Every once in a while, in the exception that proves the rule, an idea or product skips the early adopters and seems to magically entrance a different slice (witness the organic and largely hype-free start of *Harry Potter*). Or consider the very untraditional launch and growth of the

Prius. More often than not, though, the hype machine spends itself out and fails.

Authors worry too much about the hype part. We focus too much on the promo, on the article in the *Times* or the review in the *New Yorker*. I don't think publishers are particularly good at helping authors reach those who aren't looking for them, even if the book is really good.

The amount of luck in the voyage from launch to mass is huge. But it's certainly true that a product or service that delights the early adopters—delights them enough to turn them into peer-focused salespeople—is the tried-and-true path to mass success.

Short version: make great stuff, stuff that's easy or urgent to talk about and that matches a wide but vital worldview. Then share it with people who have given you permission to talk about it.

Quality, Price, Marginal Cost, and the Open Door

No one expects a Bugatti or Tesla to cost the same as a used Celica. After all, if you want a car that is silent, fast, and sexy, you will (and should) pay more for it.

No one expects that dinner at Alinea should cost the same as dinner at McDonald's. After all, even though the calories are the same, the quality, attention to detail, and costs are not.

But for books and movies, there's no correlation at all between quality and price.

A lousy movie costs precisely the same to see in the theater as *Memento* did. Even after we find out if the movie is good, the price doesn't change—a DVD of *Toy Story* is the same as the new release of *The Smurfs*.

Worse still, a used paperback copy of *Snow Crash* gives you precisely the same level of intellectual quality as the original hardcover did, at one-tenth the price.

Obviously, this lack of correlation occurs because the intellectual property rights, the ideas, are of a quality worth pursuing, while the letters on the page or the pixels on the screen cost precisely the same to deliver as they do for something lousy.

And the open door? Since the cost of quality is all up front, a digital copy is just fine—better, in fact, because it's convenient and easy to share. Can't do that with a Tesla.

The producer realizes that he has a product with a marginal cost of zero. Even a nickel or dime is better than nothing, and when producers of lower-quality products start to lower their prices to gain market share, there's pressure to keep up. (I remember when a VHS movie cost $90.)

The paradox here is that the cost of the stuff done up front, the risk and the guts and the hard work needed to make a great bit of content, is actually going up, while the price we're willing to pay for a digital copy is plummeting and will continue to plummet. We don't hesitate to pay $25 for a hardcover (yet), but there are almost no iPad apps that cost that much for similar content. Yet the original cost for the app is probably greater than it is for the book.

I think we'll always be willing to pay extra for the benefits we get from getting something first, getting it curated, or getting it customized. But for most of what gets purchased in pop culture, none of those three factors are at work.

Prepare for a continuous erosion of what you pay for digital content, at the same time that you'll see a sticky and upward trend for what you might be charged for the collectible stuff and the scarce or custom stuff. I think producers are going to fight mightily for a second (higher) tier of pricing for amazing work, but while this strategy might work for the front-list new stuff, I have a hard time seeing it sustained for the backlist titles.

How much do you expect to pay for a perfect (but used) digital copy of Prince's *Greatest Hits*? How about a penny?

Are You Feeling Lucky?

One of the biggest distinctions between old publishing and new is the nature of luck.

The fact is, in the old model, *something* had to become a bestseller. *What to Expect When You're Expecting* just hit its tenth year on the bestseller lists (520 weeks in a row, 17 million copies sold). It's a great book from a great publisher, but a run like that is as much the result of good timing, good breaks, and the fickle finger of fate as it is the result of helpful content. There's a reason the expression "surprise bestseller" is in the vernacular. Most bestsellers are, in fact, surprises.

Do the math: 170,000 real books published a year, probably 50,000 of them are commercial, well constructed, and seriously published. Of those 50,000, as many as 100 (that's two a week) hit their potential. One out of five hundred. It's got to be *some* book, but it doesn't have to be yours.

Since there doesn't appear to be a significant correlation between publishing prowess and success (even great editors, great marketers, and great sales teams at publishers don't regularly succeed), at some point it comes down to a spin of the wheel. And the author gets to take that spin at someone else's expense. Yes, she has to write a great book, and yes, she has to tour or interview or whatever the publisher asks, but it's the publisher that's putting cash and risk on the line. Why do some books from unknown authors sell well while others don't? No one knows.

Compare this scenario to the lonely life of the self-published author. This is street fighting, one reader at a time. Getting a Word file turned into an ebook is trivially easy. Getting a book into the world isn't so hard. Being discovered and talked about: really hard.

Building a tribe is not a matter of a miracle. Instead, it's about converting tiny groups of people at a time, leading them, connecting them, building an audience. When a self-published author does this, she has a new job. Not the author part, but the publisher part. She's not putting a book into the universe and hoping it will be found. She's not even putting a book into a journalist's hands and hoping it will be hyped. No, she is engaging in a yearslong journey to build a platform. It might take a decade to become an overnight success, but if you keep it up, if you keep building, the odds keep getting better and better.

That's why it's silly to compare the two ways of making a book happen. If you can get a great deal from a publisher and you're into the spin, go spin! If you want to control the building of the platform, get your hands dirty, and avoid the whims of fate, then the other path makes a lot more sense, no?

[Analogy alert: the above applies to your career, to musicians, to entrepreneurs, to VCs, to coaches, and to just about everyone who is hoping to get picked.]

Want to Buy a Watch? Patronage, Scarcity, and Souvenirs

A hundred years ago, if you wanted to know what time it was, you had to make a significant investment—in a watch.

Twenty years ago, Timex made it clear that if you merely wanted the time (not jewelry), it would cost about $15.

And five years ago, every kid with a cell phone got the time as a free bonus.

And yet there are still watchmakers. Still Rolex and Patek and the rest. Some of them are having great years.

Clearly, they don't sell the time. They sell jewelry. Exclusivity. A souvenir.

One reason to buy a watch (or a book) is because you want to possess it, show it off, give it to your grandchildren. Holding a book is a luxury, one for which you pay a premium. There are few books that contain information unavailable anywhere else, and fewer still that can't be bought more cheaply and easily as an ebook. In the nonfiction category, the reasons to buy a book are smaller still. With a novel or a significant work of nonfiction research, the book itself might be part of what you're paying for. In a busy universe, though, if all you want is information, you can probably find it faster and cheaper without the book part coming along for the ride.

And so 90% of the people who read my blog don't buy my books, figuring that they can get the information (or at least enough information) for free. This is as big a change as the time-keeping change that rocked the watch world. You no longer have to pay a book toll to get information.

Sam Harris is worried that this change means the end of authors. At some level, he's correct: the lack of a barrier means that the number of authors is skyrocketing, yet the sales per author are going down. Ebook distribution means that everyone can be everywhere, but it also means that more choice generates less income for each writer.

It's as if the watch business had 100,000 competitors in it.

Patronage is one answer. The way it makes you feel to put a dollar in the busker's guitar case, or to buy a CD even though you know how to listen for free. I get pleasure out of buying books, and I like supporting the medium (even though the vast majority of the money I spend goes nowhere near the person who took the creative risks). Patronage, though, doesn't make an industry work.

No, the future of books lies in amateur authors, together with the few superstars with a big enough tribe or a big enough reputation to earn significant advances and royalties. (And yes, a "middle class" of authors with a big enough tribe to make a living, but nowhere near what it takes to make it big.) The big middle, though, the writers who earned enough on tolls—those guys are in big trouble long term. As Esther Dyson predicted fifteen years ago, they are going to have to become troubadours again, traveling, selling live events, doing speeches, etc.

You don't have to like it, but that's how it's sorting out. Anyone know what time it is?

What Talent Wants

There are countless new publishers being created. Online podcasts, talk shows, ebook publishers, new kinds of film studios and record labels—all of them need talent.

Here are four words that create an acronym for what talent wants (along with two things it no longer needs):

MONEY: this is the easiest one, because it's simple to measure. When in doubt, pay an advance or a fee. When a publisher gives an author $850,000 for her next book, they have earned the right to call the shots. While this is clearly easy for publishers, you can see how difficult this is for authors to pull off in a long-tail, moving-toward-free world.

UBIQUITY: in an economy based on attention, the publisher that can offer talent a large platform has a significant edge. The reason virtually no one turned down Oprah during her reign was simple—she guaranteed the largest possible audience and she delivered it every single day. This is why a permission asset—a list of customers/listeners/readers just waiting to pay attention—is at the core of the publishing proposition.

STRUCTURE/SUCCOR/STANDARDS: talent often looks for someone who will care, raise the bar, shepherd the work, challenge, and generally make the good, great. This is why stories of great editors are legendary. Charlie Rose and Woody Allen both get talent for cheap for this very reason. Make a project interesting enough and talent will be interested.

EGO: rare indeed is a talented person who is uninterested in what the world thinks. If they're out there, you probably haven't heard of them. Writers want to win a Pulitzer, and jugglers want Ed Sullivan to tell them they did a great job. Hollywood publishers are fabulous at this. Producers and executives spend most of their time engaging with the talent early and often and bringing them feedback or control or interesting challenges—the things that drive better work.

The TED conference, then, thrives as a publisher (even though they don't pay a penny to the talent) because they bring a huge audience via video, because they insist on extraordinary presentations (and work with the speakers to get them), and most of all, because there is a prestigious audience, a group the talent would like to consider its peers, just waiting to give a standing ovation and to make connections for future projects.

The two letters missing from the acronym now turn MUSE into MUSEUM (sorry, couldn't help it).

UMBRELLA: talent has often avoided the vanity press, the self-published route, the notion that it's okay to pick one's self. It was unseemly. You looked for cover, for an umbrella to protect you from the criticism that you weren't good enough to be chosen. I think there are enough extraordinary successes in every field that this is clearly no longer the case.

MECHANICS: it used to be that the most obvious role of the publisher was to handle mundane, expensive, and challenging tasks like printing, binding, shipping, accounting, venue arrangements, film developing, carriage, etc. All of these elements are diminished in the digital world—some are still important, but most are easily outsourced by the talent if she chooses. Handling this role is not enough in itself, and those who can do only this are left resorting to offering money as an inducement, which doesn't really scale.

The publishing landscape is being completely reshaped—in just about every medium. The next generation will replace this landscape when they get ever better at providing at least three of the four things talent wants.

Shovelware—It's Time to Rate Publishers

Now that shelf space is infinite, now that ebooks take up no room and every seller of them has an incentive to have a nearly infinite selection, the inevitable next step shows up:

When anyone can publish a book, anyone will.

Far worse than the individuals publishing junk, though, are organizations generating literally thousands of books that no one would happily buy if they knew what was in them.

These books are created by shoveling public-domain content—often from Wikipedia, and with no human intervention, no care, no attention to detail—into ebooks. Worse, they are then mislabeled as something that feels like a pirated book or an interesting collection of essays.

While some bloggers have been doing this for a decade, surfing a blog is free and it's a natural way to browse the Web. Buying an ebook is neither.

The real losers here, in addition to the ripped-off readers (and the writers who are having their names stolen), are the ebook platforms themselves. Once the Nook and the Kindle get a reputation as dark alleys filled with mislabeled junk, it will be hard to erase.

If it were me running the store, I'd delete every single book from a publisher caught with junk like this. And I'd figure out how to rate not just authors but publishers, so it wouldn't be so easy for someone to show up and steal a brand and disappoint a customer.

Selling Vs. Reading

Back when the only way to get people to read your work was to get them to actually buy your work first, a focus on selling and a focus on being read were the same thing.

Paper costs money. You need to sell the book if you want someone to read it, so feel free to spend all your time persuading people to *buy* it.

In the digital world, there's a little bit of bluff-calling going on. If the cost of delivering one more copy of the book is zero, then choosing to sell your work is optional. You might choose to work hard merely to get people to *read* your work, leaving money out of the equation.

Money cuts both ways, of course. If someone pays for your book, perhaps they'll take it more seriously, focus a bit more energy on it. If your book is easy to get and find and discard, perhaps it's not valued as highly. On the other hand, it will certainly spread faster.

Too many choices, no doubt.

But the real question remains: Are you writing to be read, or are you writing to get paid? They are becoming ever more divergent paths, with gradations ($6? $9?) in between.

(An example of this divergence is the publishers and authors that oppose libraries and the lending of ebooks. In these cases, even though money was paid, they're apparently against being read—even though there's zero evidence that library reading hurts book sales.)

Ubiquity

Web users have been trained long enough to know what they want: everything.

That's the promise of the Web. Every book for sale at Amazon. Every search result visible on Google. Every auctioned item right there on eBay.

Not piracy. Availability.

The music industry got confused about this and decided that people merely wanted to steal music. What's clear now from the rise of iTunes, as well as ad- and subscriber-supported services like Spotify, is that people will happily pay as long as the music brings most everything along for the ride.

And Netflix shows us that subscriptions are generally more welcomed than à la carte sales.

Into this world walks the MPAA, the movie business, and the folks who make books.

And once again, there's the same mistake: they think piracy is the problem. It's not. The problem is that these providers are doing nothing to embrace ubiquity, because their heritage is all about scarcity.

When the VHS tape came along, the MPAA insisted that the movie industry would be killed by it. They finally listened to the market and made a fortune. And when DVDs came along, the same thing happened. Form factors change and the business model that supports them must change as well. The business model for an ebook can't possibly be the same as it is for a paper book, despite the best efforts and hyperventilation of a few overpaid book publishing executives.

When in doubt, move toward ubiquity. When wondering, favor subscriptions.

Readers will pay.

Moviegoers will pay.

If you give them what they want, which is everything, right now, easily found and discussed.

Knock, Knock, It's the Future (Building 59)

Why not ban digital cameras?

Kodak declared bankruptcy this week. Legislation to ban digital cameras could have saved this company, a "jobs creator," pillar of the community, and long-time wonderful brand. One wonders why they didn't make the effort? Would you have lobbied for that bill?

A friend tells a story about Kodak. Apparently, they had 59 buildings on the site that made film. As the film business started to shrink, the obvious thing for Kodak to do was to shrink as well, to reduce overhead, to become more nimble. The CEO said, "Look out at those buildings and answer this question for me: How many steps are involved in making film?"

The answer, of course, was 59. Slowly shrinking wasn't an option. The overhang was too large—crossing it was going to take a leap, not a gradual series of steps. And that's why the future is uncomfortable for most successful industrialists, including those in the media business.

It's interesting to note that the only people who are in favor of SOPA and PIPA are people who are *paid* to be in favor of it. And creators (authors like me and Clay Shirky and Scott Adams) aren't. While the folks at the Copyright Alliance pretend to be looking out for the interests of independent filmmakers and authors, the fact is that the only paying members of their lobbying group seem to be big corporations, corporations that are worried not about creators but about profits. Given a choice between a great film and a profitable one, they'd pick the profitable one every time. Given the choice between paying net profits to creators and adjusting the accounting . . .

Anyway, back to the future:

The leap to a new structure is painful for successful industries precisely because they're successful. In book publishing, the carefully constructed system of agents, advances, copy editors, printers, scarcity, distributors, sales calls, bestseller lists, returns, and lunches is threatened by the new regime of the long tail, zero marginal cost, and ebook readers with a central choke point. The problem with getting from one place to another is that you need to shut down Building 59, and it's hard to do that while the old model is still working, at least a little bit.

Just about all the people who lost their jobs in Rochester meant well and worked hard and did their jobs well. They need to blame the senior management of Kodak, the ones who were afraid of the future and hoped it would go away. There are more pictures being taken more often by more people than ever before—but Kodak leadership couldn't deal with their overhang. They were so in love with their success that they insisted that the world change in their favor, as opposed to embracing the future that was sure to arrive.

Please understand that the destruction of the music business had no impact at all on the amount of music available, and little that I can see on the quality of that music. Musicians just want to make music, thanks very much, and they'll find a way to make a living gigging in order to do so. The destruction of the film business in Rochester is going to have very little impact on people's ability to take photos. The destruction of the New York publishing establishment will make me sad, and they/we should hustle, but it's not going to have much impact on the number of books that are written.

Before we rush to the most draconian solution we can think of to save the status quo, I think it's worth considering what the function of the threatened industry is, and whether we can achieve that function more directly now that the future is arriving.

Rethinking the Bestseller List

A year ago, I explained why the Domino Project chose to reject the very broken, easily gamed *New York Times* bestseller list.

Many authors and some publishers bend over backward, changing every element of their business just to get on the list, in the mistaken belief that it still matters. It doesn't, because shelf space and discount decisions aren't based on the list the way they used to be. Add to this the fact that recent additions to the list (it now takes up many, many pages each week) have made it almost impossible to read and understand.

The key question is this: What is the list for?

If you're a publisher, what you care about is how many books you sold last week. This number isn't based on category or format; you just want to know how many. BookScan and other data sources tell you that.

For the rest of us, then, the reason we care if something is a bestseller is that *we want to know if our friends are reading it.* We want to know this so we can stay in sync with them, so we don't appear stupid, or, perhaps, because we trust their judgment. That's why you don't care a bit about what the bestsellers in New Zealand are.

The digital world opens a new window, something that was unknowable just five years ago. Tell me what other TED attendees are reading, please. Tell me what readers of *Mother Jones* or *Newsmax* are reading. Or what my Facebook friends bought last week. Or highlight for me what people who read what I read are finishing on their Kindles.

Suddenly, there isn't one bestseller list. There are a million. And almost all of them aren't relevant to you. Except the few that are, and those lists are the lists that matter.

This scenario works for music, too, of course, as well as for movies and even wines and restaurants.

No one has built this new kind of list yet; it is sort of showing up around the edges of a variety of sites and services and industries. Creating this list is a great opportunity if you can figure out the best way to source the data and then distribute it. The person who knows what's hot right now, and has permission to talk about it, has earned an asset that will be valuable for a long time.

Reading Isn't Dead, but It's Changing

What does your gut tell you about this statement: "kids in high school read more books for fun than their parents."

In fact, it's true. Young adult reading is up 20% since the last time the survey was done by the Feds, and a recent commercial survey finds the same thing.

Of course, these kids aren't reading the right books, the books we read, the *hard* books.

And go take a look at the bestseller lists for the Kindle and other e-readers. You'll see 99-cent short stories, self-published books, disgraceful genre fiction. Nothing much that was published by Knopf and others in that ilk in 1983 and is deemed literature. On the other hand, Walter Dean Myers has known this for decades. We worked together years ago.

Readership of blogs is up infinity percent in the last decade (from zero), and online journals and magazines continue to gain in power and influence.

And there's more unsettling stuff being read by readers of all ages— books that question authority and force readers to consider deeply held beliefs. The words may have gotten shorter (along with the sentences), but there's plenty of intellectual ruckus being made.

You could view this shift as the end of the world and a threat to how you publish, or you could view it as an opportunity and shift gears as quickly as you possibly can. Publish what people choose to read (at a price they want to pay), and odds are, they will choose to read it. There's plenty of room for leadership and art here, but little room for stubborn intransigence.

The End of Paper Changes Everything

Not just a few things, but everything about the book and the book business is transformed by the end of paper. Those that would prefer to deny this obvious truth are going to find the business they love disappearing over the next five years.

The book itself is changed. I'm putting the finishing touches on a manifesto I hope to share soon, and I found myself writing differently because I understood that the medium that was going to be used to acquire, consume, and share the book was different.

The first change in the creation of the ebook is that there is no appropriate length. Print books are bounded on two sides—they can't be too short, because there's a minimum price that a bookseller needs to charge to make it worth stocking. At the same time, a book can't be too long or ornate, because there's also a maximum price that readers are willing to pay (and a maximum weight we're willing to haul around).

None of these boundaries exist in ebooks. As a result, we get blog posts (which are a form of writing that was virtually unknown ten years ago—personal, short, helpful nonfiction that's serialized over time), 1000-page zombie novels, beautifully illustrated and interactive apps, and everything in between.

[Aside: How come we don't call blog posts "really short, free ebooks"? I'm not being facetious—what makes something a book? The length? The paper? The money? I don't think we know yet.]

We've gone from a very simple taxonomy of classifying (and thus creating) the thing we call a book to a taxonomy that's wide open and undetermined. This is unsettling to anyone in the media business— we know how long a movie is supposed to be, how much music goes on a record, etc. And now, because the wrapper is changed, so is the product.

The second change is that ebooks *connect.* Not so much on the Kindle platform (yet) but certainly in PDF and HTML, we see that it's almost an insult to the reader to create a nonfiction ebook that fails to include links to other voices and useful sources. Not only are the links there, but the writer needs to expect that the reader will actually click on them. A little like being a playwright while knowing that in the middle of the performance, the audience may very well pick up the phone and chat or tweet or surf based on what's going on onstage.

Beyond these two elements of what makes a book a book, there's a fundamental change in the way ebooks are being consumed. Paper meant that a book was very much a considered purchase—more expensive, more time consuming, involving shipping or schlepping, together with long-term storage. With a 99-cent ebook (or, as is the majority, if we count the Web, with a free ebook), not only is the "purchase" an impulsive act, but the number of titles consumed is going to skyrocket.

The consumption of free (or nearly free) ebooks is more like browsing through a bookstore or library and less like purchasing and owning a book. As a result, there will be significantly more unread titles, abandoned in mid-sentence. Think blogs, not *Harry Potter*.

As soon as paper goes away, so do the choke points that created scarcity. Certainly we're already seeing this with the infinite shelf space offered by the digital bookstore. Hard for the layperson to understand, but for decades, the single biggest benefit a publisher offered the independent writer was *the ability to get the book onto the shelves of the local store.*

The entire sales organization at the publishing house (amplified by the publicity department and the folks who do cover design and acquisition) is first and foremost organized around getting more than its fair share of shelf space. When my mom ran the bookstore at the museum in Buffalo, there were sales reps in her store every single day. And of course, for every book that came in, one had to go out, so it wasn't an easy sale.

Publishers cared so much about shelf space that they made bookstores a remarkable offer: don't pay for the books. We'll bill you, and if you haven't sold the book in two months, don't pay the bill, just send the book back. In other words, books were (and still largely are) a guaranteed sale for bookstores. That's how Barnes & Noble got to build such big stores—they were financed by publishers, who took all the risk.

Of course, if there's infinite shelf space (as there is for ebooks), ALL of this is worthless. <gasp>

Previously, I've written about the economics of substitution and the inevitable drop in the price of backlist nonfiction and fiction and just about anything for which there is an acceptable substitute. Since bits aren't scarce (remember, this is a post about the death of paper), it's extremely difficult to charge a premium for an ebook that has a substitute. The vast majority of books published do have substitutes, of course, so the price is going to fall.

Summary: flip scarcity with abundance and everything changes.

Effects: Hawthorne, Scarcity, and Showroom

The Hawthorne effect describes how people react to changes in their environment—particularly to the knowledge that they are being paid attention to. Turn up the lights in the factory and productivity goes up. Turn them down and productivity goes up.

It turns out that the Hawthorne effect works in retail, too. Tell the buyer for the store that you have a new edition, or a new format, or a new cover, or a new pricing strategy, and you have a new chance at getting shelf space.

The scarcity effect is surprisingly powerful in a world that's suddenly filled with abundance. We've been trained to expect that every book will be available everywhere, forever. When I had 600 copies of a book that I no longer wanted to warehouse, I blogged that I had just a few left. Sold them all in twenty minutes—and (alas) disappointed more people than I would have liked to. The interesting takeaway for me is that the book had been available for over a year, so it's not like it was hiding. Only when it became scarce did the rush happen.

The showroom effect is something we're seeing again and again online. Having your product in a store makes your online sales go up, sometimes significantly. It certainly has a huge impact on ebooks because, at least for now, ebooks are seen as a *shadow* of the real book—so if the "real" book is right there, before your eyes, it prompts you to go online and get the digital replacement.

As retail shifts within the book world, some of these effects are going to wane, but right now they matter a lot.

The Null Set

Ask a friend with a tablet (iPad or Kindle Fire) to show you her bookshelf.

More and more, you'll see nothing. Emptiness.

When we juxtapose an ebook with a movie, Instagram, or pigs that attack turtles, the ebook often loses.

One of the very real truths of our culture is being hidden in the dramatic shift from paper to ebook—lots of people are moving from paper to "no ebook." For now, this trend is being concealed by the super-readers, ebook readers who are on a binge and buying more books than ever before.

If you're a fan of reading or publishing, though, the real truth is sad. At $15 or $20 for an ebook, lots of people aren't developing the online reading habit, and the industry is going to pay dearly for that in the decade to come.

My best suggestion: every device shipped ought to come with a dozen entertaining bestsellers already on it, for free. Not all authors are open to subsidizing this seeding, but I sure am. Add five million or ten million readers to an author's fan base and she'll have no trouble at all making back the lost royalties, and publishers will soon discover that habits formed early last a long time.

Demolishing the Argument That Abundance Causes Scarcity

The only public-policy argument that can be made in favor of draconian opposition to fair-use sharing of work online is that if too many people share it, more won't be created.

Copyright is part of the U.S. Constitution NOT because the founders were trying to make Ira Gershwin's great-grandchildren happy, but because they believed that the entire community would benefit if authors of creative works benefited.

Go check out Gimmeshiny.com. One stunning photo after another. Or consider the new WordPress plug-in for the brilliant Compfight tool, which makes it easy to find and use Creative Commons photos in your blog posts.

Or take a look at all the previously unknown artists fighting to give away their music on YouTube.

Or the countless free or nearly free ebooks on the Kindle.

Is there a shortage? I think it's trivial to show that more interesting photos are being taken and published by more photographers than ever before.

And probably more interesting music is being made as well.

Sure, there's more junk than ever before, because without a curating filter, the obvious junk gets through. But you know what? In addition to junk, that conservative curator also kept us from seeing and hearing things that today we are amazed and delighted by.

Once we start running out of photos or music or writing or poems, then yes, please alert the authorities! Until then, the facts speak for themselves—sharing fair-use content (and making it easy for authors and musicians to share) *increases* the quantity and interestingness of what's out there.

It might not be fun for those that have committed to making a living at this, but that challenge only pushes us to find new ways to monetize our passion. And back to my point: making it fun for those in the field isn't the point. The point is creating a useful and interesting flow of creative works. And that's precisely what's happening.

Tracts, Manifestos, and Books

Has a nonfiction book ever changed your mind?

For me, it has happened literally dozens of times. Books have changed the way I think about sales, evolution, marketing, governance, interpersonal relationships, mindfulness, the invention of the Western world, government power, and more.

Next question: How far into the book did you get before your mind was changed?

Not a facetious question. I'm serious. *The Communist Manifesto* is 80 pages long. Certainly long enough to make an impact.

It has never taken me beyond a hundred pages to be persuaded. Sure, there are times when the pages after page 100 help me pile on, give me more depth and understanding. But a hundred (and usually fifty) is enough to get under my skin.

On the other hand, a tweet has never once changed my mind about anything.

Writing a tract that works is significantly more difficult than writing a long book filled with defensible facts and stories, which I think is one reason why authors do the latter so often. And when we finish a tract unconvinced of the author's point of view, our instinct is to point out that it just wasn't long enough! (In fact, that's rarely the problem—the problem is that it wasn't good enough, not that it was too short.)

What if the great authors of our time were challenged to rewrite their favorite works? Let them ignore the price, ignore the bookstore, and merely focus obsessively on arguing their point . . . imagine how powerful those arguments would be.

I think ebooks bring us to a new golden age of polemics, tracts, and nonfiction short works that will actually change things. Without the pressure from an editor trying to justify a $29 price point, the author can go ahead and do the work she's meant to do: change our minds, not kill as many trees as possible.

If we accomplished one thing with the twelve books at the Domino Project, this is what I was hoping to achieve: we made the world safe for manifestos. Every one of our books has changed (at least a few of) the people who experienced them.

They're not longer, because we took the time and effort to make them short. That's what I want to read next—another short book that will change the way I think.

Book Content as a Solo Endeavor

Some would argue that books need to evolve into apps or other forms of multimedia—that books won't be appreciated by large numbers of people until appreciating a book ceases to involve reading it.

While this may be an accurate discussion of the public's habits (far more people saw *The Hunger Games* than read it), it ignores the key part of the production question: books work as an art form (and an economic one) because they are primarily the work of an individual.

One person with time but no money can produce a first draft that is substantially similar to what the public will end up reading.

It doesn't matter that the technology permits animation and color pictures and hypertext and JavaScript. Just because it's possible doesn't mean it's feasible.

When we turn the book into the work of a committee, one that costs a million dollars to create and months or years of pre-pub review and planning, the medium ceases to function. The long tail doesn't work—because it's impossible to create such a huge variety if each book costs that much. And the very notion of surprising, outlying ideas can't survive the committees that those AV books would have to go through.

For a long time, we've seen popular books turned into other sorts of media, and that trend is going to accelerate. But the core driver of the book business is going to remain lone (and lonely) authors bringing their ideas to a small segment that cares.

Powerful (and Powerless) Merchants

The following things are so commonplace that they are almost beyond noticing:

A visit to Costco turns up quite a few items produced by a brand called Kirkland, which is owned, naturally, by Costco.

Check out of Barnes & Noble in many large cities and you're likely to see the *Zagat* restaurant guide near the cash register. Zagat pays a fee for this. Not to mention the huge stacks of books in the window and near the door—that display costs the publishers.

The end cap at your local supermarket features a deal from Pepsi or Coke, but never both at the same time. And the deal is paid for by the soda company. Slotting allowances generate millions of dollars a year in revenue.

These merchants have the power to increase sales of a given item (sometimes by 100% or more), and they're not afraid to use it and to sell it.

When we shop in the real world, we take it for granted that end caps and promotions and speed tables and other interactions will be there not because they are in the direct interest of us, the shoppers, but because they were placed there by the retailer to help generate income. It's a store, for goodness' sake—of course they're trying to maximize their income.

So that speed table that's covered with Maybelline eyeliner near the checkout—it's not there because it maximizes our shopping enjoyment, it's there because someone got paid to put it there. We've been trained to respond to promotions with our attention and our dollars.

Online, where stores are more like tools than like stores, this behavior rarely transfers successfully. You bristle when Twitter starts inserting irrelevant tweets in the stream you see, because you didn't ask for them.

Online merchants have done an extraordinary job of honestly presenting relevant information and drawing a bright line between editorial and merchandising. Which means that they've given up a huge amount of power. Since online merchants can't *make* a particular item sell, they have far less leverage. They make up for it by selling everything, indifferent to which item you choose. In short, they've traded their power to you, the customer, in exchange for volume.

There's no comparison between the way Macy's makes a profit merchandising shoes at the store and the way Zappos promotes shoes online. Online merchants have learned the hard way that they must take an obsessive user-first approach. This is the secret of the long-tail online merchants, including eBay, Amazon, BN.com, and others: they don't care what you buy, as long as you buy something.

This isn't a bad thing, and for most shoppers, it's actually welcome.

Which leads to the conundrum facing Amazon as they become a publisher. It's hard to make a *particular* book a hit online by using traditional merchandising tools, which means that authors (whether they're published by Harper, S&S, or Amazon) have to conclude that it's up to them (and their readers) to make books sell, because the online merchants have voluntarily ceded that power. The merchant doesn't pick the winners any longer.

Publishers have been nervous about moving from a powerful merchant that they know and understand and can motivate with cash to a set of online merchants where it appears that a bunch of power is up for grabs—they want their share. In fact, the move is to the long-tail universe, where the power isn't with the merchant but with individuals and their tribes.

Brick by Brick—Building a Digital Platform Right

Amanda Palmer (leaving out her middle name, which is a story for another day) didn't used to be a superstar.

She is now.

Her Kickstarter project is instantly oversubscribed. Her concerts sell out, wherever she goes in the world, and she goes everywhere.

Her Twitter account (@amandapalmer) has more than half a million followers.

Classic overnight success. Of course, it isn't that at all. Just a few years ago, Amanda was posing as a statue in Harvard Square, collecting dollars and quarters on the street.

And a few years after that, she was building her fan base, one listener at a time, one CD burned for one fan, and then another CD burned for another fan.

Amanda is a wonderful character, a warm and optimistic friend, and a killer ukulele player. But that's not her secret.

Amanda is an impresario in service of her art. She understands that her job is to earn the permission of her audience, to make them big promises and then to keep them. She's aware that she needs to put on a show, and she does. And most of all, she doesn't merely sell to her audience—she leads them and connects them. Amanda F. Palmer is a touchstone, the center of the circle, a living, breathing experiment in audacity, in challenging the status quo, and in having a good time while she does it.

The most amazing thing about this path is that it's open to just about anyone willing to put in the extraordinary sweat and tears it takes to be this powerful and this remarkable.

More on the Economics of the Self-Published Book

For books under $20 (which means just about all ebooks), all that matters is volume. Not margin, but volume.

A book in the hand of a reader is far more likely to lead to another book sold. Bestsellers become bestsellers largely because lots of other people are already reading them. I know that sounds silly and self-referential, but it reflects the social nature of books. *We like to read what others are reading*.

So, if you sacrifice half your volume so you can make twice as much on every copy sold, you've done nothing smart.

Second, for more and more authors, the book is a calling card. It leads to a movie deal or a speaking gig, or another book contract, or consulting, or respect, or a better class of cocktail party. Which means that the true margin on each book is more of these external benefits, not the dollar or three made on each copy.

Yes, you can make a living writing books. But you need to either write a lot of them (Asimov wrote 400) or sell a bunch of each title. Even better—make a margin on each book that has nothing to do with the selling price. The price of the book and the profit margin made on each book are secondary to this goal of making a dent in the conversation among your chosen audience.

Does Curation Work for Publishers?

One mantra heard often is, "in a world with a million ebooks, readers need curators."

Of course, traditional publishers are good at curation, because traditional books are expensive to publish, so publishers had to be picky, merely as a method of self-preservation.

That pickiness leads to widespread rejection of books like *A Confederacy of Dunces* and *Harry Potter,* but let's set that aside for a moment.

The challenge of curation by an individual publisher is this: readers have no idea who publishes which books.

If the marketplace is wide open, an infinite, endless bazaar that anyone can access, the game theory behind an individual publisher's voluntarily publishing fewer books is pretty hard to see. If the readers don't understand where the books are coming from, one organization (or even thirty) holding back isn't going to have any impact at all.

No, the only way to make curation work is to have it in place alongside permission. If the publisher has direct contact with the reader, THEN she can build trust, build a brand, build an identity, and be rewarded for her curative (curationitive?) powers. Once you associate a publisher with high-quality choices, then (and only then) the curation pays off.

One more reason why publishers have to urgently build a permission asset of readers who actually want to hear from them.

STOP STEALING DREAMS

(What Is School For?)

1. Preface: Education Transformed

As I was finishing this manifesto, a friend invited me to visit the Harlem Village Academies, a network of charter schools in Manhattan.

Harlem is a big place, bigger than most towns in the United States. It's difficult to generalize about a population this big, but household incomes are less than half of what they are just a mile away, unemployment is significantly higher, and many (in and out of the community) have given up hope.

A million movies have trained us about what to expect from a school in East Harlem. The school is supposed to be an underfunded processing facility, barely functioning, with bad behavior, questionable security, and, most of all, very little learning.

Hardly the place you'd go to discover a future of our education system.

For generations, our society has said to communities like this one, "here are some teachers (but not enough) and here is some money (but not enough) and here are our expectations (very low) . . . go do your best." Few people are surprised when this plan doesn't work.

Over the last ten years, I've written more than a dozen books about how our society is being fundamentally changed by the impact of the Internet and the connection economy. Mostly I've tried to point out to people that the very things we assumed to be baseline truths were in fact fairly recent inventions and unlikely to last much longer. I've argued that mass marketing, mass brands, mass communication, top-down media, and the TV-industrial complex weren't the pillars of our future that many were trained to expect. It's often difficult to see that when you're in the middle of it.

In this manifesto, I'm going to argue that top-down industrialized schooling is just as threatened, and for very good reasons. Scarcity of access is destroyed by the connection economy, at the very same time the skills and attitudes we need from our graduates are changing.

While the Internet has allowed many of these changes to happen, you won't see much of the Web at the Harlem Village Academy school I visited, and not so much of it in this manifesto, either. The HVA is simply about people and the way they should be treated. It's about abandoning a top-down industrial approach to processing students and embracing a very human, very personal, and very powerful series of tools to produce a new generation of leaders.

There are literally thousands of ways to accomplish the result that Deborah Kenny and her team at HVA have accomplished. The method doesn't matter to me, the outcome does. What I saw that day were students leaning forward in their seats, choosing to pay attention. I saw teachers engaged because they chose to as well, because they were thrilled at the privilege of teaching kids who wanted to be taught.

The two advantages most successful schools have are plenty of money and a preselected, motivated student body. It's worth highlighting that the HVA doesn't get to choose its students, they are randomly assigned by lottery. And the HVA receives less funding per student than the typical public school in New York. HVA works because they have figured out how to create a workplace culture that attracts the most talented teachers, fosters a culture of ownership, freedom, and accountability, and then relentlessly transfers this passion to their students.

Maestro Ben Zander talks about the transformation that happens when a kid actually learns to love music. For one year, two years, even three years, the kid trudges along. He hits every pulse, pounds every note, and sweats the whole thing out.

Then he quits.

Except a few. The few with passion. The few who care.

Those kids lean forward and begin to *play*. They play as if they care, because they do. And as they lean forward, as they connect, they lift themselves off the piano seat, suddenly becoming, as Ben calls them, one-buttock players.

Playing as if it matters.

Colleges are fighting to recruit the kids who graduate from Deborah's school and I have no doubt that we'll soon be hearing of the leadership and contribution of the HVA alumni—one-buttock players who care about learning and giving. Because it matters.

2. A Few Notes About This Manifesto

I've numbered the sections because it's entirely possible you'll be reading it with a different layout than others will. The numbers make it easy to argue about particular sections.

It's written as a series of essays or blog posts, partly because that's how I write now, and partly because I'm hoping that one or more of them will spur you to share or rewrite or criticize a point I'm making. One side effect is that there's some redundancy. I hope you can forgive me for that. I won't mind if you skip around.

This isn't a prescription. It's not a manual. It's a series of provocations, ones that might resonate and that I hope will provoke conversation.

None of this writing is worth the effort if the ideas aren't shared. Feel free to email or reprint this manifesto, but please don't change it or charge for it. If you'd like to tweet, the hashtag is #stopstealingdreams. You can find a page for comments at http://www.stopstealingdreams.com

Most of all, go do something. Write your own manifesto. Send this one to the teachers at your kid's school. Ask hard questions at a board meeting. Start your own school. Post a video lecture or two. But don't settle.

Thanks for reading and sharing.

3. Back to (the Wrong) School

A hundred and fifty years ago, adults were incensed about child labor. Low-wage kids were taking jobs away from hardworking adults.

Sure, there was some moral outrage about seven-year-olds losing fingers and being abused at work, but the economic rationale was paramount. Factory owners insisted that losing child workers would be catastrophic to their industries and fought hard to keep the kids at work—they said they couldn't afford to hire adults. It wasn't until 1918 that nationwide compulsory education was in place.

Part of the rationale used to sell this major transformation to industrialists was the idea that educated kids would actually become more compliant and productive workers. Our current system of teaching kids to sit in straight rows and obey instructions isn't a coincidence—it was an investment in our economic future. The plan: trade short-term child-labor wages for longer-term productivity by giving kids a head start in doing what they're told.

Large-scale education was not developed to motivate kids or to create scholars. It was invented to churn out adults who worked well within the system. Scale was more important than quality, just as it was for most industrialists.

Of course, it worked. Several generations of productive, fully employed workers followed. But now?

Nobel Prize–winning economist Michael Spence makes this really clear: there are tradable jobs (doing things that could be done somewhere else, like building cars, designing chairs, and answering the phone) and non-tradable jobs (like mowing the lawn or cooking burgers). Is there any question that the first kind of job is worth keeping in our economy?

Alas, Spence reports that from 1990 to 2008, the U.S. economy added only 600,000 tradable jobs.

If you do a job where someone tells you exactly what to do, he will find someone cheaper than you to do it. And yet our schools are churning out kids who are stuck looking for jobs where the boss tells them exactly what to do.

Do you see the disconnect here? Every year, we churn out millions of workers who are trained to do 1925-style labor.

The bargain (take kids out of work so we can teach them to become better factory workers as adults) has set us on a race to the bottom. Some people argue that we ought to become the cheaper, easier country for sourcing cheap, compliant workers who do what they're told. Even if we could win that race, we'd lose. The bottom is not a good place to be, even if you're capable of getting there.

As we get ready for the ninety-third year of universal public education, here's the question every parent and taxpayer needs to wrestle with: Are we going to applaud, push, or even permit our schools (including most of the private ones) to continue the safe but ultimately doomed strategy of churning out predictable, testable, and mediocre factory workers?

As long as we embrace (or even accept) standardized testing, fear of science, little attempt at teaching leadership, and, most of all, the bureaucratic imperative to turn education into a factory itself, we're in big trouble.

The post-industrial revolution is here. Do you care enough to teach your kids to take advantage of it?

4. What Is School For?

It seems a question so obvious that it's hardly worth asking. And yet there are many possible answers. Here are a few (I'm talking about public or widespread private education here, grade K through college):

To create a society that's culturally coordinated.

To further science and knowledge and pursue information for its own sake.

To enhance civilization while giving people the tools to make informed decisions.

To train people to become productive workers.

Over the last three generations, the amount of school we've delivered to the public has gone way up—more people are spending more hours being schooled than ever before. And the cost of that schooling is going up even faster, with trillions of dollars being spent on delivering school on a massive scale.

Until recently, school did a fabulous job on just one of these four societal goals. First, the other three:

A culturally coordinated society: School isn't nearly as good at this as television is. There's a huge gulf between the cultural experience in an underfunded, overcrowded city school and the cultural experience in a well-funded school in the suburbs. There's a significant cultural distinction between a high school dropout and a Yale graduate. There are significant chasms in something as simple as whether you think the scientific method is useful—where you went to school says a lot about what you were taught. If school's goal is to create a foundation for a common culture, it hasn't delivered at nearly the level it is capable of.

The pursuit of knowledge for its own sake: We spend a fortune teaching trigonometry to kids who don't understand it, won't use it, and will spend no more of their lives studying math. We invest thousands of hours exposing millions of students to fiction and literature, but end up training most of them to never again read for fun (one study found that 58% of all Americans never read for pleasure after they graduate from school). As soon as we associate reading a book with taking a test, we've missed the point.

We continually raise the bar on what it means to be a college professor, but churn out PhDs who don't actually teach and aren't particularly productive at research, either. We teach facts, but the amount of knowledge truly absorbed is minuscule.

The tools to make smart decisions: Even though just about everyone in the West has been through years of compulsory schooling, we see ever more belief in unfounded theories, bad financial decisions, and poor community and family planning. People's connection with science and the arts is tenuous at best, and the financial acumen of the typical consumer is pitiful. If the goal was to raise the standards for rational thought, skeptical investigation, and useful decision making, we've failed for most of our citizens.

No, I think it's clear that school was designed with a particular function in mind, and it's one that school has delivered on for a hundred years.

Our grandfathers and great-grandfathers built school to train people to have a lifetime of productive labor as part of the industrialized economy. And it worked.

All the rest is a by-product, a side effect (sometimes a happy one) of the schooling system that we built to train the workforce we needed for the industrialized economy.

5. Column A and Column B

Aware
Caring
Committed
Creative
Goal-setting
Honest
Improvising
Incisive
Independent
Informed
Initiating
Innovating
Insightful
Leading
Strategic
Supportive   **>**   Or   **>**   Obedient

Which column do you pick? Whom do you want to work for or work next to? Whom do you want to hire? Which doctor do you want to treat you? Whom do you want to live with?

Last question: If you were organizing a trillion-dollar, sixteen-year indoctrination program to turn out the next generation of our society, which column would you build it around?

This is more of a rant than a book. It's written for teenagers, their parents, and their teachers. It's written for bosses and for those who work for those bosses. And it's written for anyone who has paid taxes, gone to a school board meeting, applied to college, or voted.

6. Changing What We Get, Because We've Changed What We Need

If school's function is to create the workers we need to fuel our economy, we need to change school, because the workers we need have changed as well.

The mission used to be to create homogenized, obedient, satisfied workers and pliant, eager consumers.

No longer.

Changing school doesn't involve sharpening the pencil we've already got. School reform cannot succeed if it focuses on getting schools to do a better job of what we previously asked them to do. *We don't need more of what schools produce when they're working as designed.* The challenge, then, is to change the very output of the school before we start spending even more time and money improving the performance of the school.

The goal of this manifesto is to create a new set of questions and demands that parents, taxpayers, and kids can bring to the people they've chosen, the institution we've built and invested our time and money into. The goal is to change what we get when we send citizens to school.

7. Mass Production Desires to Produce Mass

That statement seems obvious, yet it surprises us that schools are oriented around the notion of uniformity. Even though the workplace and civil society demand variety, the industrialized school system works to stamp it out.

The industrialized mass nature of school goes back to the very beginning, to the common school and the normal school and the idea of universal schooling. All of which were invented at precisely the same time we were perfecting mass production and interchangeable parts and then mass marketing.

Some quick background:

The common school (now called a public school) was a brand-new concept, created shortly after the Civil War. "Common" because it was for everyone, for the kids of the farmer, the kids of the potter, and the kids of the local shopkeeper. Horace Mann is generally regarded as the father of the institution, but he didn't have to fight nearly as hard as you would imagine—because industrialists were on his side. The two biggest challenges of a newly industrial economy were finding enough compliant workers and finding enough eager customers. The common school solved both problems.

The normal school (now called a teacher's college) was developed to indoctrinate teachers into the system of the common school, ensuring that there would be a coherent approach to the processing of students. If this sounds parallel to the notion of factories producing items in bulk, of interchangeable parts, of the notion of measurement and quality, it's not an accident.

The world has changed, of course. It has changed into a culture fueled by a market that knows how to mass-customize, to find the edges and the weird, and to cater to what the individual demands instead of insisting on conformity.

Mass customization of school isn't easy. Do we have any choice, though? If mass production and mass markets are falling apart, we really don't have the right to insist that the schools we designed for a different era will function well now.

Those who worry about the nature of schools face a few choices, but it's clear that one of them is *not* business as usual. One option is smaller units within schools, less industrial in outlook, with each unit creating its own varieties of leaders and citizens. The other is an organization that understands that size can be an asset, but only if the organization values customization instead of fighting it.

The current structure, which seeks low-cost uniformity that meets minimum standards, is killing our economy, our culture, and us.

8. Is School a Civic Enterprise?

At the heart of Horace Mann's push for public schooling for all was a simple notion: we build a better society when our peers are educated. Democracy was pretty new, and the notion of putting that much power into the hands of the uneducated masses was frightening enough to lead to the push for universal schooling.

Being surrounded by educated people makes democracy stronger, and it benefits our entire society. In the words of John Dewey, "Democracy cannot flourish where the chief influences in selecting subject matter of instruction are utilitarian ends narrowly conceived for the masses, and, for the higher education of the few, the traditions of a specialized cultivated class. The notion that the essentials of elementary education are the three R's mechanically treated, is based upon ignorance of the essentials needed for realization of democratic ideals."

It's easy to see how this concept manifests itself. There are more doctors, scientists, enlightened businesses, and engaged teachers in a society that values education. Sure, education is expensive, but living in a world of ignorance is even more expensive.

For a long time, there was an overlap between the education that the professions rewarded and the education that we might imagine an educated person would benefit from. Tied up in both paths is the notion that memorizing large amounts of information was essential. In a world where access to data was always limited, the ability to remember what you were taught, without fresh access to all the data, was a critical success factor.

The question I'd ask every administrator and school board is, "Does the curriculum you teach now make our society stronger?"

9. Three Legacies of Horace Mann

As superintendent of schools in Massachusetts, Mann basically invented the public school. Except he called it a common school, because a key goal was to involve the common man and raise the standards of the culture. Right from the start:

> Building a person's character was just as important as reading, writing, and arithmetic. By instilling values such as obedience to authority, promptness in attendance, and organizing the time according to bell ringing helped students prepare for future employment.

After a self-financed trip to Prussia, he instituted the paramilitary system of education he found there, a system he wrote up and proselytized to other schools, first in the Northeast U.S. and eventually around the country.

His second legacy was the invention of the "normal school."

Normal schools were institutes that taught high school students (usually women) the community norms and gave them instruction and power to go work for common schools as teachers, enforcing these norms across the system.

His third legacy, one with which I find no fault, was banning corporal punishment from schools. As further proof that his heart was ultimately in the right place, the man who industrialized the public schools he created left us with this admonition,

> . . . be ashamed to die until you have won some victory for humanity.

Unfortunately, that part of his curriculum is almost never taught in school.

10. Frederick J. Kelly and Your Nightmares

In 1914, a professor in Kansas invented the multiple-choice test. Yes, it's less than a hundred years old.

There was an emergency on. World War I was ramping up, hundreds of thousands of new immigrants needed to be processed and educated, and factories were hungry for workers. The government had just made two years of high school mandatory, and we needed a temporary, high-efficiency way to sort students and quickly assign them to appropriate slots.

In the words of Professor Kelly, "This is a test of lower order thinking for the lower orders."

A few years later, as president of the University of Idaho, Kelly disowned the idea, pointing out that it was an appropriate method to test only a tiny portion of what is actually taught and should be abandoned. The industrialists and the mass educators revolted and he was fired.

The SAT, the single most important filtering device used to measure the effect of school on each individual, is based (almost without change) on Kelly's lower-order thinking test. Still.

The reason is simple. Not because it works. No, we do it because it's the easy and efficient way to keep the mass production of students moving forward.

11. To Efficiently Run a School, Amplify Fear (and Destroy Passion)

School's industrial, scaled-up, measurable structure means that fear must be used to keep the masses in line. There's no other way to get hundreds or thousands of kids to comply, to process that many bodies, en masse, without simultaneous coordination.

And the flip side of this fear and conformity must be that passion will be destroyed. There's no room for someone who wants to go faster, or someone who wants to do something else, or someone who cares about a particular issue. Move on. Write it in your notes; there will be a test later. A multiple-choice test.

Do we need more fear?

Less passion?

12. Is It Possible to Teach Attitudes?

The notion that an organization could teach anything at all is a relatively new one.

Traditionally, society assumed that artists, singers, artisans, writers, scientists, and alchemists would find their calling, then find a mentor, and *then* learn their craft. It was absurd to think that you'd take people off the street and teach them to do science or to sing, and persist at that teaching long enough for them to get excited about it.

Now that we've built an industrial solution to teaching in bulk, we've seduced ourselves into believing that the only thing that can be taught is the way to get high SAT scores.

We shouldn't be buying this.

We can teach people to make commitments, to overcome fear, to deal transparently, to initiate, and to plan a course.

We can teach people to desire lifelong learning, to express themselves, and to innovate.

And just as important, it's vital we acknowledge that we can *unteach* bravery and creativity and initiative. And that we have been doing just that.

School has become an industrialized system, working on a huge scale, that has significant by-products, including the destruction of many of the attitudes and emotions we'd like to build our culture around.

In order to efficiently jam as much testable data into a generation of kids, we push to make those children compliant, competitive zombies.

13. Which Came First, the Car or the Gas Station?

The book publisher or the bookstore?

Culture changes to match the economy, not the other way around. The economy needed an institution that would churn out compliant workers, so we built it. Factories didn't happen because there were schools; schools happened because there were factories.

The reason so many people grow up to look for a job is that the economy has needed people who would grow up to look for a job.

Jobs were invented before workers were invented.

In the post-job universe, workers aren't really what we need more of, but schools remain focused on yesterday's needs.

14. The Wishing and Dreaming Problem

If you had a wish, what would it be? If a genie arrived and granted you a wish, would it be a worthwhile one?

I think our wishes change based on how we grow up, what we're taught, whom we hang out with, and what our parents do.

Our culture has a dreaming problem. It was largely created by the current regime in schooling, and it's getting worse.

Dreamers in school are dangerous. Dreamers can be impatient, unwilling to become well rounded and, most of all, hard to fit into existing systems.

One more question to ask at the school board meeting: "What are you doing to fuel my kid's dreams?"

15. "When I Grow Up, I Want to Be an Astronaut Assistant"

Jake Halpern did a rigorous study of high-school students. The most disturbing result was this:

"When you grow up, which of the following jobs would you most like to have?"

The chief of a major company like General Motors
A Navy SEAL
A U.S. senator
The president of a great university like Harvard or Yale
The personal assistant to a very famous singer or movie star

The results:

Among girls, the results were as follows: 9.5% chose "the chief of a major company like General Motors"; 9.8% chose "a Navy SEAL"; 13.6% chose "a U.S. Senator"; 23.7% chose "the president of a great university like Harvard or Yale"; and 43.4% chose "the personal assistant to a very famous singer or movie star."

Notice that these kids were okay with not actually being famous—they were happy to be the *assistant* of someone who lived that fairy-tale lifestyle.

Is this the best we can do? Have we created a trillion-dollar, multimillion-student, sixteen-year schooling cycle to take our best and our brightest and snuff out their dreams—sometimes when they're so nascent that they haven't even been articulated? Is the product of our massive schooling industry an endless legion of assistants?

The century of dream-snuffing has to end. We're facing a significant emergency, one that's not just economic but cultural as well. The time to act is right now, and the person to do it is you.

16. School Is Expensive

It's also not very good at doing what we need it to do. We're not going to be able to make it much cheaper, so let's figure out how to make it a lot better.

Not better at what it already does. Better at educating people to do what needs to be done.

Do you need a competent call-center employee? School is good at creating them, but it's awfully expensive. Do we really need more compliant phone operators, and at such a high cost?

Given the time and money being invested, what I want to know, what every parent and every taxpayer and every student should want to know, is: Is this the right plan? Is this the best way to produce the culture and economy we say we want?

What is school for?

If you're not asking that, you're wasting time and money.

Here's a hint: *learning is not done to you.* Learning is something you choose to do.

17. Reinventing School

If the new goal of school is to create something different from what we have now, and if new technologies and new connections are changing the way school can deliver its lessons, it's time for a change.

Here are a dozen ways school can be rethought:

Homework during the day, lectures at night
Open book, open note, all the time
Access to any course, anywhere in the world
Precise, focused instruction instead of mass, generalized instruction
The end of multiple-choice exams
Experience instead of test scores as a measure of achievement
The end of compliance as an outcome
Cooperation instead of isolation
Amplification of outlying students, teachers, and ideas
Transformation of the role of the teacher

Lifelong learning, earlier work
Death of the nearly famous college

It's easier than ever to open a school, to bring new technology into school, and to change how we teach. But if all we do with these tools is teach compliance and consumption, that's all we're going to get. School can and must do more than train the factory workers of tomorrow.

18. Fast, Flexible, and Focused

It's clear that the economy has changed. What we want and expect from our best citizens has changed. Not only in what we do when we go to our jobs, but also in the doors that have been opened for people who want to make an impact on our culture.

At the very same time, the acquisition of knowledge has been forever transformed by the Internet. Often overlooked in the rush to waste time at Facebook and YouTube is the fact that the Internet is the most efficient and powerful information-delivery system ever developed.

The change in the economy and the delivery of information online combine to amplify the speed of change. These rapid cycles are overwhelming the ability of the industrialized system of education to keep up.

As a result, the education-industrial system, the one that worked very well in creating a century's worth of factory workers, lawyers, nurses, and soldiers, is now obsolete.

We can prop it up or we can fix it.

I don't think it's practical to say, "we want what we've been getting, but cheaper and better." That's not going to happen, and I'm not sure we want it to, anyway.

We need school to produce something different, and the only way for that to happen is for us to ask new questions and make new demands on every element of the educational system we've built. Whenever teachers, administrators, or board members respond with an answer that refers to a world before the rules changed, they must stop and start their answer again.

No, we do not need you to create compliance.

No, we do not need you to cause memorization.

And no, we do not need you to teach students to embrace the status quo.

Anything a school does to advance those three agenda items is not just a waste of money but actually works against what we do need. The real shortage we face is dreams, and the wherewithal and the will to make them come true.

No tweaks. A revolution.

19. Dreams Are Difficult to Build and Easy to Destroy

By their nature, dreams are evanescent. They flicker long before they shine brightly. And when they're flickering, it's not particularly difficult for a parent or a teacher or a gang of peers to snuff them out.

Creating dreams is more difficult. They're often related to where we grow up, who our parents are, and whether or not the right person enters our life.

Settling for the not particularly uplifting dream of a boring, steady job isn't helpful. Dreaming of being picked—picked to be on TV or picked to play on a team or picked to be lucky—isn't helpful either. We waste our time and the time of our students when we set them up with pipe dreams that don't empower them to adapt (or better yet, lead) when the world doesn't work out as they hope.

The dreams we need are self-reliant dreams. We need dreams based not on what is but on what might be. We need students who can learn how to learn, who can discover how to push themselves and are generous enough and honest enough to engage with the outside world to make those dreams happen.

I think we're doing a great job of destroying dreams at the very same time the dreams we do hold on to aren't nearly bold enough.

20. Life in the Post-Institutional Future

In *Civilization,* his breakthrough book about the ascent (and fall) of Western civilization, Niall Ferguson makes the case that 400 years of Western dominance was primarily due to six institutions that were built over time—not great men, or accidents of weather or geography, but long-lasting, highly leveraged institutional advantages that permitted us to grow and prosper.

Competition, the scientific method, property rights, medicine, consumption, and jobs were all brand-new ideas, put into place and then polished over time. The result of this infrastructure was the alignment of institutions and outputs that enabled us to live in the world we take for granted today.

The industrial age is the most obvious example. Once the template was set for productivity-enhancing, profit-creating factories, the work of millions could be coordinated and wealth would be created.

The next century offers fewer new, long-lasting institutions (we're seeing both organized religion and the base of industry fading away), to be replaced instead with micro-organizations, with individual leadership, with the leveraged work of a small, innovative team changing things far more than it ever would have in the past. The six foundational elements are taken for granted as we build a new economy and a new world on top of them.

Amplified by the Web and the connection revolution, human beings are no longer rewarded most for work as compliant cogs. Instead, our chaotic world is open to the work of passionate individuals, intent on carving their own paths.

That's the new job of school. Not to hand a map to those willing to follow it, but to inculcate leadership and restlessness into a new generation.

21. Two Bumper Stickers

The first one is sad, selfish, and infuriating. I often see it on late-model, expensive cars near my town. It says, "Cut School Taxes."

These drivers/voters/taxpayers have given up on the schools, or they have kids who have graduated, and/or they're being selfish. None of these points of view fill me with optimism about our future.

The other bumper sticker is the one I never see. It says, "Make School Different."

I think if we followed the advice of the second, non-existent bumper sticker, we might be on to something.

School belongs to parents and their kids, the ones who are paying for it, the ones it was designed for. It belongs to the community, too, the adults who are going to be living and working beside the graduates the school churns out.

Too often, all these constituents are told to treat school like an autonomous organism, a pre-programmed automaton, too big to change and too important to mess with.

Well, the world changed first. Now it's time for school to follow along.

22. The Connection Revolution Is Upon Us

It sells the moment short to call this the Internet revolution. In fact, the era that marks the end of the industrial age and the beginning of something new is ultimately about connection.

The Industrial Revolution wasn't about inventing manufacturing, it was about amplifying it to the point where it changed everything. And the connection revolution doesn't invent connection, of course, but it amplifies it to become the dominant force in our economy.

Connecting people to one another.

Connecting seekers to data.

Connecting businesses to each other.

Connecting tribes of similarly minded individuals into larger, more effective organizations.

Connecting machines to each other and creating value as a result.

In the connection revolution, value is not created by increasing the productivity of those manufacturing a good or a service. Value is created by connecting buyers to sellers, producers to consumers, and the passionate to each other.

This meta level of value creation is hard to embrace if you're used to measuring sales per square foot or units produced per hour. In fact, though, connection leads to an extraordinary boost in productivity, efficiency, and impact.

In the connected world, reputation is worth more than test scores. Access to data means that data isn't the valuable part; the processing is what matters. Most of all, the connected world rewards those with an uncontrollable itch to make and lead and matter.

In the pre-connected world, information was scarce, and hoarding it was smart. Information needed to be processed in isolation, by individuals. After school, you were on your own.

In the connected world, all of that scarcity is replaced by abundance—an abundance of information, networks, and interactions.

23. And Yet We Isolate Students Instead of Connecting Them

Virtually every academic activity in school is done solo. Homework. Exams. Writing. The lectures might take place in a crowded room, but they too are primarily one-way.

How is this focus on the isolated individual going to match up with what actually happens in every field of endeavor? No competent doctor says, "I don't know what to do, I'll figure it out myself." No academic researcher or steelworker or pilot works in complete isolation.

Group projects are the exception in school, but they should be the norm. Figuring out how to leverage the power of the group—whether it is students in the same room or a quick connection to a graphic designer across the sea in Wales—is at the heart of how we are productive today.

24. If Education Is the Question, Then Teachers Are the Answer

Walking through the Harlem Village Academy, the first thing most people notice is the noise. There isn't any.

Please understand: it's not quiet like a morgue or a library. There are the sounds of engaged students and of motivated teachers, but there's no chaos. The chaos we've been trained to associate with an inner-city school is totally missing.

If the casual visitor walks away thinking that Dr. Kenny's secret is that she has figured out how to get eleven-year-old kids to become obedient, he will have missed 95% of what makes this school work.

On the first day, she tells the student body, "we are strict because we love you." And she means it. Most schools are strict because that's their job, or strict because it makes their lives easier. The revolutionary element of HVA isn't the strictness. It's the love.

Beginning with the foundation of a respectful (and respected) student body, Deborah Kenny has added something exciting: she lets the teachers teach.

This isn't a factory designed to churn out education at the highest speed for the lowest cost. No, this is handmade education. Teachers don't teach to the test. Teachers don't even teach to the pre-approved, standardized curriculum. At HVA, *teachers who care teach students who care.*

Simple.

Is it any surprise that this is revolutionary?

25. What If We Told Students the Truth?

Transparency in the traditional school might destroy it. If we told the truth about the irrelevance of various courses, about the relative quality of some teachers, about the power of choice and free speech—could the school as we know it survive?

What happens when the connection revolution collides with the school?

Unlike just about every other institution and product line in our economy, transparency is missing from education. Students are lied to, and so are parents. At some point, teenagers realize that most of school is a game, but the system never acknowledges it. In search of power, control, and independence, administrators hide information from teachers, and vice versa.

Because school was invented to control students and give power to the state, it's not surprising that the relationships are fraught with mistrust.

The very texture of the traditional school matches the organization and culture of the industrial economy. The bottom of the pyramid stores the students, with teachers (middle managers) following instructions from their bosses.

As in the traditional industrial organization, the folks at the bottom of the school are ignored, mistreated, and lied to. They are kept in the dark about anything outside of what they need to know to do their job (being a student), and put to work to satisfy the needs of the people in charge. Us and them.

The connection economy destroys the illusion of control. Students have the ability to find out which colleges are a good value, which courses make no sense, and how people in the real world are actually making a living. They have the ability to easily do outside research, even in fifth grade, and to discover that the teacher (or her textbook) is just plain wrong.

When students can take entire courses outside of the traditional school, how does the school prevent that? When passionate students can start their own political movements, profitable companies, or worthwhile community projects without the aegis of a school, how are obedience and fealty enforced?

It's impossible to lie and manipulate when you have no power.

26. School as a Contract of Adhesion

Friedrich Kessler, writing in 1943 in the *Columbia Law Review*, articulated a new kind of contract, one for the industrial age. Rather than being individually negotiated with each party, a contract of adhesion is a take-it-or-leave-it mass deal.

The industrialist says, use this car or this software or this telephone, and merely by using it, you are agreeing to our terms and conditions. With a hat tip to Doc Searls, here's what Kessler wrote:

> The development of large-scale enterprise with its mass production and mass distribution made a new type of contract inevitable—the standardized mass contract. A standardized contract, once its contents have been formulated by a business firm,

is used in every bargain dealing with the same product or service. The individuality of the parties, which so frequently gave color to the old type of contract, has disappeared. The stereotyped contract of today reflects the impersonality of the market . . . Once the usefulness of these contracts was discovered and perfected in the transportation, insurance, and banking business, their use spread into all other fields of large-scale enterprise, into international as well as national trade, and into labor relations.

School offers the same contract. Every student walking through the doors of the public school is by default entering into a contract of adhesion (and so are her guardians or parents). In Texas, the contract even includes tickets and fines for students as young as ten years old (and if they aren't paid by the time the student is eighteen, he goes to jail).

Beyond the draconian, barbaric frontier schooling techniques in Texas, though, we see a consistent thread running through most of what goes on in school. The subtext is clear: "hey, there are a lot of kids in this building. Too many kids, too many things on the agenda. My way or the highway, son."

Precisely what a foreman would say to a troublesome employee on the assembly line. Not what a patron would say to a talented artist, though.

27. The Decision

We don't ask students to decide to participate. We assume the contract of adhesion, and relentlessly put information in front of them, with homework to do and tests to take.

Entirely skipped: commitment. Do you want to learn this? Will you decide to become good at this?

The universal truth is beyond question—the only people who excel are those who have decided to do so. Great doctors or speakers or skiers or writers or musicians are great because somewhere along the way, they made the choice.

Why have we completely denied the importance of this choice?

28. Exploiting the Instinct to Hide

Human beings have, like all animals, a great ability to hide from the things they fear.

In the name of comportment and compliance and the processing of millions, school uses that instinct to its advantage. At the heart of the industrial system is power—the power of bosses over workers, the power of buyers over suppliers, and the power of marketers over consumers.

Given the assignment of indoctrinating a thousand kids at a time, the embattled school administrator reaches for the most effective tool available. Given that the assigned output of school is compliant citizens, the shortcut for achieving this output was fear.

The amygdala, sometimes called the lizard brain, is the fear center of the brain. It is on high alert during moments of stress. It is afraid of snakes. It causes our heart to race during a scary movie and our eyes to avoid direct contact with someone in authority.

The shortcut to compliance, then, isn't to reason with someone, to outline the options, and to sell a solution. No, the shortcut is to induce fear, to activate the amygdala. Do this or we'll laugh at you, expel you, tell your parents, make you sit in the corner. Do this or you will get a bad grade, be suspended, never amount to anything. Do this or you are in trouble.

Once the fear transaction is made clear, it can get ever more subtle. A fearsome teacher might need no more than a glance to quiet down his classroom.

But that's not enough for the industrial school. It goes further than merely ensuring classroom comportment. Fear is used to ensure that no one stretches too far, questions the status quo, or makes a ruckus. Fear is reinforced in career planning, in academics, and even in interpersonal interactions. Fear lives in the guidance office, too.

The message is simple: better fit in or you won't get into a good school. If you get into a good school and do what they say, you'll get a good job, and you'll be fine. But if you don't—it'll go on your permanent record.

Years ago, five friends and I were put in charge of 150 rowdy fifth-graders for a long weekend up in Canada. It was almost impossible to be heard over the din—until I stumbled onto the solution. All we had to say was, "points will be deducted," and compliance appeared. There weren't any points and there wasn't any prize, but merely the threat of lost points was sufficient.

Instead of creating a social marketplace where people engage and grow, school is a maelstrom, a whirlpool that pushes for sameness and dumbs down the individual while it attempts to raise the average.

29. The Other Side of Fear Is Passion

There really are only two tools available to the educator. The easy one is fear. Fear is easy to awake, easy to maintain, but ultimately toxic.

The other tool is passion. A kid in love with dinosaurs or baseball or earth science is going to learn it on her own. She's going to push hard for ever more information, and better still, master the thinking behind it.

Passion can overcome fear—the fear of losing, of failing, of being ridiculed.

The problem is that individual passion is hard to scale—hard to fit into the industrial model. It's not reliably ignited. It's certainly harder to create for large masses of people. Sure, it's easy to get a convention center filled with delegates to chant for a candidate, and easier still to engage the masses at Wembley Stadium, but the passion that fuels dreams and creates change must come from the individual, not from a demigod.

30. The Industrial Age Pervaded All of Our Culture

There has been no bigger change in 10,000 years of recorded human history than the overwhelming transformation of society and commerce and health and civilization that was enabled (or caused) by industrialization.

We're so surrounded by it that it seems normal and permanent and preordained, but we need to lay it out in stark relief to see how it has created the world we live in.

In just a few generations, society went from agrarian and distributed to corporatized and centralized. In order to overhaul the planet, a bunch of things had to work in concert:

Infrastructure changes, including paving the earth, laying pipe, building cities, wiring countries for communication, etc.

Government changes, which meant permitting corporations to engage with the king, to lobby, and to receive the benefits of infrastructure and policy investments. "Corporations are people, my friend."

Education changes, including universal literacy, an expectation of widespread commerce and, most of all, the practice of instilling the instinct to obey civil (as opposed to government) authority.

None of this could have happened if there had been widespread objections from individuals. It turns out, though, that it was relatively easy to enforce and then teach corporate and educational obedience. It turns out that industrializing the schooling of billions of people was a natural fit, a process that quickly turned into a virtuous cycle: obedient students were turned into obedient teachers, who were then able to create even more obedient students. We're wired for this stuff.

The system churned out productivity and money from the start. This result encouraged all the parties involved to amplify what they were doing—more lobbying, more infrastructure, more obedience. It took only 150 years, but the industrial age remade the entire population of the planet, from Detroit to Kibera.

The cornerstone of the entire process was how well the notion of obedience fit into the need for education. We needed educated workers, and teaching them to be obedient helped us educate them. And we needed obedient workers, and the work of educating them reinforced the desired behavior.

As the industrial age peters out, as the growth fades away, the challenge is this: training creative, independent, and innovative artists is new to us. We can't use the old tools because resorting to obedience to teach passion just isn't going to work. Our instinct, the easy go-to tool of activating the amygdala, isn't going to work this time.

31. Doubt and Certainty

The industrial structure of school demands that we teach things for certain. Testable things. Things beyond question. After all, if topics are open to challenge, who will challenge them? Our students. But students aren't there to challenge—they are there to be indoctrinated, to accept and obey.

Our new civic and scientific and professional life, though, is all about doubt. About questioning the status quo, questioning marketing or political claims, and, most of all, questioning what's next.

The obligation of the new school is to teach reasonable doubt. Not the unreasonable doubt of the wild-eyed heckler, but the evidence-based doubt of the questioning scientist and the reason-based doubt of the skilled debater.

Industrial settings don't leave a lot of room for doubt. The worker on the assembly line isn't supposed to question the design of the car. The clerk at the insurance agency isn't supposed to suggest improvements in the accounts being pitched.

In the post-industrial age, though, the good jobs and the real progress belong only to those with the confidence and the background to use the scientific method to question authority and to re-imagine a better reality.

32. Does Push-pin Equal Poetry?

Philosopher Jeremy Bentham argued that if two kids playing hopscotch or push-pin* are gaining as much joy and pleasure as someone reading poetry, they have enjoyed as much utility.

John Stuart Mill took a different approach. He argued, "it is better to be a human being dissatisfied than a pig satisfied; better to be Socrates

---

*Push-pin was a truly inane game in which kids would stick pins in a cloth or a hat brim and wrestle to knock one over. A little like Angry Birds, but without batteries.

dissatisfied than a fool satisfied. And if the fool, or the pig, are of a different opinion, it is because they only know their own side of the question."

I'm with Mill on this one. One of the things that school is for is to teach our children to understand and relish the idea of intellectualism, to develop into something more than a purpose-driven tool for the industrial state.

Fortunately for my side of the argument, the economy is now reinforcing this notion. Simple skills and cheap pleasures (bread and circuses) worked for a long time, but they no longer scale to quiet the masses. The basic skills aren't enough to support the circuses that we've been sold.

The fork in this road is ever more pronounced because there's now so much more to choose from. A citizen can spend his spare time getting smarter, more motivated, and more involved, or he can tune out, drop out, and entertain himself into a stupor. The same devices deliver either or both from the online ether—and the choice that people make is one that's going to develop early, based on the expectations of our teachers and the standards of our peers.

We can teach kids to engage in poetry, to write poetry, and to demand poetry—or we can take a shortcut and settle for push-pin, YouTube, and LOLcats.

33. Who Will Teach Bravery?

The essence of the connection revolution is that it rewards those who connect, stand out, and take what feels like a chance.

Can risk taking be taught? Of course it can. It gets taught by mentors, by parents, by great music teachers, and by life.

Why isn't it being taught every day at that place we send our kids to?

Bravery in school is punished, not rewarded. The entire institution is organized around avoiding individual brave acts, and again and again we hear from those who have made a difference, telling us that they became brave *despite* school, not because of it.

Harvard Business School turns out management consultants in far greater numbers than it develops successful bootstrapping entrepreneurs. Ralph Lauren, David Geffen, and Ted Turner all dropped out of college because they felt the real challenges lay elsewhere.

34. Responsibility

The Sudbury Valley School was founded during the hippie generation, and has survived and thrived as an independent school for forty years. From their introductory handbook:

> The way we saw it, responsibility means that each person has to carry the ball for himself. You, and you alone, must make your decisions, and you must live with them. No one should be thinking for you, and no one should be protecting you from the consequences of your actions. This, we felt, is essential if you want to be independent, self-directed, and the master of your own destiny.

While this is easy to dismiss as hype or pabulum, what if it's true? What if you actually built a school from the ground up with this as its core idea, not just window dressing? This is precisely what they did.

Students ask for teachers when they wish. They play soccer if they choose. They take responsibility for everything they do and learn, from the age of six. And it works.

If a school is seen as a place for encouragement and truth telling, a place where students go to find their passion and then achieve their goals, it is not a school we would generally recognize, because our schools do none of this.

35. Off the Hook: Denying Opportunities for Greatness

Greatness is frightening. With it comes responsibility.

If you can deny your talents, if you can conceal them from others or, even better, persuade yourself that they weren't even given to you, you're off the hook.

And being off the hook is a key element of the industrialized school's promise. It lets parents off the hook, certainly, since the institution takes over the teaching. It lets teachers off the hook, since the curriculum is preordained and the results are tested. And it lets students off the hook, because the road is clearly marked and the map is handed to everyone.

If you stay on the path, do your college applications through the guidance office and your job hunting at the placement office, *the future is not your fault.*

That's the refrain we hear often from frustrated job seekers, frustrated workers with stuck careers, and frustrated students in too much debt. "I did what they told me to do and now I'm stuck and it's not my fault."

What they've exchanged for that deniability is their dreams, their chance for greatness. To go off the path is to claim responsibility for what happens next.

Because the industrial education system makes it so clear when someone has stepped from the well-lit path, it highlights those who leave it, making it pretty easy to find those willing to speak up and connect and lead. They're noticeable at first primarily for the fact that they refuse to be sheep.

Rebecca Chapman, literary editor of a new online journal called *The New Inquiry*, was quoted in the *New York Times*. "My whole life, I had been doing everything everybody told me. I went to the right school. I got really good grades. I got all the internships. Then, I couldn't do anything."

The only surprising thing about this statement is that some consider it surprising.

Rebecca trained to be competent, excelling at completing the tasks set in front of her. She spent more than sixteen years at the top of the system, at the best schools, with the best resources, doing what she was told to do.

Unfortunately, no one is willing to pay her to do tasks. Without a defined agenda, it's difficult for her to find the gig she was trained for.

Too many competent workers, not enough tasks.

Peter Thiel made headlines when he offered to pay students *not* to attend college—to start something instead. The reason this program works, though, has nothing to do with avoiding college and everything to do with attracting those bold enough to put themselves on the hook.

Education isn't a problem until it serves as a buffer from the world and a refuge from the risk of failure.

36. Instead of Amplifying Dreams, School Destroys Them

Every day, beginning the first day and continuing until the last day, our teachers and our administrators and yes, most parents, seeking to do the right thing, end up doing the wrong one.

We mean well.

We let our kids down easy.

We tell ourselves that we are realistic.

We demand that students have a trade to fall back on, an assembly-line job available just in case the silly dreams don't come true. And then, fearing heartbreak, we push them to bury the dream and focus on just the job.

The job with a boss and an office and air conditioning and a map of what to do next. A job with security and coworkers and instructions and deniability.

And when the job doesn't come?

When all the dues are paid and for nothing?

Ouch.

37. The Curse of the Hourly Wage

Frederick Taylor is responsible for much of what you see when you look around. As the father of scientific management, he put the fine points on Henry Ford's model of mass production and was the articulate voice behind the staffing of the assembly line and the growth of the industrial age.

Armed with a stopwatch, Taylor measured everything. He came to two conclusions:

Interchangeable workers were essential to efficient manufacturing. You can't shut down the line just because one person doesn't show up for work. The bigger the pool of qualified labor, the easier it is to find cheap, compliant workers who will follow your instructions.

People working alone (in parallel) are far more efficient than teams. Break every industrial process down into the smallest number of parts and give an individual the same thing to do again and again, alone, and measure his output.

One outgrowth of this analysis is that hourly workers are fundamentally different from salaried ones. If you are paid by the hour, the organization is saying to you, "I can buy your time an hour at a time, and replace you at any time." Hourly workers were segregated, covered by different labor laws, and rarely, if ever, moved over to management.

School, no surprise, is focused on creating hourly workers, because that's what the creators of school needed, in large numbers.

Think about the fact that school relentlessly downplays group work. It breaks tasks into the smallest possible measurable units. It does nothing to coordinate teaching across subjects. It often isolates teachers into departments. And most of all, it measures, relentlessly, at the individual level, and re-processes those who don't meet the minimum performance standards.

Every one of those behaviors is a mirror of what happened in the factory of 1937.

Of course, business in the U.S. evolved over time to be less draconian than it was seventy years ago. Companies adopted a social contract (usually unstated). Union movements and public outcry led to the notion that if you were obedient and hardworking, your hourly gig would continue, probably until you retired, and then your pension would keep you comfortable.

In the last twenty years, though, under pressure from competition and shareholders, the hourly social contract has evaporated, and manufacturers and others that engage in factory work have gone back to a more pure form of Taylorism. No, Walmart and Target and Best Buy don't bring "good jobs" to Brooklyn when they build a megamall. They bring hourly jobs with no advancement. How could there be? The pyramid is incredibly wide and not very tall, with thousands of hourly workers for every manager with significant decision-making ability.

Walmart has more than 2 million employees around the world, and perhaps a thousand people who set policy and do significant creative work. Most of the others are hourly employees, easily replaced with little notice.

The bottom of our economy has gone back into the past, back into alignment with what school has perfected: taking advantage of people doing piecemeal labor.

This is not the future of our economy; it is merely the last well-lit path available to students who survive the traditional indoctrination process. If we churn out more workers like this, we will merely be fighting for more of the bottom of the pyramid, more of the world market's share of bad jobs, cheaply executed.

38. Scientific Management >
Scientific Schooling

There didn't used to be one right way, one perfected method, one step-by-step approach to production.

But in the industrial age, scientific management is obvious when you think about it: record how long it takes to make something, change the way you do it, see if you can do it faster or better. Repeat.

Frederick Taylor was right—we could dramatically increase industrial productivity by measuring and systemizing the assembly line. His method became the standard for any assembly line that wanted to become more productive (and thus competitive).

Use your left hand, not your right, to pick this up. Turn up the lights. Lower the height of the counter. Process exactly six units per minute.

Scientific management changed the world as we knew it. And there's no doubt it boosted productivity.

The rise of scientific management furthered the need for obedient and competent factory workers, individuals with enough skill and self-control to do precisely what they were told.

So it's not a surprise that schools were enlisted to train future employees in just that—skill and self-control. Of course, it's not self-control, really; it's external control. The willingness (or tolerance) to accept external instruction and become compliant.

From there, from this position of wanting to manufacture compliant workers, it's only a tiny step to scientific schooling.

Scientific schooling uses precisely the same techniques as scientific management. Measure (test) everyone. Often. Figure out which inputs are likely to create testable outputs. If an output isn't easily testable, ignore it.

It would be a mistake to say that scientific education doesn't work. It does work. It creates what we test.

Unfortunately, the things we desperately need (and the things that make us happy) aren't the same things that are easy to test.

39. Where Did the Good Jobs Go?

Hint: the old ones, the ones we imagine when we think about the placement office and the pension—the ones that school prepared us for—they're gone.

In 1960, the top ten employers in the U.S. were GM, AT&T, Ford, GE, U.S. Steel, Sears, A&P, Esso, Bethlehem Steel, and IT&T. Eight of these (not so much Sears and A&P) offered substantial pay and a long-term career to hardworking people who actually made something. It was easy to see how the promises of advancement and a social contract could be kept, particularly for the "good student" who had demonstrated an ability and willingness to be part of the system.

Today, the top ten employers are Walmart, Kelly Services, IBM, UPS, McDonald's, Yum (Taco Bell, KFC, et al), Target, Kroger, HP, and The Home Depot. Of these, only two (*two!*) offer a path similar to the one that the vast majority of major companies offered fifty years ago.

Burger flippers of the world, unite.

Here's the alternative: What happens when there are fifty companies like Apple? What happens when there is an explosion in the number of new power technologies, new connection mechanisms, new medical approaches? The good jobs of the future aren't going to involve working for giant companies on an assembly line. They all require individuals willing to chart their own path, whether or not they work for someone else.

The jobs of the future are in two categories: the downtrodden assemblers of cheap mass goods and the respected creators of the unexpected.

The increasing gap between those racing to the bottom and those working toward the top is going to make the 99% divide seem like nostalgia.

Virtually every company that isn't forced to be local is shifting gears so it doesn't have to be local. Which means that the call center and the packing center and the data center and the assembly line are quickly moving to places where there are cheaper workers. And more compliant workers.

Is that going to be you or your kids or the students in your town?

The other route—the road to the top—is for the few who figure out how to be linchpins and artists. People who are hired because they're totally worth it, because they offer insight and creativity and innovation that just can't be found easily. *Scarce skills combined with even scarcer attitudes almost always lead to low unemployment and high wages.*

An *artist* is someone who brings new thinking and generosity to his work, who does human work that changes another for the better. An artist invents a new kind of insurance policy, diagnoses a disease that someone else might have missed, or envisions a future that's not here yet.

And a *linchpin* is the worker we can't live without, the one we'd miss if she was gone. The linchpin brings enough gravity, energy, and forward motion to work that she makes things happen.

Sadly, most artists and most linchpins learn their skills and attitudes *despite* school, not because of it.

The future of our economy lies with the impatient. The linchpins and the artists and the scientists who will refuse to wait to be hired and will take things into their own hands, building their own value, producing outputs others will gladly pay for. Either they'll do that on their own or someone will hire them and give them a platform to do it.

The only way out is going to be mapped by those able to dream.

40. What They Teach at FIRST

The largest robotics competition in the world organizes hundreds of thousands of kids into a nationwide competition to build fighting robots and other technical fun.

Last year, more than 300,000 students participated, surrounded by their peers and the 50,000 mentors and coaches who make the program possible. A recent university study of past participants found that FIRST participants in college were:

> More than three times as likely to major specifically in engineering.
>
> Roughly ten times as likely to have had an apprenticeship, internship, or co-op job in their freshman year.
>
> Significantly more likely to achieve a postgraduate degree.
>
> More than twice as likely to pursue a career in science and technology.
>
> Nearly four times as likely to pursue a career specifically in engineering.
>
> *More than twice as likely to volunteer in their communities.*

When you dream about building the best robot in the competition, you'll find a way to get a lot done, and you'll do it in a team. When you dream of making an impact, obstacles are a lot easier to overcome.

The magic of FIRST has nothing to do with teaching what a capacitor does, and everything to do with teamwork, dreams, and, most of all, expectations. FIRST is a movement for communicating and encouraging passion.

41. Judgment, Skill, and Attitude

Those are the new replacements for obedience.

We sometimes (rarely) teach skill, but when it comes to judgment and attitude, we say to kids and their parents: you're on your own.

Here's what I want to explore: Can we teach people to care?

I know that we can teach them *not* to care; that's pretty easy. But given the massive technological and economic changes we're living through, do we have the opportunity to teach productive and effective caring? Can we teach kids to care enough about their dreams that they'll care enough to develop the judgment, skill, and attitude to make them come true?

42. Can You Teach Indian Food?

It's not easy to find young Anglo kids in Cleveland or Topeka who crave tandoori chicken or shrimp vindaloo. And yet kids with almost the same DNA in Mumbai eat the stuff every day. It's clearly not about genetics.

Perhaps households there approach the issue of food the way school teaches a new topic. First, kids are taught the history of Indian food, then they are instructed to memorize a number of recipes, and then there are tests. At some point, the pedagogy leads to a love of the food.

Of course not.

People around the world eat what they eat because of community standards and the way culture is inculcated into what they do. Expectations matter a great deal. When you have no real choice but to grow up doing something or eating something or singing something, then you do it.

If culture is sufficient to establish what we eat and how we speak and ten thousand other societal norms, why isn't it able to teach us goal setting and passion and curiosity and the ability to persuade?

It can.

43. How Not to Teach Someone to Be a Baseball Fan

Teach the history of baseball, beginning with Abner Doubleday and the impact of cricket and imperialism. Have a test.

Starting with the Negro Leagues and the early barnstorming teams, assign students to memorize facts and figures about each player. Have a test.

Rank the class on who did well on the first two tests, and allow these students to memorize even more statistics about baseball players. Make sure to give equal time to players in Japan and the Dominican Republic. Send the students who didn't do as well to spend time with a lesser teacher, but assign them similar work, just over a longer time frame. Have a test.

Sometime in the future, do a field trip and go to a baseball game. Make sure no one has a good time.

If there's time, let kids throw a baseball around during recess.

Obviously, there are plenty of kids (and adults) who know far more about baseball than anyone could imagine knowing. And none of them learned it this way.

The industrialized, scalable, testable solution is almost never the best way to generate exceptional learning.

44. Defining the Role of a Teacher

It used to be simple: the teacher was the cop, the lecturer, the source of answers, and the gatekeeper to resources. All rolled into one.

A teacher might be the person who is capable of delivering information. A teacher can be your best source of finding out how to do something or why something works.

A teacher can also serve to create a social contract or environment where people will change their posture, do their best work, and stretch in new directions. We've all been in environments where competition, social status, or the direct connection with another human being has changed us.

The Internet is making the role of content gatekeeper unimportant. Redundant. Even wasteful.

If there's information that can be written down, widespread digital access now means that just about anyone can look it up. We don't need a human being standing next to us to lecture us on how to find the square root of a number or sharpen an ax.

(Worth stopping for a second and reconsidering the revolutionary nature of that last sentence.)

What we *do* need is someone to persuade us that we *want* to learn those things, and someone to push us or encourage us or create a space where we want to learn to do them better.

If all the teacher is going to do is read her pre-written notes from a PowerPoint slide to a lecture hall of thirty or three hundred, perhaps she should stay home. Not only is this a horrible disrespect to the student, it's a complete waste of the heart and soul of the talented teacher. Teaching is no longer about delivering facts that are unavailable in any other format.

45. Shouldn't Parents Do the Motivating?

Of course they should. They should have the freedom to not have to work two jobs, they should be aware enough of the changes in society to be focused on a new form of education, and they should have the skills and the confidence and the time to teach each child what he needs to know to succeed in a new age.

But they're not and they don't. And as a citizen, I'm not sure I want to trust a hundred million amateur teachers to do a world-class job of designing our future. Some parents (like mine) were just stunningly great at this task, serious and focused and generous while they relentlessly taught my sisters and me about what we could accomplish and how to go about it.

I can't think of anything more cynical and selfish, though, than telling kids who didn't win the parent lottery that they've lost the entire game. Society has the resources and the skill (and thus the obligation) to reset cultural norms and to amplify them through schooling. I don't think we maximize our benefit when we turn every child's education into a first-time, home-based project.

We can amplify each kid's natural inclination to dream, we can inculcate passion in a new generation, and we can give kids the tools to learn more, and faster, in a way that's never been seen before.

And if parents want to lead (or even to help, or merely get out of the way), that's even better.

46. At the Heart of Pedagogy

When we think about the role of school, we have to take a minute to understand that we *backed* into this corner; we didn't head here with intent.

A hundred and fifty years ago, 1% of the population went to the academy. They studied for studying's sake. They did philosophy and mathematics and basic science, all as a way to understand the universe.

The rest of the world didn't go to school. You learned something from your parents, perhaps, or if you were rich, from a tutor. But blacksmiths and stable boys and barbers didn't sit in elegant one-room schoolhouses paid for by taxpayers, because there weren't any.

After the invention of public school, of course, this all changed. The 1% still went to school to learn about the universe.

And 99% of the population went to school because they were ordered to go to school. And school was about basic writing (so you could do your job), reading (so you could do your job), and arithmetic (so you could do your job).

For a generation, that's what school did. It was a direct and focused finishing school for pre-industrial kids.

Then, as often happens to institutions, mission creep sank in. As long as we're teaching something, the thinking went, let's teach something. And so schools added all manner of material from the academy. We taught higher math or physics or chemistry or Shakespeare or Latin—not because it would help you with your job, but because learning stuff was important.

Public school shifted gears—it took the academy to the masses.

I want to be very clear here: I wouldn't want to live in an uneducated world. I truly believe that education makes humans great, elevates our culture and our economy, and creates the foundation for the engine that drives science, which leads to our well-being. I'm not criticizing education.

No. But I am wondering when we decided that the purpose of school was to cram as much data/trivia/fact into every student as we possibly could.

Because that's what we're doing. We're not only avoiding issues of practicality and projects and hands-on use of information; we're also aggressively testing for trivia.

Which of society's goals are we satisfying when we spend 80% of the school day drilling and bullying to get kids to momentarily swallow and then regurgitate this month's agenda?

47. Academics Are a Means to an End, Not an End

Go back to the original purpose of school: we needed to teach citizens to be obedient (to be good workers), to consume what marketers sold them (to keep industry going), and to be able to sit still (to be good workers).

Academics are one way to reinforce those ideas. Sure, there were a few things (like basic arithmetic and the ability to read) that all civilized people needed, but we kept adding to the list, creating a never-ending list of topics that students could be confronted with as a test of their obedience. By conflating learning (a good thing) with obedience (an important thing for the industrial age) and consumption (essential for mass marketers), we confused ourselves. We came to the conclusion that increasing all three of these in tandem was what society wanted, and we often used one to get more of the other.

Of course, those who were creating the curricula got focused on the academic part.

At first, we used primers and memorization as a direct method of teaching obedience. Then, though, as we got smarter about the structure of thought, we created syllabi that actually covered the knowledge that mattered.

But mattered to whom?

School is still about obedience and compliance and consumption, but now, layered on top of it, are hours every day of brute-force learning about how the world actually works. The problem is that we don't sell it well, it's not absorbed, it's expensive, and it doesn't stick.

Now that obedience is less important and learning matters more than ever, we have to be brave enough to separate them. We can rebuild the entire system around passion instead of fear.

48. The Status Quo Pause

That feeling you're feeling (if you haven't given up because of the frightening implications of this manifesto) is the feeling just about every parent has. It's easier to play it safe. Why risk blowing up the educational system, why not just add a bit to it? Why risk the education of our kids merely because the economy has changed?

That whisper in your ear, that hesitation about taking dramatic action—that's precisely why we still have the system we do. That's how we get stuck with the status quo. When it's safer and easier and quieter to stick with what we've got, we end up sticking with what we've got.

If just one parent asks these questions, nothing is going to happen. Every parent has an excuse and a special situation and no one wants to go out on a limb . . . but if a dozen or a hundred parents step up and start asking, the agenda will begin to change.

The urgency of our problem is obvious, and it seems foolish to me to polish the obsolete when we ought to be investing our time and money into building something that actually meets our needs. *We can't switch the mission unless we also switch the method.*

49. Compliant, Local, and Cheap

Those were the three requirements for most jobs for most of the twentieth century. Only after you fit all three criteria was your competence tested. And competence was far more important than leadership, creativity, or brilliance.

If you were applying to be a forklift operator, a receptionist, an insurance salesperson, or a nurse, you showed up with a résumé (proof of a history of compliance), you showed up (proof that you lived somewhere nearby), and you knew about the salary on offer (of course).

School didn't have to do anything about the local part, but it sure worked hard to instill the notion that reliably handing in your work on time while making sure it precisely matched the standards of the teacher was the single best way to move forward.

And it certainly taught you to accept what those in authority gave you, so the wage was the wage, and you took it until someone offered you a better one.

Each student had already had a job—from the age of five, a steady job, with a string of managers giving instructions. Built right into the fabric of our lives were the ingredients for compliant and cheap. Local was a bonus.

50. The Problem with Competence

Institutions and committees like to talk about core competencies, the basic things that a professional or a job seeker needs to know.

Core competence? I'd prefer core incompetence.

Competent people have a predictable, reliable process for solving a particular set of problems. They solve a problem the same way, every time. That's what makes them reliable. That's what makes them competent.

Competent people are quite proud of the status and success that they get out of being competent. They like being competent. They guard their competence, and they work hard to maintain it.

Over the past twenty to thirty years, we've witnessed an amazing shift in U.S.-based businesses. Not so long ago, companies were filled with incompetent workers. If you bought a Pacer from American Motors, it wasn't all that surprising to find a tool hidden in a door panel of your new car. Back then, it wasn't uncommon for shipped products to be dead on arrival.

Computers changed that. Now the receptionist can't lose your messages because they go straight into voice mail. The assembly-line worker can't drop a tool because it's attached to a numerically controlled machine. The telemarketer who interrupts your dinner is unlikely to overpromise because the pitch is carefully outlined in script form on paper.

Oh, there's one other thing: as we've turned human beings into competent components of the giant network known as American business, we've also erected huge barriers to change.

Competence is the enemy of change!

Competent people resist change. Why? Because change threatens to make them less competent. And competent people like being competent. That's who they are, and sometimes that's all they've got. No wonder they're not in a hurry to rock the boat.

If I'm going to make the investment and hire someone for more than the market rate, I want to find an incompetent worker. One who will break the rules and find me something no one else can.

Nothing in the world is more dangerous than sincere ignorance and conscientious stupidity.

—Dr. Martin Luther King Jr.

51. How They Saved LEGO

Dr. Derek Cabrera noticed something really disturbing. The secret to LEGO's success was the switch from all-purpose LEGO sets, with blocks of different sizes and colors, to predefined kits, models that must be assembled precisely one way, or they're wrong.

Why would these sell so many more copies? Because they match what parents expect and what kids have been trained to do.

There's a right answer! The mom and the kid can both take pride in the kit, assembled. It's done. Instructions were followed and results were attained.

LEGO isn't the problem, but it is a symptom of something seriously amiss. We're entering a revolution of ideas while producing a generation that wants instructions instead.

52. The Race to the Top (and the Alternative)

The real debate if you're a worker is: Do you want a job where they'll miss you if you're gone, a job where only you can do it, a job where you get paid to bring yourself (your true self) to work? Because *those* jobs are available. In fact, there's no unemployment in that area.

OR do you want a job where you're racing to the bottom—where your job is to do your job, do as you're told, and wait for the boss to pick you?

School is clearly organized around the second race. And the problem with the race to the bottom is that you might win. Being the best of the compliant masses is a safe place (for now). But the rest? Not so much.

53. The Forever Recession

There are two recessions going on.

One is gradually ending. This is the cyclical recession. We have them all the time; they come and they go. Not fun, but not permanent.

The other one, I fear, is here forever. This is the recession of the industrial age, the receding wave of bounty that workers and businesses got as a result of rising productivity but imperfect market communication.

In short: if you're local, we need to buy from you. If you work in town, we need to hire you. If you can do a craft, we can't replace you with a machine.

No longer.

The lowest price for any good worth pricing is now available to anyone, anywhere. Which makes the market for boring stuff a lot more perfect than it used to be.

Since the "factory" work we did is now being mechanized, outsourced, or eliminated, it's hard to pay extra for it. And since buyers have so many choices (and much more perfect information about pricing and availability), it's hard to charge extra.

Thus, middle-class jobs that existed because companies had no choice are now gone.

Protectionism isn't going to fix this problem. Neither is the stimulus of old factories or yelling in frustration and anger. No, the only useful response is to view this as an opportunity. To poorly paraphrase Clay Shirky, every revolution destroys the last thing before it turns a profit on a new thing.

The networked revolution is creating huge profits, significant opportunities, and a lot of change. What it's not doing is providing millions of brain-dead, corner-office, follow-the-manual, middle-class jobs. And it's not going to.

Fast, smart, and flexible are embraced by the network. Linchpin behavior. People and companies we can't live without (because if I can live without you, I'm sure going to try if the alternative is to save money).

The sad irony is that everything we do to prop up the last economy (more obedience, more compliance, cheaper yet average) gets in the way of profiting from this one.

54. Make Something Different

I don't know how to change school, can't give you a map or a checklist. What I do know is that we're asking the wrong questions and making the wrong assumptions.

The best tactic available to every taxpayer and parent and concerned teacher is to relentlessly ask questions, not settling for the status quo.

"Is this class/lecture/program/task/test/policy designed to help our students do the old thing a little more efficiently, or are we opening a new door to enable our students to do something that's new and different?"

School is doing the best job it knows how to create the output it is being asked to create.

We ought to be asking school to make something different. And the only way to do that is to go about it differently.

55. Make Something Differently

The simple way to make something different is to go about it in a whole new way. In other words, doing what we're doing now and hoping we'll get something else as an outcome is nuts.

Once we start to do schooling differently, we'll start to get something different.

56. 1,000 Hours

Over the last three years, Jeremy Gleick, a sophomore at UCLA, has devoted precisely an hour a day to learning something new and unassigned.

The rules are simple: it can't be related to schoolwork, and reading a novel doesn't count.

Since he's started on this journey, he has read Steven Pinker and Stephen Hawking books, watched documentaries about ants and astrophysics, and taken courses in blacksmithing (in person) and card tricks (online). He has done this with rigor and merely had to sacrifice a little TV time to become smarter than most of his peers.

There are two things I take away from this:

a. This is a rare choice, which is quite disturbing. Someone actually choosing to become a polymath, signing himself up to get a little smarter on a new topic every single day.

b. The resources available for this endeavor have increased by several orders of magnitude. Available resources and instruction have gone from scarce to abundant in less than a decade, and the only barrier to learning for most young adults in the developed world is now merely the decision to learn.

My argument is that the entire schooling establishment can be organized around this new widely available resource.

57. The Economic, Cultural, and Moral Reasons for an Overhaul

There's an economic argument to make about schools and the world of dreams. Small dreams are hurting us like never before. Small dreams represent an attitude of fear; they sabotage our judgment and they keep us from acquiring new skills, skills that are there if we're willing to learn them.

There's a societal argument to make as well. All of us are losing out because we've done such a good job of persuading our future generations not to dream. Think of the art we haven't seen, the jobs that haven't been created, and the productivity that hasn't been imagined because generations have been persuaded not to dream big.

And there's a moral argument, too. How dare we do this, on a large scale? How dare we tell people that they aren't talented enough, musical enough, gifted enough, charismatic enough, or well-born enough to lead?

58. The Virtuous Cycle of Good Jobs

Industrial jobs no longer create new industrial jobs in our country. A surplus of obedient hourly workers leads to unemployment, not more factories.

On the other hand, creative jobs lead to more creative jobs. Self-starting, self-reliant, initiative-taking individuals often start new projects that need new workers. In my opinion, the now politicized role of "job creator" has nothing at all to do with tax cuts and everything to do with people who trained to have the guts to raise their hands and say, "I'm starting."

An economy that's stuck needs more inventors, scientists, explorers, and artists. Because those are the people who open doors for others.

59. The Evolution of Dreams

Fairy tales tell us a lot about what people want. Girls want to be princesses, boys want to be heroes. And both girls and boys want to be chosen. They want to have the glass slipper fit, or the mighty gods from another planet give them a lantern that energizes their power ring.

In a monarchy or similarly authoritarian system, there was no way in the world you were going to accomplish much of anything unless you were picked. Picked by the chief or the local ruler or the priest or the nobleman in search of a wife.

It was the best you could hope for.

We've heard of Mozart because he was picked, first by Prince-elector Maximilian III of Bavaria, and then by a string of other powerful royalty. Michelangelo was picked by the Pope. Catherine of Aragon was picked by one man after another (with plenty of dowry politics involved) until she ended up with Henry VIII.

When life is short and brutish, and when class trumps everything, fairy-tale dreams are about all we can believe we are entitled to.

The Industrial Revolution created a different sort of outcome, a loosening of class-based restrictions and the creation of new careers and pathways.

Suddenly, folks like Andrew Carnegie and Henry Ford became the pickers. Now there were far more people who could pick you (and offer you a job), and thus the stakes were even higher because the odds were better. Not only were there more ways to be picked, but suddenly and amazingly, there was a chance that just about anyone could become powerful enough to move up the ladder.

Our fairy tales started to change.

When the economy hit its stride after World War II, it led to an explosion in dreams. Kids dreamed of walking on the moon or inventing a new kind of medical device. They dreamed of industry and science and politics and invention, and often, those dreams came true. It wasn't surprising to get a chemistry set for your ninth birthday—and it was filled not with straightforward recipes, but with tons of cool powders and potions that burst into flame or stank up the entire house.

A generation dreamed of writing a bestseller or inventing a new kind of car design or perfecting a dance move.

We look back on that generation with a bit of awe. Those kids could dream.

60. Dreamers Are a Problem

And then schools refocused on mass and scale, and the dreams faded. While these new heroes created generations of kids who wanted to disrupt the world as they did, they also sowed the seeds for the end of those dreams.

It turns out that industry scales. Little businesses turn into big ones. One McDonald's turns into ten thousand. One scientist at Pfizer creates a pathway for one hundred or one thousand obedient assistants and sales reps.

Fifty years ago, businesses realized that they were facing two related problems:

They needed more workers, more well-trained, compliant, and yes, cheap workers willing to follow specific instructions . . .

and

They needed more customers. More well-trained, pliable, eager-to-consume customers watching TV regularly and waiting to buy what they had to sell.

Dreamers don't help with either of these problems. Dreamers aren't busy applying for jobs at minimum wage, they don't eagerly buy the latest fashions, and they're a pain in the ass to keep happy.

The solution sounds like it was invented at some secret meeting at the Skull and Bones, but I don't think it was. Instead, it was the outcome of a hundred little decisions, the uncoordinated work of thousands of corporations and political lobbyists:

School is a factory, and the output of that factory is compliant workers who buy a lot of stuff. *These students are trained to dream small dreams.*

What about the famous ones we hear about? Surely the successful people we read about have something special going on . . .

Majora Carter grew up in the 1960s in the South Bronx. She wasn't supposed to have dreams; neither were her classmates. The economic impediments were too big; there wasn't enough money to spend on schools, on support, on teachers who cared.

And yet Majora grew up to be, according to *Fast Company,* one of the hundred most creative people in business, a TED speaker, a community activist, and a successful consultant. Her fellow students are still waiting to get the call.

Dreamers don't have special genes. They find circumstances that amplify their dreams. If the mass-processing of students we call school were good at creating the dreamers we revere, there'd be far more of them. In fact, many of the famous ones, the successful ones, and the essential ones are part of our economy despite the processing they received, not because of it.

The economy demands that we pick ourselves. School teaches us otherwise.

I'm arguing for a new set of fairy tales, a new expectation of powerful dreaming.

61. Is It Possible to Teach Willpower?

After all, willpower is the foundation of every realized dream.

Dreams fade away because we can't tolerate the short-term pain necessary to get to our long-term goal. We find something easier, juicier, sexier, and more now, so we take it, leaving our dreams abandoned on the side of the road.

But is willpower an innate, genetic trait, something we have no say over?

It turns out that (good news) willpower can be taught. It can be taught by parents and by schools. Stanford researcher Kelly McGonigal has written about this, as has noted researcher Roy Baumeister.

If willpower can be taught, why don't we teach it?

Simple: because industrialists don't need employees with willpower, and marketers loathe consumers who have it.

Instead of teaching willpower, we expect kids to develop it on their own. Colleges and others have to sniff around guessing about who has developed this skill—generally, it's the students who have managed to accomplish something in high school, not just go along to get along. In other words, the ones who haven't merely followed instructions.

62. Pull Those Nails: The Early Creation of Worker Compliance

Years ago, I sat in on a fifth-grade class ostensibly working on a math project.

Mary Everest Boole was a mathematician in the 1800s, the wife of the inventor of Boolean logic. One of her legacies was string art, a craft designed to teach math to students. The project took the nub of Mary's idea and industrialized it into a make-work craft project.

My job was to bring the hammers, twenty-four of them, which I had bought for cheap at the local hardware store. The students were using little brass nails to create patterns on inexpensive pine boards—and then they were going to use string to interlace modulo-nine patterns on the nails, creating (ostensibly) both learning and art.

At the start of the class, the teacher gave the students instructions, including the stern advice that they needed to be sure that the nails went in quite firmly.

For the next half hour, I sat and listened to twenty-four students loudly driving nails. I'm not sure if more nails led to more learning, but it was certainly noisy. (One thousand nails, thirty strikes per nail—you get the idea.)

Then the teacher interrupted the class and called a student (ten years old) to the front of the room. "I said," she intoned, raising her voice, "that all the nails had to be put in *firmly*." She made him wiggle a few nails. They were loose.

I will never forget what happened next. She didn't ask him to hammer the nails in a little tighter.

No.

She stood there, and with the entire class watching and with the little kid near tears, took each and every loose nail out of the board. A half an hour of solid (and loud) hammering, for nothing. She intentionally humiliated him, for one clear reason. The message was obvious: I am in charge, and my instructions matter. You will conform and you will meet the quality standards or you will be punished.

If there's a better way to steal the desire to dream, I'm not sure what it is.

63. Is It Too Risky to Do the Right Thing?

Do parents mean well?

It's about at this point in the discussion that parents get a bit squeamish. We all want the best for children—and many parents are willing to go to extraordinary lengths to get the best. We will hire tutors, track down better schools, fret over report cards, go to parent-teacher conferences, and drive ourselves crazy worrying about homework or the kind of felt used to complete a school project.

But the sanctity of performance/testing/compliance-based schooling is rarely discussed and virtually never challenged.

It's crazy to imagine a suburban school district having serious talks about abandoning state standards, rejecting the SAT, or challenging the admissions criteria at famous colleges (more about famous in a minute).

There's a myth at work here, one that cannot and will not be seriously questioned. The myth says:

Great performance in school leads to happiness and success.

And the corollary:

Great parents have kids who produce great performance in school.

It doesn't matter that neither of these is true. What matters is that finding a path that might be better is just too risky for someone who has only one chance to raise his kids properly.

64. Connecting the Dots Vs. Collecting the Dots

The industrial model of school is organized around exposing students to ever-increasing amounts of stuff and then testing them on it.

Collecting dots.

Almost none of it is spent in teaching them the skills necessary to *connect* dots.

The magic of connecting dots is that once you learn the techniques, the dots can change but you'll still be good at connecting them.

65. The Smartest Person in the Room

David Weinberger writes,

> As knowledge becomes networked, the smartest person in the room isn't the person standing at the front lecturing us, and isn't the collective wisdom of those in the room. The smartest person in the room is the room itself: the network that joins the people and ideas in the room, and connects to those outside of it. It's not that the network is becoming a conscious super-brain. Rather, knowledge is becoming inextricable from—literally unthinkable without—the network that enables it. Our task is to learn how to build smart rooms—that is, how to build networks that make us smarter, especially since, when done badly, networks can make us distressingly stupider.

This is revolutionary, of course. The notion that each of us can assemble a network (of people, of data sources, of experiences) that will make us either smart or stupid—that's brand new and important.

What is the typical school doing to teach our students to become good at this?

66. Avoiding Commitment

A by-product of industrialization is depersonalization. Because no one is responsible for anything that we can see, because deniability is built into the process, it's easy and tempting to emotionally check out, to go along to get along.

When the factory owner treats you like you're easily replaceable, a natural response is to act the part.

It's no surprise to read quotes like this (from *Wired*):

"This is something to commit to," he says. He takes a break and gives me the tour, pointing out different people in the community, tells me who they are and what they do for Occupy Boston. The community gives them something to care about, he explains. "That's what a lot of this is. We're rediscovering our self respect."

At school, we have created a vacuum of self-respect, a desert with nothing other than grades or a sports team to believe in or commit to. The only way for a student to get respect inside the system of school is to earn temporary approval from a teacher he won't likely see again any time soon. If that teacher is mercurial, petty, or inconsistent, the student is told to deal with it.

The notion that humans want to commit to something is ancient and profound. And yet we work overtime to keep students from doing just that.

67. The Specter of the Cult of Ignorance

Here's a note I got after a recent blog post used the word *bespoke*, a much better fit than the word *custom* would have been:

> *Bespoke? A word used only for sending people to the dictionary to discover how literate you are—a word they'll use only for the same purpose. Right?*

> Andrew

Really?

My blog is hardly filled with words most educated citizens would have trouble understanding. And yet a cable TV–inoculated audience wants everything dumbed down to the Kardashian level. This relentless push for less (less intelligence, less culture, less effort) is one of the boogeymen facing anyone who would mess with the rote rigor of mass schooling.

"If we spend more time training inquisitive humans, we'll have to give up on the basics, and that will mean nothing but uneducated dolts who don't even know who Torquemada was."

Not to mention all those missing apostrophes.

I'm worried too. But one thing is clear: the uneducated *already* don't know who Torquemada was. The uneducated have already dumbed everything down to sound bites and YouTube clips. The industrial school had several generations and billions of dollars to drill and practice us into game-show champions, and it has failed, miserably.

Cultural literacy is essential. A common store of knowledge is the only way to create community, to build and integrate a tribe of people interested in living together in harmony. But that store of knowledge will never be infinite, and what's more important, we cannot drill and practice it into a population that has so many fascinating or easy diversions available as alternatives.

I'm concerned about fact ignorance and history ignorance and vocabulary ignorance.

I'm petrified, though, about attitude ignorance.

If we teach our students to be passionate, ethical, and inquisitive, I'm confident that the facts will follow. Instead of complaining that I'm using a seven-letter word when a six-letter one might be sufficient, the inquisitive reader thanks me for adding a new, better word to his lexicon. No need to memorize that word—it's now, and forever, a mouse click away.

68. The Bing Detour

Here's a simple example of the difference between pushing kids to memorize a technique and selling them on a process and an attitude:

The Bing search engine is owned by Microsoft—it's their alternative to Google. In order to increase usage, they've built it into the home page that shows up in Microsoft Explorer, the Web browser built into Windows, the operating system installed on most PCs.

It turns out that one of the most popular items searched for on Bing throughout 2011 was the word "Google."

Users type "Google" into Bing to get to Google so they can do a search (the very search they could have done in Bing, of course).

And then, when they get to Google, one of the most popular terms? Facebook.

They're typing "Facebook" into Google to get to the social networking site, because they don't know how to use the address bar at the top of the browser to type www.facebook.com, and they don't know how to bookmark their favorite sites.

Clueless user: Bing ❯ "Google" ❯ Google ❯ "Facebook" ❯ Facebook

Motivated user: hit bookmark

Should you memorize this tip? Of course not. What's missing is that millions of Americans, people possessing computers that would have cost a million dollars just ten years ago, are operating out of habit and fear and treating the computer like a magic box. They're afraid to wonder if they can replace Bing with Google. Afraid to ask how to get rid of Internet Explorer and install Firefox. Too lazy to ask their colleagues if there's a better way. They don't look for tips or ways to break or open or fix or improve. They self-describe as Dummies and give up, not for lack of genetic smarts, but for lack of initiative and because of an abundance of fear.

They weren't sold on a forward-leaning posture when it comes to technology, so they make no effort, acting out of fear instead of passion. For the rest of their lives.

That forward-leaning posture is teachable.

69. But What About the Dumb Parade?

I know the feeling. You see the young mom feeding her infant a can of Sprite from a baby bottle. The blog reader who thinks *bespoke* is too difficult a word (and not worth looking up). The financially afraid who get tricked into losing their houses because they don't understand simple arithmetic . . .

What about them?

How can we possibly argue about forcing students to memorize fewer facts when the world doesn't even know who's buried in Grant's tomb, doesn't know the difference between *write* and *right*, and can't balance a checkbook. What about them?

For a really long time, I thought more drilling, more schooling, and more homework was the only way. That schools lacked rigor and were failing students by not pumping them with enough data.

Then I realized that all of the people in this parade have already been through school. They've received the best their community could afford, but it didn't work because our effort was based on the wrong strategy.

The bad decisions we see every day aren't the result of lack of data, or lack of access to data.

No, they're the result of a schooling culture that is creating exactly what it set out to create.

Along the way, we teach students to be open to and trusting of marketing messages. Not only is the school day primarily about students accepting the messages marketed to them by the authority figures in the school, but the fashions, gadgets, and trends of teen culture (all delivered by marketers) are the glue that holds the place together. We mix obedience with marketing culture, why are we surprised at what we get?

School is successful . . . at the wrong thing.

70. Grammr and the Decline of Our Civilization

I need to come back to this again, because deep down, the educated people reading this aren't sure yet. The argument for rote, for primers, for drill and practice, and for grammar is made vivid within ten seconds of checking out YouTube. Here's a sample comment:

NOW UV STARTED READIN DIS DUNT STOP THIS IS SO SCARY. SEND THIS OVER TO 5 VIDEOS IN 143 MINUTES WHEN UR DONE PRESS F6 AND UR CRUSHES NAME WILL APPEAR ON THE SCREEN IN BIG LETTERS. THIS IS SO SCARY? BECAUSE IT ACTUALLY WORKs

We're all going down the drain. Too much profanity, no verb conjugation, incomplete thoughts, and poor analysis, everywhere you look, even among people running for president.

I don't think the problem is lack of access to role models, or to Strunk & White, or to strict teachers.

I think the problem is that kids don't care. Because they don't have to. And if someone doesn't care, all the drilling isn't going to change a thing.

The way we save the written word, intellectual discourse, and reason is by training kids to care.

Only 3% of Americans can locate Greece on a map. (That's not true, but if it were, you wouldn't be surprised, because we're idiots about stuff like that.)

The question is: Will spending more time drilling kids on the map of the world solve this problem? Is our apathy about world affairs a function of a lack of exposure to the map in school?

Of course not.

No, the problem isn't that we haven't spent enough hours memorizing the map. The problem is that we don't want to.

Teachers aren't given the time or the resources or, most important, the expectation that they should sell students on *why*.

A kid who is into dinosaurs has no trouble discussing the allosaurus/brontosaurus controversy. A student interested in fixing up his dad's old car will have no trouble understanding the mechanics of the carburetor. And the young Hillary Clintons among us, those who are fascinated by the world, understand quite clearly where Greece is.

If you're running an institution based on compliance and obedience, you don't reach for motivation as a tool. It feels soft, even liberal, to imagine that you have to sell people on making the effort to learn what's on the agenda.

I'm not sure it matters how it feels to the teacher. What matters is that motivation is the only way to generate real learning, actual creativity, and the bias for action that is necessary for success.

OPEN BOOK, OPEN NOTE

Futurist Michio Kaku points out that soon, it will be easy for every student and worker to have contact lenses hooked up to the Internet.

One use will be that whatever you're reading can be instantly searched online, and any questions that can be answered this way, will be answered this way. Already, there are simple plug-ins that allow you to search any word or phrase in the document you're currently reading online.

Forget about futurists and contact lenses. This is something we can do right now, on any text on any screen on just about any computer.

What's the point of testing someone's ability to cram for a test if we're never going to have to cram for anything ever again? If I can find the answer in three seconds online, the skill of memorizing a fact for twelve hours (and then forgetting it) is not only useless, it's insane.

In an open-book/open-note environment, the ability to synthesize complex ideas and to invent new concepts is far more useful than drill and practice. It might be harder (at first) to write tests, and it might be harder to grade them, but the goal of school isn't to make the educational-industrial complex easy to run; it's to create a better generation of workers and citizens.

71. Lectures at Night, Homework During the Day

Sal Khan, founder of the Khan Academy, has a very different vision of how school can work. He's already raised millions of dollars from Bill Gates and others, and his site currently offers more than 2,600 video lectures that (for free) teach everything from Calculus to World History. To date, the lectures have been delivered almost a hundred million times.

None of the videos are as good as they will be in two years, just as Wikipedia, Google, and Amazon started as mere shadows of their current selves. But as each video is replaced by a better one, as others start competing to increase the quality, here's what will happen:

There will be a free, universal library of courses in the cloud online, accessible to anyone with an Internet connection. Every lecture, constantly improved, on every conceivable topic. This means that students will be able to find precisely the lecture they need, and to watch it at their own speed, reviewing it at will.

The next day at school, teachers can do what they want to do anyway—coach and help students in places they are stuck. In a school like this, the notion that every student will have to be in sync and watch the same (live!) lecture at the same time will become absurd. And for good reason.

The most visible symptom of the death of traditional schooling is going to be the rise of online video lectures. Not just online, but specific. Specific to a topic, to a problem, to a student's status. With the long tail of the Internet at our disposal, why settle for a generic lecture, the local lecture, the lecture that everyone else needs to see?

And most important, why settle for an amateur lecture, not very good, given by a teacher with a lot of other priorities? It's a bit like requiring teachers to write their own textbooks.

72. Beyond the Khan Academy

Check out Udacity.com, co-founded by Sebastian Thrun, who until recently, was a tenured professor at Stanford. His goal is to teach courses that have 200,000 simultaneous students. And why not?

He reports that in the last class he taught at Stanford, every single person in the class who got a perfect grade wasn't in the classroom at all—all the A students were remote, some as remote as Afghanistan. Many of the students would watch a lecture twenty or more times because they were so focused on learning what he had to teach.

I've shared one example after another of what happens when we combine motivated students with specific and refined educational assets delivered digitally. It's easy to see how it works for computer programmers and math students, for those that want to learn a craft or understand a novel (not for a grade, but because they actually care).

And yet, like all things associated with the ever-increasing yield of the networked economy, the examples are discounted. "Yes," people said after Amazon sold a few books, "it works for specialty books, but it will never work for novels." And then, after novels started selling a third or more of their copies online, the skeptics said it would never work for DVDs or MP3s or chocolate bars. But it did.

Just as online shopping scaled, an inexorable rise due to the efficiencies of the connections created by the 'Net, so will the digital delivery of information permeate every nook and cranny of what we learn.

What we can't do, though, is digitize passion. We can't force the student to want to poke around and discover new insights online. We can't merely say, "here," and presume the students will do the hard (and scary) work of getting over the hump and conquering their fears.

Without school to establish the foundation and push and pull our students, the biggest digital library in the world is useless.

73. Here Comes Slader

Slader is a new website that further clarifies the future teaching process. Slader hired dozens of nerds, and together they solved every homework problem in hundreds of editions of dozens of math textbooks.

Want to see the answer to any math homework problem? It's free.

Want to see it worked out? That'll cost a few pennies.

It's CliffsNotes for math (and soon, they'll be doing English assignments as well).

This, it seems to me, is a ridiculous subterfuge when the efficient answer is obvious (though difficult to reach). Instead of playing cat and mouse with textbook publishers (who will quickly renumber the assignments and change numbers here and there in order to break Slader), why not interact directly with the teachers?

Find the best homework questions ever devised and create world-class tutorials in how to solve each one.

Go one step further and generate useful reports about which assignments were answered easily and which ones frustrated each student. Connect the data with people (human tutors and teachers and parents) who can actually pay attention when attention is needed.

When teachers nationwide coordinate their homework, we don't waste the time and energy of thousands of people. When students can get patient, hands-on, step-by-step help in the work they're doing, they learn more.

All of this was impossible five years ago. Now it's obvious.

74. The Role of the Teacher's Union in the Post-Industrial School

It's not surprising that early on, many teachers found support in unions. The industrial nature of schooling set up an adversarial system. Management (the board, the administration, and, yes, the parents) wanted more productivity, more measurability, and more compliance, not just from students but from teachers as well. Spend less money, get more results—that's the mantra of all industries in search of productivity.

In the post-industrial model, though, the lectures are handled by best-in-class videos delivered online. Anything that can be digitized, will be digitized, and isolated on the long tail and delivered with focus. What's needed from the teacher is no longer high-throughput lectures or test scoring or classroom management. No, what's needed is individual craftsmanship, emotional labor, and the ability to motivate.

In that world, the defend-all-teachers mindset doesn't fly. When there is no demand for the mediocre lecture reader, the erstwhile deliverer of the state's class notes, then school looks completely different, doesn't it?

Consider the suburban high school with two biology teachers. One teacher has an extraordinary reputation and there is always a waiting list for his class. The other teacher always has merely the leftovers, the ones who weren't lucky enough to find their way into the great class.

When we free access to information from the classroom setting, the leverage of the great teacher goes way up. Now we can put the mediocre teacher to work as a classroom monitor, shuffler of paper, and traffic cop, and give the great teacher the tools he needs to teach more students (at least until we've persuaded the lesser teacher to retire).

The role of the teacher in this new setting is to inspire, to intervene, and to raise up the motivated but stuck student. Instead of punishing great teachers with precise instructions on how to spend their day, we give them the freedom to actually teach. No longer on the hook to give repeat performances of three or four lectures a day, this star teacher can do the handwork that we need all star teachers to do—the real work of teaching.

When the union becomes a standards-raising guild of the very best teachers, it reaches a new level of influence. It can lead the discussion instead of slowing it down.

75. Hoping for a Quality Revolution at the Teacher's Union

The Harlem Village Academy, like most charter schools, has no teacher's union. No tenure, no contract-based job security.

The thing is, the teachers here are more engaged and have more job satisfaction across the board than just about any school I've ever visited.

And the reason is obvious: they are respected professionals working with respected professionals. There's no one holding them back, and they work in a place where their bosses measure things that matter.

I've spent hours talking with school administrators, and when the union comes up, they invariably sadden and shake their heads. So many great teachers, they say, held back by a system that rewards the lousy ones. The union is held hostage by teachers in search of a sinecure instead of driven forward by those that want to make more of an impact.

And the message of the Harlem Village Academy becomes crystal clear when held up against the traditional expectation that the union will protect the bureaucracy wherever it can. What happens when the great teachers start showing up at union meetings? What happens when the top 80% of the workforce (the ones who truly care and are able and willing and eager to get better at what they do) insist that the union cut loose the 20% that are slowing them down, bringing them down, and averaging them down?

In a post-industrial school, there is no us and them. Just us.

76. Emotional Labor in the Work of Teachers

Lewis Hyde's essential book *The Gift* makes a distinction between work and labor.

> Work is an intended activity that is accomplished through the will. A labor can be intended but only to the extent of doing the groundwork, or of not doing things that would clearly prevent the labor. Beyond that, labor has its own schedule. Things get done, but we often have the odd sense that we didn't do them.

> Paul Goodman wrote in a journal once, "I have recently written a few good poems. But I have no feeling that I wrote them." That is the declaration of a laborer . . .

> . . . One of the first problems the modern world faced with the rise of industrialism was the exclusion of labor by the expansion of work.

Labor, particularly emotional labor, is the difficult task of digging deep to engage at a personal level. Emotional labor looks like patience and kindness and respect. It's very different from mechanical work, from filling out a form or moving a bale of hay.

Every great teacher you have ever had the good luck of learning from is doing the irreplaceable labor of real teaching. They are communicating emotion, engaging, and learning from the student in return. Emotional labor is difficult and exhausting, and it cannot be tweaked or commanded by management.

As our society industrialized, it has relentlessly worked to drive labor away and replace it with work. Mere work. Busywork and repetitive work and the work of Taylor's scientific management. Stand just here. Say just that. Check this box.

I'm arguing that the connection revolution sets the table for a return of emotional labor. For the first time in a century, we have the opportunity to let digital systems do work while our teachers do labor.

But that can only happen if we let teachers be teachers again.

77. Making the Cut, the Early Creation of the Bias for Selection (Early Picks Turn into Market Leaders)

The fun things that matter in school have no shortage of applicants. School government, the class play, and, most of all, school sports are all about tryouts and elections.

Those who run these organizations are pretty sure they're sending the right message—life is a meritocracy, and when a lot of people try out for a few slots, we should pick the best ones. After all, that's how the world works.

So if you want to have a speaking part in the play, try out (even if you're eleven years old). If you want to get any time on the field, better play well (even though it's time on the field that may lead to your actually playing well). If you want to find out if you can contribute to budget discussions in the school government, better be preternaturally charismatic so that you can get elected (even though this creates a cycle of shallowness that we all suffer under).

The freshman soccer team at the local public school has a fairly typical coach. He believes that his job is to win soccer games.

Of course, this isn't his job, because there isn't a shortage of trophies, there isn't a shortage of winners. There's a shortage of good sportsmanship, teamwork, skill development, and persistence, right?

There are sixteen kids on the squad. Eleven get to play; the others watch. One popular strategy is to play your top eleven at all times, and perhaps, just maybe, if you're ahead by five or more goals, sub in a few of the second-string players. (Actually, this isn't just a popular strategy—it's essentially the way nearly every high school coach in the nation thinks.)

The lesson to the kids is obvious: early advantages now lead to bigger advantages later. Skill now is rewarded; dreams, not so much. If you're not already great, don't bother showing up.

If the goal of the team was to win, that would make sense. But perhaps the goal is to teach kids about effort and opportunity and teamwork. Isn't it interesting that the movies we love about sports always feature the dark horse who dreams, the underdog who comes off the bench and saves the day?

What would happen to school sports if the compensation of coaches was 100% based on the development of all the players and none of it was related to winning the game at all costs?

Malcolm Gladwell has famously written about the distribution of birthdays in professional sports, particularly hockey. It turns out that a huge percentage of hockey players are born in just three months of the year. (About *twice* as many NHL players are born in March as in December.)

The reason is simple: these are the oldest kids in youth hockey in Canada, the ones who barely made the birthday cutoff. Every year, the peewee leagues accept new applications, but those applicants have to have been born by a certain date.

As a result, the kids born just after the deadline play in a younger league. They're the biggest and the strongest when they're seven or eight or nine years old. What a terrific advantage—to be nine months older and five pounds heavier and two or three inches taller than the youngest kids. The older kids (remember, they are still eight years old) get picked for the all-star squad because they're *currently* the best.

Once picked, they get more ice time. They get more coaching. Most of all, they get a dream. After all, they're the ones getting applauded and practiced.

The rest of the kids, not so much. Dreams extinguished, they realize they have no right to play, so they settle for a job, not their passion.

The hockey parable extends to so many of the other things we expose kids to as they're seeking for something to dream about. Be good now, and you'll get even better later.

78. First Impressions Matter (Too Much)

"Maybe your son should do something else. He's not really getting this."

That's what Brendan Hansen's coach said to his mom. When he was four. In the pool for his third day of swim lessons.

You can already guess the punch line. Brendan has won four Olympic medals in swimming.

The industrialized system of schooling doesn't have a lot of time to jump-start those who start a bit behind, doesn't go out of its way to nurture the slow starter. It's easier to bring everyone up to a lowered average instead.

In Hansen's estimation, it's easy for natural gifts to escape the notice of people who aren't focused on finding them and amplifying them.

79. Why Not Hack?

Much of this manifesto echoes the attitude of the hacker. Not the criminals who crack open computer systems, but hackers—passionate experimenters eager to discover something new and willing to roll up their sleeves to figure things out.

Check out this sixteen-year-old student from Georgia: http://boingboing.net/2012/02/04/16-y-o-girl-accepted-to-mit.html

After getting admitted to MIT at the age of sixteen, she did what any hacker would do—she turned her admissions letter into a space probe, wired a video camera into it, and sent it more than 91,000 feet in the air. And made a movie out of it.

Someone taught Erin King how to think this way. Who's next? Isn't that our most important job: to raise a generation of math hackers, literature hackers, music hackers, and life hackers?

80. American Anti-Intellectualism

Getting called an egghead is no prize. My bully can beat up your nerd. Real men don't read literature.

We live in a culture where a politician who says "it's simple" will almost always defeat one who says "it's complicated," even if it is. It's a place where middle school football coaches have their players do push-ups until they faint, but math teachers are scolded for giving too much homework.

Ben Franklin and Thomas Jefferson were legendary intellectuals. Bill Gates and Michael Dell are nerds. But still, the prevailing winds of pop culture reward the follower, the jock, and the get-along guy almost every time.

Which is fine when your nation's economy depends on obeisance to the foreman, on heavy lifting, and on sucking it up for the long haul.

Now, though, our future lies with the artist and the dreamer and, yes, the person who took the time and energy to be passionate about math.

81. Leadership and Followership

John Cook coined the phrase "leadership and followership" when he described a high school student practicing his music conducting skills by conducting the orchestra he heard on a CD. When you are practicing your leadership in this way, you're not leading at all. You're following the musicians on the CD—they don't even know you exist.

This faux leadership is what we see again and again in traditional schools. Instead of exposing students to the pain and learning that come from actually leading a few people (and living with the consequences), we create content-free simulations of leadership, ultimately reminding kids that their role should be to follow along, while merely pretending to lead.

Leadership isn't something that people hand to you. You don't do followership for years and then someone anoints you and says, "here." In fact, it's a gradual process, one where you take responsibility years before you are given authority.

And that's something we can teach.

82. "Someone Before Me Wrecked Them"

It doesn't take very much time in the teacher's lounge before you hear the whining of the teacher with the imperfect students. They came to him damaged, apparently, lacking in interest, excitement, or smarts.

Perhaps it was the uncaring parent who doesn't speak in full sentences or serve a good breakfast. The one with an accent. Or the teacher from the year before or the year before that who didn't adequately prepare the student with the basics she needs now.

And the boss feels the same way about those employees who came in with inadequate training. We sell teaching and coaching short when we insist that the person in front of us doesn't have the talent or the background or the genes to excel.

In a crowded market, it's no surprise that people will choose someone who appears to offer more in return for our time and money. So admissions officers look for the talented, as do the people who do the hiring for corporations. Spotting the elite, the charismatic, and the obviously gifted might be a smart short-term strategy, but it punishes the rest of us, and society as a whole.

The opportunity for widespread education and skills improvement is far bigger than it has ever been before. When we can deliver lectures and lessons digitally, at scale, for virtually free, the only thing holding us back is the status quo (and our belief in the permanence of status).

School serves a real function when it activates a passion for lifelong learning, not when it establishes permanent boundaries for an elite class.

83. Some Tips for the Frustrated Student

1. Grades are an illusion
2. Your passion and insight are reality

3. Your work is worth more than mere congruence to an answer key

4. Persistence in the face of a skeptical authority figure is a powerful ability

5. Fitting in is a short-term strategy, standing out pays off in the long run

6. If you care enough about the work to be criticized, you've learned enough for today

84. The Two Pillars of a Future-Proof Education

Teach kids how to lead
Help them learn how to solve interesting problems

Leadership is the most important trait for players in the connected revolution. Leadership involves initiative, and in the connected world, nothing happens until you step up and begin, until you start driving without a clear map.

And as the world changes ever faster, we don't reward people who can slavishly follow yesterday's instructions. All of the value to the individual (and to the society she belongs to) goes to the individual who can draw a new map, who can solve a problem that didn't even exist yesterday.

Hence the question I ask every teacher who reads from her notes, every teacher who demands rote memorization, and every teacher who comes at schooling from a posture of power: are you delivering these two precious gifts to our children? Will the next generation know more facts than we do, or will it be equipped to connect with data, and turn that data into information and leadership and progress?

85. Which Comes First, Passion or Competence?

One theory is that if you force someone to learn math or writing or soccer, there's a chance she will become passionate about it and then run with what she knows.

The other theory is that once someone becomes passionate about a goal, she will stop at nothing to learn what she needs to learn to accomplish it.

The question, then, is: Should we be teaching and encouraging and demanding passion (and then letting competence follow)? In other words, if we dream big enough, won't the rest take care of itself?

I think that part of effective schooling is helping students calibrate their dreams. Big enough doesn't mean too big—so big that your dream is a place to hide.

The student who dreams of playing in the NBA, starring in a television show, or winning the lottery is doing precisely the wrong sort of dreaming. These are dreams that have no stepwise progress associated with them, no reasonable path to impact, no unfair advantage to the extraordinarily well prepared.

School is at its best when it gives students the expectation that they will not only dream big, but dream dreams that they can work on every day until they accomplish them—not because they were chosen by a black-box process but because they worked hard enough to reach them.

86. "Lacks Determination and Interest"

Here's an interesting question: When a good student gets a comment like that on a report card from a teacher in just one of his classes, who is at fault?

Does it matter if the student is six or sixteen?

If the teacher of the future has a job to do, isn't addressing this problem part of it? Perhaps it's *all* of it . . .

87. Hiding?

It's human nature to avoid responsibility, to avoid putting ourselves in the path of blame so we can be singled out by the head of the village for punishment. And why not? That's risky behavior, and it's been bred out of us over millions of generations.

The challenge is that the connected economy demands people who won't hide, and it punishes everyone else. Standing out and standing for something are the attributes of a leader, and initiative is now the only posture that generates results.

We're clever, though, and our amygdala and primitive lizard brain see a way to use big dreams to *avoid* responsibility. If the dream is huge, we get applause from our peers and our teachers but are able to hide out because, of course, the dream is never going to come true, the auditions won't pan out, the cameras won't roll, the ball won't be passed, and we'll never be put on the spot.

School needs to put us on the spot. Again and again and again it needs to reward students for being willing to be singled out. Learning to survive those moments, and then feel compelled to experience them again—this is the only way to challenge the lizard.

The lights go out and it's just the three of us
You me and all that stuff we're so scared of

—Bruce Springsteen

88. Obedience + Competence ≠ Passion

The formula doesn't work. It never has. And yet we act as if it does.

We act as if there are only two steps to school:

Get kids to behave

Fill them with facts and technique

Apparently, if you take enough of each, enough behavior and enough technique, then suddenly, as if springing from verdant soil, passion arrives.

I'm not seeing it.

I think that passion often arrives from success. Do something well, get feedback on it, and perhaps you'd like to do it again. Solve an interesting problem and you might get hooked.

But if it takes ten years for you to do math well, that's too long to wait for passion.

89. A Shortage of Engineers

We can agree that our culture and our economy would benefit from more builders, more people passionate about science and technology. So, how do we make more of them?

We need more brave artists, too, and some poets. We need leaders and people passionate enough about their cause to speak up and go through discomfort to accomplish something. Can these skills be taught or amplified?

90. Reading and Writing

In the connected age, reading and writing remain the two skills that are most likely to pay off with exponential results.

Reading leads to more reading. Writing leads to better writing. Better writing leads to a bigger audience and more value creation. And the process repeats.

Typical industrial schooling kills reading. Among Americans, the typical high school graduate reads no more than one book a year for fun, and a huge portion of the population reads zero. No books! For the rest of their lives, for 80 years, bookless.

When we associate reading with homework and tests, is it any wonder we avoid it?

But reading is the way we open doors. If our economy and our culture grows based on the exchange of ideas and on the interactions of the informed, it fails when we stop reading.

At the Harlem Village Academy, every student (we're talking fifth graders and up) reads *fifty books a year*. If you want to teach kids to love being smart, you must teach them to love to read.

If the non-advantaged kids in Harlem can read fifty books a year, why can't your kids? Why can't you?

If every school board meeting and every conversation with a principal started with that simple question, imagine the progress we'd make as a culture. What would our world be like if we read a book a week, every week?

Writing is the second half of the equation. Writing is organized, permanent talking, it is the brave way to express an idea. Talk comes with evasion and deniability and vagueness. Writing, though, leaves no room to wriggle. The effective writer in the connected revolution can see her ideas spread to a hundred or a million people. Writing (whether in public, now that everyone has a platform, or in private, within organizations) is the tool we use to spread ideas. Writing activates the most sophisticated part of our brains and forces us to organize our thoughts.

Teach a kid to write without fear and you have given her a powerful tool for the rest of her life. Teach a kid to write boring book reports and standard drivel and you've taken something precious away from a student who deserves better.

91. The Desire to Figure Things Out

Consider the case of Katherine Bomkamp, a twenty-year-old who will never struggle to find a job, never struggle to make an impact.

She's not a genius, nor is she gifted with celebrity looks or a prodigy's piano skills. What she has is the desire to make things, to figure things out, and to make a difference.

In high school, she spent a fair amount of time with her dad at Walter Reed Army Hospital. Her father is disabled and he had to visit often for his treatment. While sitting in waiting rooms with wounded soldiers, Katherine learned a lot about phantom limb syndrome. Like many idealistic kids, she thought she'd try to help.

What makes this story noteworthy is that Katherine actually did something. She didn't give up and she didn't wait to get picked. Instead, she got to work. Entering her idea in a school science fair, Katherine spent months finding experts who could help make her idea a reality. This is a revolutionary notion—that there are experts just waiting to help. But, as she discovered, there *are* people waiting to help, waiting for someone interested in causing change to reach out to them. Some are there in person, while others are online. The facts are there, the vendors are there, the case studies are there, just waiting to be found.

It was the science fair and the support of those around her that gave her an opening to do something outside of the path that's so clearly marked. Katherine did what so many kids are capable of doing but aren't expected to do.

A few years later, the Pain Free Socket is about to be patented and may very well become a life-changing device for thousands of amputees. Katherine's life is already changed, though. She called the bluff of the system and didn't wait. What she learned in high school is something that precious few of her peers learn: how to figure things out and make them happen.

92. Because or Despite?

That's the key question in the story of Katherine Bomkamp and so many other kids who end up making a difference.

Did they reach their level of accomplishment and contribution *because* of what they are taught in school, or *despite* it?

That question ought to be asked daily, in every classroom and at every school board meeting. The answer is almost always *both*, but I wonder what happens to us if we amplify that positive side of that equation.

93. Schools as Engines of Competence or Maintainers of Class?

Or possibly both.

Public schools were the great leveler, the tool that would enable class to be left behind as a meritocracy took hold.

At schools for "higher"-class kids, though, at fancy boarding schools or rich suburban schools or at Yale, there's less time spent on competence and more time spent dreaming. Kids come to school with both more competence (better reading and speech skills) and bigger dreams (because those dreams are inculcated at home). As a result, the segregation of school by class reinforces the cycle, dooming the lower classes to an endless game of competence catch-up, one that even if it's won won't lead to much because the economy spends little time seeking out the competent.

Give a kid a chance to dream, though, and the open access to resources will help her find exactly what she needs to know to go far beyond competence.

94. College as a Ranking Mechanism, a Tool for Slotting People into Limited Pigeonholes

The scarcity model of the industrial age teaches us that there are only a finite number of "good" jobs. Big companies have limited payrolls, of course, so there's only one plant manager. Big universities have just one head of the English department. Big law firms have just one managing partner, and even the Supreme Court has only nine seats.

As we've seen, the ranking starts early, and if you (the thinking goes) don't get into a good (oh, I mean famous) college, you're doomed.

This is one of the reasons that college has become an expensive extension of high school. The goal is to get in (and possibly get out), but what happens while you're there doesn't matter much if the goal is merely to claim your slot.

When higher education was reserved for elite academics, there was a lot of learning for learning's sake, deep dives into esoteric thought that occasionally led to breakthroughs. Once industrialized, though, college became yet another holding tank, though without the behavior boundaries we work so hard to enforce in high school.

In the post-industrial age of connection, though, the slotting and the scarcity are far less important. We care a great deal about what you've done, less about the one-word alumnus label you bought. Because we can see whom you know and what they think of you, because we can see how you've used the leverage the Internet has given you, because we can see if you actually are able to lead and actually are able to solve interesting problems—because of all these things, college means something new now.

95. The Coming Meltdown in Higher Education (as Seen by a Marketer)

For four hundred years, higher education in the U.S. has been on a roll. From Harvard asking Galileo to be a guest professor in the 1600s to millions tuning in to watch a team of unpaid athletes play another team of unpaid athletes in some college sporting event, the amount of time and money and prestige in the college world has been climbing.

I'm afraid that's about to crash and burn. Here's how I'm looking at it.

1. *Most colleges are organized to give an average education to average students.*

Pick up any college brochure or catalog. Delete the brand names and the map. Can you tell which school it is? While there are outliers (like St. John's, Deep Springs), most schools aren't really outliers. They are mass marketers.

Stop for a second and consider the impact of that choice. By emphasizing mass and sameness and rankings, colleges have changed their mission.

This works great in an industrial economy where we can't churn out standardized students fast enough and where the demand is huge because the premium earned by a college grad dwarfs the cost. But . . .

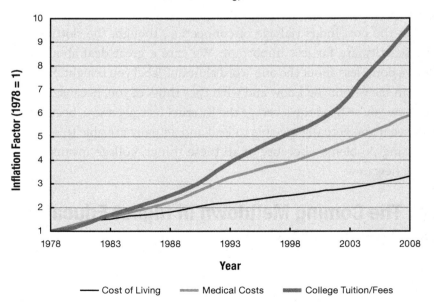

Inflation of Tuition and Fees (Private Four-Year Colleges), Medical Costs, and Cost of Living, 1978–2008

2. *College has gotten expensive far faster than wages have gone up.*

As a result, there are millions of people in very serious debt, debt so big it might take decades to repay. Word gets around. Won't get fooled again . . .

This leads to a crop of potential college students who can (and will) no longer just blindly go to the "best" school they get into.

3. *The definition of "best" is under siege.*

Why do colleges send millions (!) of undifferentiated pieces of junk mail to high-school students now? We will waive the admission fee! We have a one-page application! Apply! This is some of the most amateur and bland direct mail I've ever seen. Why do it?

Biggest reason: so the schools can reject more applicants. The more applicants they reject, the higher they rank in *U.S. News* and other rankings. And thus the rush to game the rankings continues, which is a sign that the marketers in question (the colleges) are getting desperate for more than their fair share. Why bother making your education more useful if you can more easily make it **appear** to be more useful?

4. *The correlation between a typical college degree and success is suspect.*

College wasn't originally designed to be merely a continuation of high school (but with more binge drinking). In many places, though, that's what it has become. The data I'm seeing shows that a degree (from one of those famous schools, with or without a football team) doesn't translate into significantly better career opportunities, a better job, or more happiness than does a degree from a cheaper institution.

5. *Accreditation isn't the solution, it's the problem.*

A lot of these ills are the result of uniform accreditation programs that have pushed high-cost, low-reward policies on institutions and rewarded schools that churn out young wannabe professors, instead of experiences that help shape leaders and problem solvers.

Just as we're watching the disintegration of old-school marketers with mass-market products, I think we're about to see significant cracks in old-school schools with mass-market degrees.

Back before the digital revolution, access to information was an issue. The size of the library mattered. One reason to go to college was to get access. Today, that access is worth a lot less. The valuable things people take away from college are interactions with great minds (usually professors who actually teach and actually care) and non-class activities that shape them as people. The question I'd ask: Is the money that mass-marketing colleges are spending on marketing themselves and scaling themselves well spent? Are they organizing for changing lives or for ranking high? Does NYU have to get so much bigger? Why?

The solutions are obvious. There are tons of ways to get a cheap, liberal education, one that exposes you to the world, permits you to have significant interactions with people who matter and to learn to make a difference (start here). Most of these ways, though, aren't heavily marketed, nor do they involve going to a tradition-steeped, two-hundred-year-old institution with a wrestling team. Things like gap years, research internships, and entrepreneurial or social ventures after high school are opening doors for students who are eager to discover the new.

The only people who haven't gotten the memo are anxious helicopter parents, mass-marketing colleges, and traditional employers. And all three are waking up and facing new circumstances.

96. Big Companies No Longer Create Jobs

Apple just built a massive data center in Malden, North Carolina. That sort of plant development would have brought a thousand or five thousand jobs to a town just thirty years ago. The total employment at the data center? Fifty.

Big companies are no longer the engines of job creation. Not the good jobs, anyway.

What the data center does, though, is create the opportunity for a thousand or ten thousand individuals to invent new jobs, new movements, and new technologies as a result of the tools and technology that can be built on top of it.

There is a race to build a plug-and-play infrastructure. Companies like Amazon and Apple and others are laying the groundwork for a generation of job creation—but not exclusively by big companies. They create an environment where people like you can create jobs instead.

Pick yourself.

97. Understanding the Gas Station Question

"How many gas stations are there in the United States?"

Yet another one of those trick questions that William Poundstone writes about. Companies like Google and Microsoft are renowned for using obtuse questions (what's the next number in this sequence: 10, 9, 60, 90, 70, 66 . . .), often to make job seekers feel inadequate and pressured.

That wasn't my goal. Years ago, when doing some hiring, I often asked the gas station question because in a world where you can look up just about anything, I found it fascinating to see what people could do with a question they couldn't possibly look up the answer to (because, in this case anyway, they didn't have a computer to help them).

Those are the only sorts of questions that matter now.

If the training we give people in public school or college is designed to help them memorize something that someone else could look up, it's time wasted. Time that should have been spent teaching students how to be wrong.

How to be usefully wrong.

That's a skill we need along with the dreaming.

PS: After asking this question to more than five hundred people in job interviews, I can report that two people mailed me copies of the appropriate page from the Statistical Abstract (what a waste), and two other people said, "I don't have a car" and walked out of the interview.

98. The Cost of Failure Has Changed

In an industrial setting, failure can be fatal—to the worker or to the bottom line.

If we're building a giant factory, the building can't fall down. If we're hauling 10,000 pounds of ore, we need to move it the right way the first time. If we're changing the legal conditions on a thousand life insurance policies, we can't afford the class action lawsuit if we do it wrong.

Noted.

But if we're trading hypotheses on a new scientific breakthrough, of course we have to be wrong before we can be right. If we're inventing a new business model or writing a new piece of music or experimenting with new ways to increase the yield of an email campaign, of course we have to be willing to be wrong.

If failure is not an option, then neither is success.

The only source of innovation is the artist willing to be usefully wrong. A great use of the connection economy is to put together circles of people who challenge each other to be wronger and wronger still—until we find right.

That's at the heart of the gas station question: discovering if the person you're interviewing is comfortable being wrong, comfortable verbalizing a theory and then testing it, right there and then. Instead of certainty and proof and a guarantee, our future is about doubt and fuzzy logic and testing.

We can (and must) teach these skills, starting with kids who are happy to build towers out of blocks (and watch them fall down) and continuing with the students who would never even consider buying a term paper to avoid an essay in college.

99. What Does "Smart" Mean?

Our economy and our culture have redefined "smart," but parents and schools haven't gotten around to it.

Some measures are:

SAT scores
GPA average
Test results
Ability at Trivial Pursuit

These are easy, competitive ways to measure some level of intellectual capacity.

Are they an indicator of future success or happiness? Are the people who excel at these measures likely to become contributors to society in ways we value?

There's no doubt that Wall Street and the big law firms have a place for Type A drones, well educated, processing reams of data and churning out trades and deals and litigation.

The rest of the straight-A students in our society are finding a less receptive shortcut to prosperity and impact, because smart, this kind of smart, isn't something that we value so much anymore. I can outsource the ability to repetitively do a task with competence.

And what about the non-dreamers with C averages? Those guys are in *real* trouble.

100. Can Anyone Make Music?

Ge Wang, a professor at Stanford and the creator of Smule, thinks so. The problem is that people have to get drunk in order to get over their fear enough to do karaoke.

Ge is dealing with this by making a series of apps for iPhones and other devices that make composing music not merely easy but fearless.

He's seen what happens when you take the pressure off and give people a fun way to create music (not play sheet music, which is a technical skill, but *make* music). "It's like I tasted this great, wonderful food," he says now, "and for some reason I've got this burning desire to say to other people: 'if you tried this dish, I think you might really like it.'"

His take on music is dangerously close to the kind of dreaming I'm talking about. "It feels like we're at a juncture where the future is maybe kind of in the past," he says. "We can go back to a time where making music is really no big deal; it's something everyone can do, and it's fun."

Who taught us that music was a big deal? That it was for a few? That it wasn't fun?

It makes perfect sense that organized school would add rigor and structure and fear to the joy of making music. This is one more symptom of the very same problem: the thought that regimented music performers, in lockstep, ought to be the output of a school's musical education program.

It's essential that the school of the future teach music. The passion of seeing progress, the hard work of practice, the joy and fear of public performance—these are critical skills for our future. It's a mistake to be penny wise and cut music programs, which are capable of delivering so much value. But it's also a mistake to industrialize them.

As we've learned from Ben Zander (author and conductor), real music education involves teaching students how to hear and how to perform from the heart . . . not to conform to a rigorous process that ultimately leads to numbness, not love.

101. Two Kinds of Learning

Quick, what's 8 squared?

My guess is that you know, and the reason you know is that someone drilled you until you did.

The same is true for many of the small bits of knowledge and skill we possess. We didn't learn these things because we believed we needed them right then, and we didn't learn them because they would change our lives; we learned them because it was required.

Here's a second question:

It's third down and four. There are five defensive linemen running straight at you and you have about one second to throw the ball. What now?

There's just no way you learned this in a classroom.

Of course, this sort of learning covers far more than football. You need to give a speech. What should it be about? You have to work your way through an ethical dilemma involving your boss. What should you do?

The instinct of the industrial system is to force the bottom rung to comply. It's the most direct and apparently efficient method to get the work done—exercise power. In fact, it's not efficient at all. Real learning happens when the student wants (insists!) on acquiring a skill in order to accomplish a goal.

We've inadvertently raised generations that know volumes of TV trivia and can play video games and do social networking at a world-class level. The challenge for educators is to capture that passion and direct it to other endeavors, many of which will certainly be more useful and productive.

102. History's Greatest Hits: Unnerving the Traditionalists

In his book *Civilization,* Niall Ferguson complains,

> A survey of first-year history undergraduates at one leading British university revealed that only 34 per cent knew who was the English monarch at the time of the Armada, 31 per cent knew the location of the Boer War and 16 per cent knew who commanded the British forces at Waterloo. In a similar poll of English children aged between 11 and 18, 17 per cent thought Oliver Cromwell fought at the Battle of Hastings.

He bemoans the fact that kids only know the greatest hits of history, recognizing the names of Henry VIII, Hitler, and Martin Luther King Jr., uncomfortably juxtaposed without the connecting facts well remembered.

My first answer is, "so what?" It's even easier for me to be dismissive since he's talking about British history and I know not a thing about the Battle of Hastings.

The real question, though, in an always-on world, a world where I can look up what I need to know about the Battle of Hastings faster than I can type this, is, "how many of these kids leave school *caring* to know?"

The top-down, command-and-control, authoritarian, pedagogical approach to cramming facts into our kids is an unqualified failure.

When forced to comply, the smart kid plays along, the stupid one is punished, and neither of them produces much of value as a result.

To be as clear as possible here: In which situation does knowledge of the Boer War help society? And does it help because it means the student was obedient and attentive enough to play along to get ahead (in other words, it's a marker, a symptom of something else)? Or do we actually need the trivia?

Trivia? Yes, I think knowing the year that the Battle of Hastings was fought is trivia. On the other hand, understanding the sweep of history, being able to visualize the repeating cycles of conquest and failure, and having an innate understanding of the underlying economics of the world are essential insights for educated people to understand.

When access to information was limited, we needed to load students up with facts. Now, when we have no scarcity of facts or the access to them, we need to load them up with understanding.

If we're looking for markers, we need better ones.

103. This Is Difficult to Let Go Of

Those of us who have successfully navigated the industrial education system like it when people are well informed, when sentences are grammatically correct, and when our peers understand things like what electrons do and how the scientific method works.

Does the new economy demand that we give this up?

No. But applying ever more effort and rigor to ensure that every kid knows every fact is insane.

We've failed at that. We've failed miserably. We set out to teach everyone everything, en masse, with embarrassingly bad results. All because we built the system on a foundation of compliance.

What if we gave up on our failed effort to teach facts? What if we put 80% of that effort into making huge progress in teaching every kid to care, to set goals, to engage, to speak intelligently, to plan, to make good decisions, and to lead?

If there's one classroom of beaten-down kids who scored well on their PSATs due to drill and practice, and another class of motivated dreamers, engaged in projects they care about and addicted to learning on a regular basis, which class are you going to bet on?

If we can give kids the foundation to dream, they'll figure out the grammar and the history the minute it helps them reach their goals and make a difference.

104. The Situation

Real learning happens in bursts, and often those bursts occur in places or situations that are out of the ordinary. Textbooks rarely teach us lessons we long remember. We learn about self-reliance when we get lost in the mall, we learn about public speaking when we have to stand up and give a speech.

In *Thinking, Fast and Slow* by Nobel Prize winner Daniel Kahneman, we discover that we have two brains—the primordial, hot-wired, instinctive brain and the more nuanced, mature, and rational brain. When we celebrate someone who is cerebral or thoughtful or just plain smart, what we're really doing is marveling over how much he's managed to use his rational brain. This is the person who doesn't take the bait and get into a bar fight, the one who chooses the long-term productive path instead of the shortcut.

It turns out, though, that none of this happens if we haven't also trained our instinctive brain to stand down. When we practice putting ourselves into situations, we give the rational brain a better chance to triumph. That's why you'd like the doctor who sees you in the emergency room to have years of experience. Why performance in debates improves over time. And why a mom with three kids is surprisingly more calm than one with merely one.

Practice works because practice gives us a chance to relax enough to make smart choices.

A primary output of school should be to produce citizens who often choose the rational path. And that's going to happen only if we've created enough situations for them to practice in.

105. If You Could Add Just One Course

Neil deGrasse Tyson, astronomer and head of the Hayden Planetarium at the Museum of Natural History in New York, adds this one: "how to tell when someone else is full of it."

I'd augment that with: "and how to tell when you are."

106. The Third Reason They Don't Teach Computer Science in Public School

The first reason is classic: it's a new topic, and changing the curriculum is political, expensive, and time consuming. The bias is to leave it alone.

The second reason is related. Many teachers are more comfortable teaching areas in which they have significant experience and expertise, and computer programming doesn't really line up for them in those areas.

But the third reason is the most important one, and gets to the heart of the argument: just about all the important things we need to teach in computer science can't be taught by rote memorization, lectures, and tests. And school is organized around all three.

Computer programming is directed problem solving. If you solve the problem for the student by saying, "here we use this line of code, and here we use this one," you will have done nothing at all to develop the deep thinking and arrangement skills that programmers use every day.

Instead, the process involves selling the student on the mission, providing access to resources, and then holding her responsible for an outcome that works. And repeat. And repeat.

Other topics that are just like computer programming:

Fine art
Selling
Presenting ideas
Creative writing
Product development
Law
Product management
Leadership

I don't think it's an accident that there are few traditional schools that teach these topics (in a moment, an aside about law schools).

These fields used to be left to the desire and persistence of the individual. If you wanted to excel in any of these areas, you were left to your own devices. You might, like Shepard Fairey, end up at Rhode Island

School of Design, but more commonly, you either found a mentor or figured it out as you went.

107. An Aside About Law School

The apparent exception to the list above is law school. There are tons of law schools, probably too many, and they apparently churn out hundreds of thousands of lawyers on a regular basis.

What any lawyer will tell you, though, is that *law school doesn't teach you how to be a lawyer.*

Law school is a three-year hazing process, a holding tank based on competitiveness and the absorption of irrelevant trivia, combined with high-pressure exams and social pressure.

The pedagogy of law school has nothing to do with being a lawyer, but everything to do with being surrounded by competitive individuals who use words as weapons and data as ammunition. This indoctrination is precisely what many lawyers benefit from.

(The ironic aside here is that law school provides precisely the sort of situation I wrote about earlier—it puts students into a place where they can develop their rational minds at the same time they learn to calm down and do the work, whatever the work happens to be.)

The method is clever: use the trope of school, the lectures and the tests, to create an environment where a likely by-product is that person-alities are shaped and the culture of lawyering is fostered. In fact, they could replace half the classes with classes on totally different topics (Shake-speare, the history of magic) and produce precisely the same output.

Part of the make-believe academic sideshow is the role of the law reviews, publications that are produced by law schools and that feature academic treatises by law-school professors. Rather than acknowledging that law school is a vocational institution, top schools race to hire profes-sors doing esoteric research. The $3.6 billion spent each year on law school tuition goes, in large part, to these professors.

According to a study done in 2005, 40% (!) of the law review articles in LexisNexis had never been cited (never, not even once) in a legal case or in other law review articles.

The problem is that this process is an expensive waste. Top law firms have discovered that they have to take law school grads and train them for a year or more before they can do productive work—many clients refuse to pay for the efforts of first-year lawyers, and for good reason.

One more example of failing to ask, "what is school for?" and instead playing a competitive game with rules that make no sense.

108. School as the Transference of Emotion and Culture

One thing a student can't possibly learn from a video lecture is that the teacher cares. Not just about the topic—that part is easy. No, the student can't learn that the teacher cares about *him*. And being cared about, connected with, and pushed is the platform we need to do the emotional heavy lifting of committing to learn.

Learning is frightening for many because at any step along the way, you might fail. You might fail to get the next concept, or you might fail the next test. Easier, then, to emotionally opt out, to phone it in, to show up because you have to, because then failure isn't up to you; it's the system's fault.

109. What Great Teachers Have in Common Is the Ability to Transfer Emotion

Every great teacher I have ever encountered is great because of her desire to communicate emotion, not (just) facts. A teacher wrote to me recently,

> I teach first grade and while I have my mandated curriculum, I also teach my students how to think and not what to think. I tell them to question everything they will read and be told throughout the coming years.
>
> I insist they are to find out their own answers. I insist they allow no one to homogenize who they are as individuals (the goal of compulsory education). I tell them their gifts and talents are given as a means to make a meaningful difference and create paradigm-changing shifts in our world, which are so desperately

needed. I dare them to be different and to lead, not follow. I teach them to speak out even when it's not popular.

I teach them "college" words as they are far more capable than just learning "sat, mat, hat, cat, and rat." Why can't they learn words such as cogent, cognizant, oblivious, or retrograde just because they are 5 or 6? They do indeed use them correctly, which tells me they are immensely capable.

What's clear to me is that teaching first graders words like cogent and retrograde isn't the point. It's not important that a six-year-old know that. What is important, vitally important, is that her teacher believes she could know it, ought to know it, and is capable of knowing it.

We've been spending a fortune in time and money trying to stop teachers from doing the one and only thing they ought to be doing: coaching. When a teacher sells the journey and offers support, the student will figure it out. That's how we're wired.

110. Talent Vs. Education

Tricky words indeed.

Where does one end and the other begin? Are you a lousy public speaker/runner/brainstormer because you've never been trained, or because there's some mysterious thing missing from your DNA?

If you're in the talent camp, then most achievement is preordained, and the only job of school or parents is to shore up the untalented while opening doors for the lucky few.

This is a dark and lonely job, one that's appropriate for a pessimist masquerading as a realist.

Fortunately, most of us are of a different belief, willing to imagine that there are so many opportunities in our fast-moving culture that drive, when combined with background and belief, can overcome a lack of talent nine times out of ten.

If that's true, our responsibility is to amplify drive, not use lack of talent as a cheap excuse for our failure to nurture dreams.

111. Dumb as a Choice

Let's define dumb as being different from stupid.

Dumb means you don't know what you're supposed to know. Stupid means you know it but make bad choices.

Access to information has radically changed in just ten years. Kahn Academy, Wikipedia, a hundred million blogs, and a billion websites mean that if you're interested enough, you can find the answer, wherever you are.

School, then, needs not to deliver information so much as to sell kids on wanting to find it.

Dumb used to be a by-product of lack of access, bad teachers, or poor parenting. Today, dumb is a choice, one that's made by individuals who choose not to learn.

If you don't know what you need to know, that's fixable. But first you have to want to fix it.

112. The Schism over Blocks

Jean Schreiber wants kids in elementary school to spend more time playing with blocks and less time sitting at a desk and taking notes.

Is that okay with you?

Blocks for building.

Blocks for negotiating.

Blocks for pretending.

Blocks for modeling the real world.

Time spent on blocks takes time away from painstakingly learning to draw a 6, from memorizing the times tables, and from being able to remember the names of all 50 states.

Is that what school ought to be doing?

As a parent, you see what seven-year-olds in China are doing (trigonometry!) and you see the straight rows of silent students and rigor, and it's easy to decide that there's a race, and we're losing.

We are losing, but what we're losing is a race to produce the low-paid factory workers of tomorrow.

In New York, the Education Department just proposed a reading test for all third-graders—a test that would last more than four hours over two days. Clearly, playing with blocks is not part of this requirement.

But go back to the original premise of this manifesto—that what we need is not to create obedient servants with a large bank of memorized data, but instead to build a generation of creative and motivated leaders—and suddenly, blocks make a lot of sense.

Give me a motivated block builder with a jumbled box of LEGOs over a memorizing drone any day. If we can't (or won't, or don't want to) win the race to the bottom, perhaps we could seriously invest in the race to the top.

113. Completing the Square and a Million Teenagers

Every year, more than a million kids are at exactly the right age to radically advance their understanding of leadership and human nature. They're ready to dive deep into service projects, into understanding how others tick and, most of all, into taking responsibility.

And so, of course, the system teaches our best and brightest how to complete the square to solve a quadratic equation.

In case you missed it, it involves adding (b/a)[squared] to both sides of the equation and then solving from there.

It's almost entirely abstract, it is certainly of zero practical use, and it's insanely frustrating. The question worth asking is: Why bother?

One reason is that quadratic equations are the gateway to calculus, which is the gateway to higher math.

Another reason is that many of the elements of Newtonian mechanics involve similar sorts of analysis.

Both reasons are based on the notion that a civilized society learns as much as it can, and advancing math and science (and thus engineering) requires a wide base of students who are educated in this subject so that a few can go on to get advanced degrees.

Less discussed is the cost of this dark alley of abstract math. In order to find the time for it, we neglect probability, spreadsheets, cash flow analysis, and just about anything that will increase a student's comfort and familiarity with the math that's actually done outside of academia.

Also ignored is the benefit of learning how to actually figure things out. Because we're in such a hurry to drill and practice the techniques on the SAT or Regents exam, we believe we don't have time to have students spend a week to independently *invent* the method of completing the square. They don't invent it, they memorize it.

Obedience again.

Precisely at the moment when we ought to be organizing school around serious invention (or reinvention and discovery), we wholeheartedly embrace memorization and obedience instead. Because it's easier to measure, easier to control, and easier to sell to parents.

The puzzles of math and physics are among the most perfect in the world. They are golden opportunities to start young adults down the path of lifelong learning. The act of actually figuring something out, of taking responsibility for finding an answer and then proving that you are *right*—this is at the heart of what it means to be educated in a technical society.

But we don't do that any longer. There's no time and there's no support. Parents don't ask their kids, "what did you figure out today?" They don't wonder about which frustrating problem is no longer frustrating. No, parents have been sold on the notion that a two-digit number on a progress report is the goal—if it begins with a "9."

Here's the nub of my argument: the only good reason to teach trig and calculus in high school is to encourage kids to become engineers and scientists. That's it.

The way we teach it actually *decreases* the number of kids who choose to become engineers and scientists. It's a screen, the hard course schools set up to weed out the less intent. In other words, we're using the very tool that creates engineers to dissuade them from learning the material that would help them become engineers.

Advanced high school math is not a sufficient end in and of itself. If that's the last class you take in math, you've learned mostly nothing useful. On the other hand, if your appetite is whetted and you have a door to advanced work opened, if you go on to design bridges and to create computer chips, then every minute you spent was totally worthwhile. And so the question:

Is the memorization and drill and practice of advanced math the best way to sell kids on becoming scientists and engineers?

If not, then let's fix it.

(Have you ever met a math whiz or an engineer who explained that the reason she went on to do this vital work was that the math textbook in eleventh grade ignited a spark?)

114. Let's Do Something Interesting

Every once in a while, between third grade and the end of high school, a teacher offers the class a chance to do something interesting, new, off topic, exciting, risky, and even thrilling.

I'd venture it's about 2% of the hours the student is actually in school. The rest of the time is reserved for absorbing the curriculum, for learning what's on the test.

Just wondering: What would happen to our culture if students spent 40% of their time pursuing interesting discoveries and exciting growth opportunities, and only 60% of the day absorbing facts that used to be important to know?

115. Getting Serious About Leadership: Replacing Coach K

Let's assume for a moment that college sports serve an educational function, not just one of amusing alumni.

Who learns the most? I'm arguing that the quarterback and the coach take away the most lessons, because they're making significant decisions and have the biggest opportunities for intellectual (as opposed to physical) failure in each game.

A running back might learn from a fumble (hold on tighter), but the person calling the plays and managing the team and organizing the defense probably gains a greater life lesson.

So let's de-professionalize. Have a student (or a rotating cast of students) be the coach. And let students be the high school recruiters. And let students be the managers of as many elements of the stadium, the press box, and the concessions as possible.

And let's have the director of the college musical be a student as well. And the person in charge of logistics for homecoming.

Just about all of these jobs can be done by students. What would that lead to?

Well, first we'd have to get truly serious about giving these students the background and support to do these jobs well. Interesting to note that kids in college plays have taken ten years or more of drama classes, but the student director probably has no mentor, no rigor, and no background in doing his job. We've rarely taught students how to do anything that involves plotting a new course.

Would you be interested in hiring the kid who coached the team that won the Rose Bowl? How about working for someone who had handled logistics for 500 employees at a 50,000-seat stadium? Or having your accounting done by someone who learned the craft tracking a million dollars' worth of ticket sales?

Is there a better way to learn than by doing?

116. Higher Ed Is Going to Change as Much in the Next Decade as Newspapers Did in the Last One

Ten years ago, I was speaking to newspaper executives about the digital future. They were blithely ignorant of how Craigslist would wipe out the vast majority of their profits. They were disdainful of digital delivery. They were in love with the magic of paper.

In just ten years, it all changed. No interested observer is sanguine about the future of the newspaper, and the way news is delivered has fundamentally changed—after a hundred years of stability, the core business model of the newspaper is gone.

College is in that very same spot today.

Schools are facing the giant crash of education loans and the inability of the typical student to justify a full-fare education. It will be just a few years after most courses are available digitally—maybe not from the school itself, but calculus is calculus. At that point, either schools will be labels, brand names that connote something to a hiring manager, or they will be tribal organizers, institutions that create teams, connections, and guilds. Just as being part of the *Harvard Crimson* or *Lampoon* is a connection you will carry around for life, some schools will deliver this on a larger scale.

I guess it's fair to say that the business of higher education is going to change as much in the next decade as newspapers did in the prior one.

117. This Is Your Brain on the Internet: The Power of a Great Professor

Cathy Davidson teaches at Duke and her courses almost always have a waiting list. Interesting to note that in the first week, about 25% of the students in the class drop out. Why? Because the course doesn't match the industrial paradigm, can't guarantee them an easy path to law school, and represents a threat to established modes of thinking.

Bravo.

In her words, "Sometimes the line outside my office was as long as those at a crowded bakery on a Saturday morning, winding down the hall. Students wanted to squeeze every ounce of interaction from me because they believed—really believed—that what they were learning in my classes could make a difference in their life."

The astonishing thing about this quote is that only one professor in a hundred could truly claim this sort of impact.

Davidson doesn't use term papers in her class—instead, she has created a series of blog assignments as well as a rotating cast of student leaders who interact with each and every post. Her students write more, write more often, and write better than the ones down the hall in the traditional churn-it-out writing class.

She is teaching her students how to learn, not how to be perfect.

118. Polishing Symbols

Just about everything that happens in school after second grade involves rearranging symbols. We push students to quickly take the real world, boil it down into symbols, and then, for months and years after that, analyze and manipulate those symbols. We parse sentences, turning words into parts of speech. We refine mathematical equations into symbols, and become familiar with the periodic table.

The goal is to live in the symbolic world, and to get better and better at polishing and manipulating those symbols. That's what academics do.

If

$$f(x) \geq g(x) \geq 0$$

$f(x) \geq g(x) \geq 0$ $\qquad$ $[a, \infty)$ [a, ∞)

then,

If $\displaystyle\int_a^\infty f(x)\, dx$ $\int_a^\infty f(x)\,dx$ converges, then so

does $\displaystyle\int_a^\infty g(x)\, dx$ $\int_a^\infty g(x)\,dx$

If $\displaystyle\int_a^\infty g(x)\, dx$ $\int_a^\infty g(x)\,dx$ diverges, then so

$\displaystyle\int_a^\infty f(x)\, dx$ $\int_a^\infty f(x)\,dx$

I love stuff like this. The manipulation of ever-increasing levels of abstraction is high-octane fuel for the brain; it pushes us to be smarter (in one sense).

But at another level, it's a sort of intellectual onanism. For a few math students, it's a stepping stone on the way to big, new insights. For everyone else, it's a distraction from truly practical conversations about whether to buy or lease a car, or how to balance the federal budget.

The reason we make fun of advanced research papers with titles like "Historic Injustice and the Non-Identity Problem: The Limitations of the Subsequent-Wrong Solution and Toward a New Solution" is that the academics are focusing all their attention on symbol manipulation—and since we, the readers, have no clue how the symbols relate to the real world, we're lost.

Symbol manipulation is a critical skill, no doubt. But without the ability (and interest) in turning the real world into symbols (and then back again), we fail. Pushing students into the manipulation of symbols without teaching (and motivating) them to move into and out of this world is a waste.

It doesn't matter if you're able to do high-level math or analyze memes over time. If you're unable or unwilling to build bridges between the real world and those symbols, you can't make an impact on the world.

Back to the original list of what our society and our organizations need: we rarely stumble because we're unable to do a good job of solving the problem once we figure out what it is. We are struggling because there's a shortage of people willing to take on difficult problems and decode them with patience and verve.

119. My Ignorance Vs. Your Knowledge

> There is a cult of ignorance in the United States, and there has always been. The strain of anti-intellectualism has been a constant thread winding its way through our political and cultural life, nurtured by the false notion that democracy means that "my ignorance is just as good as your knowledge."
>
> **—Isaac Asimov**

School is not merely vocational. It used to be, a long time ago, but then, in addition to work training creeping up, the Academy crept down. It became important to our culture for even the street sweeper to know what a star was, to have a basic understanding of the free market, and to recognize Beethoven when he heard it.

In the rush to get a return on our investment, sometimes we forget that having knowledge for the sake of knowledge is a cornerstone of what it means to be part of our culture.

The shift now is this: school used to be a one-shot deal, your own, best chance to be exposed to what happened when and why. School was the place where the books lived and where the experts were accessible.

A citizen who seeks the truth has far more opportunity to find it than ever before. But that takes skill and discernment and desire. Memorizing a catechism isn't the point, because there's too much to memorize and it changes anyway. No, the goal has to be creating a desire (even better, a need) to know what's true, and giving people the tools to help them discern that truth from the fiction that so many would market to us.

> I don't know what your destiny will be, but one thing I know: The only ones among you who will be really happy are those who sought and found out how to serve.
>
> **—Albert Schweitzer**

120. Seek Professional Help

There seems to be a cultural bias against getting better at things that matter. School has left such a bad taste that if what we need to do to improve feels like reading a book, attending a lecture, or taking a test, many of us tend to avoid it.

Consider how easy (and helpful) it would be to get better at:

Giving a presentation
Handling a negotiation
Writing marketing copy
Shaking hands
Dressing for a meeting
Making love
Analyzing statistics
Hiring people
Dealing with authority figures
Verbal self-defense
Handling emotionally difficult situations

And yet . . . most of us wing it. We make the same mistakes that many who came before us did, and we shy away from the hard (but incredibly useful) work of getting better at the things that matter.

Not because we don't want to get better. Because we're afraid that it will be like school, which doesn't make us better but merely punishes us until we comply.

121. Homeschooling Isn't the Answer for Most

Thousands of caring and committed parents are taking their kids out of the industrial system of schooling and daring to educate them themselves. It takes guts and time and talent to take this on and to create an environment that's consistently challenging and focused enough to deliver on the potential our kids are bringing to the world.

There are several problems, though—reasons for us to be concerned about masses of parents doing this solo:

The learning curve. Without experience, new teachers are inevitably going to make the same mistakes, mistakes that are easily avoided the tenth time around . . . which most home educators will never get to.

The time commitment. The cost of one parent per student is huge—and halving it for two kids is not nearly enough. Most families can't afford this, and few people have the patience to pull it off.

Providing a different refuge from fear. This is the biggest one, the largest concern of all. If the goal of the process is to create a level of fearlessness, to create a free-range environment filled with exploration and all the failure that entails, most parents just don't have the guts to pull this off. It's one thing for a caring and trained professional to put your kids through a sometimes harrowing process; it's quite another to do it yourself.

122. Some Courses I'd Like to See Taught in School

How old is the Earth?
What's the right price to pay for this car?
Improv
How to do something no one has ever done before
Design and build a small house
Advanced software interface design

123. The Future of the Library

This is an issue very much aligned with the one we're dealing with here. The very forces that are upending our need for school are at work at libraries as well. Here's my most retweeted blog post ever:

What Is a Public Library For?

First, how we got here:

Before Gutenberg, a book cost about as much as a small house. As a result, only kings and bishops could afford to own a book of their own.

This situation naturally led to the creation of shared books, of libraries where scholars (everyone else was too busy not starving) could come to read books that they didn't have to own. *The library as warehouse for books worth sharing.*

Only after that did we invent the librarian.

The librarian isn't a clerk who happens to work at a library. A librarian is a data hound, a guide, a sherpa, and a teacher. The librarian is the interface between reams of data and the untrained but motivated user.

After Gutenberg, books got a lot cheaper. More individuals built their own collections. At the same time, though, the number of titles exploded, and the demand for libraries did as well. We definitely needed a warehouse to store all this bounty, and more than ever we needed a librarian to help us find what we needed. *The library is a house for the librarian.*

Industrialists (particularly Andrew Carnegie) funded the modern American library. The idea was that in a pre-electronic media age, the working man needed to be both entertained and slightly educated. Work all day and become a more civilized member of society by reading at night.

And your kids? Your kids need a place with shared encyclopedias and plenty of fun books, hopefully inculcating a lifelong love of reading, because reading makes all of us more thoughtful, better informed, and more productive members of a civil society.

Which was all great, until now.

Want to watch a movie? Netflix is a better librarian, with a better library, than any library in the country. The Netflix librarian knows about every movie, knows what you've seen and what you're likely to want to see. If the goal is to connect viewers with movies, Netflix wins.

This goes further than a mere sideline that most librarians resented anyway. Wikipedia and the huge data banks of information have basically eliminated the library as the best resource for anyone doing amateur research (grade school, middle school, even undergrad). Is there any doubt that online resources will get better and cheaper as the years go by? Kids don't schlep to the library to use an out-of-date encyclopedia to do a report on FDR. You might want them to, but they won't unless coerced.

They need a librarian more than ever (to figure out creative ways to find and use data). They need a library not at all.

When kids go to the mall instead of the library, it's not that the mall won; it's that the library lost.

And then we need to consider the rise of the Kindle. An ebook costs about $1.60 in 1962 dollars. A thousand ebooks can fit on one device, easily. Easy to store, easy to sort, easy to hand to your neighbor. Five years from now, electronic readers will be as expensive as Gillette razors, and ebooks will cost less than the blades.

Librarians who are arguing and lobbying for clever ebook lending solutions are completely missing the point. They are defending the library-as-warehouse concept, as opposed to fighting for the future, which is librarian as producer, concierge, connector, teacher, and impresario.

Post-Gutenberg, books are finally abundant, hardly scarce, hardly expensive, hardly worth warehousing. Post-Gutenberg, the scarce resources are knowledge and insight, not access to data.

The library is no longer a warehouse for dead books. Just in time for the information economy, the library ought to be the local nerve center for information. (Please don't say I'm anti-book! I think through my actions and career choices, I've demonstrated my pro-book chops. I'm not saying I *want* paper to go away, I'm merely describing what's inevitably occurring.) We all love the vision of the underprivileged kid bootstrapping himself out of poverty with books, but now (most of the time), the insight and leverage are going to come from being fast and smart with online resources, not from hiding in the stacks.

The next library is a place, still. A place where people come together to do co-working and to coordinate and invent projects worth working on together. Aided by a librarian who understands the Mesh, a librarian who can bring to bear domain knowledge and people knowledge and access to information.

The next library is a house for the librarian with the guts to invite kids in to teach them how to get better grades while doing less grunt work. And to teach them how to use a soldering iron or take apart something with no user-serviceable parts inside. And even to challenge them to teach classes on their passions, merely because it's fun. This librarian takes responsibility or blame for any kid who manages to graduate from school without being a first-rate data shark.

The next library is filled with so many Web terminals that there's always at least one empty. And the people who run this library don't view the combination of access to data and connections to peers as a sidelight—it's the entire point.

Wouldn't you want to live and work and pay taxes in a town that had a library like that? The vibe of the best Brooklyn coffee shop combined with a passionate raconteur of information? There are a thousand things that could be done in a place like this, all built around one mission: *take the world of data, combine it with the people in this community, and create value.*

We need librarians more than we ever did. What we don't need are mere clerks who guard dead paper. Librarians are too important to be a dwindling voice in our culture. For the right librarian, this is the chance of a lifetime.

124. Thinking Hard About College

If there's a part of the educational system that should be easier to fix, it's higher education. We've seen really significant changes in the physical plant, the marketing, and the structure of many universities, usually in response to student demand.

University presidents are responsive to application rates, donations, and football attendance—they understand that their seven-figure salaries are often a reflection of how the world of alumni, parents, and students feel about them. Unlike local high schools, colleges compete. They compete for students, for professors, and for funding.

Colleges have an opportunity to dramatically shift what it means to be educated, but they won't be able to do this while acting as a finishing school for those who have a high-school diploma. College can't merely be high school but louder.

So, that said, here are some thoughts from a former adjunct professor, an alum, and a parent of future college students (no football here, sorry).

125. The Famous-College Trap

Spend time around suburban teenagers and their parents, and pretty soon the discussion will head inexorably to the notion of going to a "good college."

Harvard, of course, is a good college. So is Yale. Add to the list schools like Notre Dame and Middlebury.

How do we know that these schools are good?

If you asked me if a Mercedes is a good car compared to, say, a Buick, by most measures we could agree that the answer is yes. Not because of fame or advertising, but because of the experience of actually driving the car, the durability, the safety—many of the things we buy a car for.

The people who are picking the college, though, the parents and the students about to invest four years and nearly a quarter of a million dollars—what are they basing this choice on? Do they have any data at all about the long-term happiness of graduates?

These schools aren't necessarily good. What they are is *famous*.

Loren Pope, former education editor at the *New York Times*, points out that colleges like Hiram and Hope and Eckerd are actually *better* schools, unless the goal is to find a brand name that will impress the folks at the country club. His breakthrough book, *Colleges that Change Lives*, combines rigorous research with a passion for unmasking the extraordinary overselling of famous colleges.

If college is supposed to be just like high school but with more parties, a famous college is precisely what parents should seek. If we view the purpose of college as a stepping stone, one that helps you jump the line while looking for a good job, then a famous college is the way to go. The line for those good jobs is long, and a significant benefit of a famous college is more than superstition—associating with that fame may get you a better first job.

A famous college might not deliver an education that's transformative to the student, but if that's not what you're looking for, you might as well purchase a valuable brand name that the alumnus can use for the rest of his life.

But is that all you're getting? If the sorting mechanism of college is all that's on offer, the four years spent there are radically overpriced.

It turns out that students who apply to Harvard and get in but don't go are just as successful and at least as happy throughout their lives as the ones who do attend. Try to imagine any other branded investment of that size that delivers as little.

Steve Jobs and Bill Gates both dropped out of college (one more famous than the other). It turned out that getting in was sufficient to give them a credibility boost.

Famous colleges are part of the labeling and ranking system but have virtually nothing to do with the education imparted or the long-term impact of the education received. If you need the label to accomplish your goals, go get the label. Either way, we ought to hold colleges to a much higher standard when it comes to transformative education.

For starters, though, start using the word *famous* when your instinct is to say *good*.

126. The SAT Measures Nothing Important

Here's the essential truth: the only reported correlation between the SAT scores of a seventeen-year-old student and the success or happiness of that student when he's thirty is a double counting of how the brand name of a famous college helped him get a better job early on. Double count? Sure. Because normalizing for the fame of the college in the short run, lousy SAT scores lead to just as much (if not more) life happiness, income, leadership ability, etc.

The circular reasoning, of course, is that the fame of college determines the number of students who apply, which determines the "selectivity" (carefully put in quotes), which raises the typical SAT score of incoming students.

Kiplinger, normally a reality-based magazine, ranked the fifty "best" private universities in the USA. The criteria were: admissions rate, freshman and graduating senior retention rate, and students per faculty member.

As we've seen, the admissions rate is nothing but a measure of how famous the college is, how good it is at getting applications. That's the key reason that so many middle-level (there's that ranking again) colleges spend a fortune on high school outreach. They do direct-mail campaigns to boost applications, which boosts their statistics, which boost their ratings, which lead to more applications because they are now famous.

What about retention rate? Well, if a school tells its students the truth and gives them tools to proceed and succeed in the real world, you'd imagine that more of those students would leave to go join the real world, no? If retention rate is a key metric on the agenda of a university's leadership, I wouldn't be surprised to see grade inflation, amazing facilities, and, most of all, an insulation from what will be useful in the real world. Why leave? Indeed, how can you leave?

To be clear, it's entirely likely that some students will find a dramatic benefit from four years of college. Or six. Or perhaps three. But measuring retention as a way of deciding if a college is doing a good job is silly—if students are leaving early, I'd like to know where they're going. If they are leaving to do productive work and are satisfied with what they've learned, I put that down as a win, not a failure.

The most surprising irony of all is that the average debt load of a student leaving the top fifty schools on graduation is less than $30,000. Princeton, ranked first, has an average debt of less than $6,000. No, the famous schools aren't saddling their graduates with a lifetime of debt, one that's crippling. In fact, it's the second-, third-, and fourth-tier schools that lack the resources to offer aid that do this.

The lesser-ranked schools are less famous, net out to be more expensive (less aid), and, because many of them struggle to be on the list of the top fifty, offer none of the character-stretching that Loren Pope so relished.

A trap, caused by the power of marketing and the depth of insecurity among well-meaning parents raised in an industrial world.

127. "I'm Not Paying for an Education, I'm Paying for a Degree"

In the words of a Columbia University student, that's the truth. If you choose to get an education at the same time, well, that's a fine bonus, but with free information available to all, why pay $200,000 for it?

Of course, once a college student realizes this truth, the entire enterprise loses its moorings. The notion of motivated students teamed up with motivated professors falls apart, and we're back to the contract of adhesion, to compliance-based education, to a scarce resource (the degree) being dispensed to those who meet the measurable requirements.

Hofstra University spent more than $3.5 million sponsoring a presidential debate in 2008. In exchange, they got 300 tickets for students (that works out to about $10,000 a ticket) and, as they're happy to brag, a huge boost of publicity, apparently worthwhile because it makes their degree more valuable (famous = good). That famous degree then leads to more applicants, which allows the university to be more particular about their SAT scores and admission rate, which leads to better rankings in *U.S. News*, which leads to more applications and, ultimately, more donations and a raise for the university's president.

But did anyone actually learn anything?

128. Getting What They Pay For

Over the last twenty years, large universities discovered a simple equation: winning football and basketball teams would get them on television, which would make them more famous, which would attract students looking for a good school. Once again, it's the marketing problem of equating familiar with good.

Since 1985, the salary of college football coaches (at public universities) has increased by 650%. Professors? By 32%.

There is no question that over this time, the quality of football being played has skyrocketed. Attendance at games is up. Student involvement in sports spectating has gone up as well. And the fame of the schools that have invested in big-time sports has risen as well.

What hasn't improved, not a bit, is the education and quality of life of the student body.

In fact, according to research by Glen Waddell at the University of Oregon, for every three games won by the Fighting Ducks (winners of the Rose Bowl), the GPA of male students dropped. Not the male students on the team—the male students who pay a fortune to attend the University of Oregon.

Further research by Charles Clotfelter, a professor at Duke, found that during March Madness, schools that had teams in the playoffs had 6% fewer downloads of academic articles at their libraries. And if the team won a close game or an upset, the number dropped 19% the next day. And it never rose enough later to make up for the dip.

We get what we pay for.

Colleges aren't stupid, and as long as the game works, they'll keep playing it. After the University of Nebraska entered the Big 10, applications at their law school went up 20%—in a year when applications nationwide were down 10%. As long as students and their parents pay money for famous, and as long as famous is related to TV and to sports, expect to see more of it.

129. Access to Information Is Not the Same as Education

Universities no longer spend as much time bragging about the size of their libraries. The reason is obvious: the size of the library is now of interest to just a tiny handful of researchers. Most anything that we want access to is available somewhere online or in paid digital libraries.

Stanford University has put up many of their courses online for free, and some have more than 30,000 active students at a time.

MIT just launched MITx, which will create ubiquitous access to information. The finest technical university in the world is going to share every course with any student who is willing to expend the effort to learn.

Measured by courses, MIT is going ahead and creating the largest university in the world. If you could audit any class in the world, would you want to?

A university delivers four things:

Access to information (not perspective or understanding, but access)
Accreditation/a scarce degree
Membership in a tribe
A situation for growth (which is where you'd file perspective and understanding)

Once courses are digitized, they ought to be shared, particularly by nonprofit institutions working for the public good. Given that all the major universities ought to/should/will create a university of the people—giving access to information and great teachers to all (and if they don't, someone should and will, soon)—which of the other three really matter?

Accreditation: a degree from an Ivy League school is a little like real estate in a good neighborhood. It makes a lousy house better and a great house priceless. We make all sorts of assumptions about fifty-year-old men (even fictional ones—Frasier Crane went to Harvard) because someone selected them when they were eighteen years old.

With so much information available about everyone, it gets ever harder to lump people into categories. Graduating from (or even getting into) a prestigious institution will become ever more valuable. We need labels desperately, because we don't have enough time to judge all the people we need to judge. It's worth asking if the current process of admitting and processing students (and giving a "gentleman's C" to anyone who asks) is the best way to do this labeling.

But there's really no reason at all to lump the expense and time and process of traditional schooling with the labeling that the university does. In other words, if we think of these schools as validators and guarantors, they could end up doing their job with far less waste than they do now. They could be selectors of individuals based on the work they do elsewhere, as opposed to being the one and only place the work has to occur.

Membership in a tribe: this is perhaps the best reason to actually move to a college campus in order to get a degree. While access to information is becoming ever easier (you'll soon be able to take every single MIT course from home), the cultural connection that college produces can be produced only in a dorm room, at a football stadium, or walking across the quad, hand in hand. Catherine Oliver, an Oberlin graduate, remembers living in one of the co-ops, planning a menu, cooking, baking, washing dishes, mopping floors, and sitting through long consensus-building meetings.

All of it builds tribes.

For centuries, a significant portion of the ruling class has had a history with certain colleges, been a member of the famous-college tribe, sharing cultural touchstones and even a way of speaking. The label on a résumé is more than a description of what you did thirty years ago—it's proof, the leaders say, that you're one of us.

Until that changes, this tribe is going to continue to exert power and influence. The real question is how we decide who gets to be in it.

A situation for growth: and here's the best reason, the reason that's almost impossible to mimic in an online situation, the one that's truly worth paying for and the one that almost never shows up in the typical large-school, laissez-faire experience. The right college is the last, best chance for masses of teenagers to find themselves in a situation where they have no choice but to grow. And fast.

The editor at the *Harvard Lampoon* experiences this. I felt it when I co-ran a large student-run business. The advanced physics major discovers this on her first day at the high-energy lab, working on a problem no one has ever solved before.

That's the reason to spend the time and spend the money and hang out on campus: so you can find yourself in a dark alley with nowhere to go but forward.

130. Whose Dream?

There's a generational problem here, a paralyzing one.

Parents were raised to have a dream for their kids—we want our kids to be happy, adjusted, successful. We want them to live meaningful lives, to contribute, and to find stability as they avoid pain.

Our dream for our kids, the dream of 1960 and 1970 and even 1980, is for the successful student, the famous college, and the good job. Our dream for our kids is the nice house and the happy family and the steady career. And the ticket for all that is good grades, excellent comportment, and a famous college.

And now that dream is gone. Our dream. But it's not clear that our dream really matters. There's a different dream available, one that's actually closer to who we are as humans, that's more exciting and significantly more likely to affect the world in a positive way.

When we let our kids dream, encourage them to contribute, and push them to do work that matters, we open doors for them that will lead to places that are difficult for us to imagine. When we turn school into more than just a finishing school for a factory job, we enable a new generation to achieve things that we were ill-prepared for.

Our job is obvious: we need to get out of the way, shine a light, and empower a new generation to teach itself and to go further and faster than any generation ever has. Either our economy gets cleaner, faster, and more fair, or it dies.

If school is worth the effort (and I think it is), then we must put the effort into developing attributes that matter and stop burning our resources in a futile attempt to create or reinforce mass compliance.

131. How to Fix School in Twenty-four Hours

Don't wait for it. Pick yourself. Teach yourself. Motivate your kids. Push them to dream, against all odds.

Access to information is not the issue. And you don't need permission from bureaucrats. The common school is going to take a generation to fix, and we mustn't let up the pressure until it is fixed.

But in the meantime, *go*. Learn and lead and teach. If enough of us do this, school will have no choice but to listen, emulate, and rush to catch up.

132. What We Teach

When we teach a child to make good decisions, we benefit from a lifetime of good decisions.

When we teach a child to love to learn, the amount of learning will become limitless.

When we teach a child to deal with a changing world, she will never become obsolete.

When we are brave enough to teach a child to question authority, even ours, we insulate ourselves from those who would use their authority to work against each of us.

And when we give students the desire to make things, even choices, we create a world filled with makers.

The best way to complain is to make things.

—James Murphy

BLOG TITLE INDEX

Printed in the United States
by Baker & Taylor Publisher Services